W9-BLT-912

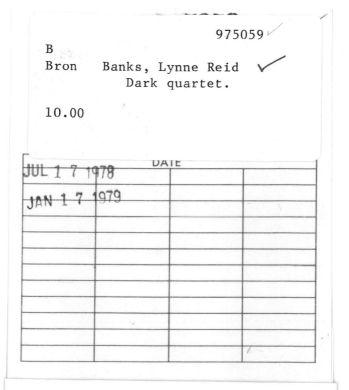

975059

B
Bron   Banks, Lynne Reid
          Dark quartet.

10.00

	DATE		
JUL 1 7 1978			
JAN 1 7 1979			

Department of Library & Archives
Box 537
Frankfort, Kentucky 40601

3/30/78

© THE BAKER & TAYLOR CO.

Also by

Lynne Reid Banks

THE L-SHAPED ROOM
HOUSE OF HOPE
CHILDREN AT THE GATE
THE BACKWARD SHADOW
TWO IS LONELY
ONE MORE RIVER
SARAH AND AFTER

Dark Quartet

DARK QUARTET
The Story of the Brontës

by
LYNNE REID BANKS

DELACORTE PRESS / NEW YORK

Originally published in Great Britain
by George Weidenfeld & Nicolson Limited

Copyright © 1976 by Lynne Reid Banks

All rights reserved. No part of this book may be reproduced in
any form or by any means without the prior written permission of the Publisher,
excepting brief quotes used in connection with reviews written
specifically for inclusion in a magazine or newspaper.

Manufactured in the United States of America

Second Printing—1977

Designed by MaryJane DiMassi

Library of Congress Cataloging in Publication Data

Banks, Lynne Reid.
Dark quartet.

1. Brontë family—Nonfiction.   I.   Title.
PZ4.B2173Dar3   [PR6003.A528]   823′.8′09   [B]   76-29727
ISBN 0-440-01657-6

β
Bron

HENDERSON

TO MY MOTHER, PAT REID BANKS,
AND MY HUSBAND, CHAIM STEPHENSON.

CONTENTS

FOREWORD

*W*HEN IT WAS FIRST SUGGESTED
that I should write a biographical novel about the Brontës, I
was daunted at the prospect, though not as much, in retrospect,
as I should have been. Had I known what lay before me, I would
undoubtedly have had to refuse the commission.

I knew very little about my subject to begin with, and by the
time I had spent six months bent over book after book, I was
convinced that not only was there no more to be said, but that
if there were, it would need not a novelist, not even a scholar, but
some kind of archaeologist to find it: someone who would creep
into the parsonage garden by night and dig up the letters that
might be buried there, or burrow like a mole into the moorsides
nearby for new, "original" sources. For a time, I despaired.

But among all these heaps of known and documented facts,
there are a great many unanswered questions—unanswer*able*,
surely, at this stage, except in terms of speculation. Every scholar
who has ever written about the Brontës has felt free to speculate
a little. May I, as a self-confessed writer of fiction, not be bold
enough to speculate without apologetical phrases such as, "We

may easily imagine the scene . . ." or "We ask ourselves whether at this point . . ." or "Surely they must have thought, felt, said . . ."?

At the same time, much *is* known, and nothing that is authentic may be altered (though certain incidents must inevitably be left out). Since I didn't want to include too many letters, which are published elsewhere, I used the convention of making characters say what, in fact, they wrote. Thus some of the conversation— Charlotte's in particular—employs the characters' own words.

With regard to the novels, I have gone into very little detail, for the obvious reason that these are available for all to read. What I have tried to do, without drawing deliberate attention to it in the narrative, is to introduce backgrounds, settings, influences and incidents in their proper places, which the reader can relate to the novels. Unfortunately it has not been possible to include all such sources for lack of space, but the observant reader can spot a good many.

So the facts were my stepping-stones, and sometimes, when there were enough of them, my straight path through these four lives. Where there was no solid factual ground, I have felt free to guess, to use my novelist's insight—in a word, to invent. Who has studied this family and not longed to be a fly on the parsonage wall, to watch and listen and find out what really happened, what they said to each other, what they did, what motivated them? But I have not let my imagination run riot. I have kept it harnessed to the truth. For the rest, I offer *my* answers to some of the mysteries. Let anyone who is not satisfied with these brave the wrath of the curator of the Brontë Museum by digging up the parsonage garden!

I must add my humble thanks to a number of Brontë experts, living and dead, who laid the stepping-stones down for me: first and foremost, the redoubtable Mrs. Elizabeth Gaskell, without whom nothing; second (only just), kind, wise and scholarly Winifred Gérin, whose definitive studies of my four protagonists provided me with my most fruitful field of study. Phyllis Bentley, Margaret Lane, Fanny Ratchford and Daphne du Maurier are others to whom I am deeply indebted for their scholarship, their insights and their researches. My thanks also to Norman Raistrick, the curator, and to all at the Brontë Museum who have helped me.

LYNNE REID BANKS
London, 1976

PART I

The Unchildish Years

1821–25

1

THE PARSON'S
FAMILY

*I*T WAS DECEMBER. HAWORTH PAR-
sonage on the Yorkshire moors stood like a rock in the river
of wind, foursquare on a hill, where it caught the wildest blasts
of any storm. The unchecked currents of air eddied past its
windows in noisy torrents, flattening the few poor shrubs in the
garden and swirling over the wall among the green gravestones,
to be brought up short by the massive bulk of Haworth Church.
Beneath the aisle, in the vault reserved for the incumbent's
family, lay a new coffin which bore the inscription:

MARIA BRANWELL BRONTË
WIFE OF THE REVEREND PATRICK BRONTË

—together with the dates, which enclosed, like quotation marks,
the short years of her life: 1783 to 1821. It had been a good life,
gay, virtuous and unselfish, terminated by an undeservedly protracted and agonizing death.

In the parsonage dining room, five of the six children she had
borne in almost as many years were sitting around the table; the
baby, Anne, was asleep in her cradle. There was Maria, the eldest

at seven, Elizabeth, Charlotte, then Branwell (the only boy) and finally Emily Jane. She was a pretty child, taller at three than Branwell at four, and as tall as five-year-old Charlotte. They ate heartily—what there was to eat, for poor parsons' families didn't get meat every day.

The father of the family was not present. He suffered from digestive difficulties and had years ago elected to eat alone in his study. The carving-chair was occupied by his sister-in-law, Elizabeth Branwell. She had come up from Cornwall out of a sense of duty, to bring up her deceased younger sister's children.

She sat straight and firm in the chair facing the window. It had no curtains, only shutters, which kept out some of the wind but augmented its moaning with creaks and rattles. A fire burned in the plain grate, putting out a mixture of sweet and acrid smells, but not as much heat as even that small room needed to prevent shivers. Aunt Branwell, accustomed to the balmy warmth of the West Country, drew her shawl more tightly around her with every rude gust outside.

Her face was narrow, austere; her eyes were fishlike, her forehead domed. Her rather thin lips were pinched, and the tight lines around them and down her fleshless cheeks bespoke a rigid inner discipline. She was a devoutly religious woman, a follower of Calvin. The children suffered from the rigors of her beliefs, but also, indirectly, they benefited, for nothing less compelling could have brought their aunt away from her beloved Cornish home to this inclement moorland wilderness.

Just now she was looking disapprovingly at Branwell. He had an odd little face—asymmetrical and narrow, with the beginnings of a strong nose and a weak chin—like two faces blended into one contradictory collection of features. Small brilliant eyes; soft flyaway red hair like his Irish father's.

"—I made them fight, and Bonaparte killed Wellington, and after supper we can have a state funeral—"

Aunt tutted loudly. Maria was supposed to have the floor. She was describing, between mouthfuls, a debate in the House of Commons, as reported in the newspapers and related to her by her father. She poured it all out in high excitement, as if the perennial quarrels between Whigs and Tories, far away in London, were of the most urgent importance to her. Aunt Branwell was fascinated; she still hadn't got used to a niece of seven who read and discussed the political columns—such a phenomenon went some way to cancel out the child's perpetual untidiness.

Now Charlotte also interrupted, answering Branwell. "But Bonaparte can't kill Wellington! You must bring him back to life. Kill your beloved Bony, if you like, and tomorrow we'll bury him in the churchyard."

"I won't kill him!" shouted Branwell excitedly, half jumping up from his place. "Have your own soldiers and kill who you like! You can't tell me who I can kill—"

"Children!" The back of a fork descended ringingly on the table edge. Branwell sank back into his seat. Even Maria stopped, but went on again when her aunt turned to her: "I am listening, Maria. Who spoke next?"

Charlotte bent to her brother and they continued their argument in whispers. She was another queer-looking child. No beauty—jaw too pronounced, upper lip too short under a big nose, disproportionately bulging forehead and a poor complexion. Her eyes redeemed her—huge gray pools of expressiveness, and what they expressed now was defiance. Branwell was not going to kill her hero off if she could help it.

Emily Jane was bored, and covertly stretched her hand down to the region of her ankles, where a dog was serving as her footrest. Her eyes strayed longingly in the direction of the window with its quivering shutters. Elizabeth leaned to her and whispered:

"You can't go out tonight, Emily—Aunt will never allow you."

Emily said nothing to that, but asked in a clear, loud voice:

"May I leave the table, Aunt?"

"No, Emily, you may not. Be still till we have finished."

Emily didn't ask again, but waited until her aunt's attention was occupied with Maria. Then she slipped from her seat and moved silently to the door. The dog's claws, clicking on the carpetless flags, gave her away.

"Emily Jane! Did I not say you were to wait?"

"He has to go out, Aunt. _He_ can't wait."

The door closed quietly and firmly behind child and dog, leaving Aunt defeated and purse-lipped. It was incomprehensible to her how the Reverend Patrick could allow dogs in the house at all.

Spring came late. The winter had seemed endless for the children, shut in the dark, cold parsonage, adjusting to Aunt and getting over the death that had brought her. But now the rough moor was flecked with racing cloud-shadows; the holly tree had stopped weeping; the green mold on the graves had dried to an unsuggestive gray.

The church could never look cheerful. It was too black, and its voice, the bell, always said "Fu-ner-al . . . fu-ner-al . . ." even when it was only calling them to hear one of their Papa's dramatic sermons. Some said that Haworth Moor was also bleak and depressing; but when you ran up over its first brow and stopped at the top to look down at the village, nestling (where in winter it cowered) on its slope, the prospect could be joyful indeed. Even the dark-gray parsonage looked quite jaunty, set in its broken, sunlit frame of graves, which had no morbidity from afar when the spring light was on them. Life was sublime, especially when there was liberty to bang out of the back door and run and run, holding hands in a long line with Elizabeth first and Maria at the end to see that Anne didn't get pulled clean off her feet.

Emily never stayed in the line long. Her dog rushed ahead and she had to follow: her thin legs began to carry her forward, in a rush of tingling wind; her hair tore from its ribbons, her hands from the hands on either side. On and up she went, disappearing over the first hilltop in a billow of skirts and cloak, her hastily tied bonnet coming adrift and flying back like a winged messenger to the others. Anne, who couldn't really run, sometimes cried to see her nearest and most beloved sister vanishing from sight, as it seemed to her, into the clouds that sat on the hill.

Often they stumbled home windblown, wet and filthy. Aunt

Branwell remonstrated in vain. She scrubbed them with a hard brush, telling them that God desired them to be clean and gentle, not rough and wild, although she did not convince them. But she said less to Branwell than to the girls. Branwell was, after all, a boy.

There was not always freedom, for Aunt had to give them lessons. Then the four elder girls would sit in her bedroom and Miss Branwell would read the Bible to them while they poked their needles wearily into their squares of linen.

Maria hated the detailed work of samplers. It was not in her nature to be neat and orderly. But not one to accept defeat in a matter so important, Aunt Branwell drove her hard, forcing her to sit unpicking and reworking for an hour after the others had been released to roam the moors or help in the kitchen or, best of all to Charlotte, to sit in the little room and "make out" with Bany.

"Making out" was one of their chief joys. To interpret "making out" as simply pretending would be to degrade the kind and degree of their make-believe. It was no mere playacting to them; they had begun to believe in it utterly. The little room they called their "study" was a world far wider than the whole rest of the house, with garden, village, graveyard and more besides. The moors were not part of the world, but like outer space, a glorious, limitless infinity at whose edges they had so far merely nibbled.

Aunt Branwell didn't like it. She would come and rap sharply on the door. "Children! Cease this caterwauling! Cease at once, the whole village can hear you!"

Silence—the frozen silence of intense concentration rudely broken into. Then, from Bany, "But it's not Sunday, Aunt."

"Sunday! I should hope it is not! Were it Sunday, I would not expect to find you shut in there at all, engaged in battle-games and other godless goings-on! But Sunday or no, you are to stop now. Your poor father is working below you. Have some thought for him in his bereavement."

There would be a reduction of the noise within the study to

whispers, but it couldn't last long. Soon they would be joined by Maria, when her sewing was done, and Elizabeth, who had been helping in the kitchen. Sometimes even Emily crept in. The room became overcrowded, and soon the whispers would rise through a swift progression to shouts and bellows. Footsteps on the stone stairs . . . Now it was Papa's voice, the ultimate accent of authority.

"Children!"

The Reverend Patrick opened the door and gazed at his brood, and they at him.

They were frozen into statues, a strange group of infant grotesques: an arm uplifting an invisible sword; a corpse on the floor with flounces awry; one pursued, backing against a chest; a fugitive crouched under the table.

He stood erect, his fine pale-blue Celtic eyes ablaze with a mixture of annoyance, pride and wry amusement well concealed, all shadowed in an engulfing sadness. His hair was like reddish fur, beginning to turn gray; his face was long and narrow, with a high-bridged nose and small but sensual mouth. His clerical collar cut high under an angular, domineering, obstinate jaw.

"What's all this noise? Is it possible you are quarreling in earnest?"

The statues melted and edged toward him, uncertain of his mood. In a rage he could be terrible—terrible! Did he not load a pistol each night against intruders, and every morning fire it through his bedroom window at the church tower, making everyone jump? Did he not occasionally go roaring and stamping through the house, forcing them all to run and hide? Once (but this was only one of the tales of Nancy, their maid, and might not be true) he had stuffed a hearthrug into the fire, where it had smoldered sickeningly all day, and they all remembered him in a fit of fury sawing the back off a chair to improve Maria's posture.

"No, Papa! Indeed no one's really cross."

"But Bany is very vexing, all the same. He *always* tries to make Napoleon come off best. I say Caesar was greater and could have thrashed Bony soundly, if they'd ever met."

"Prove it! Caesar was a fool and no one liked him!"

"Napoleon is a tyrant and a villain," put in Charlotte shrilly. "Anyway, we're not talking of who was stronger, but of who was the greater hero. No one can say the Duke of Wellington is not *that*!"

The Reverend Patrick sighed. He was in the middle of writing a poem. But he took off his pince-nez and beckoned his children to him with both hands.

"Come downstairs. We will talk over the problem together, and when each has made claim for his own hero, I shall judge between them."

They clamored around him eagerly, each one pressing for a place nearest Papa. They had, unconsciously, touched the right spring, for in matters of intellectual discussion and judgment Patrick Brontë delighted in participating with them, whereas if he had been asked to crawl on the floor, or demean his mind to some fatuous level, he could not have done it. Luckily for all, these children didn't require this of him; they knew nothing of children's games, for they mixed seldom with others of their age, and so their examples had been all of maturity.

No effort was made by any adult to modify language or rules of behavior to suit these small children. They were expected to conform. They didn't—no children do, or can. But the expectation continued, and the struggle to mold and contain the wayward outlines of childhood within the strict silhouette of adulthood was unabating.

The children's memory of their poor mother and her sufferings faded with time. Maria and Elizabeth alone remembered her clearly; for Charlotte, try as she might, there remained only one image, and that not a personal association—her mother sitting in the parlor one evening playing with Branwell.

But the Reverend Patrick did not forget so easily. When his dear wife was alive, before her illness, his home had been very different. Not only was there warmth in it for the children, but much for himself, for which no frosty Calvinist sister-in-law was any substitute. Altogether apart from the cozier aspects of domesticity, there were his more intimate needs, which his Maria, with her warm Cornish temperament (so different from her sister's) amply satisfied, raising no protest as child after child was conceived. Now all these legitimate delights, which as a passionate husband Patrick had taken for granted, were withdrawn from him. No wonder that he discharged his pistol each morning with such a sense of inward tension and tumult; no wonder there were times when the very sight of those children, so pleasurably and innocently begotten, was more than he could bear, so that he turned from them and shut himself away in his study, closing his mind to their need of him.

No solution to his loneliness presented itself. But before long the Reverend Patrick was feeling profoundly grateful to a kindly providence that had offered him a tailor-made solution to another major dilemma—how to educate his daughters. On a fixed stipend of £200 a year he could hardly have provided this out of his own resources. He had given them a certain grounding himself over the past year or two; but to be frank, he wanted to concentrate on his only son. This boy of his . . . ! Well, they were all extraordinary, all his children. But Branwell! Branwell was brilliant, no other word for it. He was also naughty, willful, headstrong, nervous to the point of hysteria—but these were forgivable faults in a lad.

Who should forgive them if not Patrick himself? He hadn't forgotten his barefoot childhood in Ireland and how he'd rebelled against the constrictions of his humble family. If he had not broken free of their severely limited expectations, would he ever have learned anything, would he have become a tutor, earned the respect and patronage of the Methodist, Dr. Tighe, who sent him on to Cambridge? Would he, in a moment of passionate ambition, have changed his surname from the commonplace Brunty to the Brontë which Nelson had adopted when he was make a Duke? No. That spirit, that fire which had driven him, he delighted to see flashing in his son's small bright eyes. Surely the boy would be a scholar or an artist—perhaps both.

But what about the girls? They, too, deserved an education, and he couldn't do justice to all of them.

And now, a miracle! A new school had opened at Cowan Bridge in Lancashire, especially for the daughters of impecunious clergymen. Patrick hardly believed his good fortune when the prospectus arrived and he saw that a figure of only £14 per annum for each girl was required for a complete education. He was so overjoyed at this that he forgot his own loneliness.

Maria was already eleven years old, and Patrick knew that his sporadic and unsystematic efforts to school her had done little more than fill her head with a ragbag of disordered and, from a scholastic point of view, useless information and ideas. She understood politics almost as well as he did; she was well acquainted with poetry, including his own efforts, of which he was prouder than their quality strictly warranted. She had some scattered knowledge of recent history, particularly of the outstanding figures in it, of whom she and indeed all the children spoke as if they were family acquaintances. She had read widely but without direction or system, and like the others, she wrote and painted with more energy than neatness.

Neatness was Maria's great failing. Aunt was perpetually pulling and tugging and straightening her. Patrick pursed his lips each time he thought of how this darling untidy creature would fare under the strict regime of a well-run boarding school. But faults must be corrected.

Anxiously Patrick watched his two eldest daughters, and asked their aunt if she thought their little frames and delicate constitutions could stand the strain of a regime which, however necessary and salutary to discipline, could not fail to be a shock to children who until now had been so free.

"Too free," commented Aunt Branwell. "It must be to their good, Brother-in-law. If they are strong enough to roam the moors in all weathers, they can withstand anything, I should think. Besides, you have been wise enough not to pamper them with too much warmth, rich food and fine clothes. In material matters their upbringing has been quite Spartan."

"I hope you don't think I have denied them anything they need, Elizabeth," he said uneasily.

"Far from it!" she returned crisply. "I am saying that you have prepared them well for the life they will have at school. Physically, at least. Intellectually, and in accomplishments . . ." She shrugged and flared her nostrils, a habit she had when disapproving. "Well, you have your own ideas, no doubt. They may not find that their precocious intimacy with the Houses of Parliament will be much appreciated by their teachers, but at least their brains have not lain idle . . . It remains for the school to mold their exceptionally active minds more in the pattern of other girls of their station, about which, Brother-in-law, you must allow me to say you seem to know too little."

And she went off to the kitchen, where she was soon grappling with a mound of dough. She had not yet got over missing the busy social round of her native Penzance, her cheerful relations and the warm climate. Occasionally, as if to torment her, her shriveling heart conjured up for her a young girl of Maria's age, hair flying, actually running *barefoot* upon velvet lawns with the sweet scent of flowers and the tang of the sea wafting in her face like the very breath of heaven. That same face, altered now by disappointment, spinsterhood, the demands of duty, the rigors of piety and perhaps most of all by the cold of the moors, which caused all her muscles to contract, would soften for a moment at the incredible recollection—then toughen again. For who can live with such a loss?

I was a different person then, she would think firmly, and dismiss the barefoot child. She tried to dismiss everything that was bad for discipline. And when Emily crept up beside her and stood on tiptoe to peep into the bowl of dough, Aunt Branwell smacked away the little finger before it had ventured beyond the brown rim.

"Emily Jane! Don't tell me you've washed those hands since you were fondling that smelly animal!"

2

SCHOOL

*J*UNE WAS ALMOST PAST, AND the time was approaching when Maria and Elizabeth must take up their places in Cowan Bridge. The weather was all balmy warmth and fresh, tantalizing bracken-scented breezes. But for the two eldest Brontës there was little freedom; instead, there was the "List."

The school would supply (at a modest price) the outer uniform garments—the nankeen and white Sunday summer dresses, purple merino frocks and capes for winter, brown holland pinafores, bonnets and plaid outdoor cloaks. But the underthings must be brought from home in a box. Night shifts, day shifts, night caps, stays, *five* petticoats in assorted weights, pairs of pockets, a spencer, some extra pinafores . . . Endless list! Aunt helped; she sat with them in her stuffy bedroom, stitching with an almost fanatic intensity, urging them on. Deficient in accomplishments her nieces might be, but deficient in petticoats, *that* they should not —not if Aunt Branwell had aught to say.

Sarah, Nancy's sister, who helped with the housework, was their only succor in this difficult time. She came knocking on the door on all sorts of frail excuses, tut-tutting and flapping her hand through the air as if it were thick with smoke, inventing urgent errands or tasks to get a temporary parole for the prisoners. Then, when she had them safely downstairs and out of sight, she would shoo them through the back door for ten minutes' joyous, though necessarily silent, play in the kitchen garden until the sharp voice called down the stairs.

"Sarah! Where are those girls? Time is wasting! They must get on with their lists!"

But in the evening, when the sun was down and the moors had stopped calling, they were released, and then all six of them clustered together and played their secret games with a passion and energy that would have frightened their Aunt had she seen them. It was as if they were playing now for all the rest of their lives, not only for the deprived hours of each working day.

There was an engraving by John Martin hanging in the dining room, called *Belshazzar's Feast*. Branwell in particular could stand before it for twenty minutes at a time—Branwell who as a rule couldn't stay still for two minutes before his restless daemon twitched him off to some other pursuit. But the children were all fascinated by the picture.

It was probably chiefly the contrast between the grandeur, the pagan luxury and spacious extravagant perspectives of Martin and the narrow, square-walled austerity of their home surroundings, that pierced the children's minds like a vision of endlessly opening doors leading to infinity.

Emily was in love with these illimitable distances, and Branwell with the intimations of power and luxury. But its charm for Charlotte was the feast itself: the raised dais or balcony in front, with an elaborate table set with silver goblets and a centerpiece of exotic fruits; the wide steps, up which terrified guests were fleeing; and the heroic central figure, who was surely Daniel.

Another aspect Charlotte dwelt on, but secretly, was the clothes. They were shockingly rich and splendid, especially the women's dresses. She was not aware, as Maria was, that most of these women were something unspeakable called concubines, a word Aunt stuttered over and would not explain; but even an eight-year-old could see that these were no ordinary ladies. Their hair, their head-dresses, their voluminous skirts and veils, their very gestures, bespoke a voluptuous, indecent sensual richness that choked Charlotte and almost made her feel ill whenever she contemplated it. Yet she stroked the wicked finery through the glass whenever she was alone, and sometimes she dreamed that one of those entrancing forms was somehow enveloping her puny homespun self.

Yet this was wrong—very wrong! Wrong to want to be rich, weighted down with jewels, smothered in perfumed silks and velvets. Aunt said these women were *damned* . . . Damned! Damned! Charlotte would hug herself with delicious horror at the word.

Maria was unaware of any pagan undercurrents in the picture. To her it magnificently represented a scene from the Old Testament, so she felt quite free to look at it and enjoy its soul-expanding panoply and its message. Elizabeth liked the excitement in it, the scurrying figures, the wild gestures, the mysterious fires in the background.

Now, in their last days together before Maria and Elizabeth went away, they gathered before the picture in its gilded frame and projected themselves into it, each in his or her own style, each telling his feelings or making up a story for the others. Even Anne was lifted up and told to say her thoughts, but she only stared for a while and remarked, "I've seen it at meals, and it's not pretty." They all laughed and hugged her, their baby and their pet, and Maria said competently, "Come, Anne, it's your bedtime." Then they all looked at each other, and at the picture, and slowly came away.

There was one evening left. They were to spend it with Papa.

He'd told them he had a special game for them, that after supper they were to come to his "study" (the parlor), for he wished to talk to them.

It seemed to all of them a special occasion. Without being told, right after supper they repaired upstairs to their rooms to tidy themselves. Even Maria brushed her hair and refastened the little cameo that held her fichu in place. Then they went down and washed their hands in the kitchen, after which, nudging and giggling with excitement and some nervousness, they clustered at the parlor door. Maria knocked.

"Come in."

They entered, half timid, half bold: timid because this was Papa's place, which they usually entered only as intruders; bold because tonight they were invited and expected. Another Martin loomed down from above the fireplace, in which a coal fire was glowing cozily. Its flames were reflected in the wood of the piano (which they were allowed to practice on at special times) and Papa's table, where his papers and books, his quill and several of his long clay pipes were tidily arranged, "put to bed" for the night.

Usually when one of them had cause to knock and enter, it was to find Papa at work, bent over his table. His spectacles, perched on his nose, often slipped off as he raised his head with a frown to see why he had been interrupted. But tonight he stood before the fire, his hands behind his back, looking genial and rather excited.

They ranged themselves before him in order of their age, and he looked at them with fond—no, fond is too mild a word—with violent love and pride. Their heads descended regularly, like a profile of steps, except for Emily, who made a single long step with Branwell. The girls in their pretty summer dresses, with cool scooped necks and puffed sleeves, decorated with rows of tucks and buttons and patterned with minute flowers, were pictures of demure yet unrestricted girlhood. He was glad they were small; he liked their doll-like fragility, which was so feminine (if only it did not mean they lacked robustness!). As for his son—well, time enough later for him to grow tall and strapping like his father. Some boys of six still wore long curls. Patrick was in no way dissatisfied.

"Tomorrow is an important day," he began, and the children, all at once, were reminded of his manner in the pulpit. "My two big daughters are off to school. A great step and a great adventure! Heh? Are you not excited, you two?" They nodded solemnly, prey to separate feelings. "And soon it will be Charlotte's turn, and then Emily's. You are growing up, all of you. Now, this being our last evening together until next summer (for the girls' school allows no holidays, you know, at Christmas), I have made a little plan. I know you like to dress up and to act plays. So see what I have here."

He brought out his hands from behind his back, and they all gave a gasp. In them he held a thing they had never seen before, a mask made of papier-mâché and painted in cracked but still-lurid colors. It had eye holes and a turned-down mouth. Papa held it up before his own face, which instantly became alien, tragic, and yet at the same time wildly funny. They stared at this strange being, entranced. He laughed at their faces and, reaching across the table, handed the mask to Maria.

"I found it among some things we brought from Thornton," he said. "It must have belonged to your mother. Now then. Maria, hide your face."

She put the mask up at once, and all the others looked at her. Anne was the last to laugh.

"I shall ask each of you a question and you shall answer from behind the mask. Is it agreed?"

Entering into the spirit of his game, they all fairly shouted agreement.

"On second thoughts, let me begin with the youngest."

The mask was handed down the line to Anne, each of them irresistibly compelled to try it on along the way. Branwell had to have it wrested from him by Emily. By the time it reached Anne her fear of it had passed, and she put it on as eagerly as the rest.

"What does a child like you most want?"

Into the sudden silence, the little voice piped out of the sinister mask, "Age and experience."

The father looked dumbfounded, as well he might. He stared for some time at the quaint, small figure with the grotesque face.

"Age and experience," he repeated at last, and passed his hand bemusedly across his head. "Indeed, that is all you lack, my girl! Next."

The mask passed to Emily. In some way it suited her better.

"Let's see . . . What had I best to do with your brother, Branwell, when he is naughty?"

The answer came promptly. "Reason with him, and when he won't listen to reason, whip him."

A general laugh acclaimed this piece of wisdom, but Branwell, unable to see the joke, looked sulky and snatched the mask.

"Me now, Papa! Ask what you had best do with Emily."

"No—I know your answer to that already. What is the best way of knowing the difference between the intellects of men and women?"

There was a long pause, and heavy breathing from within the mask. Patrick got ready to withdraw this too-difficult question and substitute another. But the answer forestalled him.

"You must look at how they are different in their bodies."

"What do you mean, lad?"

"Women being softer and smaller, their minds must be so, too."

The girls exchanged looks of pride. A brilliant reply! They all recognized it, they all shared in the wonder of this prodigy in their midst. Patrick swelled visibly. Only Emily seemed unmoved, and remarked, "I am as big as you, and as strong, and I daresay my mind is equal to yours."

"That only proves that his answer was correct," said Patrick. "Next."

Charlotte assumed the mask, after a short struggle with Branwell.

"What is the best book in the world?"

"The Bible," she answered at once.

"I meant, the next best."

"The Book of Nature."

A murmur of approval, and this time Emily added her approbation: "Yes! If nature were one big book, that would be the best, indeed! I would read it all day and leave the Bible quite alone."

Maria tutted, scandalized, but Papa only smiled.

Elizabeth's question came next. "What is the best mode of education for a woman?"

"Whatever would make her rule her house well."

"For that you need not go away to school," said Branwell cheekily.

"Maria . . . What is the best mode of spending your time?"

Maria's reply needed only a little thought, and came out, calmly and incongruously, through the mouthpiece: "By laying it out in preparation for a happy eternity."

The mask came down, and Patrick looked into the sweet face he loved and must part from—*must,* in order that the quick bright mind, which lay behind it as surely as this face behind the mask, might be filled and polished like a holy chalice, developed and employed as the talent in the parable.

He came around the table and kissed them all, his soul aglow with pride and wonder.

"I wish your dear mother had been with me to hear your answers," he said softly.

The children fidgeted and looked at him expectantly. Was that all the game? They wanted more. But abruptly, perhaps because of a surfeit of emotion, Patrick's stomach took him in a painful grip. A spasm passed across his face, and he said with a change to his usual brisk, even terse, tone, "Bed, children. Early rising tomorrow."

As they turned obediently to file out, he added, "I will be up as usual to bid you each good-night in bed."

Hands were squeezed, their steps quickened. Soon they were scampering upstairs in a flux of excitement and laughter, so that Aunt Branwell's sharp cough of disapproval from behind her door passed unheard.

Below, the Reverend Patrick sat at his table and slowly filled his pipe. *I don't give them enough of myself,* he thought. He had enjoyed the interlude past expression. Why do I always let the demands of the parish, and my own writing and reading, take precedence? Now the two eldest are going; soon Charlotte and Emily will follow. Who knows when we'll have another chance to be thus together? I wish . . . The smoke curled around his head and around the lamp-chimney. He ruminated. The germ of a poem came into his mind. There was a sermon there, too, somewhere, a theme, a lesson. "Be not sparing of yourself to those who need you, lest sooner than you dream, they need you no longer." No, that had a morbid hint in it which he did not intend. He picked up his pen and began drafting a few notes.

The time had come.

Maria and Elizabeth, in cloaks and bonnets, surrounded by the family including Nancy and Sarah and all the livestock, were ready at the door, their boxes beside them. The Haworth gig was coming to take them to Keighley, there to catch the coach that would transport them to school.

The soon-to-be-abandoned four clustered around to say goodbye. Maria kissed them all, holding Branwell the tightest and longest. He alone broke down and sobbed as she tore herself away at last and was lifted into the gig beside her father and sister. She and Elizabeth waved and waved as the gig jerked forward and moved cautiously down the steep cobbled street to disappear around the corner of the church.

The four waved back; so did Nancy and Sarah, both in tears. Aunt Branwell stood motionless, dry-eyed, her hands folded. *It is needful*, she thought. *It is for the best.* But she felt a strange, unwonted stress in her tightly corseted breast as the gig clattered out of sight, and she turned to herd the children indoors, away from a sudden chilly wind that blew back up the empty street.

Much later, she sat alone in her room staring out into the twilight. Her thoughts formed themselves almost automatically into a rigidly formalized prayer. She did not know how to talk to God. She spoke to Him in respectful formulas memorized from authorized books of devotion. She did not look for an answer, or even a faint easing of her anxieties, by way of beneficent acknowledgment. So she felt a mild surprise when, in the midst of her stilted devotions, there was a tap on the door and Anne came in.

Anne was her favorite. She was little, gentle and tractable, lacking the disturbing quality of suppressed wildness that all the others—even Maria—displayed to some degree. Aunt Branwell was so glad to see Anne at this moment that she behaved uncharacteristically. She put out her hand to her and smiled the warmest smile that her taut, narrow mouth could form. The child almost, but not quite, ran to her, and pressed herself to her side.

"What is it, Anne?"

Anne couldn't answer. She was tense and trembling. An impulse seized the woman to lift her onto her knee, but her arms did not know the way. She stiffly bent her head, in its lace bonnet, down to her instead.

"What's the matter? Tell Aunt."

After a moment, Anne whispered, "Nancy and Sarah are gone out. And Charlotte and Bany are 'making out' and don't want me."

"And Emily?" Anne was forever with Emily except when she needed more adult security, and then it had always been to Maria that she had run.

"She is gone walking. She wished to be by herself."

There was something in the forlorn little figure that would have melted stone. Aunt Branwell was not stone, and she loved this littlest niece. But how to be to her what Maria was—how to supply her need? She was emotionally inadequate and she knew it. Only God could make good her insufficiencies, and unlike Maria, she had no confidence in His omnipresence. She was too humble to believe in His intimate concern for her. It was not the results of prayer, but the performance of it that gave comfort. So she urged Anne firmly to her knees and said:

"Come, let us ask God to look after the girls on their journey."

"But they are there by now," objected Anne, though she knelt willingly enough.

"While they're at school then."

But the prayer she led had nothing to say about Maria and Elizabeth, or school either. It was all about sinners and repentance and the frail hope of glory to come. It was not what Anne had wanted to say to God; but the rich, mystical words flowed over her. Sin seemed to her like a thin black fissure in the earth, a crack big enough to fall through, leading down into some unspeakable dark regions of terror and anguish called Guilt. Only God could lift you back onto the sunny, known earth again, and He did not always want to. It was called "being saved," but you could not do it for yourself. You must just lie down there in Guilt, until His hand, called Repentance, or sometimes Grace, chose to lift you out.

Anne listened, there on her knees on the chill boards, as darkness deepened in Aunt's room. The long doctrinaire prayer frightened her almost senseless, and yet it was True, it was Right, she was not permitted to doubt it. She must learn these magic words and say them, for they were the all-powerful key—not to anything as positive as heaven, but to a way of avoiding hell.

Watching Aunt's thin lips moving in the dusk, Anne, aged four and a half, caught a word here and there and repeated it, like a sorcerer's apprentice learning the ultimate spell.

The next two months passed very slowly for Charlotte and Emily, waiting to join the older girls at school; slower still, though no one at home knew it, for Maria and Elizabeth, who were there already.

Letters home, written weekly, said nothing of trouble or homesickness. Elizabeth might let slip an occasional hint, but Maria would not let it pass. "How can we dare to complain?" she scolded as she struck out the offending words from the paper. "What matter if the food is—well, simple? What if the air is damp and we shiver a little? And if we are spoken to angrily by our teachers, who is at fault? Look how we are taught—hours and hours of lessons each day, each one blotting out a little area of our ignorance. We are so lucky! We must *never* complain, *never* let Papa think we are not happy."

Elizabeth sighed and wrote the letter out again. She couldn't rise above physical discomfort quite so easily. She had the imagination to project herself forward into winter, when the cold fogs would rise from the marshes and the snow would pile in drifts around the low-lying school buildings. If they were shivering now as they walked to church on Sunday mornings in their white cotton frocks, how would they feel in December, despite the merino and the plaid cloaks? How then would they survive the mornings in the ill-heated schoolrooms on oatmeal porridge, a dish Elizabeth loathed even when it was well cooked but could not stomach when, as frequently in Cowan Bridge, it came to the table burned?

Maria ate the minimum needed to keep up her strength and seemed indifferent to taste and smell. Her mind was on her religion and her studies. Elizabeth was of a more practical, earthly bent. But this at least kept her out of trouble with the teachers. Maria, inwardly absorbed—her whole being entangled, as it were, in her intellect and her spirit—often didn't hear what was said to her, or notice when the other girls left her to answer some routine summons. Her body, untrained to perform from habit those tasks of personal attention that Aunt had strived to impart, could sit or stand idle while her mind was feverishly active, digesting all that was new and stimulating in her lessons. But suddenly a shout or a tug would bring her back to herself—often too late to brush her hair, button up her frock properly, or tidy her drawer.

And so she was rebuked, even punished. By Miss Taylor in particular, a little black-haired woman like a malignant beetle, who had conceived a violent detestation of Maria for what she repeatedly, and publicly, called her "dirty and slovenly habits." This woman taught history, a subject in which Maria excelled; but this excellence did not outweigh, in the teacher's eyes, those irregularities of appearance, those moments of absentmindedness, upon which she pounced with a sort of energetic mercilessness. She banished Maria from her merited place at the top of the class to ignominy at the bottom, heaping abuse on her head, and even, on occasion, hanging a placard around her neck on which was inscribed the word "SLATTERN."

But Maria had no complaint. She regarded her punishments as well deserved. Even in her prayers there were no murmurings, only gratitude for a mind full, at last, of good, solid, wholesome learning.

If Maria had been nervous of going to school, how much more so was Charlotte! Terror would be a better word for what she felt as she stood with her father outside the massive gate in the grim, prison-spiked outer wall—a wall so high that it appeared to Charlotte to support the lowering clouds which, that late summer evening, had rolled down from the distant Cumberland fells. Charlotte's chief fear, however, was not of the interior of the place, however gloomy. It was of the inhabitants. One would never have guessed—her father, for one, did not—from seeing Charlotte freely playing and quarreling and acting with her brother and sisters at home, exchanging banter with the servants, or speaking up for herself to her grown-up relatives, how shy, how terrified, she was of strangers, young or old.

The gate opened; the Reverend Patrick picked up the small bag, indicated the box to the servant, who shouldered it, and taking Charlotte's limp little hand once more in his, led her up the path to the front door. They were both stiff and tired. The trip from Keighley was fifty miles in a bucketing coach on bad roads; they walked the last three miles from the nearest stopping-place, Patrick with the box on his back. Charlotte's legs ached, and she trembled from weariness as much as from dread.

They were met in the hall by the headmistress, Miss Ann Evans, a tall woman with dark-brown hair. She had a kindly eye for Charlotte, who, as she explained to Patrick, would be the youngest girl at the school. "We must try not to spoil you," she said, stooping to look into the pale, averted face. "The poor child, look how tired she is! Come, you must have some supper and go to bed."

Charlotte cast a beseeching look at her father, who, mercifully, understood.

"May she see her sisters tonight?"

Miss Evans was about to refuse, but something in Patrick's manner—a sudden fierce tension on the angular face, a flash in the pale eyes—made her bend the rules and call the two girls from the dormitory where they were getting ready for bed.

The ensuing reunion would have moved a far sterner nature than Miss Evans'. The little figures in their nightshifts fairly flew down the narrow stairway, and in a moment the three were all but indistinguishable. Their father watched their transports for a moment or two, almost overcome himself, before wrapping both arms around the sobbing, hugging trio. Only then did Maria disentangle herself and seek her old place near his heart.

Ashamed of his own tears, Patrick was brisker than he would have been if Miss Evans had not been standing there. After a single hug he put his dearest gently away from him, embraced Elizabeth, and then, sitting down, drew them to his knees.

"Is all well, my loves?"

"Yes, yes, Papa!" cried Maria at once, rubbing her face against his waistcoat to dry it. "Now all is perfect!" But her excitement made her cough, and quite a racking, prolonged spasm it was, so that he held her and she leaned against him when it was over. Then, before the sudden anxiety on his face could evolve into a question, she broke into a hasty laugh.

"It's nothing, Papa! Just a little leftover from the whooping cough that I have all but shaken off. I have not coughed like that since my arrival, and that is the truth, is it not?" She turned to Elizabeth for confirmation. Elizabeth, between devil and deep, was silent.

Miss Evans filled the breach. "She has been mildly troubled by little coughing fits," she said, "but we have dosed her with linctus and I believe she is much improved. Maria, you and Elizabeth run up to bed now and get warm. Say good-night to your Papa."

They kissed him again, and Maria whispered, "When will we see you, Papa?"

"In three months I will come with Emily." He held her shoulders and whispered, just above his breath, "Have you aught to tell me? I can send her away."

Maria shook her head vehemently. He did not trouble to repeat his inquiry to Elizabeth. He wanted and needed everything to be all right. In the wilderness, when the Israelites complained that the manna was not meat, God grew angry and punished them severely. Patrick passed the night at the school, and after the briefest farewells, caught the early coach back to Keighley with the set features of determined optimism.

Too young to put the premium on education for its own sake that sustained Maria through her trials, yet even more sensitive physically than Elizabeth, Charlotte was tormented from the first days by the Spartan arrangements promulgated at Cowan Bridge by its founder. An ardent believer in the Puritan ethic that underlay his Evangelical persuasion, Mr. Carus Wilson aimed to wean his girls away from any notion that bodily comforts mattered in the great scheme of things. He was training them for careers as dependents of one kind or another; they must, first and foremost, be made aware of their humble status. Any pride or spirit or wanton individualism must be broken out of them for the good of their future peace, as well as of their souls. To this end he not only kept them perpetually on the borders of hunger and cold, but sometimes, as the bitter weather crept on, well beyond those borders.

On Charlotte's second day at Cowan Bridge, long before she had grown accustomed to the privations, her stomach was growling with hunger and her soul already harbored the sprouting seeds of rage and rebellion. That morning she had witnessed Miss Taylor publicly holding Maria up to contempt for some trifle and banishing her from the top of the class to the bottom. (All the classes were held in one big room around separate tables, and so every child could watch what happened to every other out of the corner of her eye.)

At teatime—following a burned breakfast, no "lunch" (as the uncertain mid-morning snack was called, when they did get it) and a dinner of hotchpotch, quite uneatable—the girls lined up for their meager portions of oatcake and hot coffee. Nothing much could go wrong with this in the kitchen, and Charlotte was frankly longing for it. Her turn came; the crunchy texture of the oatcake, the smooth, promising warmth of the mug were in her hands. She hurried off to the window seat with her treasures. But no sooner had she settled there, **her** back to the folded shutters, when one of the big girls came and stood over her.

"You're new," she said. "New girls aren't allowed to have tea. Give it to me."

"But it's mine!" Charlotte cried. She clutched the mug to her thin chest.

"Nevertheless," said the girl, a big, buxom, hungry creature of an age to be the mother of two. "Come on, be sharp now, give them up, or you'll have trouble in the dormitory tonight."

She put out her hand commandingly. Charlotte, helpless, glanced around for Maria, but she was not to be seen. In any case, what could she do against this Amazon? Burning with rage as much as with thwarted hunger, Charlotte yielded up the biscuit and the mug. Her persecutor bolted half the oatcake in one bite and swilled it down with coffee. Tears of chagrin rolled down Charlotte's cheeks as she watched.

On one occasion she saw Maria being not so much menaced as coaxed out of her breakfast by one lubberly girl, who contrived, even in these surroundings, to be quite fat.

"Why did you give it to her? Fat pig! *You* need it! She can't hurt you!"

"Oh . . . It doesn't matter. She feels her hunger so much, I'm sorry for her."

Charlotte's habitual worship of Maria was sometimes tinged with exasperation. To endure persecution at stronger hands was one thing, but to submit patiently to unwarranted coercion was another. It hurt her in a peculiar way. She resented the fact that during breaks she herself couldn't creep to one of the fires that burned at either end of the long classroom, because of the double row of broad backs that encircled it; but much more, she hated to watch Maria shrug mildly and walk quietly away, wrapping her cold arms in her pinafore, to sit in a chilly corner with a book. There, Charlotte knew, her sister grew oblivious; her cough became quiescent and her flushed cheeks grew paler, as if the feverish blood were flowing more peacefully through her veins. However Charlotte might long for her company, she didn't disturb her then.

Charlotte had been tested and found to "read tolerably, write indifferently, cipher a little and sew neatly." Thus the teachers wrote in her record. As she was considered clever for her age, though "knowing nothing systematically," she was not kept in the lowest class, but put in a higher one among bigger and older girls. They treated her with disdain, until one day, when they were making remarks about her smallness and "queer-looking face," she burst out, "Well, small as I am, I have written a whole book before coming here, which is more than one of you has, I'm certain!"

They stared at her. "What sort of book?" one asked at last.

"It was only a small one, but there was lots in it."

"Writing?"

"Writing—a story—and drawings, too, of ladies walking their dogs, and a picture of a lake—but that I copied—and of our room at home. There was a church ruin in it, too," she added defiantly.

The other girls looked at her curiously.

The general rules and restrictions, the clang of the bell which divided up the day into arbitrary segments, were as irksome to Charlotte as the hunger and cold. She had grown up in an atmosphere of freedom. Now it was clang-clang! Get up. Clang-clang! Downstairs for an endless session of prayers and Bible readings. Clang-clang! Breakfast. Clang-clang! Hurry to stand behind your chairs. In came the teachers. Another clang, and all must sit; books were opened; lessons began. Charlotte hated that bell. It jangled directly on her nerves. It made her feel like a clockwork doll; her limbs jerked when the bell caught her un-awares. "Why can they not just tell us what to do?" she asked Maria; but that obedient creature only remarked, "The bell is easier and can always be heard. Not all the girls are as untalkative as we are, you know."

On Charlotte's first Sunday they dressed in their best white frocks, their bonnets trimmed with green, their light cloaks and gloves. Their lunch, cold meat and bread, was put into their hands with their prayer books, and right after breakfast they set off for church.

It was still August, and a fine, blowy day. The scenery was beautiful beyond that monstrous wall. Charlotte could hardly restrain her delight as she twisted her head this way and that, afraid of missing any element of this day of freedom—as it seemed to her. No lessons, no restricted play in the walled garden or veranda; instead, a glorious walk across the crests of the hills to Mr. Carus Wilson's church at Tunstall. "Why, it's like being at home!" she exulted to Elizabeth.

In the valley below sparkled the Leck, a tributary to the river Lune, rustling shrilly even in this dry season. Far away, the high Cumberland fells rose majestically toward the ponderous white clouds; their purple shadows darkened the white dresses of the line of girls every now and then, accentuating the bliss when the sun returned. Underfoot the moorland grass was dry and tussocky, giving a spring to their steps. Sweeping downward between them and the river was lush pastureland, measured out by hedges and flowery lanes, with an occasional farmstead or cluster of trees.

The air up here was tangibly different from the dank breath of the valley. Charlotte felt better as soon as her nostrils caught the dry tang of the uplands; Maria, behind her, coughed. Charlotte dodged ahead in the line, wanting to leave the others and run free as they used to at Haworth. A teacher spotted her and sent her back to her place. Never mind! It was all-beautiful, all-smiling Nature, welcoming her back.

The church was two miles from the school. Some girls grumbled, but Charlotte covered the distance without effort; for her the walk was all too quickly over. The church was dark and chilly inside where the sun could not reach, but Charlotte didn't mind. The feel of a church, too, was familiar, part of home, part of Papa. Quite contented, she sat through the service, annoyed and troubled only by the sound of coughing. There was a girl called Sarah Bicker sitting beside her. She really looked ill, much iller than Maria. Charlotte noticed that Miss Evans kept looking at the girl anxiously.

Mr. Carus Wilson gave the sermon. It was the first time Charlotte had ever seen her benefactor, though they were reminded every day about his goodness to them. He was a large, florid man with well-trimmed side-whiskers and a powerful cleft chin. His red lips smiled and his eyes twinkled benignly as he looked over his flock of white lambs massed below the pulpit. He discoursed on the necessity of selflessness and obedience, meekness and piety, taking as his text a verse that Charlotte had never liked, about woman being the weaker vessel. However, there was nothing else in the sermon to offend her, as the Reverend Wilson seemed to have taken Maria as his model, and he did not even mention her untidiness.

For their dinner they ate the contents of their parcels standing up in the gallery. Charlotte sneaked away and ate hers outside in the sun. The long, brisk walk and the longer service had sharpened her appetite, and the solitary piece of bread and slice of cold mutton were wholly inadequate.

She was puzzled. Could it be that that kind-looking clergyman did not *know* about the cook? Had not Miss Evans told him that there wasn't enough to eat?

The following Sunday, the Reverend Mr. Wilson preached his sermon on death.

"On Thursday last," he began with great solemnity, "died in our Clergy School your schoolfellow Sarah Bicker, aged eleven years. Her complaint was inflammation in the bowels, and her sufferings were very great. I had heard from the teachers that she had expressed a desire to depart and to be with Christ, and I

61293

was anxious to assure myself that her hopes were well founded. I came to the school especially to interview her. 'Sarah, are you happy?' I asked her. 'Yes, very happy, sir,' she replied. 'And what makes you happy?' 'Because Jesus Christ died to save me and He will take me to heaven.' 'And will He save all men?' 'No, sir,' answered Sarah, calmly despite her agony of body. 'Only those that trust in Him.'

"I left her, reassured, for she evidently was well acquainted with the tenets of her faith. As to her deserts in the life to come, some investigation set my mind at rest upon this head also. She was ever a good and virtuous pupil. She worked industriously. She was neat and tidy in her person, a great point with me as with God, who requires cleanliness in all things. More than this, she was devout, even to the point of praying with her school-fellows on Saturday nights, offering up long prayers, especially for three girls whose bad conduct gave her—as indeed it gives me—cause to be anxious for their souls should they, too, be called away." He fixed his bright eyes upon some point or points in the crowd. Charlotte, her heart thudding with sudden alarm, turned her head to see if Maria might be the recipient of that pointed stare, but she could not see. The whole tenor of the address was distressing her in some deep way that she could not fully understand.

Mr. Wilson kept up his peroration for some twenty minutes, dwelling upon Sarah's merits, her torments and her ultimate joyful and blessed release. He finished by urging them all to their knees for this prayer:

"I bless God that He has taken from us the child of whose salvation we have the best hope, and may her death be the means of rousing many of her schoolfellows to seek the Lord while He may be found."

When they mounted the gallery to eat their lunch, Charlotte's was not the only face to bear traces of frightened tears, nor was she alone in being unable to eat. Creeping to Maria's side, she was forced to ask:

"Maria . . . If Sarah had been a bad girl, lazy, perhaps, or . . ."

(but she couldn't bring herself to say "untidy") "and she had died as she did, in such pain, would she not have gone to heaven? Would her suffering not have paid for her badness in this life? Surely God would not send her soul to hell!"

"God is kind and merciful, perhaps more than Mr. Wilson supposes," said Maria. She was sitting in a corner on a bench, leaning against the wall with her eyes closed. Charlotte noticed the rings under them.

"Aunt says that God will not take to heaven any but those He has chosen. How are we to know if God has chosen us or not?"

Maria opened her eyes and put her arm around Charlotte comfortingly. "Charlotte, don't fret about it. There's nothing to fear in death. God is our friend. Papa says only the truly wicked will not get to heaven in the end, and we do not know anyone who is as wicked as that."

"Except Miss Taylor!" interrupted Charlotte hotly.

Maria smiled. "Not even she. She does her duty as it appears to her. She doesn't mean to be unkind."

"Not unkind—cruel! My heart could burst when I see how unjustly she treats you, who are so good and clever, far more than she is! Is she blind that she can't see that your faults are nothing beside your goodness?"

"Nonsense, Charlotte. I am full of faults. You don't see them because you love me, and Miss Taylor sees them clearly because she does not. That's all. Now eat your dinner and be cheerful."

"I can't eat it. I can't eat meat anymore."

"Eat the bread then. Why can't you eat meat?"

"It's because of that stuff we're given on Saturdays, that— that—mess which the girls say is made of all the scrapings off the plates for the week, heated up together in some dirty pot. The smell of it the first time it was put before me made me sick. I'm sure I'll never eat meat again, even the good boiled beef Nancy makes at home."

"Here, then. Change with me. Have my portion of bread, and let me eat your mutton."

3

PERSECUTION

*A*S AUTUMN DREW ON INTO THE awful beginnings of winter, each Sunday became more of a misery to Charlotte. No longer did she look forward to them, but dreaded them throughout the week—not only for herself, but for Maria. After each of those long, long days spent with sodden feet and shivering bodies in the unheated church—not to mention the perishing walks there and back in the face of vicious winds, rain, or lately, even snow—Maria's cough worsened.

In the mornings the bell now rang before dawn, and the girls had to get out of bed and wash and dress by the light of a taper. Down the middle of the long dormitories were washstands with washbowls and pitchers—one set for every six girls. One of the worst physical miseries was standing in line for the use of a basin, shivering in a shift, hugging mottled arms and shifting from foot to foot on the bare floor.

One morning in November—the very day on which Papa was at long last due to bring Emily, the day the three sisters had dreamed and talked of for months—Charlotte, tired of being pushed to the end by bigger girls, forced herself early from her bed and arrived at the basin first. But she was appalled, on trying to tip the heavy jug, to find that the icy northeast wind, which made her shiver all night, had frozen two inches of water at the top of the pitcher. All the containers being in the same condition, there were loud complaints. Only the hardiest managed to wash, by forcing the lump of ice downward and pouring out the chilling water underneath. Charlotte wiped her hands and face gingerly and considered herself as clean as anyone had any right to expect.

However, Maria had not the willpower to wash her clammy face and chilblained hands in ice water. She dressed as fast as her aching limbs would allow and hurried down to prayers, anxious only to avoid incurring another punishment for being late. Miss Taylor might easily forbid her to come downstairs this evening to see Emily and Papa when they arrived. This she would not risk, not only because of her longing to see them, but because, this time, Charlotte had persuaded her that she ought to mention her cough to Papa. Not in any complaining spirit, but so that perhaps he might ask Miss Evans if, on particularly windy or wet Sundays, she might stay in the school.

This dispensation was given only in the case of very sick girls, and Maria felt guilty at her weakness in wanting it; but she was becoming secretly frightened about the way she often felt. Of course she was not alone in her physical sufferings, to which, in general, she tried to be indifferent. It was much harder for her to bear the heartache of watching Charlotte, her feet a mass of chilblains, forcing her swollen toes into her shoes each morning. Maria was aware, without conceit, that she was important to her sisters. For herself, she was not afraid; God would take care of her. It seemed odd, even to her, that she was less sanguine about His power to take care of her sisters and brother, if anything should happen to her.

Seated at the table, suffering alternate fits of sweating and shivering, Maria looked at Charlotte across the big, cold candle-lit room. How small she looked sitting bolt upright on her chair, her hands folded under her pinafore, her eyes gazing ahead. There was a tightness in her lips which Maria rightly interpreted as impatience for the prayers to end and breakfast to be served; the smell of porridge, unburned for once, was beginning to tantalize them all. With a modest effort of her vivid imagination, Maria could see Emily, even smaller, younger, even more vulnerable and less fitted for this harsh, demanding life than Charlotte, seated beside her, her little head hardly rising above the tabletop. She was barely six years old. Oh, no, it was too hard! The thought of it sent pangs through Maria's body so that she clutched her arms to quell them.

Her gratitude to the school for its inexpensive educational opportunities had been undermined by watching the effects of the soul-quenching regime on Charlotte. Listening as well as she could with a hot and aching head to the interminable Bible reading, Maria suddenly changed her mind. When she saw Papa that night, she would say nothing of herself. She would swallow her linctus to check the cough and bathe her face in cold (even icy) water lest he notice her temperature. And instead of weak and selfish complaints she would concentrate on urging him not to leave Emily here, to take her back with him where she would be—*safe*, she almost let herself think, but changed the word in her thoughts to *happy*.

As always, in or out of crisis, Maria turned to God—the kind, paternal God in whom her entire being was bound up—and appealed to Him to come to her help.

But God seemingly had other concerns on that day, for even while Maria was petitioning Him, Miss Taylor, who was prowling about the room checking that each girl was in her place and attentive to the devotions, stopped short behind Maria.

Maria felt her there. Cold prickles beset her bent neck and she quickly raised her head; but it was too late.

The moment the reading had finished, the hatchet-voice snapped:

"Brontë! Stand."

Maria rose meekly. The whole school turned its many faces toward her submissive figure.

"Show me your hands, but be assured, if their condition resembles that of your neck, you will be chastised."

Maria slowly put out her hands. Large, hard fingers pulled them forward, turned them sharply once, like documents, for inspection, then let them drop.

"Abominable! Your nails are filthy. You lazy, sluttish girl! Why can you not rise early enough to wash yourself? It's disgraceful."

Charlotte, trembling all over with rage, opened her mouth to cry out, but something choked up her breath and she could not speak.

"Fetch the rod."

Maria turned and walked into the storeroom where the bundle of twigs was kept, returning with it at once and handing it to Miss Taylor.

"Undo your pinafore."

But Maria was already unbuttoning it at the back. She bent her neck. Miss Taylor raised the birch twigs.

"No! No! You shall not, you shall not!"

It was a scream from Charlotte. She flew to Maria, and stood, a frail little warrior, her arms outstretched to protect her. Tears streamed down her face.

"Charlotte Brontë! Return instantly to your place!" cried Miss Taylor, more in astonishment than anger.

"I won't! You shan't beat her! The water was frozen, the water was frozen, and she is ill. Leave her alone!"

The girls broke ranks, milled about, shouted, gesticulated and in general enjoyed a moment's freedom, which the other teachers tried in vain to control. It was only when Miss Evans came hurrying in to see what was happening that something like order was restored.

When she located the center of the trouble, she removed the twigs from Miss Taylor's hand almost gently, although her indignation was apparently reserved for Maria and Charlotte. Maria was ordered to bed, whether as punishment or out of kindness was not clear. Charlotte was rebuked and sent back to her place. But the worst blow came last.

"I cannot allow these outbreaks of indiscipline," she said. "When your father comes tonight, you will not be allowed to see him."

Maria swayed in the doorway and went so deadly pale that Miss Evans hurried to her side to support her. For a moment she regretted her words, but they had gone from her; the whole school had heard them.

From Charlotte came one more gasping sob:

"But the water! The water was *frozen!*"

"As to that," said Miss Evans quickly, glad of a chance to mollify, for she saw in the eyes of every girl who dared to look at her that glitter of repressed anger, that conviction of injustice, which hurt her heart, "it is against Mr. Wilson's beliefs to pamper the flesh with such things as warm water to wash in, but ice in the jugs is another matter. The jugs henceforth will be filled in the mornings, albeit with cold water, and brought up when the bell rings. Several of the senior class will rise early to help the servants with this task."

This was scant consolation to Maria. Unless . . .

At dinnertime, when Elizabeth crept up to bring her something to eat, she clutched her. "Lizzie! You are not to be punished, you will see Papa! You must tell him not to leave Emily here. She will never endure it! You must make Papa take her away."

Elizabeth was dumbfounded. "I shan't be able to, Maria! I know I shan't. Besides, Miss Evans will be there, and that will keep me silent even if I know what to say."

"You must try, Lizzie, you must try." A fit of coughing seized Maria. Elizabeth coughed in sympathy and soon both were helpless under the seizure. Her eyes running, Maria finally gasped out: "If Papa but hears you cough like that, no more will need saying . . ."

But Elizabeth was destined to say nothing. On her way down from Maria's dormitory, on the stairway, dark even by day, her eyes still watering from her cough and her misery, she tripped and fell, banging her head badly on a newel post. Some of the big girls found her there half an hour later, unconscious and bleeding from a severe cut.

Immensely distressed, Miss Evans carried her off to her own room, where she dressed the cut herself and put Elizabeth to bed in a crib beside her own bed. When the Reverend Patrick arrived that evening with Emily fast asleep in his arms, he was told that Maria and Charlotte had incurred punishment. The details were explained to him, not omitting the matter of the ice and the rectification of this excess of Spartanism that Miss Evans had decided upon; but as a bracing environment was quite in keeping with his own ideas, he was not too appalled by this circumstance. He was also told that Elizabeth had hurt her head, and was taken to see her, but she was asleep and did not wake when he stooped to kiss the pale, but by no means alarmingly livid, face under the bandage. The doctor had been, he was truthfully assured, and pronounced the wound superficial. Patrick handed the small sleeping figure of his next-to-youngest child into the arms of Miss Evans. He was deeply distressed not to see Maria and Charlotte; but he knew Maria's faults and Charlotte's impetuous temper. No doubt their punishment was just. He spent the night at the school, kissed Elizabeth again in the morning, and set off just after dawn to walk to the coach-stop three miles away, with a frugal but sufficient breakfast under his belt and Miss Evans' cheerful reassurances of his daughters' excellent scholastic progress ringing in his ears.

Winters are always long and nearly always hard at Haworth. The Reverend Patrick, whose home now seemed relatively empty with four of his daughters away, resolutely shut his heart to its loneliness for them and concentrated upon the many tasks at hand. He had his parish duties, but also he had the long-anticipated delight of teaching Branwell.

This proved, though it was long before Patrick would admit it, not to be the unalloyed pleasure he had expected. The scintillating mind shut up in that bright-eyed fluffy head was not to be called forth merely by uttering the words "Come, Branwell, it is time for your lessons." The rock before the treasure cave frequently remained quite motionless; the eyes wandered, the vivid mouth declined into reluctant sighs, the hands fiddled, the feet fairly itched to wander.

Sometimes, of course, all went well: the boy's imagination was caught, the busy brain concentrated its powers; the anxious, ambitious father saw instant, flying and effortless progress, which seemed to have little to do either with teacher or pupil but with some power channeled through the boy's brain, emerging from mouth or fingers. "That's it, my boy, that's it!" Patrick cried exultantly on these occasions. "Would you always worked so well! There is nothing you cannot do when you apply yourself!" But just as suddenly the mystic power to learn could be withdrawn, and lessons often ended in annoyance, frustration and dissatisfied words.

But the Reverend Patrick would not give up. To send Branwell to school would leave him only with Anne. Anne always looked so . . . frail. He was afraid to love her too much. Who better than a clergyman was aware of how many little children died young in that harsh climate? All his children were small for their age, except Emily. Sometimes he thought of the ice water in the jugs at Cowan Bridge. It troubled him even though he knew it was an isolated occurrence. Yet the letters from the girls spoke of Elizabeth's recovery from her injury, of Emily's settling down "as happily as one may expect." It never occurred to him that their letters might be subject to overseeing by the teachers.

Thus the news that arrived in early February burst upon him like a thunderclap. It was waiting for him when he came home at the end of a long day spent tramping the muddy hollows and snowy heights to visit two or three outlying cottagers. His sister-in-law had already opened the letter and was waiting for him.

"Brother-in-law! At last you are come! There is such bad news arrived by the post from the school. Pray read it quickly and act upon it, for I am quite beside myself with worry!"

Maria was ill, so seriously that Miss Evans could no longer accept responsibility. Mr. Brontë was requested to come and fetch her away.

He did not sleep all night.

The gig was at the door at first light and hurried him to Keighley, where he caught the coach to Lancashire, light-headed and numb with apprehension. It was dark by the time he arrived at Cowan Bridge. He bribed the coachman to let him descend between stops. As the coach clattered away, the wild, mocking sound of the Leck chuckling over the rocks in the darkness filled the silence. He felt the unwholesome damp in the foggy air that surrounded him; a rotten, marshy stench rose to his nostrils. He was appalled. It had not been thus in the summer—yet why had he not looked about him at the low-lying situation of the school and realized how unhealthy its vapors must make it when the sun withdrew its warmth from the site? What if his eagerness to accept the school had so blinded him to its drawbacks that he had jeopardized the life of his daughter?

The sight of Maria lying in her narrow bed in the infirmary, conscious but obviously terribly weak, stunned him.

Sick with dread, he sank to his knees beside her.

"My dearest! My dearest! Why was I not told? Why was I not sent for before?"

Miss Evans stood at his side. "It was Maria's own wish that we try every remedy before disturbing you, Mr. Brontë. She has behaved with quite exceptional fortitude. I thought until the very day I wrote to you that her will and her constitution would triumph—I still believe so—but something—some . . ." She hesitated, swallowed, and continued with difficulty. "There was an unfortunate occurrence with one of the staff which, when I heard of it, convinced me that Maria would be better at home."

Patrick turned to look at her. "What occurrence? What was done to her?"

Miss Evans was quite unable to meet his eyes.

"I cannot tell you. I feel the shame of it in every fiber of my body, Mr. Brontë. Rest assured only that the guilty teacher has been dismissed. I am deeply sorry for it, believe me . . ."

"I will remove them, all of them! If—"

"No, Mr. Brontë, I beg you will do no such thing. There is no cause. Let Maria be nursed back to health at home, and entrust the other three to me. They shall have my personal attention, be certain."

"Let me see them."

Elizabeth, Charlotte and Emily were brought. They ran to him; they bewailed Maria's decline. Charlotte seemed quite speechless with sorrow and anger, and it was Elizabeth who told, though not as graphically as Charlotte might have done had she been able to marshal her words, how Miss Taylor one morning had dragged Maria from her bed when she was too ill to get up, and despite the raw blister that had been raised on her side by the doctor, flung her on the floor with words of abuse about her laziness and bad habits. All three girls were so filled with indignation and anxiety about this episode and Maria's condition generally, that not one found time or breath to speak of her own ailments or anxieties about the school.

With deep inner reluctance, Patrick forced himself to ask, "Do you wish me to take you home? Do you wish to leave the school?"

"Yes, yes!" they all cried. "We want to be with Maria!"

It was not a total condemnation, and Patrick breathed a sigh of relief. He talked to them tenderly but firmly of their duty to become educated, of the near-impossibility of achieving this anywhere else, of the need to overcome hardships and even hatreds.

"This Miss Taylor will not trouble you more," he said. "As for Maria, she will be better off if there is peace and quiet in the house, which there cannot be if you are all at home. Aunt will want to concentrate all her attention upon nursing your sister. It will surely be best if you remain here and await good news of Maria's recovery. Meanwhile, work hard, and pray hard. God will be more inclined to hear you if He sees you are courageous and dutiful."

They pleaded, but without conviction. They were too accustomed to obeying him.

Thus Mr. Brontë, with Maria on a litter, traveled back to
Haworth the following day, leaving three other daughters behind.
His mind was sorely troubled in doing so; he was uncertain even
as to why he had persuaded himself to this decision. His mind
was set upon their education. But there was more. Just as he had
craved to have Branwell to educate alone, now he must have
Maria to cherish—alone. Her needs were paramount. For the
rest, he trusted in a seemingly immutable course of action that
God had put into his mind, and was holding him to, no matter
what attempts fate made to deflect him.

4
THE
FUNDAMENTAL
LOSS

*W*ITH MARIA REMOVED, CHARLOTTE did not rebel anymore. She often felt rebellious, but to act on those feelings, now the incentive of Maria's persecution was no longer before her, would have been out of character. Elizabeth attracted no special notice, incurred no special opprobrium or punishment, any more than Charlotte herself did in normal circumstances.

As for Emily, a surprising thing happened. The spoiling that never materialized in the case of Charlotte, enveloped her from her first day. "A darling child," was Miss Evans' instant verdict as she led her, a quaint, self-possessed little figure in her buff nankeen and pinafore and doll-like cap, to her place at the bottom of the lowest class. And, "Ah! The pet!" gurgled all the girls, reaching out to touch and stroke her. No question of *this* new girl not getting her tea; extra tidbits were even pressed on her by the very hoydens who had once tyrannized Charlotte. Watching, Charlotte thought philosophically, *Well. She is pretty. And then, she would not mind if they were unkind to her—she would not even notice.* At a very young age Charlotte had begun to analyze people, to realize that the human animal only gets sport from tormenting the weak. And Emily, even at six, was not weak. She had the strength of imperviousness.

But only two months after Maria's departure from the school, just as the elder two remaining sisters were beginning to look forward to spring after the physical hardships of winter, there was a change. They were busy at their lessons one day when a girl from a higher class got up to fetch something for the teacher, hesitated halfway across the room, and quietly collapsed on the floor.

It was typhus.

Now, indeed, Charlotte became accustomed to death. Many pupils, weakened by the insufficient, dirty food, damp buildings and wholly inadequate sanitary arrangements (one stone privy for upward of seventy people), succumbed like flies to the fever, and a number died of it, either in their homes or before they could be fetched away. The mournful tolling of the Tunstall bell, calling the girls to put on their Sunday frocks and attend another graveside, became a commonplace that no longer had power to make Charlotte shiver.

The epidemic had its good side. With the school routine upset and all discipline at a standstill, while every adult effort was spent on nursing, those pupils who managed to remain healthy were enjoying exceptional freedom. Every morning—and it was spring, so the mornings were now an open invitation—the unafflicted were almost pushed outdoors, and not merely into the walled gardens to tend their allotments, but right out into the countryside to roam at liberty until hunger brought them back.

There was another good thing that had attended the "plague." The doctor sent for by Mr. Wilson, recognizing the debility of many of the girls, had at once demanded access to the kitchen, and there picked up a ladle and sampled the stew. The next moment he had spat it out.

"What in the name of the Almighty is this filthy stuff?" he roared. "It is not fit for pigs, let alone growing girls!" It happened that this forthright man was one of the founder's near relations. The slatternly cook left the premises, bag and baggage, the next morning.

Her replacement was a very different member of her calling. It might have helped, too, that Mr. Wilson was now spending a good deal more money upon foodstuffs. Mealtimes became a pleasure. The pupils' health, and consequently their high spirits, blossomed. Charlotte, despite her worry about Maria (reported in Papa's letters to be "much the same"), had seldom enjoyed life more.

Each day when they woke, the three sisters asked each other, "Have you got it?" They felt each other's foreheads, and then laughed with a relief quite unconscious of its own callousness, for always there were others less lucky. They dressed quickly, took their breakfasts chattering (no more Bible readings, only the briefest prayers) and then were off and out, often equipped with a rough but ample cold dinner to eat in the woods or fields as they liked. They could thus escape the gloomy sights and smells, the darkened rooms and anxious, hurrying steps that filled the school. When they ran free across the newly sprung grass of the fields and hills, jumping the flashing streams and wandering through woods and lanes all misting up with buds and glossed over with spring flowers, they felt the joy of it even more keenly than on the moors at home, for here there was contrast to lend edge to their pleasure. The staff of the school, who regarded Charlotte as a grave, taciturn little girl, would not have known her here.

And thus in pleasant, unexpected liberty passed the end of April and the first days of May, until the day which, unknown to them (it passed delightfully like the others) brought the end of an era in their lives: the day when Maria died.

For days before the end came, the bedroom in which she had lain ill for so long had been darkened, and so had her father's mind. He continued to pray, but he was tortured by the image of Cain's sacrificial smoke trailing upon the ground. Sometimes, when he had lost hope completely, and sat by her bed holding her wasted hand in both of his, waiting for the inevitable, he imagined he could see his dreary, hopeless prayers falling from his lips and lying inert at his feet. How could they rise to God, how could he think of God at all, when he knew what was coming? At last his prayers lost all order and formality, and he was reduced to one dismal repetition that went on and on with every intonation of pleading. "Do not take her from me. Do not take her from me." But one look at her face robbed even that simple appeal of all point and logic.

At last the fragile beating of her heart stopped, the breath was stilled. Patrick refused to notice it at first, but Aunt Branwell, bending over the bed, felt the motionless chest and put her cheek down to the gray lips. Then she straightened up, stood still for a moment with her eyes upraised, and with a slow, deliberate movement drew the sheet up over the dead face.

From then on Aunt Branwell took over. Patrick was like a child in her brusque, capable hands. She raised him, led him to his own room, helped him out of jacket and boots and laid him on his bed. Then she went about the business of death, commencing with the closing of the shutters all over the house. This would notify the handful of watchers outside that the child had departed; soon the whole district would know. The sexton would be here within the hour; mourners would come to the house with offers of meats and pies for the funeral; the whole train of sad, necessary events would be touched off by that simple action of closing the eyes of the house.

And at the first creak of the first shutter, Nancy and Sarah burst into loud weeping in the kitchen. They would have rushed to Miss Branwell for comfort if she had had any to give; as it was, they fell into each other's arms and then hurried upstairs, sobbing and crying, to kiss the dead face and lay out the body.

And Branwell and Anne? They were in the house, too, for the moment forgotten in the children's study. They, too, heard the creak of the shutters below and understood at once that Maria was dead. They froze in their play and stared at each other aghast.

For a long moment they did not move or speak. Then Anne whispered:

"Are we to close these shutters, too? But it will be dark if we do! Oh—" she gasped as she saw with horror Branwell's face, which was slowly turning white.

"Don't look so, Bany. She has gone to heaven! I do wish Emmie were here, I do so wish she were!" Her sobs brought Nancy and Sarah running in, and she was swept up by the tear-streaked pair and borne off to the kitchen to be nursed and petted and cried over until they were all wept out. Then they brewed tea and talked about Maria's goodness endlessly until Anne was fast asleep on Sarah's lap and the two girls felt a great deal better.

But Branwell had not wept, and no one had paid much attention to him. Patrick was asleep; Aunt Branwell was much occupied; the kitchen door was shut upon the cozy, extroverted mourners. Branwell sat in the study until it was getting dark. He did not cry, or move about, or busy himself; he simply sat still, staring at the wall that divided him from Maria.

At last he got up, his cramped legs buckling under him. He walked to the door, opened it, crossed the short space and opened the adjoining door. The room was dark. Two candles burned at the head and foot of the bed. In it lay a shrouded figure. He stared at it for a long time, struggling with himself. He wanted to see her face, to convince himself that death was a real thing, that she had really gone—also just to see what death looked like. But he could not go nearer, and no power on earth could have made him lift that sheet.

Suddenly there were footsteps on the stairs.

"What are you doing there, Branwell?" asked Aunt in a sharp voice. "Come away at once; it is not time to see her yet."

She led him away, and when he had submitted limply to be put into his shift, he was firmly set upon his knees at his bedside.

"Now," said Aunt Branwell, "repeat after me. Kind and merciful God, who hast taken my sister Maria to be Thy brightest angel—"

Suddenly a flame of absolute hatred blazed up in Branwell's

heart. His face, so expressionless for so many hours, contorted abruptly into a wild grimace of rage, and he turned on his Aunt and shouted:

"He is not, He is not kind or merciful! He is cruel and greedy to take her! She is ours, our very own, and God has enough angels, while we had only her! If this is what God does, He is nothing but a robber! I won't pray to Him—I will hate Him always!"

Horrified, Aunt Branwell let him get these blasphemous words out before she could do anything to stop him. But the paralysis passed and she clutched him to her, muffling his wide-open mouth with her hand.

"Branwell! Enough! Be silent," she muttered. She glanced around her, almost as if fearing some instant visitation. "Go to bed and ask God to forgive you."

"I won't!" screamed Branwell the second his mouth was free.

"Then I will," said Aunt. "Be quiet, you will distress your father, who has enough to bear."

When the letter arrived at Cowan Bridge, several days delayed by Patrick's utter inability at first to write it, it caused a flurry in the staff room—not merely because it ticked up yet another on the school's mounting death-roll, but because only a few days before its arrival the second Brontë sister had suddenly shown signs of a decline.

Mr. Carus Wilson wrung his hands when he was informed. Those wealthy philanthropists whose generosity made the school, and Mr. Wilson's power over it, possible, had recently begun to ask unfortunate questions.

"Elizabeth must be sent home," he decreed. "We cannot accept responsibility for her. As for the other two . . . I will send them to my own seaside home at Morecombe Bay."

But this information, when it reached Patrick, did nothing to reassure him. He took only one look at the face of his second daughter as she lay on the litter in the parsonage hall and saw written there the same black message he had seen on the face of Maria, so recently laid in her coffin. Leaving Elizabeth in the care of Aunt Branwell, he rushed from the house in a frenzy of guilty apprehension. The following morning, after a long, terrible journey and an agonized search of the town of Silverdale, he found the house he had been told about, called "The Cove." As he stood trembling on the doorstep, banging on the knocker, all the blood rushed to his head. He knew suddenly that if they died, if they all died, he alone would be responsible. For he had known. He had known all the time, from the moment he saw that wall, smelled the evil smell of bad food and misery in the dank hall, heard Maria's cough, saw the faces of the others as they begged to go home. Leaning on the doorpost, he longed to strike his head there, again and again, and cry out, "Fool! Blind, wanton, selfish folly! Oh, God! Do what You will to me, but punish *me* and not them—no more, oh God, no more!"

The door opened and—almost to his surprise—Charlotte and Emily, both healthy and ruddy-cheeked, flew to his arms. He looked at them, held them, listened to them, and allowed his heart a little respite. But when he returned home with them, it was to find Elizabeth already sunk into unconsciousness. Two weeks later she was dead.

Charlotte's immense loss did not take hold of her at once. The last weeks at Cowan Bridge, with their repeated experiences of death, had made her almost immune to its terrors; and not having seen Maria for some time before her death, it seemed as if she had already suffered for, and said good-bye to, that most adored sister months ago.

Elizabeth was another matter. She actually saw Elizabeth die, and what was worse, saw her (as they all did) laid out in her small coffin on a trestle in the hall, with the servants sobbing over her, and parishioners pressing through the open doorway to pay their last respects. She saw Branwell literally dragged to the side of the coffin, and his head forcibly turned toward the corpse in an effort to make him kiss the dead face.

To Charlotte, there was nothing terrible about the sight of Elizabeth's body. It was sweetly dressed in her white school frock, with little white-shod feet peeping out beneath the hem she had so carefully sewn. Her hands were folded on her breast with a trailing wreath of late spring flowers twisted in among the small, cold fingers. Her hair—still short from its Cowan Bridge cropping—had been lovingly brushed and arranged in curls on her forehead. When it was Charlotte's turn to bend and kiss her cheek, only its unnatural marble coldness repelled her, and by that time the mandatory ritual was accomplished. The two little ones seemed to regard the corpse as a sort of image or statue of their sister. They were lifted by Aunt and each gave Elizabeth's cheek a peck. Anne reached out curiously to touch her, but her hand was firmly drawn back.

But Branwell had been through this before, less than a month ago. On that occasion, too, he had had to be forced to go through with it. Aunt would not let him off. It was customary, it was fitting and therefore it must be done, and those who shrank from it shrank from a duty to the dead. Such a thing could not be tolerated. So she was firm with Branwell, even though last time he had been sick and hysterical. However, when she felt the strength of his resistance, and saw the embarrassed and shocked looks of others standing by, her determination left her and she let Branwell go.

The second her hands were off him he fled upstairs to the study, where he shut himself in. Nothing would bring him out. He missed the funeral. It was only afterwards, when Charlotte, still in a turmoil from the events of the day and shaken by the scene at the side of the coffin, came to him with the right words of love—the wonderful, magic words of the secret language of "making-out" they had developed between them—that he recovered enough to eat a little and be helped (by Charlotte, not by Aunt, whom he would not look at) to bed.

From that day, Branwell felt himself growing closer and closer to Charlotte. Maria was gone; her absence from the world was a sort of blanketing, infinitely puzzling pain for him, like a missing limb to which the brain goes on trying to send messages.

He still sought her—sometimes frantically, sometimes in simple bafflement—in his thoughts, or even in reality, wandering through the rooms of the parsonage half hoping she might appear. Even her ghost would have been welcome if he could just have been near it for a few moments and convince himself she was not wholly lost to him. Only Charlotte understood this, and would search with him, holding his hand, playing it like one of their not-quite-games.

"Let's tiptoe to the door and open it suddenly, perhaps we can catch her—"

In this way Charlotte hoped to help Branwell get over his loss, but it had the opposite effect on herself; for her imagination produced Maria all too easily as they threw open the door. She saw her there, only not at all as she used to be in life when at home, but as Charlotte had last seen her in those atrocious days at school. She saw her lying on the floor in her shift, where she had been thrown by the hated Miss Taylor, or struggling to dress with her breath coming short, or kneeling in church stealthily rubbing at her poor inflamed, itching chilblains and trying to hide her tears. Then Charlotte had to leave the game and run away to weep alone. In this way her loss of the dearest person in her life was made slowly and painfully clear to her until she began to feel it more and more as time passed, rather than less.

She took the growing obsession to her father.

"Perhaps Maria died so that she should never have to suffer as we are suffering for her loss. Have you thought of that? She'll never know what it is to lose a beloved child—" He stopped speaking abruptly, and turned his face away.

Aunt's creed was harder, but less confused.

"This world is a vale of tears. We are put here to suffer. The more terrible our trials in this world, the greater may be our reward in the next. Be glad you are called on to endure pain. It should bring you closer to God. Tell me, do you compare your little heart-pangs to what Christ suffered on the Cross, when He took upon Him all our sins? Away with you! Be brave, say your prayers, do your duty. It is all part of living."

PART II

The Creative Years

1826–35

1

THE MINIATURE
WORLD

*B*RANWELL WAS WAKING UP. IT
was a slow process as a rule; he liked to sleep, and when he woke
he kept his eyes closed for some time to savor the aftertaste of his
complex, fantastic dreams.

His bed was now in his father's room in the front of the house.
This meant Patrick could no longer discharge his pistols, loaded
every night against possible intruders, out of the window over
the graveyard. Now he performed this morning exercise out
through the back door, at the first hill of the moor; in whose
placid, insentient side many bullets were already lodged.

Branwell rolled over and his hand dropped off his narrow bed
and trailed on the bare floor. Or—no, what was this? In a second
his eyes were wide open, his fingers groping about the unfamiliar
object they had met. It was a box—a long, flat box with words
on it. He didn't stop to read them before pulling off the top.

Toy soldiers! Twelve of them, made of wood, beautifully
painted in red, blue and black.

Hardly stopping to gloat over this treasure, Branwell snatched it up and ran barefoot (it was June and even the parsonage floors were warm) across the hall to the room shared by Charlotte and Emily. Bursting in, he began to shout:

"Tally, Emily, look! Papa must have brought them back from Leeds. And, see? You have presents, too, only just look at mine—see—they're soldiers, twelve, and no two exactly alike! Did you ever see anything so grand?"

Charlotte was out of bed in a flash and snatched up the tallest and handsomest of the little men.

"This is the Duke of Wellington!" she cried. "This shall be the Duke!"

Emily, kneeling on the floor by the box, ran her hand cautiously along the rank and then selected one.

"I want this one," she said. "I shall call him Parry, after the great explorer."

"He's got a face to match yours, Emmy—all solemn and grave. I'll call him Gravey!"

Emily shrugged. "Call him what you please. To me he is Captain Edward Parry." She carried him to the door and in a moment or two returned with Anne, who, at seven years old, still slept in Aunt's room.

"Oh, may I have one, Bany?"

"If you've all finished picking over *my* present, may I choose now? This will be my special one, and his name is—"

"Bonaparte!" shouted all the girls in one breath.

They were all late down to breakfast that morning, for the girls' presents—Charlotte's was a model farm—had to be inspected and played with, and no one bothered to think of dressing until Aunt came to the door and said that Tabby would be getting cross if breakfast was allowed to sit. That stirred them as nothing else could have done, for Tabby's cross fits were not to be trifled with; she was not above administering cuffs with her sharp words if pushed, as she would say, "beyond enough." Since her astringent regime had replaced the flabbier one of Nancy and Sarah, the house was better managed, and so were the inmates.

So then there was a scramble to get dressed and they all tumbled down the stairs with their new toys in their hands and rushed into the kitchen to mollify Tabby by showing them to her.

She was not in the mood for toys, however. "Be off wi' ye and yer silly playthings! There's a time for play and 'tis not wi' breakfast half an hour on t'table! I may look at 'em after—not as I've time to be messin' wi' toys, I'm not idle like some fowk."

The morning was given over to lessons. Papa had been teaching them more or less regularly for a year now. He was well suited to the task: his own education, poorly begun in an Irish village school, climaxed against all the odds at Cambridge, and he had, besides, a good didactic manner. The trouble was, he had no system and scant discipline. One subject, begun according to a precise plan and with determined intentions, led off at tangents. Sometimes it was an association, a recollection, a tale of his own youth perhaps; or a reminder of something recently read in *Blackwood's Magazine*, their favorite periodical, or in the *Leeds Intelligencer* (Tory), the *Leeds Mercury* (Whig) or even in the *John Bull* (high Tory, and very violent, thought Charlotte). The pile of back numbers had then to be gone through and searched for the reference, and the article was read aloud and discussed, with each adding his comment or argument until the original point of departure was completely forgotten. A whole morning's lesson time could be easily and delightfully got through in this fashion; twelve o'clock struck, and they might be too deep in discussion to realize it was officially time to break off and repair to Aunt's room for sewing or to sweep the floors for Tabby, allowing their father to go about his parish affairs. It was often only when Tabby came banging loudly on the parlor door shouting, "Am I to feed thi dinners to't geese, or to't dog?" that they remembered they had other elements in their lives besides this free-ranging delight that passed, *faute de mieux*, for schooling.

This morning, of course, all they wanted to do was talk about the presents, and to this end they began by a little impromptu chorus of thanks and praise to Papa for his thoughtful generosity. Naturally gratified, he was quite willing to settle down to examine the toys for himself.

It had not escaped the children's sharp eyes that Papa had a sneaking fondness for things military. There was something in his manner and bearing that suggested the army officer *manqué*—his crisp manner of issuing commands, his liking for order and promptness, his strict adherence to certain aspects of his routine. There was also the firing of his pistols, and certain moments of explosive wrath suggestive more of gunpowder and touchpaper than of the fire and brimstone associated with clerical ire. Thus his eagerness to set up the "young men" and arrange them in a double rank as if ready for drill was not only for Branwell's benefit. But so as not to seem partial to the "manly" toy, he cheerfully assembled Charlotte's farmyard too, equipping it realistically with Emily's wooden animals and Anne's model people. They were disproportionately tiny in comparison with the soldiers; but undeterred by this problem, Patrick suddenly began making the troops march through the farmyard, scattering chickens and ducks and even farmhands, beside whom they were as giants. They set up camp in the center of the yard, and before long Patrick had begun to tell the bit of history of which this game reminded him.

"Why, it might be the aftermath of the Battle of Adwalton Moor, nearly two hundred years ago. The Civil War between the Royalists and the Parliamentarians was raging. Many were killed in the encounter, which, we're told, was witnessed by a little boy who hid up a tree and watched the whole slaughter."

"Oh, how lucky for him! How I wish there were such things nowadays, that I might witness!" exclaimed Branwell. "How I'd cling on tight, and cheer on the Royalists—they did win, Papa, did they not?" Patrick nodded. "Then when all was over, I'd slip down and capture some tokens—a sword, or a standard, prized from a dead hand—"

"What! Would you rob a corpse, Branwell?" asked Charlotte, shocked.

"Why not? I'd need proof! Then I'd mount a charger that had belonged to some dead officer, and gallop off across the blood-stained moor to the town, and there, surrounded by breathless, eager listeners, I'd tell my tale."

"With embellishments, I don't doubt," remarked Patrick drily. "These happenings are as important as anything you can learn of. I'm heartily glad they interest you so much. We will hire the gig next Saturday week, and I shall show you where it happened."

This he did, and a fine outing they had. They visited Oakwell Hall, to which the defeated Roundheads had fled for refuge. Its present owner welcomed in the neighboring parson and his family with surprise, well concealed by deference. They were shown the hall, which seemed vast and magnificent to them, with its heavy black paneling, somber pillars and overhanging gallery. Branwell instantly ran around to the back to look at the garden, but Charlotte stood in the middle of the hall and gazed around as if entranced.

Emily shivered uneasily, like a dog.

"I hate it here," she whispered. "It's cold. Let's go."

"It's all that black paneling," Charlotte whispered back. "I would like to see it all painted. Pink. Wouldn't that put paid to any ghosts? They wouldn't know how to go on at all!"

"Look!" cried Anne suddenly. She was standing at the window. "There's something cut into the window glass. Can anybody read it? I can't."

They crowded to the corner of one of the big leaded windows. Branwell, who had returned somewhat disappointed from the trim, unbloodied garden, read the cramped words with difficulty:

> *"Kings are but slaves when by their passions held,*
> *But who commands himself commands the world."*

"And that's true!" he added. "You all used to call me 'Little King' when I was younger. But when I'm grown up, I shall be my own king, master of myself!"

"Then let's hope you grow up soon," remarked Emily, "for at present you can't give yourself a single order and get it obeyed."

"You don't know how I *feel*," said Branwell haughtily. "I am like a wild, nervous animal. If I am too harshly broken in, I will be ruined for life. People must be patient with me, and tame me gradually. Not that I will ever become truly tame," he added, disliking the word for its overtone of spiritlessness. "But I shall command myself, and my powers shall flow from me in all directions! Then you'll all be proud of me. You, too, Emmy, and you'll be sorry, then, that you often jeered at me."

"I'm proud of you now, and I don't jeer. I know you're very clever," replied Emily matter-of-factly. "I just wish you wouldn't fly into tempers as often as you do. Your screaming goes through my head."

Branwell went scarlet—a poor match for his carroty hair—and was about to offer a sharp reply when their father interrupted:

"Don't quarrel. Our host tells me there is a fair in Keighley on Michaelmas. If you're good children and work hard and don't quarrel between now and then, we shall go . . ."

So good behavior became the temporary rule, for Papa never said anything he didn't mean. Branwell in particular held himself rigidly within bounds, and never a scream or a furious word or a single piece of mischief emanated from him between that day and Michaelmas. But the three-week abstinence from tantrums resulted in a pent-up reservoir of emotion, seething for release.

The Fair, with its sideshows and food stalls, catchpenny games, gawdy troubador entertainers and an assortment of performing animals, was a positive assault upon the senses of the children. There were horrors as well as delights—a poor, muzzled dancing bear, a tentful of freaks, which Branwell insisted upon describing—but for the most part the outing was a feast for their eyes, ears, noses and imaginations.

As darkness began to fall the rowdy scene was lit with torches and lanterns, taking on an even more fabulous aspect. Branwell, grasping after a last thrill, begged a ride on the swing-boats. Not even Emily was brave enough to risk what she knew well would be a wild ride, with Bany pulling the tufted rope; but a ragged country lad who was hanging about was happy to take the opposite place, and soon the little craft was riding the air as if it were mountainous seas. Up and up Bany forced it, dragging on the rope as if each swing meant survival itself over yet another comber; his bright hair and the double circles of his spectacles caught the torchlight on each descent, while his slight, straining figure became a crested silhouette as the boat flew up against the stars. Below in the crowd his sisters and their father watched him and marveled at his fearlessness.

But suddenly the boat went just that bit too high for Branwell. The excitement burst its bonds and turned into a moment's agonizing terror, which flashed out along his skin like a burn. He dropped the rope and crouched down, clinging frantically to the boat's sides, and began to scream at the top of his voice.

"My nerves—my nerves—my nerves—!"

By the time the braking board had been hastily lifted and the ride brought to a rasping sudden end, Branwell had been overtaken by a strange seizure. He lay limp on the grass, his eyes rolling, his teeth clenched. Bending over him, his father recognized this as an exaggerated form of what happened during the temper bouts. But there was something else, something he had often obscurely feared in his unstable, high-strung son. It was a brainstorm, a "fit." Struggling to crush down the awful fear in his heart, Patrick picked up the limp body and ran with it to the hired gig, with the girls streaming out behind him against the lights of the fair.

Until this time Patrick had been toying with the advice he had been given by various people, that he should send Branwell away to school. Aunt was one of the proponents of this plan. He had for some time been nearly beyond her control. Ordinary naughtiness she could manage; but there was something almost demonic about Branwell in certain uncontrolled moods that alarmed her. The spoiling and indulgence he got at home were obviously increasing his willfulness and inability to acquire self-control.

But since the terrifying incident at Keighley Fair, Patrick turned his back on all such well-meant advice. For what was it that had always pushed his son toward this fatal edge of breakdown, but the least show of harshness or anger or opposition? Better, far, that he should continue being indulged, that the treasures of that budding mind be gently husbanded, rather than risk breaking altogether what Patrick now feared was the slender mesh that contained the treasure. Besides, what if he had a fit at school? It hardly bore thinking about. Such attacks were looked upon by the ignorant as the next step to madness. He might suffer unspeakably at the hands of masters and pupils alike if he ever displayed those symptoms in an unsympathetic environment. No. No. Such a step was now out of the question.

But now he was fairly under Branwell's thumb, for at the least sign of irritation or impatience on Patrick's part, the boy grew tense, wild-eyed, shrill-voiced. Patrick was never quite sure how much was put on and how much was genuinely to be feared as an oncoming symptom. But he dared not take risks.

Somehow the coming of "The Twelves," as they called Branwell's soldiers, triggered off something much more dynamic, more organized and directed, than any games they had previously attempted. The "plays" were secret. Not because there was anything in them—as yet—of which the adults would disapprove. But the secrecy added spice; their own private world, which they shared with their "young men," could not be shared with anyone else. No explanations about their make-believe world must ever be demanded, for none could be given.

The "young men" had begun to transcend the original concepts that their simple shapes suggested to their four inventive human puppet masters. No longer one-dimensional personalities, they became living, changing beings with a dozen characters apiece—not just explorers, warrior-dukes and emperors, but poets, politicians, sea captains, lovers and tyrants.

Before long England became too small to hold this swelling cast of actors. So their manipulators sent them forth on a voyage of discovery, to Africa of course, the exploration of whose west coast and interior (by Mungo Park among others) was currently the subject of intensive and fascinated study in the parlor.

Whatever the children learned, down in Papa's parlor, or up in Aunt's bedroom, or out on the moors, or alone with their own choice of books, was not merely absorbed by the minds of the four scholars. It was channeled through them and poured out immediately into the new and ever-expanding world of the Twelves. Not only the explorations going on in Africa, but news of the English court or the exiled French nobility; political upheavals which they followed as keenly as ever Maria had; descriptions and criticism of current art exhibitions, and all else contained in *Blackwood's*, their journalistic window on the world. Then there were the books from their father's library: Scott's *Life of Napoleon*, Goldsmith's *History of Rome*, the works of Milton, and the poetry of Southey and Cowper and the divine Lord Byron. Their father had also taken out a subscription to Keighley Mechanics' Institute Library, from which they could obtain all the latest literature. And, of course, on their own bookshelves such dog-eared treasure houses as *Aesop's Fables* and *The Arabian Nights* lay always ready to feed their insatiable imaginations with delights both old and new.

It was from the latter book that Branwell got the idea of their each becoming a genie, or "genius," a huge monster that could command even the highest rulers among their "young men" and mastermind the doings of the new kingdoms with the help of magic powers.

"Mine shall be ten miles high and perfectly fearsome to look at. Wherever I go—I am the genie myself, of course—the world shall get dark and streams of fire shall flash ahead of me, and the whole earth shall shake, like the moor did that time we were caught in the earth tremor, only much worse, so that everyone shall turn pale and fall on their faces before me." The others stood around him, staring, for his own angular face had turned pale and his eyes were glazed with some pulsing inner excitement. "I shall protect all that I love, if they give me respect, and even if the Ashantis eat part of a dead hero I shall make him whole again."

From then on, the "plays" took a new lease of life. In the shape of the genii, the creators of the dramas could take a subjective role. The Twelves flourished in Africa. As the months passed, the children's minds expanded; their lessons, their conversations, their reading, were all imagination's elixir, which they sucked into their systems through the numberless little gaping pores of their eager sensibilities. Once shut into their private chamber, they squeezed each other dry, mingled the resulting outflow with their own private sources of inspiration, and half drowned themselves in a seething deluge of creativity.

"Look, Charlotte!" Branwell was flushed, shrill-voiced and trembling.

"In a minute, Bany. I'm busy."

"You're not, you're not! You're just trying to vex me! Look, *look!*"

"All right, what is it?"

He could barely restrain himself from dancing about as he handed her a little booklet, its pages, only an inch or two in size, cut from an exercise book and folded down the middle. Its frontispiece was a tiny replica of *Blackwood's*, and inside were pictures and regular-looking scribbles which might have been minute words.

Charlotte took it from his hand and carried it to the window.

"It's—it's—why, it's excellent, Bany! I made something like this when I was little, but this is better. How did you contrive such tiny pictures? This writing, though. It looks so real, as if—but wait!" She peered closer. Then she turned to look at Branwell in open-mouthed admiration. He was grinning and panting and capering with glee and triumph.

"But Bany! This *is* real writing."

"Of course it's real! Every word can be read. Look, look how I did it—with this hair-nib I got from Papa. I had to put my nose almost to the paper. But don't you see, Charlotte, it's for *them*." He pointed to the soldiers, scattered on the floor. "It's *their Blackwood's*, just the right size for them. And the best of it is, nobody but us can read it. I'm sure Papa cannot, even with his glasses;

and as for Aunt, why she'd never trouble herself. So it's just between us. What do you think? Isn't it brilliant?"

She stood turning the little leaves over and over in her fingers,
unable to speak for admiration.

"But it will come apart," she said, suddenly seeing how she
could make her contribution and claim some share in this
diminutive wonder. "Wait!"

She dashed from the room and ran down to the kitchen, where
she began to beleaguer Tabby. Branwell, unable to grasp why
she should suddenly want a sugar-bag, stood at the door ready
to fall upon her if she should dare show his treasure to any alien
adult.

"But Tabby darling, you'll only throw them on the fire. You
might as well give them to me."

"Oh, leave off pitter-potterin' round me feet! Here then, take
thy blessed sugar-bags, but if I catch thee—"

But Charlotte, with a quick hug and kiss, had grabbed the
brown-paper bag and fled the kitchen.

Back up in their sanctuary, Branwell watched, his small eyes
glittering avidly behind their steel-rimmed glasses, while
Charlotte with her sewing scissors cut a brown-paper cover for
the little book and fitted it on. Then she took a needle and thread
from her pocket workbag and carefully stitched the whole thing
together up the fold.

"There."

Branwell whisked it from her hands and stood, trembling all
over like a nervous fawn, caressing it.

"It's a real magazine now," he breathed.

"Let's show the others."

Instinctively Branwell darted to the door, but then he stopped.

"No—not just yet. Not just yet," he said oddly.

"Why?"

"I want to keep it—just between us—only for an hour,
Charlotte," he said beseechingly. "We'll show it to them later.
Emmy and Anne have secrets sometimes, and you and Emmy talk
by yourselves in bed and keep it till the morning. I want you

and me to have a secret!" And his voice strained upward again in that strange shrilling of tension, like a taut violin string. Whenever that note sounded in the ears of any in the parsonage, it was a signal to give way.

Play upon play, world upon fecund world, the life-within-a-life expanded until it seemed it must burst the narrow confines of the real existence in the parsonage. But if the strain was great, so were the satisfactions. The four children seemed to thrive on the contrast between their overt and their covert lives. The moors were there to give release to body and spirit after hours spent indoors working, or stretched on the testing rack of compulsive creativity; Tabby was there, so ordinary, so normal, to love and scold and nurture them; Aunt and Papa were still firmly cast in their familiar roles. If Branwell, who slept in Papa's room, occasionally woke in the night to hear his father groaning out prayers for help in some strange, adult affliction, it did not trouble him too much; for by day Papa was Papa, the affectionate if sometimes remote guide and guardian at home, the electrifying mediator with God in the pulpit. Memories of their dead sisters were buried too deep to trouble them at present, though they lurked in the subconscious of Charlotte and Branwell like sleeping leviathans.

As for the "world below," it commanded them as much as they it. The four Chief Genii ruled supreme, built great cities out of dust, revived the dead, inspired their favorites and oversaw titanic battles and the rise and fall of empires; yet they, too, were in thrall to their creatures.

They named their chief city Glass Town, and the whole expanding world of the Twelves in Africa became the Great Glass Town Confederacy. Branwell drew a detailed map of the whole area and concocted and chronicled epic scenes of warfare with a background of tumultuous political intrigue. But Charlotte, who had gradually taken over the editorship of the little magazines, was more concerned with the physical settings and supernatural happenings of their society.

Aunt was increasingly anxious. They were too isolated, she kept saying. In the end, Patrick reluctantly allowed Branwell to mix with some of the village boys—"Only the ones who come to Sunday school, mind!" But he need not have worried. All Branwell's attempts at contact with his contemporaries in Haworth failed. They were thickheaded and seemed to understand nothing he said to them. They mocked him for his smallness, his bookishness, his strange adult speech. He would run home to Charlotte with a sense of escaping a foreign for a native environment. Only with much older lads, such as John and William Brown, did he find any common ground. They were the sexton's sons, and Branwell, several years their junior, worshipped them. John, who was learning stonemasonry and who therefore spent much time in the churchyard, could be counted on for some pleasantly grown-up conversation—much of it mingling the macabre with the ribald. This was a combination that appealed strongly to Branwell, who sometimes read some of his more hair-raising verses to John, and was hugely flattered to see him shudder.

And sometimes there would be visits to neighbors, specifically to Mrs. Franks of Thornton (to whom Patrick had once proposed, but whom he now regarded as a sympathetic friend) or Charlotte's godmother, Mrs. Atkinson. Branwell enjoyed these visits, since he loved showing off and attracting notice. But for the girls, they were a burden. These three articulate, lively creatures became morose in company, tongue-tied and recalcitrant from a shyness they could not conquer. All Aunt's hopes—that her nieces would learn social graces, would "extend their range," as she put it, by visiting high-toned families—were doomed to disappointment. It exasperated her to see how, having made a shamingly poor show of themselves among their hosts, they would break out into dazzling gaiety, mimicry and merriment almost the moment they set off for home.

When Charlotte was approaching her thirteenth birthday, she sat in the kitchen one morning and set out to sum up the status quo and review the year gone by:

History of the year 1829.

Our plays were established: *Young Men*, June 1826; *Our Fellows*, July 1827; *Islanders*, December 1827. These are our three great plays; they are not kept secret. Emily's and my best plays were established the first of December 1827; the others, March 1828. Best plays mean secret plays; they are very nice ones. All our plays are very strange ones. Their nature I need not write on paper, for I think I shall always remember them.

She paused. The paper itself was secret, and not to be seen by anyone. Should she try to transcribe the utterly private mysteries that were hers and Emily's alone? To see these whispered, forbidden happenings in writing would be a thrill, the mere thought of which caused a curious burning sensation low down in her body. With a sideways glance at Tabby (but she couldn't read anyway) and Anne (who was far too young for such things), she curved a protective hand tentatively around the paper and poised her pen to write. But at that moment she heard the front door open and Papa's and Branwell's voices in the passage. She caught herself up in a flush of something like terror, which turned her face first scarlet, then pale and cold. No! It would be too dangerous; besides, Emily would not forgive her. For the things they talked about in the dark together were about the doings of men and women, based uncertainly upon sights glimpsed occasionally in hidden dips of the moors, hinted at in books or overheard during Tabby's gossips at the back door with other servants. It would be unthinkable to bring them to the light of ink and paper.

Removing the shielding hand, she continued primly and innocuously:

The Young Men's play took its rise from some wooden soldiers Branwell had. I will sketch out the origin of our plays more explicitly if I can . . .

When Papa came in to find her, she felt virtuous delight in continuing her writing, knowing that when he bent down to kiss her his eyes might fall freely upon her work.

"Ah, good, Charlotte! I see you are following my advice and

writing in a clear, legible hand. Mind, I absolutely forbid these little cramped monstrosities you and Branwell have been ruining your eyes upon. Here, I have bought a new notebook for you. See that everything you write in it can be properly and easily read, or I shall take it back."

Charlotte took the notebook—a most precious object, for paper was scarce and dearly come by in this household, like most other things—and thanked him warmly. But when he actually wrote these stern injunctions into the front of it, all the pleasure of anticipation left her. How could she circumscribe her writing? She knew she would not obey him—the little books *must* continue. It was as if he had said, "You must henceforth live only in the world of reality, and visit Glass Town no more." Fortunately he knew nothing of Glass Town, for to forbid her to go there would have been like cutting out her soul.

No, Patrick knew nothing of Glass Town. But he would have had to be deaf and blind not to have had some inkling of the secret world of the imagination into which his children retreated as often as they were not occupied with the daily routine of housework and study. It worried him, and not merely because of the strain upon the eyes of his two eldest which had made their need of spectacles greater year by year. Patrick knew the value of daydreaming, but he also knew the menace that lurked under its tempting, voluptuous surface. How very easily could he himself be lured into that treacherous marshland of inactivity and life-paralysis! He had felt its tugging when sitting alone and idle in his parlor-study with a poem dancing just out of reach before him; or at night, when his wife, or, to his shame, some other woman he had seen or imagined, came to his bed in his dreams. He was sensible enough to know that he must not upbraid himself too harshly for these manifestations of his lonely condition; but by the same token he knew that just as he was a man of passion and had been so from boyhood, there was no reason to doubt that Branwell, at twelve, was experiencing equivalent stresses. As for the girls, Patrick did not delude himself that a young, burgeoning body was immune to turbulence simply because it was female.

Thus when he heard Emily and Charlotte whispering and stifling little shrill, excited laughs in their bedroom at night, he was concerned. When he saw Branwell in a reverie over some book written in a more permissive age, Patrick wondered if he was wise in allowing his children access to any volume in his library or that at Ponden Hall, which they frequently visited to borrow books. At first he had felt they were safe from the grosser allusions in Shakespeare, for instance, by virtue of an inability of their essentially innocent minds to understand. Now he was no longer so sure. Patrick would have liked to think that Branwell respected his sisters' purity too much to pass on to them any of the cruder facts, words or fantasies he might pick up beyond the bounds of the parsonage, from John and William Brown, for instance, but the relationship between Branwell and Charlotte was so preternaturally close that he could not be quite certain. Charlotte's secretiveness and her fits of blushing made Patrick wonder uneasily about the tendency of her imaginings.

None of these worries, needless to say, could be shared or even hinted at to the only partner he had in the demanding task of raising his children. Aunt Branwell, if she had ever allowed an impure thought to venture across the threshold of her consciousness, would undoubtedly have scotched it with the same vigorous promptness with which she slammed shut her window upon the intrusion of the faintest wind from the moors, or thrust the mice she trapped into a bucket of cold water.

Byron, ever a favorite, took hold of Charlotte, then in her fourteenth year, and Emily, then in her twelfth, in a subtly different way. He was no more proscribed than any other poet or author; they had always read him openly before. Yet now, when they felt the urge coming upon them, they secreted the book and stole away with it to some private place—for preference a hollow in the moors, under an open sky—where they might utterly abandon themselves to his unrighteous enchantment.

Byron's insidious ghost, through his poems, "stole like a snake within their walls" and implanted in Emily and Charlotte the mounting conviction that love and loathing, vitality and vengeance, tenderness and cruelty, were inextricably linked. What was gentleness worth, if it were not bedded in strength? What good were virtue and restraint where there was no craving, brutal appetite?

Thus, a man essentially of violence, passion and savagery by no means always under strict control became their secret ideal.

As the Glass Town saga developed, a gradual metamorphosis took place in the chief characters. Charlotte's original favorite, the Duke of Wellington, first evolved into her private version of the real Duke's son, the Marquis of Douro—a toweringly masculine figure, modeled on the heroic Duke himself mingled with Charlotte's idea of the satanic, seductive Byron.

As her preoccupations became more maturely feminine, so the Marquis, to satisfy these, had to make his way by conquests that were by no means solely military. Beautiful women, based on the voluptuous creatures in Martin's engravings, appeared on the scene, channeling all Charlotte's buried longings for luxury. There was Marian Hume, a sad and tormented girl; but the chief of these women was Zenobia Elrington, a fiery black-haired beauty who, as time went on, played a fundamental role in the complex amours of Charlotte's and Branwell's heroes.

Rejected by the fastidious Marquis, Zenobia married his archenemy, Alexander Percy. Percy was to Branwell what Douro was to Charlotte. He, too, went through a number of manifestations. He began, of course, as an extension of Bonaparte; but when "Bony" passed out of favor he metamorphosed into a fictional conqueror of extreme ruthlessness. As Branwell drew his character blacker and blacker, he nicknamed him "Rogue"—and a thoroughgoing villain he became, without heart or pity.

Charlotte found him repellent yet fascinating, a fit mate for her wild Zenobia. She contrived for him a daughter, Mary, to wed to her own hero, the Marquis. This gentle, vulnerable, virtuous and long-suffering girl balanced Zenobia (and other ladies of doubtful morals) in Charlotte's creative conscience, which was not, for the time being, much troubled by her male creations. She took it for granted that men were vice's natural prey.

Charlotte's godmother, Mrs. Atkinson, had had her charitable eye on the family for some time before she hit upon a way to help them.

Her own niece was enrolled at what careful inquiry assured her was a very suitable school for Charlotte. It was called Roe Head and was run, in a large, comfortable house on Mirfield Moor, by five maiden sisters, the Woolers. The location on a hill was wholesome, the selection of girls small and exclusive, the management impeccable. In a word, it was a very far cry from the unforgotten horrors of Cowan Bridge. All that remained was to gain Mr. Brontë's agreement.

This proved far easier than Mrs. Atkinson had dared to hope. It was Charlotte who turned gray and breathless at the prospect of leaving home.

"Now then, Charlotte," said her father, "this opportunity is not to be lightly refused." They were gathered in conference around the parlor table. "You are fourteen and a half and you know *nothing*."

"Papa! That is not true! I read a great deal and I'm sure I—"

"My dear, until you go to school and see the standards that prevail there, you *cannot* know how you compare with your contemporaries. Don't look so stricken. You'll make friends there—"

"I am not in want of friends, Papa!"

"We all need friends in later life, my love," said Patrick, throwing a look of gratitude to Mrs. Atkinson. "You will see that I'm right. Besides . . ." He paused. "My illness last winter made me very uneasy about the future. You must not depend entirely upon Branwell's prospects, however bright we believe them to be."

"I know, Papa, but—"

Aunt intervened. "Charlotte, I have taught you all I can. You must take this generous offer and show your gratitude by making the most of it."

Charlotte bowed her head, her thin hands clenched in her lap. With difficulty she restrained her tears until she could escape upstairs. There she threw herself on her knees and wept helplessly into Emily's warm heather-and-dog-scented lap.

"Don't cry, Charlotte. It may not be so bad."

"How can *you* say that? You would rather die than leave home!"

"But I shall have to at last, I expect. We can't live here safe and happy forever. You're the eldest so you must go first—that's all."

Charlotte cried afresh. "I don't want to meet other girls! They will be buxom and hearty like the ones in the village, and they'll laugh at me for my smallness and because I can't see properly!"

Emily stiffened.

"If they dare to so much as smile at you, they are ignorant little worms," she said with quiet passion. "Take no account of any who don't see your value."

At this moment, Branwell burst in without knocking. His face was scarlet with agitation and his red hair stood on end.

"Charlotte! What's this about you going away to school?"

"Yes, in January. Godmother is sending me."

"Then cursed be Godmother by all the genii in the firmament! I shall sweep down on her like—like a river of red-hot lava and sear her to a cinder! I shall consume her in slow torments until all that's left is a shrieking mound of blood and boiling fat—"

"Bany! Don't!" burst from a horrified Charlotte.

Emily only grinned scornfully and said, "If she was just a mound of fat she couldn't be shrieking, and if the fat were boiling it would all run away."

But Branwell was in full spate and not to be stopped. His voice rose higher and higher in his blood-curdling threats against poor well-intentioned Mrs. Atkinson until Emily suddenly decided she had had enough—enough of Branwell, and enough, too, of Charlotte's feeble and futile "shushes." She stepped suddenly up to Branwell and shook him.

"Be quiet, Bany, you're the one that's shrieking. You'll have one of your fits in a moment. Now get hold of yourself, sharp, or I shall slap you."

For a moment he looked at her like a mad thing, panting and wild-eyed, a little froth in the corners of his lips. Then the dangerous choler drained from his face little by little, and suddenly he collapsed on the floor in a flood of tears and moaning.

"Tally! Don't go, don't leave me, don't go!"

Both girls crouched by him, cuddling and consoling. Aunt Branwell, fussed and angry (for the shrieks, if not the actual threats, had been reaching the party in the parlor below), bustled into the room and helped lift him up and take him into his and Patrick's bedroom, where he was laid on the bed. He wouldn't release Charlotte's hand, and even after a dose of sal volatile he clung to her and sobbed weakly, "If you leave me, I'll die, I'll kill myself, I won't bear it . . ."

"Don't be so naughty, Bany! Did you think we could be together forever? I have to study so that I may keep myself when I'm grown up."

"But you won't need to! I am going to keep you all. Papa knows that, he's often said so. I am the clever one, I am the gifted one! Oh, you're clever too, I know that, cleverer than me sometimes, but you're a girl. It's my place to have a great career and make money for all of you. I shall be an artist. I shall, Tally! I shall, I shall!"

"Ssh, Bany! Don't begin again. We all believe in you. But we don't want to be helpless and like stones around your neck all our lives. We must all have careers. I want to! I don't like the idea of going away either—you don't know how I shall miss you—and the plays, how can I live without the plays?" She almost broke down again herself, but Branwell's sudden look of terror made her control herself. "But it's only half a year, Bany. In summer I shall be back, with lots of new ideas for Glass Town, Verdopolis I mean—" (Branwell had changed its name since beginning his study of Greek.)

"No!" Branwell sat up, trembling all over, and clutched her with an expression of iron hardness on his face. "No! If you're going, Verdopolis must be destroyed! I won't keep it up without you. It shan't exist without you. If God went away from the world, it would die, wouldn't it? Well, you're a god of the Confederacy, and if you're abandoning it, it will die, too. We won't let it die. We'll finish it. One great—great—" He groped frantically, striking his sweating forehead with his fist. "Charlotte—what's the *word*—"

"Cataclysm?"

"Yes!" he cried. "One great, final cataclysm! We'll do it like in Martin's picture of the *Fall of Babylon*—"

"Or Byron's 'Destruction of Sennacherib,' " whispered Charlotte, awed by the magnitude of the concept—undoing in one grand, ruthless gesture of tyrannical godhead what they had built up over four and a half years.

"You agree then?"

"I don't know . . . We must ask the others . . ."

"No, we needn't! They haven't helped much. The kingdoms and the great city, and the magazines, too, are mostly ours."

"You—you don't want to destroy the magazines?" asked Charlotte in sudden fear.

"No. We'll keep those as relics, the chronicles of an extinct civilization, for the genii to read when they grow old."

So two of the genii sat in solemn conclave, and between Christmas and the day of Chief Genius Tallii's departure for Roe Head, the Angel of Death passed over the great city.

2

SEPARATION

*I*T WAS LATE IN A DULL, DARK day in January. Huddersfield, far below Roe Head school, was lost in smoky fog. The wide lawns were snow-covered; the beautiful trees under which the pupils sat in summer were bare and weeping. Into this gloomy atmosphere, from the still darker interior of the covered cart which had brought her from Haworth, Charlotte's little figure emerged. She was helped down, and stood there, shrinking into herself from the raw air and from a misery and fear she could not conquer. Her box was lifted out, and the driver rang the doorbell of the school.

The pupils watching through the tall bow windows noticed her stillness and the spasmodic shivers that shook her.

"What a funny-looking creature! She looks about eight years old. Or, no, more like a shrunken-up little old woman . . ."

Some time later the newcomer was shown into the same oak-paneled, ground-floor room from which her arrival had been watched. She no longer wore the dress she had traveled in, but another, equally unsuited to her age, shabby and ten years out of date. Her brown hair was frizzed by the damp; her eyes, which were one of her few good features, were screwed up in an effort to see without her glasses, which, on a sudden panicky impulse, she had removed just before entering the room. They lay now in her pocket, and there they would remain, a hidden tribute to pride—a pathetic blunder. For now she peered around, and the faces and figures she dreaded loomed at her through the mists of short-sightedness like fearful figures in a nightmare.

Actually, their intentions were quite friendly, though there were one or two stifled giggles at the myopic way the undersized new girl turned her face about and tentatively reached out a defensive hand as a fair-haired pupil seemed to rush toward her.

"Hello. Who are you?"

"Charlotte Brontë."

"My name's Mary Taylor. This is my sister Martha, and Susan Ledgard, Hannah Haigh, Leah Brooke . . ."

Charlotte shook every proffered hand in silence when she felt it touch hers. To the girls, every shake was like a nervous spasm.

"Where have you come from?"

"From Haworth."

"That's twenty miles off! We all live nearer."

They gathered around her and asked her questions, which she answered in monosyllables, and told her about themselves. As they came and went within her narrow range of vision, Charlotte observed their hair styles, their pretty, ruddy faces and their fashionable dresses.

"Is your family rich, too?" she asked Mary, suddenly gauche in her nervousness.

The girls tittered at this lack of form, but Mary's outright laugh was not at all unkind.

"Ah ha! A frank question, which earns a frank answer. They *were*. But now, I'm afraid, we are as poor as—" She just stopped herself saying "country clergy" and substituted the cliché "churchmice—or nearly. My father is a banker and manufactures clothes, and until recently we were well-off indeed. Then, poor man, he went bankrupt because the army, which had placed huge orders with him, did not pay him; and now we are ruined!" She

tossed her pretty head and laughed with slightly forced carelessness.

"We are so poor, Mama makes us stitch all over our new gloves,
so they'll wear longer. But don't be sorry for us. We still have our
lovely house; we all have our health; and knowing Papa, he will
not rest till all our debts are paid."

Martha, who was a pert little thing about two years younger
than her sister, broke in, "None of it was Papa's fault, and lots
of other men were ruined by the war who will stay ruined longer."

"When will you take your exam?" another girl asked Charlotte.

"Exam?"

"Everyone takes an exam on entering the school, to see if she
belongs in the junior or the senior class. How old are you?"

"I am fourteen and nine months."

There was a murmur of astonishment at this, for she was so
small they had thought her much younger.

"Oh, well, you will go into the senior class then, for you are
almost the oldest in the school. Miss Wooler would not put you
down with Martha and the little ones who are mostly only
eleven."

It had never occurred to Charlotte that any of her anticipated
humiliations would be scholastic, despite Papa's warnings. But
when she was examined, the questions were so completely beyond
her that her heart was full of misgivings.

"Name the principal rivers of Europe."

"In what year did the Romans invade Britain?"

"Parse the following sentence . . ."

She could not. She could not! Why did they not ask her about
poetry, or the history of the Peninsular Campaign, or about politics? But such questions were as far beyond the Misses Wooler's
expectations of her as parsing was beyond her ability.

"I'm sorry, my dear," said Miss Margaret Wooler, the eldest sister and headmistress of the school, at the end of one of the most
agonizing half hours Charlotte could remember. "Your knowledge
of geography and the theory of grammar seem woefully behind

those of our senior girls. I'm sure you will catch up, for your godmother told me you are a most clever child; but for the moment we will have to put you in the junior class."

This was too much for Charlotte, who broke into a tempest of sobbing.

"No, pray don't do that to me, I shan't bear it! Don't put me with the little ones, I should die of shame—"

The senior Miss Wooler handed her a handkerchief and quite kindly bid her calm herself.

"I don't wish to start you off in what you clearly see as a humiliating position, Miss Brontë," she said. "If you promise to apply yourself seriously, and not assume that you know a great deal more than you do, I am prepared to give you a trial in the senior class."

Charlotte choked out her thanks and struggled to restore her face to order with hands that trembled violently. When she had wiped her eyes, she looked up at the stout white figure, topped by a firm, plain squarish face. Though she saw nothing intrinsically lovable in it, yet she felt such a wave of gratitude for her flexibility and understanding that she wanted to seize the headmistress's hand and kiss it.

At first, Charlotte was only happy in one place, in one circumstance—in the schoolroom, when she was learning.

The rest of the time she was tormented by homesickness. Not only separation from the parsonage and all the people in it, but separation from the surroundings in which she could escape into what she and Branwell had lately begun to call "the infernal world."

Sometimes, lying in bed at night, she tried to rediscover the way in, but it was as if the secret doorway could only be found in the study in Haworth. She thought about all her people, summoning them continually to rescue her and bear her away; but although she could visualize them—the Marquis, tall, with a Grecian profile, proud; Zenobia with her flashing half-mad eyes and bounteous black hair; poor Marian, pining in her gracious woodland estate and playing heartsick songs on her harp—they would not come alive for her, they would not enact their stories before her or empower her to be their Genius again.

Perhaps it's because we had them killed, thought Charlotte, stricken by physical pangs of anguish at the thought of them all being dead. Death had always been so mutable in their plays till now; no one had ever really died. But Branwell had said this time it was for good and all . . . Surely he did not mean it! Could they not be brought to life, could Verdopolis not be restored, if the Genii wished it so? She must write to Branwell and ask him to join her in rescinding the doom they had laid upon their great city.

At the end of her first week, the sun came out and thawed the snow. The girls put on their pattens and warm cloaks and rushed out onto the muddy lawn to play.

"Come on out, Charlotte," urged Mary. "We're going to play 'French and English.' We need another on our side, for we're only nine altogether if you don't play. Oh, enough of this shrinking, I say you must and shall! It's not healthy to be forever indoors with your nose in a book. Come on, Martha, help me to pull her out!"

Her pattens were forcibly put on, her cloak wrapped around her, and between them Martha and Mary Taylor dragged her forth into the dazzling sunlight.

"No, Mary, leave me! I *cannot* play, I tell you I *cannot*!"

But they insisted. They stood her on one side of the lawn and told her that she must catch the ball when it came to her and run with it to the other side, dodging all comers. Charlotte was absolutely paralyzed with a sense of advance incompetence. The game began. She stood immobile. After the ball had hit her twice, Mary came panting up. She was clearly beside herself with exasperation.

"What is the *matter* with you? Why do you not at least try to catch it?"

"I can't see it," muttered Charlotte, hanging her head.

"Can't see a great ball like that! Then you should be wearing glasses. They couldn't make you any uglier than you are without." She gave her a push. "Oh, go back to your book! You are worse than useless."

Charlotte jerked like a puppet, and turning, walked slowly back to the entrance. Martha ran across to her sister and hit her hard on the arm.

"You're cruel! How could you tell her she's ugly?"

Mary stared at her sister for a moment. She would have been ashamed sooner or later anyway, and did not need this attack, which consequently she bitterly resented.

"Oh . . . !" she exclaimed in guilty vexation. "It is her fault, too, for being so clumsy and odd! I will make it up to her though, for saying she was ugly."

Crouched on the window seat weeping bitterly, Charlotte didn't hear someone come quietly into the big room. The yells and laughter outside, emphasizing her own ostracism, drowned out the soft footsteps. She did not hear them until they were right next to her.

"Why are you crying?"

Charlotte jumped. A strange girl was standing there. She was quite an ordinary-looking girl, with wide-apart, sleepy eyes and brown curls and a passive expression quite at odds with Mary's vivacity. Charlotte didn't want to talk to her, or anybody; but when the question was repeated, in tones of sympathy, she found herself answering:

"I'm so unhappy . . ."

"Are you homesick?"

For answer, Charlotte threw herself face down upon the window seat, distraught with misery. Some barb, some new agony, had pierced her and was already beginning to throb and fester—not that she could ever say it to a soul, let alone this calm-faced stranger in her beautiful dress. *Ugly—I am ugly!* She groaned through her sobs.

The other girl sat by her and touched her tentatively.

"I've just arrived," she said in her uninflected Yorkshire voice.

"I left my home only today. I'm homesick myself, and could easily cry too, if you don't stop."

Charlotte sat up and bent over to hide her ravaged face. The other girl sat waiting until she had recovered a little, and then said, "I'm Ellen Nussey. Who are you?"

"Charlotte—Brontë."

The girls put out their right hands, but when they met, they fastened to each other and stayed hand in hand for several moments. Charlotte clutched Ellen through the simple, animal need to hold onto something warm and alive. Ellen held her hand in an instinctive response to Charlotte's need of her.

"I hope we'll be friends," she said placidly.

There was an unmistakable note of relief in Branwell's reply to her appeal. He, too, had evidently been feeling the loss of Glass Town and its inhabitants. He suggested eagerly that they regard its destruction in the light of the Flood—a punishment for wrong-doings—and revivify everybody. This news had a cheering effect on Charlotte. Though it was still impossible to "make out" much at Roe Head, at least she could feel that it was all still waiting for her at home. This lifted her spirits amazingly, and to celebrate she carefully extracted the center page from one of her school notebooks and began to work on a "magazine." She'd just written a miniature advertisement, inserted by a firm of Verdopolitan booksellers for the Marquis' new volume of poems, when a strong voice broke over her like a bucket of cold water.

"Well, Miss Brontë! And what is that you are resting your nose on? It doesn't look like your *devoirs* to me."

It was Mary, copying the voice of Miss Eliza, the youngest and strictest of the five Wooler sisters. A gasp of nervous giggling was forced from Charlotte when she saw she had been teased. But her hand had clapped down automatically upon the little book, and Mary's curiosity was naturally aroused.

"What is that—really? It looked like printing."

Reluctantly, Charlotte answered, "It's a miniature magazine."

"Oh! Do show it to me! Are there stories in it?"

"Stories, and poems, and criticisms, and reports—"

Mary's eyes were wide. "Please show me—oh, please! I'll keep it such a secret. Oh, do!"

In a way, Charlotte wanted to. She knew the magazines were unique, that the response could not be other than admiring. Praise, especially from Mary, and a sense of her special qualities to compensate for her utter hopelessness at games was something she craved. Her hand almost lifted of itself, as Mary's reached out . . . But no. The taboo on sharing the secrets was too strong.

"It's hardly begun. When it's finished I'll show you—perhaps." But she never did.

As spring advanced, Charlotte settled in better and better. Her fears vanished—this was no Cowan Bridge. She rose smoothly to the top of the senior class, where her only challengers were Mary and Ellen. The three were friends, although so different, and Martha, "Miss Boisterous" as she was nicknamed, danced like a marshlight around them.

Charlotte could not forget what Mary had said to her. It was never referred to, but it remained there between them, even after Mary, trying to make amends, insisted on brushing the old-fashioned curls out of Charlotte's hair, praising its silky beauty as she arranged it in a smoother, more attractive style.

During lessons, Charlotte's special mastery of certain subjects soon shone through her more general ignorance. Though the curriculum did not take much account of current affairs, the girls and teachers were soon astonished to discover how wide and deep was Charlotte's knowledge of all that related to politics and recent events at home and overseas.

In this, however, she found an equal in Mary—an equal in interest, but an unexpected opponent in opinion. For Mary's family was as staunchly Radical as Charlotte's was Tory. This dichotomy led to many heated arguments.

One day, after Miss Wooler had led a walk through the district, enlivened by a "mobile lesson" touching on the Luddite riots, Charlotte unwarily mentioned to Mary and Ellen that her father had had some marginal involvement in the events Miss Wooler had been talking about. Quick as a flash, Mary exclaimed:

"Yes, and we can be sure *he* was not on the side of the croppers! None of the clergy were, for all they are supposed to be followers of Jesus. It takes a good nonconformist like my father to understand the workers' side. *He* did not put machinery into his mills at a time when he knew it would break the men's spirits and blight all their hopes, and cause them to do such desperate deeds that many of them came to be hanged! I hate everyone who looks down on working men as mere animals to be used to make them richer."

"Then you need not hate *my* father," said Charlotte hotly. "And you are quite wrong if you assume he was hardhearted about the rebels, for although he could not approve of their wild crimes he was still full of pity for them." She lowered her voice. "It may interest you to know that some of those hanged men were from my father's own parish, the one he had before we were born, Hartshead. Their families came and begged him to allow them to bring their dead men back from the scaffold in York and bury their bodies in the consecrated ground of his church-yard—*and he allowed it.* He even performed the funeral service, in the dead of night. He believed those poor people had suffered enough."

"And so they had, indeed!"

"I wonder how your father would feel, if some of his workers tried to murder him and break up his mill. It would be the end of all stability if such acts went unpunished."

"And who caused them to act in that way? Greedy, ruthless men who wanted money and were ready to walk over poor people's bodies to get it."

Ellen, who had been listening, hardly knew which of her friends had scandalized her most.

"Your father did very wrong, Charlotte! How could he give Christian burial to murderers? Miss Wooler told us they shot a millowner in broad daylight as he crossed the moors—she showed us the spot! And Mary, did you say your father is a Nonconformist?"

"Yes," said Mary. "He despises all brands of orthodoxy. If he worships God he does it quietly, in his own way, not in public to get credit for it. And he's the proof that you don't have to be a churchgoer to be good, for my Papa is the most honorable, kind and generous man alive, whom I wouldn't change for either of yours, however pious they may be!"

"My Papa is dead," said Ellen quietly.

"Oh," said Mary. "Well, I'm sorry for that of course. But that doesn't alter my opinion. A man need not be pious to be good. Nor need he be a Tory to be respectable and sound in his views."

"But he does need to be a man in order to be a Papa," put in Martha gravely. "And that you cannot deny, Mary, however much of a Nonconformist you are."

They all looked at each other and then burst into giggles.

"How silly you are, Martha! Why can't you talk sensibly?"

"Oh, when you are all getting so solemn and red in the face about politics and religion, you just *ask* to be forced to laugh. Come on, let's go out and play something lively!"

"I will stay here and read," said Charlotte firmly.

They knew better by now than to argue with her. She would never come out, even now in the spring when the grounds of Roe Head were loud with birdsong and velvety with new growth, the flower beds like lines of colored cushions and the trees still almost lemon-tinted. While the others played in the clear, scented air, Charlotte sat on the window seat, bent over her book, and worked and worked. Even her two best friends were in awe of her capacity to sacrifice pleasure for learning.

If she was driven out for her health's sake by one of the Miss Woolers, she didn't join the games, but stood quietly under one of the big trees, a quaint little figure in her prim, shabby dress, with her hands folded in front of her, usually staring at the wall or at the big gate, her mind straining after the old dreams.

Mary's home, the Red House at Gomersal, was quite near the school, and at weekends she could go home. Occasionally Charlotte went, too. In the Taylors' elegant but unpretentious drawing room, with its beautiful fireplace and comfortable, generous furnishings, Charlotte could not help feeling at home. Mr. Joshua Taylor, Martha and Mary's father, was a strong-featured, outspoken man, like her own father, but the features themselves, and the opinions voiced, were all so at variance with Patrick Brontë's as to make his daughter smile to herself as she compared them.

The four sons of the house were equally lively-minded and self-opinionated; arguments were a matter of course, even at the dinner table. Nor did the two sisters sit mum and let the boys do all the shouting. Even Martha bounced up and down in her chair trying to get her word in, and her father, who clearly adored her, would override the noise and oblige all contestants to be silent in order that Martha's shrill little voice might have its say.

The opinions expressed by the Taylors in general were all so astounding, being so at odds with Charlotte's own very firmly held views, that in the end it was impossible for her not to take issue with them. Mr. Taylor kept a fatherly eye on her, and when he saw her bent head come up and her mouth open despite herself, to counter some particularly outrageous piece of Whiggery or nonconformism, he would do no less for his little guest than for his favorite child.

"Be silent, you pack of demagogues, and let Miss Brontë speak, for I see she has something to say that may challenge us all at our roots!"

Then they all looked at Charlotte, and Mary gave her a prod to get her started, and with a great effort she spoke her mind. Her views, being so out-of-the-ordinary for the Taylors, often had such a stimulating effect on the conversation that not a distinct word could be heard for five full minutes afterward.

When driving the girls back to school, Mr. Taylor often took Charlotte's hand and said, "You do us all good, my dear Miss

Brontë, by bringing the Opposition so articulately into our midst. You prevent us becoming complacent. Come again soon."

On the rare occasions when Ellen was there, she sat in awed and somewhat scandalized silence, listening to everybody; but when deferred to for her opinion she only shook her head.

"I am for Miss Brontë," she said, "though I can't talk as well as she does." Later, in private, she said to Charlotte: "It is hard to understand how Mary can be so nice. I suppose there must *be* radicals in England for the Tories to oppose, but the dissension is dreadful—it's not much better than outright heresy."

"So the Catholics say about the Protestants. Were *we* not a kind of Dissenters to begin with?"

"How *can* you, Charlotte? That is quite different!"

"Oh, I'm not so sure. It's comfortable to think, as we have always been taught to think, that our religion is the only true one; but when I begin to look around me at all the good people who do not belong to it, my feeling of security comes to seem mere smugness. Why must we be right and so many others wrong? Couldn't there be several paths to God? Are we really to think Mary and her family will not get into heaven because they are not Methodists or Calvinists?"

"But should we go to her house? I'm sure my Mama would not like it if she knew the way they speak, nor your Papa either."

"I have often heard my Papa disputing with Dissenters; he doesn't forbid me to listen, any more than he forbids me to read whatever I like. He told me once that if my religion would not stand up to a little argument it was not the prop to my life that it ought to be. The opinions of the Taylors can't affect me."

"I think they have affected you already," said Ellen quietly.

"Charlotte—Charlotte! Are you asleep?"

"No."

"But you were, before. I came up to get you. We were having such fun, sitting down by the fire, we thought you *must* leave your books and come to join us. But there you were, your head on your arm, fast asleep . . ."

"My eyes grew tired, I closed them for a minute to rest them, and—"

"Oh, Charlotte! You don't have to explain to *me*. I think you work far too hard, you never give yourself any pleasure. What is the sense of doing double lessons all the time? You are at the top of the school now."

"Mary, you don't understand. My father was seriously ill last autumn with his lungs. At times we thought he wouldn't recover. What if he had died? How would we live? He is in any case older than you might suppose—he is fifty-four—one has to face probabilities. He has never been strong, and if he died we should be put from our house, for it goes with the pastorate. Where would we go? Who would care for us?"

"Your aunt?"

"She has a little money of her own put by, but she has already done far more for us than she need. I would not like to depend upon her. I *must, must* prepare myself to be a governess."

"A governess! You? Charlotte, you never could do it. You are so very shy, you would be in agony, living among strangers. And besides, how much patience would you have with naughty, fractious, stupid infants? All children are not like you and your family, you know. At home, when we were little, we did nothing but squabble—we were most desperately silly, and you of all people could not tolerate silliness."

"Don't you think I've thought of all that? But what else will answer? I must do what work is open to me, and there *is* only that if I am not to lower myself in the eyes of society."

Suddenly Mary burst out, "The eyes of society! How I hate those eyes, watching all the time, watching to see that nobody steps over those little invisible lines they were born between. Who is 'society' that it may say where and at what I may work? I tell you, Charlotte, whether Papa mends our fortunes or not, *nobody* shall tell me what I may work at, *nobody*, not even Mama. *She* supposes that Martha and I will sit mim and prim at home doing our fancywork until some gentlemen of good breeding oblige her by carrying us off to do more fancywork by *their* firesides. But I shall not suffer my brain, nor even my strong, healthy body, to waste away in such child's pap. Work I must have, and so long as it be honorable—*my* idea of honorable, *not* society's—I shall put my hand and mind to it, and be proud to earn my own bread by doing it well, and Mama may scream her head off for all I care, it will make no difference—I shall go my own way."

Charlotte gazed through the candlelight at her friend, half shocked, half admiring, wholly fascinated.

"But I am not like you, Mary," she said slowly. "I couldn't go against Papa, nor bring a sense of disgrace to him. Perhaps you're right, perhaps it *is* no disgrace to do other work than governessing, but while *he* thinks it wrong, I could not do it."

She was quiet for a few moments, and Mary grew restless.

"Come on, anyway, let's go down to the others."

But Charlotte hardly heard. "*If only* Maria were still alive," she said softly.

Mary was astonished to see tears in Charlotte's eyes.

"Gracious, Charlotte! Are you still crying for her?"

"While I was sleeping just now, I had a dream. I was in my bedroom at home, and Nancy—the maid we used to have—came in to say there were people come to see me. I felt a catch at my heart and ran downstairs and into the parlor, and there they were, Maria and Elizabeth, standing before the fire . . ."

She stopped, but the tears did not. Mary, brusque and unromantic though she was, could not help being moved, though mainly by curiosity.

"Go on—what then?"

"Nothing."

"Of course that was not the end! And even if it was, you could 'make out' the rest, as you call it. Go on, Charlotte, make it out. You know you can!"

Charlotte shook her head. "I wish I had not dreamed," she said with difficulty. "It didn't go on nicely. They were not—as they were in life—simple and loving. They were fashionably dressed, and they began criticizing the room, and my clothes . . ." She put her head suddenly down upon the table and began to sob wretchedly.

"Oh—oh, Charlotte, for goodness' sake, stop! It's very wrong to keep crying for the dead forever. One must look forward with hope, not backward with all this sadness! I'm sorry I asked you. And look, here come the others to bed, and we've missed all the fun. Now blow your nose and cheer up, for they're going to get you to tell us a story tonight."

"No, I can't—"

But the others were not to be put off.

"Oh, please, Charlotte! Tell us the one about the sleepwalker on the battlements—you didn't finish that last time—"

"She didn't finish it," said Martha, "because Miss Walker had a fit of the vapors and started going 'eek—eek—eek' like a mouse in hysterics until Miss Wooler came running in and spoiled all the fun."

"How could I help it? When Miss Brontë tells stories of ghosts and tottering walls and raging seas, someone as sensitive as I cannot sleep a wink afterward."

"Then I had better be silent," said Charlotte. "Miss Wooler forbade me, in any case."

A chorus of pleading, however, overcame her scruples, and soon, bundled up in twos and threes on their own and each other's beds, with a single candle flickering over their wide-eyed faces, they were listening enthralled to the finest tale of terror that Charlotte could devise. While she screwed the tension up to the highest pitch, she was lost to sorrow for the past and anxiety for the future. She had her tale, and she had her audience. She was happy.

"Miss Brontë, there's someone come to see you."

Charlotte raised her head from its customary horizontal position over a book, and asked who it could possibly be.

"A very weary-looking young man who claims to be your brother."

She pushed back her chair so eagerly that it fell on its back, and flew into Miss Wooler's parlor, where Branwell, his bright hair darkened with perspiration and his legs dusty to the thighs, was standing awkwardly near the fireplace. At her precipitate entrance he straightened and looked around. For a moment they stared at each other, lips parted, eyes shining; then they flew to each other's arms, Branwell's spectacles slipping off in the process.

"What are you doing here? How did you come?"

"How strange you look, your hair—"

They laughed some more, and Branwell explained that he couldn't wait till the "half" ended in July to see her, but had decided to walk from Haworth, have a visit with her and walk back.

"But how tired you must be!"

"I'm not a bit tired, really."

She hugged his arm. "Tell, tell me about all at home! Are they well? How is Papa? How are Emmy and Anne?"

"Well, all well, except Papa is still suffering from the results of his bronchitis last winter, and of course the weather is not warm enough to suit Aunt . . ." They both glanced out at the sunlit view and burst out laughing from sheer happiness. "Emily and Anne are much together. Too much, I think. I'm beginning to suspect they have a design to break away from our play and start one of their own. I hear them whispering together sometimes, and the name Gondal keeps recurring. Emily says she's tired of Verdopolis and Africa altogether. She says she would rather make out a more real sort of place, and I think if their Gondal goes forward it will turn out to be more like our own moors, or those in Scotland—very dreary and ordinary. But you know how Emmy is: for her, no country could be more exciting than Yorkshire, and no landscape more stimulating than what we see out of our windows."

"And what about *our* play? I have added nothing, but—"

"Oh, I have, though it's not the same at all without you. I've been going on with my *Letters from an Englishman*, describing all the ongoings of the great city as an outsider might see them. Look, I've brought you some, and the rest I will send you as I write them, for I can't bear not to share them with you. It was mainly for that I came, to read some of them to you and have your opinion. Listen, here's how Bellingham—my Englishman, you know—watches Rogue's execution."

"You haven't killed him?"

"Yes! For the present. Listen!"

Charlotte listened, her eyes fixed on her brother's face with an intensity of feeling that knotted her fingers together and made her heart beat faster. She loved him, she loved him so much—they were like one person! The magic of Verdopolis reclaimed her; she felt herself being swept away again on tides of fantasy; the desire to abandon herself to its call and leave the harsh demands of reality behind all but overwhelmed her. She even felt a little faint as he finished, and looked up with veiled anxiety.

"Bany—" she said weakly. "It's good, very good, I love it . . ."

He relaxed. "Yes, it is good, isn't it? I really feel I am learning to write well. You know, I've been thinking. When I grow up I might like to write for *Blackwood's*. I shall write a letter to Christopher North and ask him to read some of my work."

"The Editor?"

"His real name is John Wilson, and he is quite a young and handsome fellow. One of his chief interests is in pugilism, Charlotte! Just think of it. And he has quite a reputation as a cocker."

"A what?"

"A cockfighter. He likes drinking, too, and horse racing—he's an out-and-outer, a real sportsman. I like that! I am learning to box, you know, from John and William, and they say I am quite good, and that soon they'll be taking me into the Black Bull for a drink after we've had a bout."

"Branwell! Does Papa know?"

"About the boxing? Of course. He approves. And so should you. I needn't tell you, your dear Lord Byron—"

"That is different," said Charlotte primly. "Lord Byron did a great many things I wouldn't care for you to do. And I don't like the idea of you drinking in the Bull with rough men like the Browns."

"Oh, stuff, Charlotte! You think you know more about life

than I do, but by the time you come home from school you'll find John Brown will have made such a man of me that you will have to give me great respect." He grinned impishly, and then changed the subject. "Well, and what are you learning in this old maids' institution? I bet you could teach *them* a bit about politics, for such out-of-the-way spinsters care nothing for the high events of the day, but only for dry, dusty history."

"Oh, I've half forgotten my interest in Parliament—there's been so much else to think of—"

"Forgotten Parliament?" cried Branwell in unfeigned amazement. "You can't mean that, Charlotte! With all that is happening, why, nothing could be more interesting! We talk of little else at home but the Reform Bill, and the fate of Earl Grey. The Reform Bill was thrown out of the Lords—"

"Good! Good! Oh, how cross Mary will be when I tell her."

"Who's Mary?"

"A friend—her family are Canningites to a man."

"A *friend*, you say, and a Canningite? Horrors! As for Earl Grey, he has been expelled, we believe, or perhaps he has resigned—at least, he has left the House. It's said he asked the King to create enough new peers to pass the Bill through the House of Lords, but the King very rightly refused, and so the Bill was defeated."

"What will happen now?"

"Papa is very anxious. He says there may be riots, because so many people were for the Bill. Even Papa is for it now, saying *temperate* reform is inevitable, though I can't see why."

But Charlotte could, for she had heard the matter discussed at the Taylors' dining table.

"It is because so many people in the big cities are unrepresented, while in some boroughs the landowners may return whatever candidate they choose. My friend's father calls them 'the rotten boroughs' and says they are so corrupt they make a mockery of elections."

"Charlotte! You sound as if you are becoming a Reformist yourself!"

"If even Papa is coming around, that would be no disgrace," retorted Charlotte. "Yet I am still against. There may be a few abuses, but no system is perfect, and if the Bill had gone through, many villages would have been disfranchised while allowing hundreds of representatives from the towns, who would have all been Whigs. But it's good to hear the other side well argued, Branwell. Till I met Mary, I thought all sensible people believed as we do."

"I would like to meet this Mistress-Mary-quite-contrary. I would soon set her right about how the garden grows!"

And Branwell did meet Mary, and Ellen, that very day. But no "setting right" was done, for brother and sister only had eyes and words for each other. Afterwards, Charlotte wandered arm in arm with Branwell through the grounds, and they talked without stopping until it was time for him to start his long walk home.

His visit put Charlotte into a mood of such high gaiety that all her schoolmates were astonished, and Amelia Walker said, "If I were so fond of my brother that a trifling call from him could bring such color to my cheeks, I doubt if I should bother to flirt at all!"

And when Ellen asked, "Is he so dear to you? For of all my nine brothers, I cannot say I love any so *very* particularly," Charlotte answered intensely:

"He is dearer to me than anyone on earth, except my sisters."

And Branwell, trudging home up hill and down, a journey of nearly five hours, hardly noticed his growing fatigue for the happy tumult in his head. Charlotte's presence had had the same stimulating effect on him as his on her: his flagging creativity had been revived, their combined weight of inspiration had pushed the secret door wide open again. What did he care now that Emily and Anne were withdrawing from him into a creative country of their own? He and Charlotte were still of one mind, of one soul; and if perhaps she would not totally approve of every action he took, every friend he had in Haworth, what did that matter? In the sphere of the "plays," they were, and would forever be, together.

3

REUNION

$\mathcal{C}$HARLOTTE'S WELCOME HOME after three "halves" at Roe Head was an occasion not soon to be forgotten. She arrived in the same covered cart that had taken her to school eighteen months before. She had changed little. She could even wear the same dresses as those the girls had laughed at when she first came from home. Her face was a little older, her eyes a little more tired-looking. But she was no taller. Her hands and feet still fitted the diminutive gloves and boots Aunt had bought for her when she was fourteen. Only inwardly had there been changes.

But her family knew nothing of these. They saw only their beloved Charlotte descending from the cart in her rusty-green stuff dress and her old bonnet, her glasses on her nose; and they rushed to her, almost smothering her with their embraces, crying out so loudly in their excitement that the cottagers came to their doors to see what was going on. Aunt had to shepherd them in, shushing, while they all hugged and chattered and laughed and Emily's current dog barked madly around them. And there in the doorway was Papa, grinning broadly, his pale face flushed with pleasure, his arms outstretched. Behind him in the passage hovered Tabby, clapping her hands every moment as she did when she was bursting with some strong feeling she couldn't express.

There was a special celebration meal spread in the dining room, and Charlotte amazed them all by agreeing to take a little beef.

"Charlotte! Do you eat animal food now?"

"I was persuaded to try it at school, for my health, and little by little I've overcome my dislike of it."

Tabby was overjoyed, and so, for another reason, was Patrick.

"So the ghost of that terrible place has been laid," he said to her softly.

"In part, at least, Papa." She smiled, and their eyes met. He was looking older. His hair was snowy white now, and she noticed with distress that one eye had a strange milkiness when it caught the light. His cravat, which he wore high under his jaw, was more prominent than she remembered, swathed in layers of white silk. But the firm grip of his hand, resting on hers, was, as always, strong, vigorous, comforting.

"So, my dear," he went on jauntily. "The Misses Wooler found they had nothing more to teach my clever daughter. Ah, Charlotte, what a glowing report I have had of you! They will miss you indeed, so they say. And you made friends, too, did you?"

"Yes, Papa, as I told you. Two in particular. Ellen Nussey—*not* the radical one, but the one whose views you would find quite unexceptionable—has invited me to stay with her family in September. I hope you will not object?"

"Naturally not. I shall be delighted. I have heard of the Nusseys. Very respectable people, of considerable property. And she has a great many brothers, didn't you tell me? Excellent! I shall become a regular Mrs. Bennett soon, machinating to get my daughters settled."

Everyone roared with laughter. Papa was in wonderful spirits.

After supper they sat talking for an hour, till Papa, hearing the clock on the landing strike nine, got up, and so did Aunt.

"It is my bedtime," he said. "I am too much a slave to my routine to break it even for your homecoming, my love."

"May we stay up a little longer, Papa?"

He looked over his spectacles at them, one by one. His eyes lingered on Charlotte.

"Half an hour—no more. *You* may be feeling very grown-up and independent, Miss Brontë, but you must not keep your brother and sisters up too late. They are partly in your care now, you know, for you are to begin teaching them on Monday next. A teacher is a responsible being. Good-night, children."

As they were withdrawing, Charlotte jumped up impulsively, flung her arms around Patrick's neck and kissed him. She kissed Aunt, too, though more circumspectly.

"It is so good to be home!"

Then the four were alone.

Charlotte could not sit still—she was too excited. The exhaustion of the journey had only made her restive. While the others sat by the fire—Branwell in the best chair, Anne opposite him, Emily on the rug with the dog's big head in her lap—Charlotte began to walk slowly around and around the table in the center of the little room. Easily, without effort, they began to draw close to each other's minds again. The conversation took in everyday happenings at the parsonage, gossip about friends in the village, descriptions of the school from Charlotte; and, mingled with these mundanities, the secret names crept in: Marian Hume; Bellingham; Young Soult, the poet; Alexander Rogue, arch-villain —and, of course, the Duke of Wellington and his sons.

"Mary could never understand my devotion to the Duke," said Charlotte, "any more than she, or any of her family, could sympathize with my love of poetry. That was the only thing I did not like in their house: they really scorned poetry, calling it romantic rubbish. And that is the more strange, since they are a most cultivated household in all other areas. Mr. Taylor has a fine collection of paintings and he has books in the several languages that he speaks fluently. Though to hear him talking and roaring in his Yorkshire brogue, one would often mistake him for a common self-made millowner with no culture whatever. It is the same with their politics. Mary knows all that can be known about Sir Robert

Peel and all the Whig faction, but when I began praising the Duke to her she had no answer and was not ashamed to admit she knew nothing of him."

"This Mary, for all she is so pretty, strikes me as a silly girl," said Emily. "How can civilized people scorn poetry?"

"How do you know she is pretty?" asked Charlotte.

"Branwell told me."

"Indeed!"

Branwell went scarlet. "Don't tease me, Charlotte! John Brown says there is nothing to be ashamed of in admiring girls, indeed he says it is a shame not to."

"Now, now, Bany, don't get excited," said Anne pacifyingly. "No one is teasing you."

"No one would dare to," murmured Emily, stroking the dog's back with long, slow strokes.

Later, when they were in bed and had at last blown the candle out, Emily whispered, "You must be very careful with Branwell. Instead of gaining command over himself, his passions are getting more and more out of control. Aunt can do nothing with him, and Papa *will* do nothing—at least, not usually. But about a month ago there was a most dreadful scene. Papa found out Branwell had borrowed money from William, to pay for supper at the Bull, he *said*, though I believe it was to bet on a cock. Anyhow, Papa flew into a rage—a real roaring fury, Charlotte, as in the past. Do you remember how we used to run and hide from him? Well, Anne and I ran and hid in the storeroom, but we could still hear him, crashing his fist on the table and shouting at Branwell that if he ever heard of him getting into debt again, even to the slightest degree, he would forbid him to leave the house at all. And Branwell shouted back—screamed, rather, for his voice still goes up like a girl's when he's aroused—that it was impossible for him to live or respect himself if he were given not a penny of his own, that he could not be forever accepting drinks and meals from his friends, and that he had not even a shilling to pay for the hire of his boxing gloves. In the end he went into a fit and flung himself on the floor. We were afraid to go near, but Aunt was not. She rushed down and ordered Papa back into his study while she applied her smelling salts to Branwell and got him up to bed. Papa was very shaken and has treated him most gently ever since. He hardly says a word when Branwell comes home with the smell of beer on his breath, though I know he has spoken with John, telling him to remember that Bany is only fifteen, and begging him not to lead him into company that is too old for him."

"Perhaps if he could make friends of a different sort—"

"Yes. But who is there, in our village? There are the Heaton boys at Ponden, but they're all younger than Branwell. Though he might have associated with them more, if John and William had not spoiled him for young companions. Now he thinks such 'children' are beneath his new manhood." Emily sighed in the darkness. "Well, at least now you are back he'll want to make you approve of him. I don't suppose he will carry on as he has been at the Bull, now you're here to see him."

Sessions in the upstairs study became almost frenzied in their intensity. Sometimes Branwell and Charlotte worked separately, but more often she dictated to him and he added and interpolated his own sides of the plots and characters as he wrote. They thrilled to the joys of their renewed collaboration; closer than they had ever been before, their minds interlaced; and productive as soil and seed, their themes raced on, each one striving, beneath all the surface effort and cooperation, to outpace the other in maturity, output—and daring.

While in thrall to this nether world, Charlotte could forget all her piety, all her scruples, all her prim "missishness," as Mary had called it. Nothing, it seemed, so long as it concerned her imaginary people, could shock or repel her inner self; nothing was too bold, too dark or too wicked to emerge in the tiny and and safely undecipherable print of the little books. Branwell, far from censuring her, egged her on, and fed her with facts and fictions culled from conversations in the Black Bull. Alas for Patrick's trust in her purity, in Branwell's brotherly protectiveness of it! There was no "pure" or "impure" in the world below, no prudery, no inhibitions; above all, no religion.

The morals of Charlotte's beloved Marquis began to decline, following the pattern set for her by Lord Byron. He acted out, irresistibly, her profoundest fantasies, and she chronicled them with helpless relish. But at the same time she began to develop the character of his brother, Lord Charles Wellesley, and using him as a mouthpiece, she could make critical and censorious comment upon the scandalous behavior of the Marquis. This eased her mind at times when she was reflecting, *out* of thrall, on what she had written: she could not be dead to all virtue when, through the eyes of Lord Charles, she could see and censure the faults of the fascinating, all-conquering Douro.

A Few Words to the Chief Genii

When a parent leaves his children, young and inexperienced, and without cause absconds, never more troubling himself about them, those children are by no means bound to believe that he has done his duty to them as a parent, nor are they required to own or treat him as a parent. We believe that two of our readers will understand our aim in thus speaking.

A Child of the Genii.

This veiled accusation Branwell inserted in a magazine and pointedly read aloud to Emily and Anne. They glanced at each other, smiled serenely and said nothing. Infuriated, Branwell exclaimed:

"Well? Have you nothing to say? It is you two I mean! If you don't come back into our play, your favorites shall be allowed to die. Or worse, I shall make them into inglorious nobodies; I shall let them fade into insignificance if you desert them!"

Silence.

"Then at least read us what you are writing! We know about Gondal. It's not fair of you to keep it a secret! We read ours to you."

Emily and Anne looked at him. They appeared to be about

to speak at once, but Anne deferred to Emily, who said, "Gondal is an island in the Pacific Ocean. It's a wild, rough place, without any of the magnificence of Glass Town. There are no Genii there. We've decided not to have magic or people who die being made alive again. It's a real place, isn't it, Anne?"

"It's real to us. We couldn't believe in the Genii anymore. They are too fabulous. But Gondal has a queen, and—" Here she stopped.

"Oh, don't tell us then, if you don't want to," snapped Branwell. "And if you think Verdopolis is so childish, you need not hear more of it!" He was bitterly hurt. But Charlotte was wiser. She, too, had shared secrets with Emily, and her collaboration with Branwell was now so close and exclusive that she persuaded him that they needed no help from the others, that Emily and Anne were entitled to create a world of their own in privacy.

Charlotte tried not to wait for a letter from Ellen, for, despite all protestations of eternal friendship, Charlotte expected to be forgotten as soon as she was out of sight. But when in mid-July a warm, gossipy letter did arrive, she was overjoyed. She also gratified her friend's wish to know how she spent her days, and replied:

> . . . An account of one day is an account of all. In the morning from nine o'clock till half-past twelve, I instruct my sisters and draw, then we walk till dinner, after dinner I sew till tea time, and after tea I either read, write, do a little fancy work or draw, as I please. Thus in one delightful, though somewhat monotonous course my life is passed.

Truth . . . How vital is truth to true friendship? Charlotte reflected on this as she read over the letter before sending it. She had not lied to Ellen in describing her day, but she had deceived by omission, for she had made it sound as if her writing were of no more importance than her embroidery or her drawing, between mention of which she had squeezed it.

Yet how could she say more without betraying not only the secret bond with Branwell but something even more clandestine within herself? For the writing had resumed its hold over her, a hold so powerful and compelling that she was afraid of it at times. Only by using every ounce of self-command that she had mustered over the past two years could she stick to an orderly outward routine such as the one she had outlined so casually to Ellen. Below, all was seething tumult and a sort of possession; the craving to get back to her writing was like a drug. She had dreams for the future of her work—she could see herself creating great poetry, or perhaps a novel.

In the Infernal World a whole new country, called Angria, had been opened up east of the original Glass Town. Charlotte's favorite, the Marquis of Douro, became its king and changed his title to Duke of Zamorna. This name appealed to his creator as much as Percy's new style, Earl of Northangerland, appealed to Branwell, and it was by these names that they were known from then on.

The opening up of this new imaginary territory set in motion the full force of their creativity. All that the two young writers had taught themselves about plot, structure and character over the years enabled them to launch out now unhesitatingly, and in full confidence of their powers, upon the joyful task of fabricating an entire new society.

Throughout these years when Angria was becoming the most important facet of her inner life, Charlotte continued to write prim, gossipy letters to Mary and Ellen and exchange pleasant visits with them.

In September she paid her promised visit to Ellen.

Branwell, to his delight, was sent by Papa to escort her in the Haworth gig. When he was happy, no one could be more high-spirited and charming, and he quite captivated the entire large family of Nusseys. His ebullience entirely smoothed over the awkwardness of arrival and Charlotte's painful shyness; and soon they were all strolling in the fine grounds of the house, with Branwell dashing hither and yon, beside himself with enthusiasm for everything he saw.

Charlotte, however, could not help finding the Nusseys (except Ellen) rather dull. Those of her brothers who were at home were nice enough young men but too conventional to be exciting, although she took a liking to George. Henry, twenty and about to begin his second year of theology at Cambridge, was attentive to her, but she found him frankly stodgy.

The house was very grand, even magnificent in the eyes of the parsonage children; yet it lacked much that they took for granted in the way of books, paintings and music. And the conversation —once Branwell had reluctantly taken leave—followed the conventional pattern with stultifying predictability. However, before he left Branwell had whispered to her, "I am leaving you in paradise! If you are not happy here, you will be happy nowhere." So happy she was; but it was mainly due to being again with her dear Ellen.

This continuing friendship puzzled her. Why should Ellen like her? Something in Charlotte's nature made her skeptical of any proffered friendship. She thought herself both stunted and ugly. She lacked wealth, background, assurance—even the attraction of good looks and pretty clothes. Yet Ellen insisted on being her friend.

She won every heart in the parsonage on her first visit there. Anne felt an instant affinity for her; Emily liked her for befriending Charlotte; Patrick approved of her quiet, gentle manners, and Aunt of her well-bred courtesy (though Ellen did not quite manage to hide her surprise when Aunt brought out her little snuffbox after dinner). As for Tabby, she was more than touched when Ellen came into the kitchen to chat to her and help with the baking while the girls did their morning housework and study.

"Only a proper lady," she announced later, "could do such, wi'out demeanin' herself or makkin' me feel servantish."

Branwell had recently become fanatically interested in painting. One of the back bedrooms of the parsonage had been turned into a studio for him, and up there he devoted himself to his brushes with a great air of mystique. He was painting his sisters' portrait, with himself in their midst, looking so much taller than Emily that she had told him he must be standing on a chair. In a fit of pique he painted himself out.

Ellen admired the picture, but ventured to suggest that the girls all appeared too solemn.

"They *are* solemn," said Branwell. "Why, Charlotte only smiles when you are here, Anne once a month on first Sundays, and Emily never."

"They do not strike me like that," said Ellen. "When we go walking on the moors, they laugh and chase like children without a care on earth. Did Emily not smile yesterday when she led Charlotte past the fox's den, and only told her when she had her right outside it? Poor Charlotte screamed with fright, and Emily laughed then like—"

"That was not human merriment, but eldritch mirth. My sister Emily is not a real girl, but a kind of moor-witch. I assure you, you don't know them. They have not an ounce of true gaiety or humor between them; they are as censorious of liveliness and natural human folly as a trio of hags. When you hear them laugh it sounds like the witches in *Macbeth*."

"That's a calumny! Look, they are smiling now."

"Only to deceive you into disbelieving me."

The visit was such a success that all four young Brontës were loath to see Ellen go, and arranged an outing a few weeks later at a well-known beauty-spot about fourteen miles from Haworth. Aunt and Papa clubbed together for the hire of the gig, and on a lovely September morning the four set out, with Branwell driving, in the highest spirits. As they trotted along the pleasant country lanes, enjoying the breeze, the sunshine and the changing but ever-lovely view, Branwell kept up a continual *badinage*. The girls occasionally got in a riposte, but for the most part were delighted to listen to him, for in this mood they found him wholly admirable. The brilliancy of his mind, brought to a high polish by study (the Latin and Greek tags, the erudite quotes, shot like sparks from his monologue), and enlivened by warmth and good humor, banished all their doubts about his character. Who could fail to succumb to his charm? All gates would surely fly open, all walls fall before him, when he entered upon the world. The sisters basked in the security of this conviction and flung back waves of love and admiration that fed him as an actor is fed by a responsive audience. The two-hour journey passed joyously, and soon the meeting place, an inn near Bolton Abbey, came in sight. And suddenly they fell silent.

For Ellen had not come alone, or with just a brother to escort her, as they expected. In her eagerness to bring the Brontës out of their narrow world, which Mary once described as being "like growing potatoes in a cellar," she had planned a far more expansive outing than anything they had envisaged or prepared themselves for.

Branwell's horror, as he saw a large party of smart and sophisticated young men and women gazing at him, was such that if he had dared he would instantly have turned his horse's head about and driven home at a brisk gallop. The dismay of the three girls was scarcely less. Branwell's first thought was, *Dear Lord! What a dolt, what a bumpkin I must look!* Charlotte's, which she breathed to Emily: "Oh, how could Ellen? Doesn't she know me better?" Emily simply withdrew her spirit straight back along the way they had come, letting it take refuge beside her favorite waterfall. Anne turned pale, but determined to make the best of it for Ellen's sake.

Ellen was not oversensitive, but she would have needed to be a block of wood not to realize her blunder at once. For her friends, whose relaxed laughter had been heard above the clop of hooves until the moment their gig rounded the bend, were now withdrawn, silent, barren of poise or conversation. Charlotte visibly trembled as she shook hands with the waiting party; Branwell's stumbling, stuttering awkwardness was agony to watch. The other two clung to each other; Anne's eyes were like a frightened deer's, and her words, such as they were, emerged in whispers. Emily said nothing at all, and looked blank.

Their lovely, longed-for day out was all but ruined. As they drove home silently at the end of it—an end they had thought would never come—Branwell suddenly announced, shrilly, "That will never happen to me again. I won't let it! Among such company I become contemptible. Until I can hold my head up with the cream of achievers in this world, I refuse to put myself among those who can humiliate me."

"What do you mean to do then?" asked Emily, somewhat caustically, for she had suffered least of any of them. "Mix only with your inferiors, with those in whose eyes you glitter and whom you can eclipse?"

"Oh, Emily, don't!" Charlotte exclaimed, before a flushed and tearful Branwell could answer. "He hated it so! Those callow young Cambridge men patronized him shamefully. He is right to vow to avoid them! What can they do for him, anyway? He is better off with us, who appreciate him."

"It is not what they can do for him, but what we cannot," said Emily. "If Branwell means to avoid all challenging society—"

"And did *you* not avoid it?" asked Anne quietly. "I saw what you did. You as good as ran away from them all. So leave Branwell alone."

Branwell's future career as a painter was now sufficiently settled for his father to undertake the expense of bringing an art-master, Mr. Robinson, from Leeds to teach him. But Branwell by no means felt it necessary to concentrate on painting to the exclusion of his other enthusiasms.

He continued to write, of course, as prolifically as ever; the evolution of Angria, and particularly of Northangerland, whose demonic personality was beginning to obsess his creator, absorbed much of his free time. But he was also violently in love with music, especially church music. Even the sound of Emily practicing a hymn on the piano in the parlor intoxicated him. A wild ebullience seized him, making it impossible to sit still; he was compelled to strut, stiff-legged, about the room, conducting with extravagant gestures, beating time on the backs of chairs as he passed them and singing loudly. As for what overtook him when he heard organ music in the church, it was often beyond his power to contain himself. His head throbbed; his chest swelled; he felt he would explode with the pressure of his rapture.

Once, when a new organist of unusual skill came to the parish, Branwell became so excited that he actually flung himself about in bodily contortions—to the consternation of his sisters and the marked disapproval of his father (fortunately there was no service at the time), who told him pretty sharply to control himself. These strictures, however, could not prevent Branwell from rushing up to the organist at the end of the recital and practically groveling at his feet in an ecstasy of adulation.

Afterward, Emily accused him outright of silly and exaggerated behavior.

"You don't know how I *feel!*" was (as usual) Branwell's defensive cry. "The man is a genius! We should all revere him, worship him. Such sounds as he makes can transform mere men into angels—"

"Oh, be quiet, Branwell, what rubbish! He only transformed *you* into a toadying imbecile!"

"You have no soul," retorted Branwell sullenly, and let them walk home alone while he sought solace at John Brown's stonemason's yard.

Charlotte was disturbed. When Branwell did something foolish or wild or undignified, it was as if she herself were degraded. On these occasions, which were not infrequent, she half hated him, much as she hated herself for bad thoughts or actions.

But to add her own reproach when Emily had already so unequivocally attacked him was impossible. She felt in her own heart his pain at the rebukes. However, her exasperation with him had to find an outlet somehow. So when she settled down that day to her desk, she found herself writing him into an account, by Lord Charles, of an encounter on the route between Verdopolis and the new provincial capital of Zamorna.

She described her "Branwell" character, whom she named Patrick Benjamin Wiggins, as "a low, slightly-built man with a bush of carroty hair so arranged that at the sides it projected almost like two spread hands, and a pair of spectacles placed across a prominent Roman nose." She made him a dandy as to dress, adding to the true picture a little black rattan cane which she was sure Branwell *would* flourish if he had one. A conversation began between Wiggins and Lord Charles, in which Wiggins showed himself jaunty, boastful and ridiculous. As her pen flew in an attempt to keep up with the racing dialogue proceeding effortlessly in her mind's ear, Charlotte, as so often, experienced a sense of losing control over her creations. Though she had set out to lampoon Branwell, fully intending to read the result to him later for his improvement, the caricature grew more and more astringent; aspects of Branwell were revealed in it that Charlotte had not known she was aware of.

"Wiggins," not content with exaggerating wildly about the distance he had walked and about the size of his birthplace (which he magnified into a great city endowed with twenty grand hotels), proceeded to make an abject fool of himself at the nearby inn. When he had fairly set Lord Charles to mocking him, he began to abuse his relations.

> "I've some people who call themselves akin to me in the shape of three girls, not that they are honored by possessing me as a brother, but I deny that they're my sisters . . ."
>
> "Are they as odd as you?"
>
> "Oh, they are miserable, silly creatures not worth talking about. Charlotte's eighteen years old, a broad, dumpy thing whose head does not come higher than my elbow. Emily's sixteen, lean and scant, with a face about the size of a penny, and Anne is nothing, absolutely nothing."
>
> "What! Is she an idiot?"
>
> "Next door to it."

Charlotte hadn't realized how Branwell's jibes at them before Ellen, and on many other occasions, had galled her. If they had always treated him with respect as the most brilliant and promising in the family, was that any reason for him openly to decry and belittle them, even as a joke? Charlotte's teeth were set as she dipped the pen afresh, and with scant preamble launched into a doctored account of the episode in the church.

Explaining in grandiose terms to Lord Charles how the great opportunity of his life occurred, Wiggins described the "hopening" of a new "horgan" of large dimensions in "Howard" church. A noted musician and composer by the name of Greenwood chanced to be visiting the town.

"When I heard of his arrival I stood upon my head for fifteen minutes running. It was news almost too glorious to be believed, but afterwards, when I heard that Mr. Greenwood had been prevailed on to preside at the Horgan's Hopening, I positively fell into a fit of joy. He came—I saw him—yes, I remember the moment when he entered the church, walked up to the Organ Gallery where I was, kicked Sudbury Figgs, who happened to be performing Handel's 'And the Glory of the Lord' from the stool, and assuming it himself, placed his fingers on the keys, his feet on the pedals, and proceeded to electrify us with 'I Know That My Redeemer Liveth.' 'Then,' said I, 'this is a God and not a man.' As long as the music sounded in my ears, I dared neither speak, breathe, nor even look up. When it ceased I glanced furtively at the performer. My heart had previously been ravished by the mere knowledge of his fame and skill; but now resistlessly it was captivated, when I saw in Mr. Greenwood a tall man dressed in black, with a pair of shoulders, light complexion and hair inclining to be red—my very beau ideal of personal beauty, carrying even some slight and dim resemblance to the notion I had formed of Rogue. Instantly I assumed that inverted position which with me is always a mark of the highest astonishment, delight and admiration. In other words I clapt my pate to the ground and let my heels fly up with a spring. They happened to hit Mr. Sudbury Figgs' chin, as he stood in his usual way, picking his teeth and projecting his underjaw a yard beyond the rest of his countenance. He exclaimed so loud as to attract Mr. Greenwood's attention. He turned round and saw me. 'What's that fellow playing his mountebank tricks here for?' I heard them say. Before anyone could answer, I was at his feet licking the dust under them and crying aloud, 'O Green-

wood! the greatest, the mightiest, the most famous of men, doubt-
less you are ignorant of a nit the foal of a louse like me, but I
have learnt to know you through the medium of your wonderful
works. Suffer the basest of creatures to devote himself utterly to
your service, as a shoe-black, a rosiner of fiddlesticks, a great-coat
carrier—a port-music, in short a thoroughgoing toadie . . .'
Greenwood laughed . . . He told me I might accompany him to
Verdopolis when he went there and welcome. Before my ecstacy
of thanksgiving was over he rose and told me to pack my alls for
he was going to set off that minute for the cross-roads . . ."

Charlotte sat back and flexed her fingers, a necessary exercise
to uncramp them after writing so furiously. She reread, dismayed
at the venom, yet unable to help laughing at the vitality of her
lampoon. She had got him, to the life, indeed! But was it too
strong? Would it sting too much? She finished it off and then
took it down to Emily, who was brushing the parlor carpet, and
read it to her through a miasma of dust.

"Read it to him," was the verdict. "It will do him nothing but
good."

But when it came to it, she could not. Partly she feared his
reaction—they all lived under the domination of Branwell's attacks—but chiefly she couldn't read it to him because, though he
worried, infuriated and sometimes seriously dismayed her, she
loved him more than herself.

Yet if Branwell was tainted with false conceit, Charlotte sometimes yielded to a humbleness which, while in part genuinely
felt, appeared to Ellen (the main recipient) just as exaggerated
as Branwell's boasts.

In June of that year, when Charlotte was eighteen, Ellen went
on a visit to London. Branwell was beside himself with envy at
her good luck; but Charlotte, who equally longed to go, was
mainly distressed by a nagging fear that Ellen might be so affected
by the contrasting grandeur of the great city and its inhabitants
that she would begin to despise Charlotte. This fear—based on a
belief that Ellen was socially her superior and that their inequity
of rank and situation must one day destroy their relationship—

was often in her mind, and was only partially relieved by Ellen's letters, as cheerful, friendly and unspoiled as ever.

Ellen well knew that Charlotte's mind was infinitely superior to her own, and had for several years now been accustomed to asking Charlotte's advice on everything from the propriety of dancing to the books she should read. No modesty had held back firm and unequivocal answers on *these* points. Dancing she had allowed, and for Ellen's reading had given a comprehensive list.

> . . . Now don't be startled at the names of Shakespeare and Byron. Both these were great men, and their works are like themselves. You will know how to choose the good, and to avoid the evil; the finest passages are always the purest, the bad are invariably revolting; you will never wish to read them twice over . . .

Little did Ellen guess how many times the "bad" passages had been scanned by this arbiter of the pure and sublime, how many "revolting" (that is, impure) elements had crept into the private output of this friend to whom Ellen had once turned for a frank list of her own faults.

"How can you be so foolish!" Charlotte had then replied. "I *won't* tell you of your faults, because I don't know them." And indeed she knew of none that counted as faults besides those covert imperfections of which she was only just now becoming most uneasily aware in herself. Was piety a fault? Was simplicity? Was innocence? As Charlotte turned nineteen, and began, with heavyhearted reluctance, to brace herself for her first sortie into the battle for independence, the catalogue of her own vices of the heart began to compare more and more blackly with Ellen's unsullied virtues.

PART III

The Adult Years

1835-42

FIRST SORTIES

IT WAS NINE O'CLOCK ON A SPRING evening. The clock had just struck, and the girls, walking around and around the dining table as they had begun to do every night after supper, paused to hear the inevitable click of the parlor door as Papa came out into the hall. His slow footsteps crossed the flags; he tapped on their door, put his head around it, and said, "I am going up now, children. Don't stay up too late."

They said good-night, and he was about to withdraw when he looked around again, frowned, and asked, "Where is Branwell?"

There was no reply for a moment, and into the uneasy silence Charlotte injected a painful half-truth: "He went out for a few minutes, Papa." Then, as this was obviously not satisfactory, she added the lie direct. "I think John called for him."

The frown deepened. But they were not their brother's keepers. He nodded briefly; the door closed. His steps mounted the stone stairs and paused on the landing; the faint musical squeak of the clock-key reached them. Then the steps turned the corner and faded into the closing of an upper door.

Subdued hubbub broke out.

"Charlotte! You told Papa an untruth. It wasn't John at all, but Mr. Sugden's boy, come to fetch Branwell to the Bull to 'help some stranger with his bottle,' as he called it!"

"Well, could I say that?"

"Papa *ought* to be told where Branwell is—where he goes."

Charlotte, after a moment's guilty silence, retorted, "Branwell's eighteen—he's grown up. If Papa wasn't able to stop him going to the public house at fifteen for fear of his tempers, what good will it do him to know how often he goes down there now to entertain Londoners with his so-called 'witty and learned' conversation?"

"Oh, stuff!" put in Emily. "Papa and Aunt are not fools. They know all about it. Branwell has Papa fairly under his thumb with all his nonsense about fits." The other two exchanged a shocked look. "Oh, come! Are you afraid of the word? If you ask me, it was all put on at first. If Papa had dared to be firm, it would have stopped. As it is . . ." She shrugged. "*Now* his fits are real enough, and we're obliged to bow to them. But soon he'll be off to London, to the Royal Academy, where he must take his chance like any ordinary man. Who knows, it may be the making of him. Meanwhile, perhaps it's as well for him to get a bit of practice! If he can't stand the test of a few visitors from the city, plying him with drink and flattery in the back room at the Bull, I dread to think how he'll fare against the temptations of a whole townful of taverns and gambling halls and 'sportsmen,' as he calls them. Well, if we must sit up to wait for him, let's at least entertain ourselves. Come on, Charlotte, read us the day's developments from the *Verdopolitan Intelligencer.*"

So Charlotte, with one nervous ear open to catch the stumbling footsteps up the front steps, or worse, the singing of a ribald song in the lane, sank into the electric atmosphere of the Angrian General Parliament on the night of its opening session.

Zamorna, whose relationship with his sinister father-in-law had seriously deteriorated of late, rose and addressed him in bitter terms. He accused him of pretended partiality toward himself that masked deep hatred; of possessing a cold and vitiated soul, incapable of friendship or even toleration for his fellow-creatures; of hating Zamorna's true friends and loving his enemies. At last he vowed to revenge himself in the only way open to him— through his wife, Mary, Percy's daughter.

When this diatribe ended there was a moment's charged silence, and then Emily and Anne burst into avid discussion.

"But he wouldn't carry out such a threat, surely?" cried Anne. "Why, Charlotte, what's happening to him? He used to be your hero, noble and fine-souled—and now, to avenge himself on his enemy, he says he will harm his own wife! Surely it's not meant?"

Charlotte kept an enigmatic silence. Truthfully she didn't know the answer to her own riddle of the change in Zamorna's character.

Emily answered for her. "Certainly he means it. Northangerland is a villain of iron. His armor of cold-heartedness and indifference is impregnable, except at that one point. If Mary is such a fool as to die merely because she is put aside by her husband, her death will be good riddance."

"What else should she do? He's all the world to her!" said Anne.

"What she should do is plan some revenge of her own. She'd find plenty of chinks in Zamorna's armor—*he's* not yet dead to all feeling."

"Northangerland is."

"Well, but that's where Branwell goes wrong in his characterization. One can create a tyrant without a redeeming feature, but one must see the vulnerable soft core of the man which causes his outer hardness, or it is not true to life," said Emily.

"I sometimes feel," said Anne slowly, "that we're in danger ourselves when we allow our people to be so wicked."

Emily was silent, looking at Anne. They communicated with their eyes, as Charlotte sometimes could with Branwell—or had, once. She looked on now with envy; even Ellen had noticed the profound sympathy between these two and said they were "like twins."

"I don't meddle with the afterlife," said Emily at last, as if they had continued their discussion silently. "Even if I agreed with all Aunt has taught us about spiritual cause and effect, people in real life don't live by Aunt's rules. There would be little excitement or romance if they did! And if we invent people who are passionate, even wicked, we should record their doings truthfully, and we *can* do it without any wrong attaching to us."

"Are you sure?" said Charlotte. "Aren't they part of us? Where do they draw their sinfulness, if not from some source within us?"

"Oh, nonsense!" exclaimed Emily. "They are not *you*, they're themselves—don't you know that? You're not responsible for what they do. Have you never felt them move and heard them speak, as really as if they stood before your eyes?" Charlotte nodded. "Well, then! I can't interfere with what my people do, any more than God can change the way I comb my hair."

"Emily, what are you saying? That God *cannot change* things on earth?"

"If Aunt is right, all we do is preordained. Or perhaps we are all Marys and Zamornas in His imagination—a divine play!"

She stretched both her arms above her head, yawning and spreading her long fingers in perfect animal contentment.

"Oof! I'm tired. I walked ten miles today, up to Top Withins and beyond. How it poured! I wish Branwell would be good enough to stagger home. I want my bed."

"My dear, I cannot like your taking employment."

Papa had summoned Charlotte into his study. They sat together companionably, but Charlotte could see Papa was disturbed.

"That my little one should have to go upon the world as a teacher, when she herself is barely out of the schoolroom—"

"But, Papa, I'm so fortunate to have been offered this position! If dear Miss Wooler hadn't asked me, I should have had to be a governess among strangers. Teaching at Roe Head will be quite an easy start for me."

"Relatively easy, my dear, only relatively!"

"Now, Papa, don't fret. I won't deny it's hard to leave home, but I'd never choose to stay here forever as a dependent. I must make my contribution, at least until Branwell becomes established."

"When he does so, he will have you to thank. I could never afford to send him to study at the Royal Academy if you weren't making yourself responsible for Emily's education. I fear it will mean you'll have precious little left over for yourself, when her tuition at Roe Head has been subtracted from your salary . . ."

Charlotte said nothing to this. It was a sore point between them that, while she had been living at home, he had never allowed her any pocket money. It was not only books and writing-paper she wanted to buy, but clothes. At home she could rub along well enough on the old-fashioned dresses Aunt made her; but with Ellen, or Mary, she could not help feeling a frump. And how would the smart young ladies at the school—her pupils— react to her drab garments?

This was just one of her anxieties; another separation from Branwell and the loss of their mutual "world below" was a far more serious one. But when she watched Emily moving her limbs stiffly as if she were growing numb with apprehension and sinking into silences so deep one had to shout to rouse her, Charlotte forgot her own fears.

Anne spoke to her on the subject before they set off.

"It's good of you to do this," she began. "It's a terribly hard thing."

"Oh, nonsense, you'd do the same."

"Would and *will*," said Anne determinedly, "when my turn comes. But I'm worried about Emily."

"Oh . . . she'll manage, I'm sure. She's very strong."

"Strong? What do you mean? Oh, she's strong enough to wrestle with her dog or walk all day without food, or carry Branwell to bed when he's drunk. But the kind of strength she'll need now is something quite different. You know, Charlotte, I sometimes think—don't laugh, will you?—that Emily's strength comes from the moors. She's like a tree, planted there, and if she's uprooted it won't matter how tough her trunk is, she'll wither and die."

"Nonsense," said Charlotte again, uneasily. "No one dies of homesickness."

"But you will watch her, Charlotte, won't you? Oh, I know you mean to, but your lives will be separate—you being a teacher and she a pupil. And you'll have your own troubles," she added, gazing at Charlotte anxiously.

Charlotte glanced at her. She'd grown prettier lately, with her lovely wax-doll skin and blue eyes and soft fair hair. Unexpectedly, the fleeting agony of Maria's loss passed across Charlotte's heart, leaving a long, stinging scratch.

Charlotte thought she had anticipated the worst she would have to face in this, her first professional position. She had not expected to *enjoy* teaching, but she had not braced herself against an actual dislike of it. The routine, though not particularly demanding, left little time free for her private world of invention and creative writing; besides, she felt instinctively a terror of letting herself lapse into it, as an alcoholic, realizing the insidious weakness in his blood, fears to take even a small drink that may destroy his ability to live a normal life and carry out his duties. Sometimes, in unguarded moments, Charlotte felt "her people," whom she had banished into the shadows of her mind, crowding closer, calling upon her to receive them. Though she hungered and thirsted for the escape they offered her, she thrust them back as if they had been so many howling demons. Then she could have howled herself in bitter sorrow for having rejected them.

When she had been here before, she had cried to them to come and rescue her from her loneliness, and they had melted from her fingers' ends. Now, when she had grown up enough to see that they menaced her new, unfree and disciplined life, perversely they jostled and pushed and clamored to come to her, leaving her no peace, no idle moment that was safe.

Emily's pain was different from her own. She could sense it. She didn't need to be told in words that Emily's wretchedness came because she *could not* do as Charlotte was doing and keep the dreams at bay. Emily's dream-world was impossible to banish, as impossible as cutting off a part of her living flesh. Charlotte knew little of Gondal except that it was as real to Emily as anything in life, much more real than anything at Roe Head. And yet the unreal world of school, the routine, the lessons, the discipline (mild as it was) *had* to be obeyed. There was no way out. She could not simply sit on her bed or walk about the grounds all day. The world of Gondal was constantly being broken into, hacked to pieces, by the insubstantial phantom world around her.

She could not learn. She hardly ate. She moved from place to place in a haze of anguish, as if stupefied by some great grief. Charlotte thought of Anne's words. Yes, just so does a plant wilt, become limp, dehydrated, lusterless, when it is pulled out or chopped down. *It is true*, thought Charlotte. *If she stays here she will die, for she is not getting any spiritual food.*

When Charlotte spoke to her she answered dully, her voice creaking out of her like some rusty mechanism.

"I'm trying, Charlotte. But it's no use. I can't get away at all, you see. That's the worst. I can't make journeys. There's a moment when I—come back—which is terrible, it's indescribable, nothing could be more painful . . . that's what I thought. But this, being chained up, is like that shock of returning, going on *all the time*. I feel I can't, can't, can't bear it."

"What do you mean, Emily, journeys? You mean walking on the moors?"

Emily jerked and looked at her with weird, dead eyes. She should have been weeping, yet her face spoke of a pain beyond tears.

"No. What did I say? I didn't speak aloud, did I?"

She stood up abruptly and walked out of the room in that strange, stiff-gaited way, almost as if she might suddenly fall over. Charlotte was left alone, disturbed and bewildered. Could they *both* be going mad, each in her own incommunicable fashion?

Yet certain things Charlotte held to her heart for comfort. The chief of these was that she was helping Branwell. In the autumn he was going to London—actually going to London, alone—there to present letters of introduction from his art teacher, Mr. Robinson, to some of the influential artists of the day. And then he was to apply for admission to the Royal Academy! In her blackest moments Charlotte could always sustain herself by imagining the rapture Branwell must experience in seeing London at last. He had been studying maps until he boasted that he could find his way to any landmark in the city without asking directions. His twin Meccas were St. Paul's and the National Gallery. Charlotte's self-prohibition upon dreaming excluded the dream of receiving Branwell's letters describing his impressions of the city, picturing for her his first steps to success in his chosen vocation. With this goal before her, it was just possible for Charlotte to stay upon an even keel, and even to give Emily some little comfort.

For some days after Branwell's hectic departure, Anne pursued her quiet routine at home as cheerfully as she could. She sat in the unattractive bedroom she still shared with Aunt, and sewed, and read to that now aging lady. She practiced the piano, studied her French, cleaned the brass for Tabby; she faithfully tended Emily's "dependents," and when Papa had time for her she tried to be lively enough to make up for the absence of the others.

In her leisure time she retreated to the "study," where she wrote poems.

These were utterly private. She might show them later to Emily, but to no one else, so she was able to express in them her secret sorrow—her depression and belief that the best part of her life, the freest part, was over. For soon she must take employment as a governess. She had determined on that, no matter what Papa said against it.

Once a day, with Grasper, Emily's dog, dashing ahead, her pilgrim feet would follow the invisible path left by Emily across the moors. But without her, everything was different. It was impossible to experience the old, ecstatic feelings. Being with Emily had lent to her perceptions of nature a preternatural acuteness, as if Emily's mystic communion with the moors had concentrated piercing rays of sensation through herself and thence into Anne. Without this burning-glass companion beside her, Anne might strain her hardest to recover the rapture of those past walks, but it was hopeless. Every sight, sound and smell was muffled and tainted with a sadness that sometimes verged on panic, for she could sense, from a dragging on her heart, that all was far from well with Emily.

Because of this conviction piercing through a more unspecified loneliness, Anne had her own ordeal to contend with. She missed Branwell because they had been much thrown back on each other since the other two had gone; and now he, too, had left her. But she did not think about him very much, beyond wondering how long they must wait for that first fascinating, ebullient letter.

Branwell trudged up the long cobbled hill toward home. As he walked, he wept.

It was night—he had had wit enough left to make sure it would be—and he had walked all the way from Bradford to save the fare to Keighley. The guineas that had weighted down his pocket so comfortably and promisingly on his outward journey were gone. Within his bewildered brain, a long dialogue was taking place on this matter.

"I was robbed . . . *I was robbed* . . . I cannot be blamed . . . It was not my fault!"

"You were not robbed. You merely allowed yourself to be duped out of your money by tavern companions. You bought drinks for them, you bet against them and lost, you willingly connived at their taking advantage of you—"

"They took advantage of me! That's the truth. Wicked, disreputable scoundrels, they knew I was young and inexperienced in the ways of the city, and they deliberately—"

"Yet you knew it. You invited it. You returned day after day, night after night. That tavern, and others—the cockpit, the ring —were the only places where you felt at one with yourself and your surroundings."

"How could I help that? What in all my life in this tiny village has prepared me for the terrible reality of a great city? The noise alone half stupefied me!"

"Then why go to taverns if you sought silence? The National Gallery was not noisy. St. Paul's, when you finally drove yourself to mount its steps, contained the tranquility of paradise itself."

"I cannot bear to think of those places! Oh, for God's sake, let me alone! I want to go home—I want to go home to Papa . . ."

But realizing suddenly how nearly home he was, he stopped abruptly, his tears streaming afresh down his pale contorted face. It had been one thing to cry inwardly after Papa when he was far from facing him in the flesh, when he was just a vague inner symbol of comfort and security. But now! Oh, heavens, another few steps and he would reach the gate of the parsonage. Another five minutes, and there would be Papa himself, and Aunt, and Anne, gazing at him in blank astonishment, waiting. *Waiting for him to explain.*

The immediacy of this desperate crisis brought poor Branwell to full sobriety and awareness. All his mental faculties, held in thrall to cowardice and confusion for ten days past, sprang alertly to attention. Now, when it was too late—his money squandered, his appointments broken or never made, his portfolio abandoned, his great opportunity forever lost—the keen, ready tool of his brain leaped to his service, and in the space of a moment had provided him with a whole story that was clever, irrefutable, commanding of sympathy. He did not even have to rehearse it.

In the shadows of the parsonage garden, he dried his eyes and stared at the moon to lessen their redness, the wheels of his mind clicking in his head like well-oiled machinery. In a few minutes he was ready to shoulder his box and approach the door. On the front steps, his hand raised, he still hesitated. Once, in London, he had thought that nothing could be worse than returning to those who had loved and believed in him, placing in him the highest confidence, and to have to confess that he had allowed himself to be robbed of all they had sacrificed for him. Yet now the truth was so much more dreadful, more shaming, that this very excuse—suitably embellished with details of his blamelessness—seemed by contrast not only perfectly acceptable, but absolutely justified.

When the worst was over, the explanations unquestioningly accepted and the mourning for the death of a great hope was subsiding, Anne waited up one night for Branwell's return from the Bull. When he came she seated him opposite her before the parlor fire and quietly demanded the truth.

Branwell was so stunned—by her audacity in disbelieving his story, and her temerity in challenging it openly—that he confessed everything.

Once started, he could not stop. Instinctively keeping his voice low, he told her, in a long monologue, how all his expectations of London and himself had crashed about him; how its fabled magnificence had turned out to be largely squalor, poverty, vice and stench; how, when he had ventured into the wealthier districts, he had been overtaken by the same feelings of hopeless inferiority that had assailed him when they had met Ellen's county friends at Bolton Abbey, only far worse, for in London the very buildings belonging to the "quality" seemed involved in a conspiracy to dwarf and humiliate him.

"It was out of the question for me to present any of those letters of introduction! How could I have knocked upon those doors? The brazen knockers would have burned my presumptuous fingers; the servants who answered would have withered me with their looks.

"And as to the artists I was to introduce myself to—to intrude myself upon, I should say—why, what arrogance, what swaggering, insolent conceit I had to suppose I deserved to come near such men. Anne, I feared above all things to go into the National Gallery. My very soul shrank from it. Yet until I forced myself to enter, forced myself to look, I didn't know why I feared it. But then I knew." He leaned forward, his face bringing back to Anne's mind the mask of tragedy her father had shown them so long ago. "Anne, *my work is nothing*. Art! My tongue shrivels at the word, for it has no right to name it. That I knew, finally and forever, when I walked awe-struck, on trembling legs, around those sacred galleries. I longed to fall on my knees and worship the great and marvelous works I saw there. Yet, far from enjoying them, I only wanted to cover my eyes and flee away, for in every fine canvas, every sketch, every trifling line drawn by one of those masters, I saw my own utter unworthiness."

Anne sat watching him, outwardly calm but inwardly a burning tumult of pity.

Early in her life she had learned that if she displayed her sensitivity too openly she would almost certainly be repelled or checked. "Wha! 'Tis only a dead bird, nowt to shed tears for!" Tabby would expostulate. "Save thy tears for dead fowk." Aunt harped more tellingly upon the same string. "A good Christian should weep only at the dread of hellfire for souls whom he cannot bring to Grace. Anything less is like railing at God's purposes." Papa, when he once caught her crying over a sad book, had remonstrated, "Have more fortitude, my love. There are enough real sorrows in the world. Don't wear out your pity on shadows." And even Branwell—who now seemed to be begging her to fling her arms around his neck and wallow in his emotions with him—had often scoffed at her too-tender reactions and ready tears.

But her slowly-mastered self-control masked the most agonizing empathy for Branwell now. How easily she could imagine the terrors that had paralyzed his will in London! How she blamed herself for not having foreseen this outcome, for taking Branwell at his own inflated estimation and sending him off with scarcely more than a word of warning! "Poor Branwell! Oh, poor, poor Branwell!" she cried out in her heart, for her timidity, which she had never had to disguise, now saw a fellowship with a similar quality in him, which in her ignorance she had never recognized before. Oh, she saw that he had behaved stupidly, that he had been a weakling and a coward. "But am I to upbraid him, I who will probably prove myself to be no stronger when my turn comes?" she thought.

Nevertheless, it was a terrible moment of disillusion for Anne. Emily had once warned her that Branwell was weak and lacked resolution, but she had not believed. He was to be their stay, their prop—and their pride. All her life she had looked up to him, dreamed of his future, supported and indulged him like the rest. Yet now as she looked at him she seemed to see, in place of her brilliant, mercurial brother, a poor wreck of a young man, permanently broken by his first failure. What more was there to hope for?

But she hid her disappointment from him. Patiently she sat there until he had got it all off his chest. Then they went out for a short walk together, after which she heated up some milk for him on the banked-up kitchen stove and saw him off to bed.

Back in the empty living room, her owns tears could be let loose, they were not primarily for Branwell, nor even for herself. They were for Papa, who must never, never be told the truth— but who, in time, must inevitably find it out.

2
FREEDOM AND
SLAVERY

"*S*IT DOWN, MISS BRONTË," SAID MISS Wooler kindly. "I think I know what you want to speak about. We are also very concerned. What *is* it? Why is she losing weight? Why is she unable to concentrate? Why, in short, is she so very unhappy?"

Charlotte's own face was pinched and white. Emily's sufferings, her mental and bodily deterioration, found a tangible echo here.

"Miss Wooler, she is dying of homesickness."

The two younger Misses Wooler who were in the room exchanged glances, but the oldest sister continued to look straight at Charlotte, showing no signs of disbelief.

"You know, my dear, I have seen many homesick girls, yet never one who—"

"Emily is not like other girls!" Charlotte burst out. "No one can understand! Home is not just the place where she is happiest. It's the place she cannot bear to live away from. Please, Miss Wooler, let me write to my father. She must go home. She *must*."

Miss Wooler leaned back in her chair and looked out of the window. She hated to admit defeat, and she had failed with Emily.

"Very well," she said. "You know her best. But the arrangement we had still stands. If your younger sister would like to substitute for Emily, you may continue teaching here on the same basis as before."

Charlotte said nothing. It was hard to think about Anne just now.

"How old is your other sister?" pursued Miss Wooler.

"Not yet sixteen."

"Well! And is she of the same—delicate temperament as Emily? Might she stand the separation from home better?"

"I'm not sure."

"Shall we try?"

"It's very kind of you. I will suggest it in my letter. May I go and write it at once?"

Miss Wooler nodded, and Charlotte hurried to the door as if she could not wait another moment to put matters under way. When she had gone, Miss Eliza sighed gustily.

"What nonsense! Dying, indeed! Well, *I* shall not be sorry when she goes. Not an attractive girl."

"Let us hope her sister proves more sensible," said Miss Susan crisply.

Miss Wooler said nothing. She was reflecting with relief that at least she had not lost Charlotte. Things were not going well for the school. It was to be hoped there was no family weakness, for Charlotte, as a member of the staff, was going to have to take on extra work and extra responsibilities in the difficult times ahead.

Emily's journey home was like the slow, exquisite lessening of some intolerable pressure. The tie that bound her to Haworth, and which had been stretched to breaking point all the time she had been away, now slackened and slackened, until, at the moment when the gig rounded the last corner, she could restrain herself no longer. Leaping down while it was still moving, she hitched up her skirts and ran like a young deer up the hill . . .

Grasper heard her coming and flung himself at the garden gate, barking frantically. Anne rushed to the door. She had another of her bad asthmatic colds; an attack of coughing brought her up short and she hung on the handle, wheezing and catching her breath, before flinging it open and running down the steps with her arms outstretched. In a moment she and Emily were holding each other tightly. Anne was crying. Emily drew away a little and looked down into her face.

"How long have we got before you have to leave?"

"No time. A few days. But never mind! Be happy, you are home, that's what matters! Oh, Emily"—seeing her face—"you've had an awful time! I knew it—"

"Don't. It's over."

They entered the house with their arms around each other. Papa had had to answer a sick call, but Aunt and Tabby were there. Tabby was overjoyed; Aunt was not. Emily read the reflection of her own bitter sense of failure in her sour face; Aunt could not countenance dereliction of duty. But Emily's pride rose up to defend her. There was defiance in her brief kiss.

"Where's Branwell?"

"Upstairs. He's ashamed to come and greet you," Anne said. "You mustn't speak about London. None of us ever mentions it. It's for Papa's sake, too."

"We'll take a vow to avoid the subject of failure altogether. Shall we not, Aunt?" asked Emily, standing straight and looking her Aunt in the face with eyes no longer dull, but bright and sharp as needles.

"You are looking better already," said Aunt drily.

Looking and feeling better. And in a matter of weeks Emily had put on flesh, regained her vigor and was striding about the house and the moors just as before. She had developed a lithe if rather gaunt figure, catlike in its limber strength. When she flung herself down on the heather (or, to Aunt's unavailing disapproval, upon the hearthrug in the dining room) and lay with her face turned up to sky or ceiling, her eyes rapt and unblinking, one hip rolled over like a curling wave and her legs thrown with unstudied grace one across the other, she was the epitome of feline relaxation. Her nature, and Nature itself, reclaimed her; the very moorland air seemed to feed her system until her once-sallow skin glowed and her limbs were vibrant with health and energy. During the mornings she swept the carpets and flags, fed her flock of creatures, polished the lamp chimneys, cleaned the windows and pounded bread dough. Tabby missed Anne's chatter, but, though Emily hardly talked, she was a tireless worker and a good listener. In the afternoons Emily was free to enjoy herself in her own way, and her own way seldom involved any other human being.

So interior and deep-seated were Emily's relief and fulfillment, simply at being at home again, that for weeks she hardly allowed Branwell's state of mind to impinge on her own. Branwell avoided everyone in the house, especially Papa, though Emily noticed that Papa went out of his way to be kind to him. Branwell only liked to be with John, and often left the house (in a furtive fashion that annoyed Emily, since who would have forbidden him?) to stroll down to the stonemason's yard and thence, as they all knew, to the Bull. With some liquor taken, Branwell had courage to return more noisily, often banging the front door in a senseless display of bravado before dashing upstairs to shut himself in the study again.

Very occasionally he would say, as if Emily had been trying to persuade him, "Oh, come on then! I'll let you drag me out for a walk, so long as you don't lecture me." Emily turned up one corner of her mouth at this, for nothing akin to a lecture had crossed her lips since each of them returned from their failed excursions into the world.

One day, however, as they were breasting the cold wind up by Top Withins, Emily as usual walking a little ahead, Branwell caught up with her and began to talk.

"I shall never be an artist now."

"Then what will you be?"

"A writer, perhaps—"

"Good."

"—if I must live to be anything."

She turned and stared at him with those eyes which showed too much white. "What rubbish is this? Do you plan to dive into an early grave?"

"Don't, Emily. You wouldn't joke if you knew. I'm not built for failure. I feel sometimes as if my whole being were plunged in despair. *Honestly*, I would rather have died than return home as I did."

"Stuff," returned Emily tartly, and turned into the wind again. "Did I not fail quite as miserably? Turn it to good account. Let it stiffen your resolve to do better."

"Oh, you may say so! You care nothing for the world. What you are doing this minute is the height of your worldly ambition. You don't know what it is to have every eye, every expectation, the hope of a whole family, pinned on you. That girl Mary used to say that women in our society are restricted, but I say they are far freer than men. Nothing is demanded of them that the stupidest can't fulfill! But someone like me—"

"Oh, Branwell, have done! Let's talk about your writing. What, if anything, have you done to advance yourself there?"

"I've not been as lax and hopeless as you suppose. I've already written twice to the editor of *Blackwood's*, asking him to read my work. I believe I might replace James Hogg, now he's dead." (Hogg was a writer whose Gothic horror tales had been much admired by both of them since childhood.)

"So you think you can match the Ettrick Shepherd? Well, why not? And what response have you had to your letters? Why two, by the way?"

Branwell flushed. "I think the first must have gone astray, as I had no answer to it, so I wrote another."

"I wish you had let me read them first," said Emily, frowning.

"Why should I? Do you think I can't write a letter?"

"Oh, you can write one all right. The question is, In what tone did you write? I hope it was not too sycophantic or exaggerated."

"On the contrary, I took a rather commanding line. They must receive many letters after such a vacancy occurs. I wanted to make my application stand out."

Emily suppressed a sigh.

"Well—let's hope for the best."

"When Charlotte comes home for Christmas, I must have something to show her," muttered Branwell. It was imperative for him to get a position soon. It was intolerable at home, enduring Aunt's pinch-lipped silences and Papa's determined patience, which did not quite mask his disappointment.

"I'm writing well now, Emmy, better than ever. Perhaps the agony of mind I am going through is deepening my character."

"So long as you do not pour too much drink into the newly-excavated depths," she replied, "you may do well yet."

But when Charlotte and Anne returned for the Christmas holidays, Branwell had nothing to "show" them. No letter had come from *Blackwood's*, and he felt with keen bewilderment the dawnings of chagrin. But Emily didn't mention it and they were all happy to be together again, though there were new undercurrents.

Anne had settled well at school, and they were all proud of her; but this success reflected poorly on Emily. Branwell was continually and poignantly aware that his sisters were suffering all these trials owing to *his* inability so far to earn anything. And Charlotte was hardest put to enter into the spirit of the reunion, for this intermission of warmth and joy was marred by the knowledge of its brevity.

Still, it was glorious to shut herself into the study after a minimum of chores (the others all agreed she had earned a real rest) and fling herself at her desk. During the hours she spent feverishly scribbling—"scribblemania," Branwell called it—she knew a total release from all tension and torment.

In between bouts of intensely personal creativity, she indulged herself in intimate talk with Branwell. She did not mention the real world, which contained their individual failures. They did not seem important now. All she wanted from him was the mutual delights of Angria and Verdopolis.

On the first of January, after much discussion, Branwell launched out on a *History* of new strife in the new territories.

Foreigners were to invade Angria, and the eternal feud between Zamorna and the Earl of Northangerland was to break forth in civil war. The wholeheartedness with which Branwell was able to throw himself into this new project, so exactly to his taste, was aided by the fact that he had secretly written a third, and—surely—irresistible letter to *Blackwood's*.

So they entered upon the new year filled with new hope in Branwell's case, contentment for Emily and quiet determination in Anne. But for Charlotte there was nothing but heavyhearted foreboding.

She was not deceived. Eighteen thirty-six was a hard year for her, the year in which her soul was first tempered by the fires of self-doubt.

Her personal crisis began as one of simple frustration. She longed to be alone, to be at home, to be free to plunge into the Infernal World and live there among her people. At the same time she began to suffer from something akin to Branwell's pre-London desire to break out of the narrow confines of the life she foresaw for herself and live out her fantasies—or something like them—in reality. Was she never to participate in, or even witness, anything great or magnificent or of moment in the world? Was her whole future to be this—this prison, or others like it? Hemmed in by petty concerns for "miniature" minds and lives such as those of her pupils, she became at times so exasperated that she thought of them as dolts, asses and fat-headed oafs. Must she forever discipline herself to be forbearing with such as these, when her aspirations strained after great people, great events, great and marvelous achievements?

These thoughts oppressed her so badly that there were times when the very air she breathed seemed stagnant and suffocating. She had a constant struggle with herself during her long working hours, to keep her mind from wandering, her eyes from glazing, her tongue from lashing out. The girls she taught were in no sense worse than others of their kind; yet, as the school "halves" wore wearily on, Charlotte came to see them as so many mopping and mowing demons, sent to persecute and oppress her. Sometimes they made her physically ill. One evening, for instance, when she was supervising their silent study period, the sight of them ranged before her with their tousled heads dropped indolently on their hands or arms, their unwilling sighs and their trivial whispers, so irritated her that she closed her eyes against them and began, irresistibly and against her sternest orders to herself, to write:

I am just going to write because I cannot help it. Branwell might indeed talk of Scribblemania if he were to see me just now. Stupidity the atmosphere, schoolbooks the employment, asses the society! What in all this is there to remind me of the divine silent unseen land of thought, dim now, and indefinite as the dream of a dream, the shadow of a shade? There is a voice, there is an impulse that wakens up that dormant power which in its torpidity I sometimes think dead. . . .

Her thoughts, out of control, swept on, and in a wild and dis-ordered script she wrote of the wind she could hear "pouring in impetuous current" through the advancing night—the wind that linked her with Branwell and Emily, for they could hear it in Haworth and might be thinking of her and Anne. "Glorious!" she scrawled, catching her breath in a gasp as a gust struck the bow windows. The wildness of the elements tore her in spirit from her prison and carried her to Angria.

Oh, it has wakened a feeling that I cannot satisfy—a thousand wishes rose at its call which must die with me, for they will never be fulfilled.

While all this blind tumult was ravishing her inwardly so that she lost all sense of where she was, she was suddenly interrupted by one of the girls, who, dared by another, came up beside her, poking some work beneath her nose and trying as she did so to peer at the writing. Charlotte came to herself with a sense of nausea; her head literally reeled, and the lamplight sparkled and whirled before her as if she would faint. This was not the first nor the last time she was to feel hatred—true, destructive, sinful hatred such as would not have been alien to the black souls of Zamorna or the tyrant Northangerland himself—for one of her harmless, insipid pupils.

Yet if that had been all—the passionate desire to escape into untrammeled creativeness that was perpetually thwarted—her sufferings at Roe Head would not have been unendurable. They would not have reduced her, as eventually they did, to a condition no better than Emily's at the time she was sent home.

The worst torment was the terrible guilt that began to prey upon her.

It started with an awareness that the hold her phantoms had on her, her love for them and their reality in her life, was morally dangerous. How often had Aunt, and Papa, too, told her that a Christian's business is first and foremost with God, but in obedience to His decrees, also with the "real" world of human beings and human duties? To try to escape from these was obviously a sin. To be angry to the point of violence with innocents whose only fault was to interrupt an illicit commerce with supernatural beings tempting her to idolatry, was another. But that was not the worst.

The worst was that she began to have some notion of the nature of her creations, and of the bodily excitement generated in her by their forbidden passions and vices.

For years she had used Lord Charles Wellesley and his high-minded criticisms of his degenerating brother to soothe her conscience. As long as Lord Charles saw the gathering evil in Zamorna, and condemned it, that meant that she, Charlotte, was still sufficiently in control to stay aloof and take a moral stand. But now, in her twentieth year, she was mature enough to recognize that her heart was with Zamorna and that her conscience, left in Lord Charles's slipshod care, was not safe.

There would be safety in her religion, if only she could return to it wholeheartedly. But the more she tried, the more strongly the forces of the Infernal World (how aptly, as she now saw, they had named it!) seemed to drag her back from salvation.

In this moral dilemma she searched for someone to cling to and seek help from, for she could not manage alone. No one in her own family could aid her, she knew. Emily, who could see no wrong in her creations, would not understand the root causes of her anguish. Branwell would affect to scorn her qualms, and Anne was still young and innocent. As for Papa and Aunt—! The mere thought of confiding in them made her shrivel with shame, for how could she utter to them a word of Zamorna and his wickedness?

She thought of telling Mary. She was far more open-minded and less censorious than anyone else Charlotte knew. But she was not religious enough to guide Charlotte back to the proper path. When she came over from Gomersal to visit, Charlotte noticed that her only questions were practical ones such as, "Why do you do so much for so little money when you could live without it?" She noticed that Charlotte was pale and unresponsive, and told her crisply that she was being overworked.

"I told you you would not stand it," she said. "You would do better to join me in some enterprise in which we could be independent. Let's open a shop!" But Charlotte could not even manage to laugh at this absurd idea.

No. Mary, whom Charlotte believed would be a tower of strength in any practical matter, could not be turned to for aid in a spiritual trial.

That left Ellen.

If only, Charlotte thought desperately, Ellen's piety could be allied somehow to Mary's broad-minded common sense! But that could not be. And as it was religious help she needed now, her thoughts tended more and more toward Ellen, who, as if sensing her friend's crisis, began to intrude into the routine trivia of her letters passages of moral uplift and even a kind of catechism. Did Charlotte fully accept the will of God, or was she perhaps com-

mitting the sin of opposing her own will to it? Was she as careful
as she should be to guard her thoughts and protect that core of
holiness which is the gift of God to all His elect?

This sort of thing—so redolent of the very sanctity that Charlotte felt she needed—threw her perversely into a turmoil of
reaction and resentment. It all sounded like cant to her ears. Was
Ellen, like Aunt Branwell, pressing Calvin's terrible doctrine on
Charlotte? If it were true that some were marked for salvation
and others for the "pit," then it would make absolute sense that
the more she struggled to come to God the more she was dragged
back. Well might the thought terrify her, for she knew what hell
was; Aunt had dinned it into her and so had Mr. Carus Wilson.
Even Papa did not deny it as a territory as real as the graveyard.
So she wrote in trembling agitation to Ellen:

"I forget God, will not God forget me? You cannot imagine
how hard, rebellious and intractable all my feelings are. When
I begin to study on the subject, I almost grow blasphemous, athe-
istical in my sentiments . . ."

But after this letter was sent, Charlotte became panic-stricken.
Wringing her hands and pacing her little room in a fever of
misery, she kept thinking, "I love her! She is an angel! And when
she reads what I wrote, she will desert me, or rebuke me, and her
rebukes burn like hot iron . . . If only we could be together, live
together for always, she would save me. Her pure goodness would
stop me from thinking these dark thoughts or giving way to my
vile imaginings."

Even as she thought this, the Duke rose up before her in all
but physical solidity, his handsome Byronic face and tall, strong
figure in its swirling cloak bent all upon her as if he would clasp
her in his arms. In horror she covered her eyes, her ears, her
mouth. She threw herself on her bed and struggled to suppress
the image. But it was inside her brain and there she could not
reach it.

"Ellen!" she cried aloud. "Ellen! I am damned! Save me, oh,
save me!" But even as she heard her own voice calling on Ellen,
her soul smote her down. Why was she not appealing to God?

Was it not because she knew she was unworthy, that His face had been turned from her from the beginning? Else why had He let Satan lead her into such a morass? Zamorna and his minions hemmed her in. She had become their creature, and they seemed intent upon destroying her utterly. And still she loved them, longed for them, tore open her heart for them to enter.

"It is them I love, it is them I belong to," she whispered. "It is no use! Calvinism is true. I am an outcast. There is no health in me. I am a liar and an idolater. I am wholly corrupted." She would have wished to die, if she had not been afraid of where her soul would most assuredly awaken.

Had she been the sort of person who is deflected from spiritual malaise by hard work, she would not have been miserable long.

By Christmas she had risen to a position amounting to deputy head of the school and had many minor duties heaped on her into the bargain, tedious and menial tasks which led the forthright Mary to exclaim:

"You are little better than a slave! You are not happy, you are not independent, you have no money to jingle in your pocket. Oh, Charlotte, what's to become of you? You can't spend your life like this!"

"What choice have I?" asked Charlotte in utter weariness.

But a choice of sorts had dimly appeared to her. She wanted to write; and although she was often contemptuous of her own work, there were other times when, lying on her school bed reveling in half an hour of leisure at the end of a day's drudgery, ideas and visions came to her of such a clarity that she knew, she *knew* that if life only allowed her the freedom to sit down at her desk then and there, she might yet produce something worthy— something *professional*.

So she nerved herself to an act of desperate presumption. She would write a letter to the Poet Laureate, Robert Southey. Her determination to do this, together with the expectation of a visit from Ellen over Christmas, lightened her gloomy spirits sufficiently to keep those at home from noticing the traces of strain and misery on her face when she returned.

For Charlotte this had been a desolate and self-destructive year. But Emily had thrived.

Tabby and Aunt now being elderly, and Branwell useless, most of the housework devolved upon her, but she dispatched it energetically and was then free to walk and write and read. She missed Anne; she worried about Charlotte; in the back of her mind she felt the stirrings of apprehension that sooner or later she must leave home again. But on the whole her view of life was cheerful and optimistic.

She was largely preoccupied by her own inner world, and with her poetry. This did not always please her. Once she wrote: "I am more terrifically and idiotically and brutally STUPID than ever I was in the whole course of my incarnate existence. The above precious lines are the fruits of one hour's most agonizing labor."

Many of her efforts she tore up in impatience without even troubling to reread them.

But there was sheer joy for her in Gondal, and recently in Gaaldine, a new island continent recently discovered by the Gondals. A whole panoply of drama began to open out, an epic that could be compared to a painter's canvas stretching from floor to ceiling, from wall to wall, closely covered in the artist's mind with explicit details before ever the loaded brush had touched it in reality.

The central figure was a beautiful queen, whom Emily could see at a glance in all phases of her life, from babyhood to death— as God (she thought) must watch us from some infinitely distant pinnacle of observation that encompasses all time and all space. She saw the birth of the child one cold, clear morning beside a Gondalian lake. Her name was Augusta Geraldine Almeda, and she grew into so perfect a girl that Emily's heart was torn when she looked ahead in the panorama at what she was irrevocably destined to become.

During that first year of "A.G.A." 's life within Emily's, she grew to womanhood and fell in love with a Gaaldine lord, Alexander of Elbe. From time to time battles rent Gondal, and these conflicts were far more terrible and elemental than anything even the martial-minded Branwell could conceive, for there was no "getting alive again" here. Nature and humanity followed their appointed courses: the mortally wounded died; the dead were buried; the living grieved and were radically deformed by loss and tragedy. In such a battle Alexander was wounded, and died in Augusta's arms, and she herself was imprisoned in a dungeon. Emily scarcely realized, as her heroine suffered to the point of lunacy in this confinement, that the agony Augusta felt was a dramatization of Emily's own agony at Roe Head.

The whole saga lay before her. When she closed in on this area or that of her epic canvas, the details she perceived that pricked her to actual creativity were often not the events, but the settings, the season, the weather: the waving grasses of the moors, the last rays of sunlight falling on a lake, the "old gray stone" or "spectral trees," with which her physical life was surrounded.

Occasionally, however, she grew morose. The humiliation of her failure at Roe Head returned to torment her. Within herself she could always feel an inviolable core of confidence, pride—a deep sureness. In her element she could defy the fates to do their worst, hating morbidity, self-pity and retreat. Yet how had she behaved at the first real test? Her collapse seemed a negation of all that she believed she was. She loathed thinking of it, and would shake herself like a dog when the recollection came to her.

"I was a weakling, a deserter!" she would think to herself, the words lancing her heart. "Next time—"

But the thought of enduring that horror again terrified her. Only during moments of special robustness—usually experienced on a ridge of the moors on a windy day, or lying on her narrow bed at night staring up through the curtainless window at the stars— could she face up to the necessity of trying again.

Emily's relations with Branwell at this time were slighty distanced by their separate life-experiences and current preoccupations. She secretly rather despised Branwell's eternal need for an audience, and although she listened patiently to his eager, praise-seeking readings from his Angrian *History*, she did not really care for it. It had too little of hard reality, too much of cold statistics and rootless fantasy.

Yet she was very interested in Branwell and was aware of watching him and listening to his turns of speech, picked up from the Masons' Lodge, the Bull or other all-male preserves. In short, it was her brother's masculinity that interested her. It fed her desire for knowledge of human beings. And when she saw him occasionally drunk, or heard him bitterly upbraided by Papa for gambling or loose speech, she would stand off and record it all, storing it in her mind with no urge to judge him. He was supplying something she needed, and though she hated Papa to be angered and distressed, and in the abstract worried about how Branwell was going on, her main concern was her own inner life and the contribution which the only young male in her immediate vicinity was making to it.

Although Branwell's sufferings and self-denigration were doing him no good, they were nonetheless real and painful. He brooded far more on his London failure than Emily did on hers at Roe Head. His unhappiness preoccupied him to the exclusion of any real effort.

He wrote a great deal, of course, and many of his poems were deeply felt: for the first time his grief and longing for Maria, long suppressed, were disinterred and endured again with the more acute emotions of young manhood. The hopelessness of his reaching out after Maria—the poignancy of the endless "If only! If only!" treadmill—drove him to two types of excess. Physically, he drank more, seeking escape. Spiritually, he began to revile the religious creed of his childhood.

Previously he had allowed himself to be comforted by the thought that Maria was in heaven, awaiting him. But that consolation now began to seem nothing but childishness. Not that he doubted God and an afterlife (though sometimes he longed to disbelieve it all and have nothing worse to face than oblivion). Yet, unable to shake off his conviction of judgment and eternity, he was led inexorably on to consider what possible chance there was for him to be assigned to paradise. Maria, the quintessential pure, brave and noble soul, could not share an eternal destiny with such as he was. That would not be just. Therefore he would never see her again; this separation must last forever. Perhaps hell itself would be no more than knowing she waited for him, and yet being unworthy to see her or to be with her.

This unendurable idea drove him into a position of appearing to despise religion altogether. Could he believe in something that condemned him so utterly? He began to identify more and more with his villain-hero Northangerland, strong-minded, cynical and brutal enough to be conscience-free, to direct his life by the laws of selfish expediency, snap his fingers in the face of damnation, grapple his graceless fate to his life, buying what he wanted at no matter what eternal cost. While Branwell explored his creation in thought and on paper, he could enjoy a few hours of spurious freedom from an otherwise almost constant spiritual pain.

But all this writing was futile. It took no real effort, developed no new or practical skills. For him it was as facile as talking; it did nothing to change the situation of dependence and drifting inefficacy that was at the root of his misery.

Thus the year fell away into waste, even while the *History* and the poems piled up on his desk—for, unlike Emily, he destroyed nothing, censored nothing, weeded out nothing. He could not apply her rigorous self-criticism, which caused her talent-tree to grow up well pruned, straight and strong.

The four of them gathered at Christmas and compared notes. But none of them told the others the whole truth.

Charlotte dared not touch upon her inner trials. She had begun to think she might be going mad, and she did not want to frighten the others. So she made wan little jokes about the tedium and the interruptions, and tried not to meet Emily's steady, penetrating eyes lest her soul be read.

Emily, active as always, did most of the cooking and least of the talking. She stayed close to Anne and answered questions about her writing briefly. When Charlotte urged her to read them her latest poems, she just said:

"Nothing is ready."

She and Anne played at Gondal, but only when they were alone. Emily did not ask Anne about school, and Anne volunteered no information. To each in a different way, the subject was painful. Only Aunt and Papa asked all the conventional questions, to which Anne made conventional replies: yes, she was working hard. The teachers were satisfied with her. The girls were pleasant. She was quite content with school life. No, not too homesick.

Emily stared at her hands in her lap and waited for the subject to change.

As for Branwell, he was too volatile and undisciplined to keep his unhappiness entirely to himself, and in long monologues tried to explain to Charlotte why the year had produced no plan, no prospect of change in his situation. At other moments he would talk eagerly about his acceptance by the local Freemasons; he even hinted about the sacred mysteries of his initiation, regardless of her muted but obvious contempt. He joked manfully about his "debaucheries" and Papa's efforts to control them. He talked on and on about himself, hardly letting Charlotte speak. But he said nothing about Maria, nothing about his religious crisis. And she said nothing about hers.

Just before Christmas, a disaster occurred. Tabby was walking down the icy cobbled street to the shops when she slipped and fell, breaking her hip. She was carried back groaning to the parsonage by two local shopkeepers.

The household promptly fell into an uproar.

"She cannot stay here," Aunt exclaimed. "She must go to her sister's in the village."

"Aunt! But her sister is as old as she is! Who is to nurse her?"

"Who is to nurse her here?"

"I will, of course," said Emily. "Who else?" She would not be gainsaid, and Aunt was swept aside almost bodily while Emily directed the men to carry the groaning Tabby upstairs.

It was only after all the to-do had simmered down that Charlotte realized the implications of this accident for herself. Ellen's visit, so passionately looked forward to, would have to be put off.

Weeping silently, she crept away to her room and wrote a letter, for once caring nothing that her self-pity weighted down every line:

"After this disappointment, I never dare reckon with certainty on the enjoyment of a pleasure again. It seems as if some fatality stood between you and me. I am not good enough for you, and you must be kept from the contamination of too intimate society . . ."

At the New Year, the four sat around the dining-room table making resolutions.

"I shall carry on just as I am," said Anne. "It's not that I'm so self-satisfied, but what I am doing takes all the strength of will that I have at present."

"I am going to do something for myself," vowed Branwell. "Another Christmas shall not find me in this pitiable state of uselessness. I shall write once more to North. I can't believe he has had my letters! He must and *shall* answer me. I shall offer to journey to his office for an interview. He can't ignore that! Only think, by this time next year I may be established on his staff, a journalist of means and influence. I shall write this very week."

"And I will write to Mr. Southey," said Charlotte quietly. They all knew of her plan and approved of it.

"And you, Emily? What do you resolve?"

Emily smiled to herself and rubbed Grasper's ears.

"Not to burn the bread, and to be kinder to Aunt."

They all laughed. But not even Anne knew of Emily's real and secret determination—to go out once more upon the world.

3

TRIALS

CHARLOTTE'S LETTER TO ROBERT
Southey was everything that Branwell's to the editor of *Black-
wood's* was not. Both appeals cried out for positive advice and
practical help; both issued from echoing depths of personal need
and anguish. Yet where Branwell's approach was arrogant and
hectoring, Charlotte's was modest, humble and utterly sincere.
Small wonder then that Southey replied, and that once again,
contemptuous silence was the only answer from Christopher
North.

Southey's letter, however, was not what Charlotte had hoped
for. It contained no encouragement to aim at a career in literature.
Even young men who sought his advice were warned that a
writer's life was perilous. As for a woman, literature could not
be the business of her life, and ought not to be. He also warned
her against day-dreaming.

"The day dreams in which you habitually indulge are likely
to induce a distempered state of mind and, in proportion as all
the ordinary uses of the world seem to you flat and unprofitable,

you will be unfitted for them without becoming fitted for anything else."

These words, when she first read them at Roe Head on a chill March morning, at first numbed Charlotte. Later the numbness wore off to reveal a raw area in her mind, like a wound. She could not recall telling Southey that she habitually day-dreamed. Yet he had understood it from the nature of the writing she'd sent him, and had felt it his duty to warn her of the moral dangers of this addiction—dangers she was already all too hideously aware of.

The words "flat and unprofitable," which she remembered from *Hamlet*, now rang out within her as the most apt description possible of her present surroundings and routine. Southey would undoubtedly say that she saw them in that dreary light *because* she indulged in her fantasies—that the dangers he was alerting her to were already taking effect. "Unfitted for the ordinary uses of the world . . ." Was this not a euphemism for the morbid mental state she had descended into, seeming sometimes to border on madness? She must grasp this advice, written to her so generously by this famous and worthy man, and impale herself on it, whatever the pain, in order to retain her reason and her power to be of use to her family. This could only mean that sooner or later, preferably sooner, she must summon up courage to cast out the beloved specters of the nether world and turn her whole heart, mind and imagination to the surface world that others called the real one.

On her birthday she wrote:

"Southey's advice to be kept for ever. My twenty-first birthday. Roe Head. April 21st, 1837."

Branwell waited ten nerve-racking days for an answer from North. When none came, he flew into a fury. Could the fool not *see*, had he no eyes nor wit to read and judge? How could he have failed to recognize Branwell's worth from the samples sent to him? He must be a small man after all, a commonplace mind, afraid to take any real talent into his employ. Branwell began to despise *Blackwood's*, which had been his reverence and delight since childhood.

Well, if there was no sympathy forthcoming from a callous journalist, there might be some from a sensitive poet. Branwell resolved to write to William Wordsworth.

This time he was wise enough to consult Emily, and his letter was moderate in tone and humbler. But alas for his tense hopes, some sentences of bombast and offensive conceit slipped in, nullifying the rest, so that the elderly poet, reading it, noticed only the shrill voice of the arrogant spoiled child and ignored the simple, well-phrased plea of the struggling young man. He returned no answer.

This blow seemed the knell of Branwell's literary hopes. While he did not stop writing—he couldn't—he turned his "professional" eyes back to art. His bedroom bloomed again with the strange clutter of the artist, and he dragged John Brown and others up there to pose for him.

John found it intolerable to be still, and after an hour or so would grow restless and urge Branwell to leave off his knavish daubing and come for a drink with him. Since the work never truly fulfilled Branwell's inner vision, he was glad enough to be persuaded, and most painting sessions ended in the bar of the Black Bull. There he could be witty and articulate enough. Men twice his age would be silent to listen respectfully as he held forth; he seemed to them very learned and dazzling. The smoky, fume-laden atmosphere agreed with Branwell, blurring his perception of his own situation. The horror was going out again into the cool, pellucid night afterward, and having to be helped up the hill by John or William. Worse still were the nights when he was so drunk that Emily had to half carry him to bed.

"Go on, say it, say it!" he mumbled to her one night, sensing her disgust at his reeking breath and shambling helplessness. "Don't be so tolerant; abuse me, tell me I am worthless and repulsive, I deserve it!"

"You are, and you do," said Emily shortly, lugging him up the stairs. "Does that satisfy your need for punishment?"

But there was much worse he could do to himself. "If Charlotte were here . . ." he breathed in an ecstasy of self-torment. *Or Maria.*

But that thought was too cruelly poignant, and he did not let it surface, even in his most wretched moments.

Sometimes the abuse came from outside.

Once he stumbled, coming upstairs, and fell against his father's door. It opened, and Patrick, in his nightshirt, appeared like an avenging angel.

"Branwell!" he thundered, in a tone that made his son quail and turn white. "Is there no end to your disgusting indulgence? Are you not ashamed to let your sister see you in this condition? You were pledged to temperance not a year since, and now look at you—your vows broken, your body half ruined, your soul—I can't bear to think of the state of your soul!" A door opened behind Branwell, and Patrick roared over his shoulder, "Get back in your bed, woman! Don't shame me by looking at him!" Aunt backed into her bedroom with a gasp. Branwell was literally cowering by the banisters, his mind almost numb, but with just enough coherent thought left to wonder what his father would feel were he to throw himself down the stairwell.

"What have you to say for yourself?" his father was shouting, and now Branwell felt the still-iron grip of Patrick's fist on his collar.

"If I were dead, that would be best—"

"Ah, you whimpering fool!" He yanked him upright. "Stand on your legs like a man, can't you? You sicken me! You stink of rum! Where's your mind, eh? That fine, that splendid mind that you're set on paralyzing with alcohol? Won't it come to your aid and show you a better way out of your troubles? Oh, get to bed. I can't stand the sight of you!"

He let Branwell go so violently that he nearly plunged down the stairwell unwillingly, and went back into his room, slamming the door. Tabby, distressed by the uproar, began to whine querulously, giving Emily an excuse to leave the scene.

Branwell stood alone, clutching the banister, staring down into the darkness. Emily had taken the candle. He felt himself utterly bereft, alone not only in body but in spirit, for he was sober now and recognized all too clearly the futility of his proceedings, the speciousness of the bolstering admiration of his pub cronies, the truth of his father's accusations. What was happening? Where were his prospects? What, indeed, had become of his fine brain, of his talents? It was in London that it all began to go wrong. If only—! If only he could have that time over again! If only North or Wordsworth had held out a helping hand to him when he had put himself at their mercy! If only someone understood, could feel for him, could truly love him! If only Maria . . .

He sank to his knees, clutching the posts, and cried in miserable, childlike anguish. He would have lain there all night, if Aunt had not emerged, as silent and cold as a ghost, and led him to bed.

In late spring, Anne took to her bed. She had been vaguely unwell for some weeks, but now she became quite seriously ill. It was not her chest but gastric fever, and as it was thought best not to move her, she lay in bed at school and was nursed there.

Patient and uncomplaining, she drank the medicines prescribed for her and did all she was told. To look at her pale, placid face, one might have supposed her quite calm inwardly; but in fact her soul was in ferment.

I am going to die, she thought constantly. I grow weaker every day. I can see by Charlotte's face that she expects me to die. And what awaits me then? Only perfection is fit for heaven and God. Aunt says we are all corrupt and sinful. Only Grace can purify us, and I'm sure God has not given me that or I should have known it. Wesley told us we should know the instant we were redeemed and made perfect. Who knows better than I do how weak I am, how I rebel inwardly against the life I have to face, how little I love my duty? Is this perfection? I am not suffering much; God must be saving my torments for my soul alone. Yet can God be so cruel, so unforgiving? I have tried to be good. Aunt has made me so afraid of death and of God, too. That cannot be right! We are supposed to love Him. Oh, surely these contradictions have some resolution, in some creed . . . But not ours! Not ours!

Her life was not actually in danger, and Charlotte, having no

idea of her fears, was startled when Anne asked if she might see
a minister.

"Not an Anglican, Charlotte. I know already, word for word,
what they will offer me, and it won't comfort me or answer my
questions. I want something else, something—kinder. I don't
believe in perfection in human beings . . . Charlotte, do you
remember Miss Wooler speaking about the Moravians? She seemed
to respect them. They believe that we are all sinful and yet that
God will help and forgive us if we have faith in Him. Can you
send for a Moravian minister?"

Charlotte might have argued with her. She was, indeed, a little
shocked that Anne seemed to reject their sect in favor of another.
But her own spiritual crisis was still upon her, and she understood Anne's need very well. So she sent a message to a Reverend
La Trobe, a Bishop of the Moravian church, and he came to
see Anne the next day.

Charlotte let them talk alone, but afterward she asked the
Bishop about the interview.

"She is fearful lest the least wrong action or thought will make
her inimical to God," he said. "I want to convince her that God
will give a haven to any sinner, providing he loves and trusts Him.
How could anyone love Him otherwise?" Leaning towards Charlotte, he said quietly, "Hope is what we all live by. The poor
child must be reassured that the impulses of her heart, to love and
trust in God, are her true guides. They are not the temptings of
pride or arrogance as she seems to believe."

After a week or two Anne grew stronger, and the Moravian
minister went quietly on his way, out of her life. She never forgot
him, or his words of pardon and peace. But the earlier influences
had struck the deepest roots. It was not possible wholly to convince herself that there was nothing to fear from God.

After the summer holidays, Emily walked into Patrick's study one
day and abruptly announced, "I have taken a position, Papa."

He started, and stood up to face her.

"My dear! After what happened at Roe Head, is that wise?"

"I don't know if it's wise. It's necessary. Charlotte can't go on carrying the whole burden alone."

"What position is it?"

"I answered an advertisement for a teacher in a large school near Halifax. It's at a place called Southowram and my employer is a Miss Patchett. Her sister has just got married and she needs help and is prepared to give me a trial."

"How many pupils are there?"

"About forty."

"That is a large establishment, then. I hope you will not be overworked."

Emily smiled her lopsided smile. "I hope not, too."

Patrick stared at her through his pince-nez, then abruptly came around the desk and embraced her.

"My dear child—what shall we do without you?"

"Well, Papa, Tabby is all mended and back in the kitchen. You and Aunt will not be neglected. Extra income is more important now, and practice in earning my living."

Patrick sighed heavily. It hurt him deeply that his daughters were driven to these harsh expediencies by his own inability to provide for them. For himself, he was quite satisfied with his humble lot in life, but when he thought of them he felt the lash of humiliation for his worldly failure.

So Emily packed her box and took her leave with a lack of ceremony that concealed her dread of another separation from home. Only Tabby, to whom she had drawn very close while nursing her, perceived her fears. She threw her old arms around Emily and wept for her, crying "Oh, my lamb—my poor bairnie— my brave lass!" At this even Emily's tears, very rare visitants to her wild, unsentimental eyes, were roused, until she tore herself away, jumped into the gig and was gone. Grasper, locked up in the kitchen, howled dismally after her.

When she arrived, wind-blown from the eight-mile drive in an open gig, a serving girl showed her directly into Miss Elizabeth Patchett's office.

Miss Patchett had not seen Emily, of course, before engaging her. Her sister's somewhat sudden marriage in September had forced her to find a replacement hurriedly, and Emily's was the only application. This hard fact obliged Miss Patchett to overlook the untidy hand and poor spelling in Emily's letter, and concentrate on something incisive, something rather dashing and splendid, in the wording.

However, her first sight of the new staff member caused misgivings. All the careless faults of the letter returned disturbingly to her mind when she glanced over the tall, gaunt figure with her uncovered and wind-blown hair, straggly skirt and general unkempt appearance.

But Emily's first impressions of her employer were surprisingly favorable. Miss Patchett was a tall, commanding woman with dark well-groomed hair and an aquiline profile. Her large bright eyes, too, had something of the eagle about them. Her clothes, though conventional, were well cut and did justice to her fine figure. Emily wondered how old she was. Not her own contemporary, of course, but certainly still young, around thirty perhaps. Later she realized she must be much older than that. Emily had the strange sense that she knew her.

Disturbed at Emily's penetrating gaze, and still more fearful that the girl would not do, Miss Patchett nevertheless assured her:

"Well, Miss Brontë, don't look so alarmed. I know this is your first situation and I shall not demand too much of you. The girls are anxious to meet you. Would you care to . . ."—here she glanced meaningfully at Emily's hair again—"tidy up in your room after your journey? Then I'll show you around my school."

She led Emily upstairs herself and showed her the small but adequate attic room where she was to sleep. Emily at once went to the window and peered out between the eaves. The view was superb. Law Hill stood on the rim of a bowl containing Halifax, which even at that time was beginning to resemble a witch's caldron with its black stone factories and mills from which smoke belched or drifted upward. But all around were the green hills speckled with farm buildings, crisscrossed with drystone walls and transfigured by the autumn sun.

"Do you dislike overlooking the town? I could give you a room at the back."

Emily shook her head. The contrast excited her. She stood there for so long that Miss Patchett, behind her, coughed and said, "Would you care for a wash? I had warm water brought up for you."

Emily turned abruptly and looked at her. Miss Patchett was startled by the strange eyes in that stark face. There was something . . . elemental about this odd creature. No, surely she would not do. And yet . . . Surely one look from these compelling eyes would put a stop to any indiscipline.

Emily was not thinking about the girls or the school. She was staring at the headmistress, who stood in a horizontal beam of sunlight. The bluish lights gleamed in her dark hair, and Emily saw in her face a restless determination, a sort of dignified nobility. Suddenly Emily was aware of the resemblance between this woman and her heroine, Augusta Almeda, Queen of Gondal.

Charlotte had very frequently had the experience of finding a live echo of one of her imaginary characters. Miss Wooler resembled Zenobia, at least at first sight; Ellen and Mary, and even Martha, were all employed to vivify Mary Percy, Marian Hume and other heroines. But Emily had never in her life seen any living person who reminded her of one of her own people. The effect upon her was staggering, as if the two worlds, which had coexisted in perfect harmony but always apart, had suddenly veered in their courses and for a moment collided.

She swayed and put out one hand to steady herself against the sloping attic roof.

"Miss Brontë! Are you ill?"

Miss Patchett was at her side; the strange double-image was actually touching her, supporting her arm. There was human warmth here, breath, physical solidity. Emily felt the impact of this woman's touch as fire and confusion. She could not speak.

"Come. Lie down for a few minutes. You have gone deadly pale."

Emily found herself lying on the narrow cot with a blanket spread over her. She was trembling and cold. Her heart was almost bursting through her ribs. She realized the woman was holding her wrist.

"Lie still. I will send you up some tea. Perhaps you'll feel better by and by."

As soon as she left the room, Emily wanted to jump up and run after her. What was she doing, lying on a bed in the middle of the day, "having the vapors" like any silly spoiled girl? Yet a strange lassitude came over her, dragging her down on the bed. A familiar sensation—quivering anticipation, delight, some degree of fear—took hold of her. Closing her eyes, she felt herself sinking down into a trancelike sleep. Her body became one with the bed beneath her and the air around, till she lost all sense of its contours and boundaries. She was now only herself, her essential self, no longer confined within solid walls of flesh but yet residing in them because she had not yet willed herself out of them.

Now she did will it.

She felt her body as a prison she was free to leave. Slowly she rose out of it. Some power of perception that no longer required eyes looked down and saw her body lying on the bed under the blanket. She perceived the room, the bar of sunlight coming to rest on the floor boards, the chest of drawers, the rug with her box standing obliquely on it. There was a blurred moment, and then the room became a roof; the whole panoply of the evening countryside was spread out below in patchwork glory around the black pit of the town.

She was aware of it all far more poignantly than if her body, equipped with all her senses, had been up there, flying, flying freely and blissfully. She felt the touch of the wind and perceived all the beauty spread beneath her in total clarity. Yet the magnificence, the effulgent glory of nature on an autumn evening, touched her in a direct way never experienced by the soul encased in flesh. *Then* perceptions were dulled, the spirit partially numbed by the blood and bone that hemmed it in; but *now* Emily received it all—every impression, every emotion roused by the impressions—sharp and clean, so piercingly clear that all the experience of her ordinary life (intense as it was) seemed to her muffled and half felt in retrospect, making her wonder how she had found it endurable.

The world expanded as she soared, until she saw it all—land, sea, sky, sun—encircling her, yet not enclosing her free-ranging spirit but opening up before her more and more, inviting ever greater participation in the magnitude of possibility. There was no limit to it, no ending, and no confusion or fear about that endlessness. Eternity, infinity, no less wonderful and mysterious than when Emily contemplated them intellectually, now became easily grasped, joyfully accepted. They were a sublime aspect of what her own spirit was; for as she reached onward and outward, leaving the world behind, she knew herself to be an intrinsic part of this greatness and of the perfect purpose uniting it. Yet still she retained her own identity, undiminished—no, stronger than ever, unencumbered by her earthbound body, perceiving and partaking of the universe in absolute communion.

But suddenly, in the midst of this ecstasy, she felt some interference. It was as if a gigantic hook had reached up for her, pierced her through, and dragged her as swiftly as a bolt of lightning down through the layers of the wind, back into the dungeon of the temporal world. She felt this piercing, dragging force as spiritual agony no less real than the torment her body would have experienced from equivalent treatment. Something like a rush of wind fled past her, buffeting her and terrifying her as though she were actually falling through space and would be hurtled upon the hard earth below.

Now she was aware of the earth, of the buildings, though it was dark. She perceived small splashes of light; she saw a black slate roof rushing toward her. Her body was there below her, and leaning over it, shaking the shoulders, was the maidservant who had let her into the school. There was a fearful wrench, a jar, as if all her soul were dislocated and torn asunder. At the same time she experienced a sense of sorrow and loss so profound that she "awoke" sobbing in anguish.

It was not the first time that Emily had made such a journey. But usually when it happened she would be lying up on the moors above Haworth, or in her own bed; her journey would be accomplished, and she would return from it in her own time, at her own will. Reluctance, loss, the dreadful fleshly check and renewed sense of incarceration—these always attended the end of such an experience; yet she had never been thus rudely awakened.

"Oh, Miss! Oh, Miss! I was that frighted! I couldn't get you to wake up!" cried the girl. Then her face changed. "Oh, Lord, are ye goin' to be sick? Hang on, I'll bring t'basin!"

The horror, humiliations and restrictions of renewed life had never been so intense. Emily lay, utterly exhausted in mind, body and spirit, for twenty-four hours before she began to recover. It was only much later, when she was able to contemplate the experience in retrospect and try to make sense of it, that she realized that the girl, in trying to rouse her, had probably nearly killed her. And strangely, although she longed to be free—not a mere spiritual parole, but a total permanent freedom, a condition she knew could only be synonymous with death—the relief she felt when spirit and body were once more fully united and she could savor the safe, familiar, though muted, pleasures of human-kind once more, made a final severance seem somehow terrible. She was not afraid of death, but she was afraid of the loss of life; dead and free, she would no longer be able to run on the moors with her dog, or talk to Anne, or savor sleep and food, or— greatest of all—hold a pencil and write her poems. And these were blessings she treasured, blessings which, while she was "in the body," she could not but dread the thought of losing.

When she was strong enough to get up and begin her duties, she was oddly eager to see Miss Patchett again. The oddness was that she could not remember ever having desired to look a second time on any human being outside her own family. Yet now she felt a longing to be in the presence of this stranger who was somehow no stranger. Weakened by her experience, she felt drawn to Miss Patchett's commanding strength, and when, tense and trembling but controlled, she entered the study once again, she was not disillusioned. Miss Patchett's terse manner—engendered by suppressed annoyance, in fact—Emily interpreted as just the queenly demeanor she desired to see.

"Ah, Miss Brontë, so you're yourself again. Good. Now let us go around the school. I do hope you will be fit for your duties, for I am extremely shorthanded."

If Charlotte's pupils at Roe Head thought her missish and quaint, Emily's found her quite otherwise. The first whispered comments as Miss Patchett led the strange scarecrow figure through the classrooms were: "How odd she looks! Like a man dressed in women's clothes. See how she strides, how she scowls! I hope she will not beat us—she'd lay on the cane like any master!"

During her first lessons, Emily made a mighty effort to conquer her natural reserve. She tried to talk to her pupils as equals, to establish common ground between herself and them, such as would make their pupil-teacher relationship a mutual enterprise, and not an authoritarian imposition. But her efforts went for nothing. These girls, daughters of the local manufacturers and merchants, were not used to such an approach and shrank from it, tittering among themselves. The distance between them, which Emily had sought to close, was widened, as much by her out-landish appearance and deep, abrupt voice as by her clumsy attempt at friendliness.

So Emily, rebuffed, went back into her shell.

Each evening she diligently prepared her lessons, leaving noth-ing to chance, for she had not the gift of extempore teaching. She would steel herself outside the door of the classroom, then stride in, slap her books down on her raised desk, fix her gaze upon some spot above the heads of those in the back row, and launch forth into her lesson as if it were a memorized recitation. The girls attended and did not interrupt, chiefly because they did not dare. But they were not impressed, only intrigued by her oddity and held in check by some wildness they sensed in her which they instinctively feared she might let loose.

She was not, in short, a good teacher. Miss Patchett realized this, yet she kept putting off dismissing her. From time to time she got some inkling of Emily's attachment to her, though she couldn't fathom its source or its nature. She had sometimes been "adored" by her pupils. She tolerantly assumed that her new teacher, barely out of the schoolroom herself and emotionally immature, had not yet emerged from that phase of adolescence which produces these passions for older members of their sex. She found it embarrassing, but unexceptionable and even rather touching. She had no conception at all of how deep it went with Emily.

To say that Emily was "in love" with her headmistress, in any physical sense, would be misleading. She was innocent of any sexual longing in connection with her. Yet her love was passionate and profound, and preoccupied her to a point where lessons ceased to be a real ordeal, where the long hours and hard work hardly impinged upon her. She wrote quite offhandedly to Charlotte that she worked from morning till night, without realizing how this would alarm her. ("This is slavery," Charlotte wrote to Ellen. "I fear she will never stand it.") In fact, Emily did not feel it as slavery. It was uncongenial, it was exhausting, it was unsatisfying; she was desperately homesick, and she should have been wretched to the point of illness, as before. But this time she was able to bear it, because here she was near the first exterior object of her heart's devotion.

From her juvenile passion for Byron had grown the character of Augusta: beautiful, domineering and ruthless, but never cold, always life-affirming and capable of feeling suffering as well as inflicting it. There was nothing calculating about her. Her sins were sins of anger and sensuality stemming from passion, never from deliberate cruelty.

Now Emily gifted the unwitting Miss Patchett with the same characteristics. When she spoke sharply to the pupils, or in the privacy of the study to Emily herself, Emily secretly rejoiced in this display of authority. When she was cheerful and kind, Emily reveled equally, seeing a reflecting of Augusta in more benign mood.

But there was one sight that kindled in Emily an intense devotion.

Miss Patchett was a fine horsewoman. Two or three times a week she would emerge in her elegant black riding-habit, sweeping across the yard with the ribbons on her bowler hat flying. From her bedroom window, Emily would watch the erect figure in its full black skirt and glossy boots cantering away, occasionally giving her big bay horse an imperious blow with her crop, as if leading her followers to hunt, to battle or to some magnificent royal pageant.

As soon as this heroic figure was out of sight, Emily would rush to her rickety attic table, there to write a Gondal poem embodying the inspiration she had derived from "A.G.A." brought to life.

Other poems she wrote at that time were simple heart-cries of longing for Haworth Moor. To inspire these, she had only to take a walk across the similar moors around Southowram—usually with a line of giggling girls trailing behind her, but occasionally, to her joy, alone.

As winter closed in, school walks were curtailed. It never occurred to Miss Patchett that anyone could feel deprived at not being sent out in such inclement weather, so she simply found tasks for Emily indoors—and wondered somewhat impatiently what was ailing her *now*? For Emily, withheld from her substitute heaven, grew silent and gray-cheeked and her lessons became more stilted and peculiar than ever.

One day in December Miss Patchett sent for her.

"Miss Brontë, you are not giving me complete satisfaction."

Emily clenched her hands and said nothing.

"The girls are bewildered by you, and so, I confess, am I. You are clearly unhappy here. Am I the cause, or are they?"

"Not you, certainly."

"The girls, then? Do they torment you? You seem oddly spirit-
less. You were not so when you first came."

Emily raised her head.

"I need the freedom to go out on the moors. Without that, I
feel cut off from life." Her voice cracked and she had to stop
speaking.

Miss Patchett's stern face broke into a relieved smile. "Is that
all? Of course you may go walking if you wish! But you must be
more relaxed. Just look at you now, verging on hysteria for lack
of a breath of fresh air! Stuff and nonsense. Now go and get your
cloak and take a short walk before the light is gone, and try to
brace yourself up a little."

During that same December, a crisis of another kind overtook
Charlotte and Anne at Dewsbury Moor, where their school had
removed.

Since Anne had recovered from her gastric attack in the spring,
Charlotte had withdrawn deeper and deeper into her own inner
world of neurosis and despair. Every ounce of self-discipline she
possessed was required just to get her through the days without
a complete moral and physical collapse. Her terrors of damnation
preyed upon her with infinitely more power than did those of
Anne or Branwell, for her conscience was a more delicate in-
strument of torture and inflicted its exquisite agonies upon a far
more sensitive and profound nature. It was to some degree the
natural inclination of both Branwell and Anne to be happy and
positive in outlook; guilts and other spiritual afflictions therefore
had to set certain fundamental traits into reverse before their
victims could seriously be brought low.

But Charlotte's nature was pessimistic, unexpectant of joy, convinced of the basic sinfulness of man in general and herself in
particular. In her case, Aunt's Calvinist tenets had far more fertile ground to grow in. Having once become convinced of her
own wickedness, and having no one to confide in, Charlotte was
in a sad state indeed by the end of that year.

But she forced herself to labor as if she could actually sweat the devil out of herself. Each night she crawled to bed too exhausted to do more than offer up a despairing prayer that she might not die in the night, weltering in her unresolved state of sin, and that morning should somehow bring a new grace into her life, a new strength to cast off the shadows that still persistently haunted her, despite her resolutions.

Thus self-occupied, Charlotte had no eyes for Anne's deteriorating health until one cold Sunday morning, as they sat in church. Charlotte, lost in a miserable reverie, suddenly heard a cough that jerked her body upright. She turned swiftly, and there in a pew some rows behind her sat Anne, suppressing as best she could with her handkerchief a persistent coughing-spasm exactly like that which had wracked Maria so many years ago in Tunstall Church.

With an effort, Charlotte restrained herself from jumping up then and there and rushing Anne back to bed. Her agony of mind through the rest of the service was of a new order: her guilt was now directed outward. How long had Anne been thus without her noticing? How *could* she have failed to see? The truth was that she had scarcely noticed anyone or any thing around her for months. But now that Charlotte had been made aware, there was no time to lose. The moment they were back at the school, she took charge of Anne.

"How long have you had this cough? Have you a fever? Have you any pains in your side? Why did you not tell me?" Her anger with her own self-centeredness burst out of her and flooded over poor Anne, who meekly submitted to being put to bed and catechized, only catching her hand and saying, "Don't be so upset, love. If it had been really bad I would have told you."

But her shadowed eyes and flushed cheeks told another story.

"Oh, God—oh, God—" Charlotte gasped as she almost ran along the corridors to Miss Wooler's room, entering with the briefest knock.

"What is it, Charlotte?" asked the headmistress, looking up in surprise as her deputy burst in.

"Anne is desperately ill!" cried Charlotte.

The note of accusation did not escape Miss Wooler. She rose with her usual dignity. Since the school she loved had had to remove to this far less salubrious location, she had become stiffer, more defensive and less approachable. But Charlotte had worked like a slave for her and she knew she owed her tolerant attention even in these occasional moments of exaggerated emotion.

"I am sorry to hear it. I will come and see her."

"We must send at once for a doctor!"

Miss Wooler could not help resenting this impetuosity. She liked to make her own decisions. "Try to calm yourself, my dear. I will see for myself first."

Refusing to be hurried, Miss Wooler sailed like a stately galleon down the corridors and up the stairs to Anne's room. She found her awake, quiet, rather flushed certainly but with no very alarming fever, as a practiced touch on her forehead told Miss Wooler.

"Well, my dear, I think you worry unduly," she said when they stood in the corridor together. "The doctor comes tomorrow in any case, and we will have him look at her, but it's my belief that he will order her a few days in bed and a blood tonic perhaps and that soon she will be quite well."

Something gave inside Charlotte, but she did not immediately give vent to her feelings. She stood quivering while Miss Wooler, with a tolerant smile, patted her shoulder and walked away. All day Charlotte sat with Anne, holding her hand; but inwardly she was churning with a rage quite unfamiliar to her—her father's temper, which she had always been able to hold in check till now. That evening she thought she perceived a worsening in Anne's condition. When she fell asleep, Charlotte, looking at her face, as still and pale as death, felt the fury mounting within her and demanding an outlet. Half running, she reached Miss Wooler's study once more and this time she did not knock.

"Well, Charlotte? How is she now? Better, I trust."

Her smile froze when she looked at Charlotte's blazing face.

"You trust she is better! She is not better, she is worse, and yet there you sit by your fireside doing your paperwork and caring nothing that my sister may be dying!"

"Dying!" Miss Wooler felt a stab of fear. "Who says she is dying? She has a cough and a cold, Charlotte, that is all, on my honor! I have seen—"

"What have you seen? Have you seen two of your sisters laid in their graves from neglected consumption? Are you wholly unaware of your responsibilities?"

Miss Wooler rose. Her face was austere and cold, but her heart was thundering in her bosom.

"Indeed I am not unaware of them! When do I give thought to anything else?"

"All I know is that my sister is very ill—has been, perhaps, for some time—and you have not noticed it or cared about it!"

"And you, my dear? If she has been so poorly, why have you not noticed?"

Charlotte stared at her in anguish. Her eyes behind the thick lenses were wild, and her small taut body trembled. There were no more words, only a rush of guilt, of reaction. She knew she was about to burst into tears. With an inarticulate cry, she fled from the room and ran back to Anne, where, kneeling by her bed, she cried out her shame and confusion till she fell asleep. She was worn out and had to be carried to bed by Miss Catherine and Miss Eliza, who found her there.

The senior Miss Wooler, however, slept little that night. She had rebutted Charlotte's accusations, but she was far too responsible and indeed kindhearted to dismiss them absolutely. So distressed was she by the whole scene that she wrote to Mr. Brontë the following morning, even though the doctor, when he came, pronounced Anne to be not in any immediate danger. Charlotte, who seemed herself to be in the throes of some kind of fever, refused to see anyone, and attended Anne to the exclusion of all other duties, behaving like some kind of watchdog and snapping at anyone who came near her.

Patrick's reaction to Miss Wooler's letter was the same as Charlotte's to hearing Anne's cough in the church. A searing wave of memory swept over him. Was history to repeat itself? Was this darling littlest daughter to be brought home to him to die? He wrote immediately, ordering both Charlotte and Anne to return home at once.

Miss Wooler carried this letter to Charlotte. She was very anxious for a reconciliation before she left, for though she honestly felt herself not to be in the wrong, she could not bear Charlotte to leave in anger. She did not speak at first, but merely handed the letter to Charlotte, who read it (with some difficulty, as her hands were violently trembling) and then looked up.

"We shall be leaving tomorrow morning," she said shortly.

"Yes. And—is it too soon to ask whether you will be returning next term?"

Charlotte turned a shade paler. Miss Wooler, looking at her, suddenly realized that she had indeed failed to notice that one of her small community was in dire trouble, but it was this Brontë sister, and not the other. Charlotte looked appallingly ill, ravaged almost, in a way Miss Wooler could not clearly identify; but she caught her breath now at the sight of her and was overcome with pity.

"My dear child—" she said with sudden heartfelt warmth, reaching out her hand.

But Charlotte stood off coldly and said:

"I shall not, of course, be returning after Christmas, or ever. I've done my best for this school, and my reward has been your indifference, your—"

Miss Wooler began to cry. She had not cried for years, but now the sight of Charlotte's face—an intuitive realization of the suffering that lay behind it and behind her behavior—called forth a compassion so strong that she forgot the distance she habitually kept between herself and her staff. Before Charlotte was aware of what was happening she found herself clasped in Miss Wooler's arms.

"Oh, you poor little thing! Poor, poor child! You are right to abuse me, I have indeed been neglectful and unobservant! Forgive me, I beg—do please forgive me, Charlotte!"

So both Emily and Charlotte returned to their respective schools after the Christmas holidays, though Anne stayed at home for her health's sake and was cosseted by Aunt and Tabby.

But neither arrangement outlasted that following year. Although Emily tried hard to approach the pupils in a more easygoing spirit, her general state of inner confusion baffled all efforts. As winter ended, the call of her moors at home became stronger; the sight of a simple flower on the heath reminded her so agonizingly of Haworth that all other feelings were inundated by a wave of longing. There were no more blissful "journeys" to relieve her earthbound, constricted soul, and she felt sure there would be none until she could get back permanently to her own place. In a word, she struggled on out of duty, but was wretched.

The end came suddenly, on a cold, bright day in April. An early spring had begun to green the rank grass in the more sheltered hollows behind Law Hill, and the gorse was putting out its first faint odors. Emily was leading a walk, or rather she was walking at the head of a line of girls, neither noticing nor caring whether they were following her. If they found her mannish and uncongenial, this was a mild opinion compared to that she held of them. She thought them trivial-minded, shallow and oafish, categorizing them in her mind as "lumps." Like Charlotte's, her childhood had spoiled her for ordinary children. Now she felt like a kite, struggling to soar and yet held back by too heavy a tail; each tuft in it was a girl dragging along in her wake, forcing her by lazy grumblings or shrill mindless laughter to remember that her task was to shepherd them on an outing and not to fly free on the intoxicating wind.

Still she kept her face forward and tried to ignore them and refresh her jaded spirits by communing with nature in the old way, until abruptly one of the girls drew level with her and importunately tugged at her cloak.

"Miss Brontë—oh, Miss Brontë! You must come back. Hannah has found something horrid!"

Jerked back into the world of obligation, Emily sighed and turned. Hannah Sunderland, a loutish girl with clumsy ways and small, cruel eyes, was standing in the midst of a group of girls who were all staring at the ground. As Emily approached, they tried to shield something from her, but she pushed into their circle and saw, in a flash of horror, that Hannah had her foot on something alive on the turf. She could see it struggling, the firm, malignant boot pinning it down.

"What are you doing?" Emily cried, in such a tone of agitation that the circle of girls fell back. But Hannah did not move, only pressed down more firmly on her victim.

"It's only a dirty verminous hedgehog, Miss Brontë," she said calmly. "It's been injured anyway. I am just finishing it off." And with a final shifting of her weight, she crushed the life out of the little creature.

Emily's reaction was instantaneous and instinctive. She caught Hannah and jerked her back from the tiny corpse. For a second she stared at it, feeling ill with rage and disbelief. Then she turned like a fury upon its killer and hit her as hard as she could, knocking her down.

A gasp of indignation issued from a dozen throats.

"Oh, Miss Brontë! You struck her!"

"How could you do so? It was only a hedgehog!"

"I shall tell Miss Patchett! I shall tell Miss Pachett!" screamed the girl on the ground, sobbing and holding her ear.

"Worthless, idle, cruel creatures!" Emily shouted, almost beside herself. "To crush an animal to death on purpose! How is it *possible*? It was hurt and helpless and you killed it. I despise you, you are lower than brutes, all of you—in fact, I think more of any poor cur than I do of you!"

With that she turned and ran down the hill to the school, leaving them aghast. Straight up to her attic she ran, taking the stairs two at a time, and packed her box, sobbing with rage. Then she put on her bonnet and carried the box down to the hall. By this time the girls had straggled back alone and were gathered around Miss Patchett, complaining about Emily in loud, defensive tones.

Miss Patchett turned as Emily came down the stairs. Their eyes met. Emily stared straight into her face and forced herself to see this woman as she really was—neither regal nor exalted, but an ordinary woman of forty trying to run a school, and steadily losing patience with an eccentric, ungifted teacher. She was not Augusta! She never had been. Emily had given her love to—to a commoner, and in that moment she regretted it deeply.

"What is this I hear, Miss Brontë? I require an explanation."

"All the explanation you'll get is that I'm leaving here today," replied Emily.

The end of Charlotte's first teaching situation was altogether less dramatic.

She returned to school after the Christmas holidays, not merely mollified by Miss Wooler's astonishing apology but with an added burden of guilt due to her own prior outburst; reflection taught her this should have been directed against herself. Somewhat strengthened by the short spell in the parsonage, during which Ellen had paid a welcome visit, she thought it at least possible that she could get through the half, as she had got through four previous halves. Surely, surely she could muster the fortitude to come to terms with her weakness and master it?

But she couldn't. Her sick conscience had begun to undermine her physically. As the term proceeded, the effort needed to surmount each day gradually became greater as her health deteriorated more and more. At last, quite unsensationally, she collapsed. A doctor was summoned who examined her and then said to Miss Wooler:

"You have upon your hands a young woman on the verge of irreparable mental damage. You must return her to her family immediately; I will not be responsible for her life otherwise."

Miss Wooler was greatly distressed. "But will she recover at home?"

The doctor shrugged. "One can't predict regarding these delicate nervous systems. The girl is a suppressed hysteric. If she allowed herself more license—relaxed her rigid hold upon herself occasionally—she would never have come to this. Now she's in serious danger. She needs her own around her." He smiled rue-fully at Miss Wooler's stricken expression. "You have put in a great deal there, I'm afraid, for scant ultimate return."

Miss Wooler's face drew into firm lines. "There you are mis-taken," she replied quietly. "I have received more than my due even so far, and if I can retain her friendship, my reward will be out of all proportion to my little investment."

4
A NEW BEGINNING, A NEW ENDING

CHARLOTTE RETURNED TO HAworth, her teaching career for the moment at an end. It was May, a month after her twenty-second birthday.

For a very short time, the four were together at home. It was a beautiful time. Anne was in as good health as she ever attained, and made so light of any residual aches or weaknesses that they might have been nonexistent. Branwell, who'd been "going the pace" quite strenuously during the past year and a half, took hold of himself on Charlotte's return and made a strong effort to reunite with her in the old, happy, creative relationship. Emily, having purged herself of Law Hill to some extent by numerous poems and prose writings involving her ambivalent loveexperience, was once more in harmony with herself and her surroundings.

As for Charlotte, with all her loved ones close to her and the sunlit summer moors around her, she could easily follow the doctor's advice to take more exercise and to distress herself less with her overheated imaginings. She and Emily tramped the moors for miles, laughing and talking. Charlotte was always a little shocked at the way Emily would walk straight through a brook, hardly bothering to lift her skirt out of the wet, and later take off her boots altogether and run about and paddle. While Charlotte sat genteelly on a rock to rest, Emily, when not clambering or poking about for wildlife, would fling herself down among the tussocks by the chuckling brook, and rolling up her sleeves "guddle" for little fish as they flashed by.

When they got home, hungry and bursting with well-being, Charlotte would take her cup of tea and a well-filled plate to Branwell's "studio" and either watch him paint, or let him read to her his own work or a recent novel. Of these he was often scathing.

"I ask you, seriously, Charlotte—was that chapter in any way superior to what *I* can do? Oh, I don't claim to be a second Sir Walter Scott, but truthfully, I think I am the equal of these paltry so-called poets and tale-tellers who get their work into print these days. I said as much quite frankly in my letter to Wordsworth: there is not a *writing* poet worth a sixpence today."

"I hope you specifically excluded him from such a general stricture." There was a brief, uneasy pause; then Branwell dismissed it.

"Oh, stuff, he must have known I didn't mean him! He must agree with me. How could he do otherwise when he and Southey are Gullivers in Lilliput? Unfortunately for me, the same can't be said of portrait painters, of whom there are many, and good ones, too. It's all such ironic nonsense, Charlotte! I cannot break into literature, although it is obviously my *métier*, and there is virtually no competition that I can acknowledge. So I am forced to try painting, and perverse as all luck is, I may yet make a mark there, though there are plenty better at that than I am."

It had been decided to set Branwell up as a painter of portraits. His teacher, Mr. Robinson, still had faith in him, and had suggested Bradford as a fertile seedbed for Branwell's career to root in; it was full of wealthy manufacturers and millowners, all, according to Robinson, desirous of having their own, their wives' and their offsprings' likenesses recorded for posterity.

So the period of being together at home was brief. In early June, Branwell was to leave home again, utterly determined this time to make good. It was to Anne he confided his resolutions:

"I failed in London, but I shall not fail now. London was too big for me, too strange and inimical to my character. I need to feel I am in scale with my surroundings. Bradford is just the right size for me. I shall work hard there, behave well, and God willing, I may flourish. What do you say, Anne?"

"I say, don't drink, don't boast and don't associate with those lower than yourself. Give the best in you a chance and you will be all right."

The weekend before he left was marked as a special occasion by Mary and Martha Taylor's visit to the parsonage. Branwell's earlier interest in young girls, stimulated by John and William's low talk, had faded as he became more and more oriented to masculine society. He was as free as his friends with his ribaldry and boasts, but they were all hollow; girls at close quarters disquieted him. He was puzzled himself by this, for had he not had every chance to get used to young female society? Yet he never saw a girl to compare with his sisters. The prettier, the more flirtatious they were, the more they embarrassed him; the plainer, shyer ones bored him. He preferred the company of men. The prospect of two strange girls in the house made him want to flee. It took a downright command from Papa (who did not fancy being the only man in a houseful of females, to two of whom at least he would have to be constantly gallant and charming) to alter Branwell's intention of dodging the visit.

In any event, it was a success. Mary was intelligent enough, and contentious enough, to attract the intellectual in Branwell. She challenged him from the start with some sly remark about the Tories, and soon he had quite forgotten her sex and was deep in argument with her. As for Martha, had she been equally clever and disputatious Branwell might have been overwhelmed; as it was, he did not feel threatened by her—she was much younger for one thing—and was able to view her antics and chatterings with an almost paternalistic tolerance. Before she left, after several happy days, Mary had a private word with Charlotte.

"Your whole family is all that you said. As for that brother of yours, I hardly dare tell you what an impression he has made upon us both. And he is not bad-looking either, when you get accustomed to him. It's a pity he has not more inches, and his nose and hair are unusual, but one forgets all that in the heat of conversation. So few men are interesting to talk to!"

"That's what he says about women."

"H'm! Perhaps we are suited!"

"Watch out, then, that Martha doesn't captivate him before you can make him fast," said Charlotte, joining in the joke. At least, she supposed it was a joke, for surely no girl who was really attracted to a man would be so unblushingly open about it—even Mary.

Branwell, for his part, gave Mary no more thought for the moment. He was off to Bradford to make his fortune.

He found lodgings in Fountain Street, with acquaintances, a Mr. and Mrs. Kirby. They were good, worthy and respectable people, who welcomed Branwell cordially and assigned to him a studio room at the top of their house. Privately they entertained some disquiet about the arrangement on the point of his being young and "an *artistic* gentleman." But Branwell gave them no cause for alarm. Here was the second chance he had prayed for; he was not about to cast it away like the first.

He did get sitters to begin with. A friend of his father's was the first of these, the second a fellow member of the cloth. When the Kirbys saw the elevated status of these patrons, first Mrs. Kirby and later her husband decided they, too, wanted to have their likenesses recorded. They thought Branwell immensely gifted and flattered him accordingly; but then, since neither of them had ever set foot in an art gallery nor had the smallest connection with any creative person or product till that time, they had little basis for judgment.

In fact, Branwell had talent. He could capture a likeness, and

often, when he knew his sitter, something of the underlying
character as well; he had managed this in the case of both John
and William. His main trouble was that he would get bored
before the end, making his finishing technique slipshod. Both
Kirby portraits remained unfinished in his studio for months.
Sometimes he would look at them and actually see them as if
they were finished; his vivid imagination could easily supply the
painstaking touches that would have completed the paintings
according to the demanding standards of his time. So when one
of his sitters would say, "And when will you complete my portrait, Mr. Brontë?" Branwell would reply airily, "It is near
enough to completion now, surely? Just another touch or two
will do it." That "touch or two," in most cases, never materialized.

For Branwell had other things to do as time went by. At first
he felt very lonely in Bradford. Not wholly estranged and terrified
as he had been in London, but just lacking in congenial society.
Miraculously, the ideal companion presented himself—one John
Thompson, an old friend and fellow student.

"I've come to take you out. There's a party of us down at the
George Hotel fomenting revolt against the Philistines. Someone
mentioned a newcomer to the artistic fraternity called Brontë.
I left my ale half drunk and ran all the way here to drag you off
to join our band."

Branwell required no dragging. His coat was on his back in a
moment, his top hat jauntily set on his flaming hair and his little
cane in his hand. Strutting along Market Street, chatting animatedly with Thompson, he looked for all the world like Patrick
Benjamin Wiggins strolling through the streets of Verdopolis,
swaggering a little, gesticulating with the cane, and darting bright
glances about him at passersby to see if they were looking his
way. At the back of his mind a warning voice was whispering to
him, "You should be at work! It is not yet dinner time, and you
are going to waste your working hours in a tavern. A tavern!
Beware!" But his hunger for company and an audience was even
stronger than his longing for a drink, and before long he was
possessed of both.

Each weekend he returned home, sometimes on the coach when he had a bit of money; at other times, when he was out of funds, walking to Haworth across the moors, sure always of a rapturous welcome and a huge tea when he got there. Emily alone did not allow herself to be so easily elated by his reported progress. It was she who would insert into the buoyant conversations leaden questions like, "And how many commissions have you on hand at the moment?"—questions which, as the months went by and the interest shown by friends began to fall off, became more and more irksome to Branwell. For although he was enjoying himself hugely, he could not in honesty claim to be overwhelmed with paying customers.

One weekend he did not go home. Something more exciting presented itself—an invitation from a friend to visit Joseph Leyland, the well-known sculptor.

Leyland's studio in Halifax was just the sort of place to inspire instant adulation in Branwell. It was lofty, spacious and orderly, three things that his own workroom never was, and there was a further, even more important distinction: Leyland's was crowded with commissioned works in various stages of completion. The most prominent of these was a half-finished study of African bloodhounds, and there on a dais lay a real bloodhound.

"Great Heavens, what a magnificent animal!" Branwell burst out. "I envy your ownership of him almost as much as I envy your possession of the great gift that is making him immortal."

Leyland found this irresistible. A smile of gratification banished the scowl of annoyance at being interrupted. No more work was done that day. The dog was invited to jump down and be petted; the surrogate dogs were exclaimed over and fulsomely admired. Soon the three young men retired to the Union Cross, where glasses of rum cemented their friendship.

When Branwell got back to Bradford next day, he was overjoyed to find that Charlotte had traveled over and was waiting for him in his studio.

"I couldn't let a weekend pass without seeing you," she explained. "I shall go home this evening on the coach. Tell—tell me about Leyland!"

Branwell was enchanted to do so, and talked so vociferously that Mrs. Kirby knocked reprovingly upon the ceiling of her room below.

"He is a stupendous artist, Charlotte! I am a shade, a specter of artistic reality beside him. Dear God! How I wish that—" He brooded for a while, but then brightened again. "Never mind. He is older than I. By his age, and perhaps with his help, I, too, may be the young lion of London! Who knows? When I was joking and laughing with him, anything seemed possible!"

While he talked, Charlotte was tidying up his things automatically and making his rumpled bed. She collected his soiled linen into a bag to take home for laundering, and unpacked the delicacies she had brought him from home. They demolished these together by way of a noon meal. Charlotte had been secretly hoping Branwell might introduce her somehow to some of his exciting-sounding new acquaintances, for after nearly a year at home she was beginning to feel the lack of stimulating new faces and views to feed into her creative melting pot. However, Branwell never thought of that. He wanted to enjoy her himself.

At last, however, his monologue ran dry, and he thought to ask after her own concerns.

"Well," she said, her eyes on her fingers, which were playing with some bread crumbs, "I did receive a proposal."

"Of what kind?" asked Branwell.

Charlotte looked up, her eyes twinkling. "Strange that the obvious should never occur to you in connection with me! A proposal of marriage."

Branwell gratifyingly dropped the saltcellar into his plate and stared at her openmouthed.

"Who? Who?" he got out at last.

"Henry Nussey."

"Who?"

"Come, come, Branwell! Ellen's brother Henry, the Reverend Henry Nussey. You met him at Birstall."

"Holy Henry? Great Heaven! Is it possible? How did he do it?"

"By letter. Here. I brought it for you to read."

Branwell snatched it and devoured it avidly, but before he got halfway through, his mouth had begun to twitch and soon he was rolling backward in his chair, torn between laughter and indignation.

"Oh, this is too rich! The unbelievable impudence of him! Call this a love letter? It is as cold and calculating as a miser's blessing! Needs a wife to look after his pupils, indeed—who ever heard of such a romantic approach? And to a girl heavens high above him in every way! He should have crawled to Haworth on hands and knees to plead for your condescension, instead of which he is offering you a position as his housekeeper. 'To work with me for the greater glory of the Lord.' Good God, what insufferable cant! I hope you gave him his marching orders promptly and without too much care for his sensibilities, Charlotte, for judging by this he has cared nothing for yours!"

Charlotte smiled at his reaction. Sitting there quietly, her glasses perched on her diminutive nose, her hair drawn back into a spinsterish bun, she really did not look like a girl to attract any but the most practical and unsentimental ardor. Yet she had refused Henry, not so much because of the want of passion in his letter, though she had felt that, but because she knew that he did not know her at all. When she tried to picture herself living with Henry Nussey, keeping a sober manner before him, subduing all that was irreverent and original and unique in herself in order to hide from him forever her true character—there could be no real doubt about her reply.

"I gave him a decided negative," she said.

"Naturally! He will no doubt record your refusal in his journal —he told me once that he kept one—in the driest terms, as if it were some minor business reverse. Don't fear that you hurt him, Charlotte. He has no nervous system, he is nothing but a ministerial machine. How such a man can suppose himself fit to do the work of God on earth, when God's first command is that we *love* each other, is beyond comprehension. How did Ellen react when you told her?"

"Oh, I haven't told her, nor shall I, unless she asks. I have told no one but you."

Ellen, however, did ask. She had engineered the whole thing. It would be so lovely to have Charlotte for a sister. But when she received Charlotte's letter explaining what had happened, she simply sighed resignedly. No. Perhaps it wouldn't have done. Still, to say, as Charlotte did, that she would have to be willing to *die* for a man before she would marry him, that she must *adore* him . . . Ellen disapproved of these exaggerated sentiments. They smacked of idolatry.

And Charlotte, for her part, brooded on the irony of the fact that she had rejected this worthy man partly because of his very goodness. A man—a real man—had to have a darker side to his nature before she could love him.

Before the end of that month, Branwell, borrowing again from several friends for the fare and cartage of his belongings, had said good-bye to Bradford. Before he went, he soothed Mrs. Kirby, who was naturally anxious about her rent, with a promise to return, to put the "last touches" to her and her husband's portraits and to varnish them. He left the town much more heavily in debt to various friends, landlords and shopkeepers than even he himself quite realized.

To his astonishment, it was Aunt who was kindest to him on his return to Haworth. He brought home a number of the portraits he had painted of friends in Bradford, as a proof that he had not wasted his time, and she thought them excellent and remembered that he had once been a favorite. She suddenly pitied him and her intolerance fell away, for she was older now, less severe and even a little mellow. He had tried—oh, he had tried! She could see it here in these canvases, painted for the pleasure of it for friends; and if Branwell was not a money-grubber, if he was not ruthless enough for the world, was that so much to his discredit?

So she praised him and comforted him, and without his having dreamed of asking for it, unexpectedly slipped some money into his hand and said, "You need a holiday, lad. You're worn out. Go off somewhere and enjoy yourself."

Branwell's spirits soared. Without stopping to consider that his debts in Bradford should be a first charge on his newfound riches, he joyfully contacted a group of friends and arranged a weekend jaunt to Liverpool.

It was a weekend that stretched to a week and a half. The town with its docklands and historic sites and art galleries, seen in the company of a picked group of his favorite Bradford cronies, proved to be all to him that London was not. He could hardly drag himself away, and was forced to do so in the end only because his funds utterly ran out and he found himself almost insensibly beginning to borrow again. He traveled home in the mood of a man who leaves a glorious sunlit scene and drives into the thundery, dark miasma of a storm. He felt instinctively, just as Anne had at sixteen, that the apex of his life was past, and that there was nothing ahead of him now but decline.

5

SITUATIONS

*A*NNE'S FIRST EXPERIENCE AS A governess was damaging. Not merely to her delicate constitution, on which any nervous strain was bound to tell, but more seriously to her innate optimism and belief in people. In the beautiful home of Mr. and Mrs Ingham at Mirfield she made the dreadful discovery that piety and respectability can be a front, hiding extremes of selfishness, callousness and error.

She had not set off on this venture without some qualms. But the family were known to Miss Wooler, who had assured Anne (sincerely, no doubt) that Mrs. Ingham was a very nice woman and the family a proper one for her to work for. Anne loved children (unlike Emily and Charlotte, who couldn't understand them) and felt sure she could do better in this field than her sisters. She longed to prove herself, especially as everyone at home persisted in treating her as a baby and opposing the whole project on the grounds that she wasn't yet grown-up enough to take responsibility for small children.

Mrs. Ingham, a pert, pretty woman with long black ringlets, was already the mother of five, of whom Joshua and Mary, Anne's charges, were the eldest at six and five. When Mrs. Ingham proudly led Anne to the nursery, the children seemed to her rather noisy and wild; even her future pupils did not stop their play to greet her, but she refused to be dismayed by that.

The house was large and solid, like its master, the local squire. Anne didn't meet him for several days. He was busy about the estate and had no particular interest in new members of his sizable staff, even one engaged to teach his children. What was a twenty-five-pounds-a-year governess to him? When he did meet Anne, he raised his eyebrows and touched hands with her in a manner she considered barely civil. But Mrs. Ingham treated her with, if not warmth exactly, then certainly adequate politeness, though her initial instructions seemed rather extraordinary to Anne.

"Are you a student of Mr. Thomas Day's theories of child rearing?" she asked. When Anne shook her head, Mrs. Ingham went on, "Ah! A pity. His ideas exactly coincide with ours. In brief, we believe that a child's character can only develop to its fullest if it is not restricted. They are nothing but young animals at first, and should not be compelled to conform to adult patterns of behavior. Of course, if these modern ideas are new to you, you may find some initial difficulty, but I'm sure you will soon prove their essential wisdom."

Anne said thoughtfully, "How are the children to be treated? How shall I control them?"

"With kindness. With persuasion. With patience."

"I see."

"They are not to be coerced or punished. I'm glad you look so mild and pretty. I'm sure they will behave well for you. I couldn't have entrusted my darlings to a harsh or tyrannical person."

Darlings, were they? Well, Anne was determined that they should be her darlings, too, and commenced her ministrations in the spirit of her instructions. But not even one day had passed before she began to realize what total license to the age of six bred in terms of misery for a young and inexperienced governess.

Joshua and Mary were not darlings at all. They *were* a pair of little wild animals. They had not even the semblance of manners, for manners come from an ingrained consciousness that other people's feelings matter. Neither of these children had an inkling that other people *had* feelings, and indeed their own were so blunted by indulgence that the concept of sensitivity to others was wholly alien to them. In the spacious indoor and outdoor playground-world provided by their fortunate circumstances, any well-brought-up children might have been happy and good from morning till night—or so Anne, raised in the cramped parsonage, believed. Yet these two found their chief recreation in fighting and quarreling, ill-treating each other, their siblings and their toys, and persecuting all the grown-ups about them—chiefly the servants. Their mother, having effectually withheld all weapons for their control from the hands of those in charge of them, then withdrew to the sanctum of her study and brooked no interruption to her placid day's routine.

Joshua and Mary had no innate sense of self-respect, as most children have, which could be used to restrain them. Anne never forgot an occasion in her own childhood when Papa, irritated beyond bearing by an overvociferous bit of play, had threatened that they should go to bed unkissed. They had all been brought up short on the instant, and had flung themselves upon him, begging him to excuse them and retract this doom. But these children cared nothing for her or her opinion of them. Although Mary, particularly, liked well enough to have her prayers heard, be read to, tucked in and kissed by Anne, it was no use Anne's threatening *not* to kiss her when she had been especially naughty. "What do I care?" she would say, tossing her head. "You are only the stupid governess."

"And besides," Joshua would add, "you smell of cheap soap, like all the servants."

Both the children had ponies, and there were a number of other animals deployed about the premises. Anne suffered acutely in witnessing the outright cruelties inflicted by her pupils upon these poor creatures.

"Why did you beat your pony so savagely, Joshua? He was going well enough."

"He caught my thumb in his teeth today when I gave him my applecore."

"But you must spread your hand flat as I showed you! He didn't do it from malice."

"He did it, that's enough. He's my pony, I may beat him when I will. Papa says I must teach him to mind me."

"Does not your Papa say that you ought to mind *me*?"

Joshua, who could look very stupid, stared at her openmouthed. "No," he said at last, "and if he did, I should say I wouldn't. You can't make me mind you."

"No, I see that—not without a whip, such as you use on Dapple," said Anne, whose temper was rising warmly.

Joshua's little face went dark with rage.

"Yes, you would like to whip me, wouldn't you? You'd like that! Well, you dare! You touch me even once, and I'll tell Papa! He's complaining already because you haven't taught me anything. Just try hitting me and you'll be sent home crying, so you will!"

With that he gave Anne a hard cut with his whip as high on her arm as he could reach and ran away laughing.

Anne gritted her teeth and struggled on. Often she was on the very verge of rushing in to Mrs. Ingham's study and giving her notice. But she would not admit defeat—she would not "be sent home crying" without her first year's money. A year! When she contemplated it, it stretched ahead like eternity to the damned. She wrote of her troubles to Charlotte, and was somehow ignobly consoled to get letters back relating Charlotte's almost equally trying lot with her family, the Sidgwicks of Stone Gappe Hall, Lothersdale.

If Charlotte's strength had been unequal to the mild demands of Miss Wooler's establishment, it was not to be expected that it could match the much more daunting (because more lonely and unregulated) regime at Stone Gappe.

Her crippling shyness, which she deluded herself she had to some extent learned to master at Roe Head, returned full force in this great house. The clan was a large and wealthy one, and the Sidgwicks loved to entertain. The withdrawn, unprepossessing little governess was totally out of her element amid the throngs of elegant visitors who came and went continually. The sound she came to dread above all others was the clopping of hooves and the crunch of carriage wheels on the drive under the second-story classroom where she was generally confined. The two youngest in the family, who were her charges, would invariably drop everything to rush to the casement, and in the beginning Charlotte would join them.

But after several weeks Charlotte no longer ran to look. She sat with a heavy heart, for she had come to associate these constant arrivals with what inevitably followed. The gaiety and party sounds betokened festivities from which she was excluded, or, if the children were summoned and she *was* expected to appear among the guests, something even more intolerable happened: she was either patronized or quite ignored by all, including the hostess. In company, Mrs. Sidgwick treated Charlotte as if she were a piece of household furniture.

Sometimes, to add poignancy to her hurt, the scene in the drawing room would be superficially much like those she had so often imagined, of high life in Verdopolis. She could easily identify this or that elegant beauty with the bejeweled Zenobia or the dulcet-voiced Marian Hume; her inner self *belonged* in such sparkling society, had inhabited it for years, yet her physical form was all but invisible and entirely contemptible to all who beheld it. Occasionally she overheard wounding remarks about her odd appearance or unfashionable clothes, spoken by these same manifestations of her own heroines. It was unendurable, as if her creations were turning on her, reducing her to insignificance in a world of her own making.

And the world abovestairs, the world her employers expected her to inhabit quite resignedly, was neither heaven nor hell, but a combination of purgatory and limbo. From its windows she could look beyond the arrivals and departures to a panorama of nature at its most beautiful and alluring; the grounds of the house were superb, and could have been a paradise for her had she been free to enjoy them, but she was seldom able to do more than glance.

Her charges were Mathilda, aged six, and four-year-old John, whom Charlotte with characteristic bite described in a letter to Ellen as "riotous, perverse, unmanageable cubs, pampered, spoiled and turbulent." To love them was out of the question; to control them, difficult. And to teach and keep them constantly amused strained every ounce of self-control Charlotte possessed.

Mrs. Sidgwick, furthermore, had very broad ideas of the duties she was entitled to exact from a governess. It was not enough that Charlotte attend her two youngest from morning till evening, and supervise their sleep as well. That she might not be idle while doing so, oceans of sewing were heaped upon her—shades of Aunt Branwell! Yet even that hard taskmistress might have been dismayed to have watched her poor, shortsighted, weary niece struggling by lamplight with what seemed like hundreds of yards of cambric to hem, nightcaps to fashion, and—the final indignity, since it seemed so trivial and unnecessary—dolls' clothes to make. It seemed that night must be about to turn into day before she might take herself to her own rest, stealing a few minutes before blowing out her candle to read the latest letters from home, or (best of all) from Ellen, or to write a few words of her own to them. Of creative escape there was virtually none. She had neither the time, the energy nor the heart for it.

And all the while, two floors below, she could hear the faint taunting sounds of laughter and enjoyment drifting up from those who, by virtue of nothing more than the accident of birth and circumstance, were so much happier and more fortunate than she was.

One day Mr. and Mrs. Sidgwick went off somewhere, leaving orders that the children were not to enter the stable-yard. No sooner were their parents out of sight than John and Mathilda made a beeline for the forbidden zone, and when Charlotte came after them and tried to drag them away, John threw a stone at her that broke the skin of her forehead and made it bleed.

This shocked them into obedience. Judging their governess by their own standards of behavior, they had no doubt she would complain of them, and this time their parents might be forced to take her side.

However, Charlotte did not complain. This was chiefly due to timidity; but the children interpreted her silence more charitably. There was a noticeable softening of attitudes for some time thereafter, and John once so far forgot her position in the household as to say publicly that he loved her. His mother was distinctly startled.

"Love the *governess*, my dear!" she exclaimed, and laughed merrily. Not unnaturally, nothing more was said on the subject of love, and soon the old spiteful manners crept back. Charlotte sank lower and lower under the oppression of her situation.

At last Mrs. Sidgwick summoned her.

"Miss Brontë, I fear you have no gift for children," she began without preamble. "Nor are you exactly a treasure of good nature and willingness about the house. In a word, I have seldom seen a young woman so sour and ill-tempered. Look at your face in a mirror! Is that a face to inspire confidence and goodwill in a child? I don't understand it. Here you are most happily placed in a situation—I must say it—in excess of what your education or experience entitles you to, and far from manifesting gratitude or satisfaction, you reward us with a demeanor more suitable for someone cast away in a dungeon! No, not a word, Miss Brontë. I must have cheerful, wholesome, outgoing people about me. Morbidity and low-spiritedness are an affliction to everyone, they are an extreme form of selfishness. Now cheer up, I beg, or I shall be forced to make other arrangements. You may go."

Charlotte's tears were flowing freely long before the end of this diatribe; she could not hold them back. She was shocked, as much by the shrill, harsh tones as by the burden of the speech. A dozen defensive questions rushed to her lips: Had she not worked harder than a slave? Did Mrs. Sidgwick allow her any support in author-

ity? Did she not rather make her task impossible by her partiality?
And—most pressing of all—Why did she treat Charlotte as if she
were dirt under her feet? Yet not a word of all this came out,
only sobs and sounds of strangled rage and despair. She flung herself from the room without the satisfaction of having said a word
in her own defense.

It was then that she decided she would give up her post when
the summer holidays came. She was somewhat comforted to suppose that Anne must be planning to do the same. What was her
chagrin, then, when Anne told her that she had decided to go
back to the Inghams and finish her year!

"But, Anne! How can you face it? With those little _monsters_!
That girl who lies on the floor like a sack when you are trying
to dress her or teach her, that boy who tortures his pets? You said
they had not an ounce of human feeling between them, and yet
you will waste more of yourself upon them?"

"I can't give up yet. It will all have been for nothing if I do."

"Well I am giving up! I refuse to endure more; it's worse than
casting pearls before swine. Oh, laugh if you like—I may make a
strange sort of pearl—but they are swine all right; and when that
woman told me I was unworthy of a place in her home, I should
have said it was she who was unworthy to have me. There!"

"You're right," put in Emily. "It sickens me to think of those
proud, stupid, worthless fools, assuming airs of superiority to
humiliate people whose refinement and intellect put them all
to shame—or should, if they had any real judgment. Don't go
back, Anne. Stay at home, and we'll find some other way to make
money."

But Anne shook her head stubbornly.

"At the end of my year, I will leave," she said, and quietly went
on with her work.

Charlotte stared at her. Here was this girl whom Charlotte had
always regarded as a child, succeeding where she had failed—or at
least, not yielding. Feeling Charlotte's eyes fixed on her, Anne
glanced up and smiled. The smile was as sweet as ever; but there
were new depths in her eyes, of sadness and disillusion. Impulses

of pity and resentful envy warred in Charlotte. The latter was so new and strange to her, in connection with Anne, that it overwhelmed the other, and turning, she ran out of the parlor and upstairs to her room. She met Papa on the upstairs landing.

"Charlotte! You're crying. What's the matter?"

"Oh, Papa. Anne is stronger than I am—I'm ashamed—"

Patrick held her. "Hush, darling! We all have our strengths."

"Life is terrible—nothing is simple, not even our most basic loves—"

"Especially not those."

Anne's and Charlotte's horror stories about their experiences as governesses not only shocked and appalled Branwell, but filled him with shame for his stay-at-home, protected life; the knowledge that he was doing his best to join them in their purgatory (he was trying to get a place as a tutor) was small consolation. He longed to drink, yet under the present circumstances his still-active conscience would not allow it. Besides, Charlotte was at home again, and when this was so, he was always more controlled.

One day in early August he sat out in the sun too long over his book and gave himself a headache. His moanings at supper table prompted Aunt to suggest that he walk down the road after the meal and buy a dose of laudanum from the chemist.

"Aunt, do you know what you do?" asked Branwell. "You urge me to set my feet on the road to a glorious addiction. Have you not read De Quincey's *Confessions of an English Opium Eater?*"

"Scandalous boy! Who mentioned opium?"

"You did. Laudanum is but opium as a liquid—didn't you know that?"

Aunt was shocked. "How can that be? It is freely available to any sufferer for a few pence."

"It is opium just the same. De Quincey proclaims it as a stimulant of the highest order, which puts crudities such as alcohol to shame. He implies that artists and writers may produce their finest works under its influence and suffer no ill-effects. Yes, indeed, I shall take your excellent advice, Aunt! Who knows? Perhaps some doses of the divine poppy are just what my latent genius has been lacking."

Aunt, realizing she was being teased, refused to be drawn further, and nothing more was said or thought about the matter. Branwell bought his "dose," took it and his headache was cured. Nor did it recur; yet Branwell visited the chemist twice more that week, and several times a week thereafter. No one knew of it. Indeed, how could they? This new indulgence produced none of the telltale signs of the old. No evil breath, no loss of stability or decorum, no wretched mornings after; and the positive results of taking it—the relaxation, the inspiration, the occasional imaginative flights that bordered on visions—were known only to the taker. Another virtue of the drug was its modest cost. No reciprocal "rounds" formed any part of this escape route, and the Bull and its clientele knew Branwell no more for some time.

Charlotte had a new anguish. Ellen had invited her to go on holiday with her to the coast, and she had accepted with the utmost excitement and joy. All her life the sea had fascinated her. To Ellen she wrote hungrily, "The idea of seeing the *sea*— of being near it—watching its changes by sunrise, sunset, moonlight and noonday—in calm, perhaps in storm—fills and satisfies my mind." Apart from that great aching desire, there was an almost desperate need to get away, to enjoy a little unalloyed pleasure. Was she not entitled to it? Having seen how others lived —the guests at Stone Gappe seemed to have nothing to live for but their own enjoyment—she was no longer willing to forgo every innocent delight without a struggle.

But Aunt and Papa were stubbornly opposed to the idea of the two girls traveling and lodging unchaperoned. There were agonizing delays while Henry, who had held a curacy near Burlington, wrote to friends there for advice. Ellen wanted to be away for several weeks, whereas Charlotte could afford barely one. Weeks passed; Charlotte's letters to Ellen took on a frantic tone:

I grieve that I should have so inconvenienced you; but I need not talk of either Friday or Saturday now, for I rather imagine there is small chance of my ever going at all. The elders of the house have never cordially acquiesced in the measure; and now that impediments seem to start up at every step . . . Reckon on me no more; leave me out in your calculations; perhaps I ought, in the beginning, to have had prudence sufficient to shut my eyes against such a prospect of pleasure, save to deny myself the hope of it.

Ellen couldn't bear it. She knew—who better?—what Charlotte had been through during the past two or three years, while she herself had been enjoying life at home or in London. It was not fair—it was not right! For once in her quiet life, Ellen would do something daring and decisive—must do something, for she realized that Charlotte was sinking into despair. So she borrowed her brother's carriage, complete with coachman, and drove boldly from Birstall to Haworth, determined to "kidnap" Charlotte and bear her off.

The clattering of the grand equipage on the quiet side-lane brought Tabby, Emily and Branwell to the doors; and when Ellen marched in and virtually demanded Charlotte's immediate departure, all the inhabitants burst into uproar. Branwell's voice rose above the rest, as he stood on the front steps and waved his arms.

"Hooray for the bold attacker! Down with the doubters and the waverers! Did ever a prettier pirate carry off a fair prize? No, Papa, no, Aunt, be silent now and concede honorable defeat at the hands of this fearless conquerer! Emily—upstairs with me instantly, and help me down with her box, which has been packed for weeks. Charlotte! Your bonnet and cloak. The carriage awaits!"

It was a memorable holiday. How could it fail to be so, after such a cavalier beginning? After a thrilling journey, partly by train—the discomfort more than compensated for by the novelty and excitement—they were met by a Mr. Hudson, an old friend of Henry's, who bore them off in his gig to his farmhouse two miles inland. Charlotte's disappointment at being lodged so far from the sea was soon assuaged; on the second day, she and Ellen found their way to the coast by following the course of a little river that bordered the Hudsons' farm. It was a beautiful day. As they climbed the cliffs which, from the farm, effectively blocked off the sight of the sea, Charlotte felt intensifying excitement. The seagulls overhead screamed a welcome to her, and the strong, lively smell of seaweed blew cleanly into her face. She suddenly became dizzy and clutched Ellen's arm.

"Ellen—I feel faint—"

"Nonsense! Come on, only a few yards more and we shall see it!"

Charlotte picked up her skirts and ran to the top of the rise.

The view of the sea burst upon her. Wide as the world, misting off into the far horizon, its magnificence seemed to seize her heart and stop its motion in her breast. The next moment it sprang to life again, like a prisoner released. Below the cliff the miniature waves raked the shore with a soft sibilance that prickled Charlotte's senses; the wind, to which she was now exposed, buffeted her quite roughly, blowing back her bonnet-brim and dragging her cloak almost straight out behind her; but she stood sturdily up to it, loving its smell, its briny taste, its very rudeness. It was the sea's messenger, like the gulls, untamed and elemental, answering some essential part of her secret self that had always craved communion with something as vast, mysterious, primitive and satisfying as this.

Ellen saw the tears start in Charlotte's eyes, and for once made no move to comfort her. Instead she had the sensitivity to move away and leave her friend alone. She, too, had cried when she had first seen the sea.

Charlotte's memories of this sublime holiday, and particularly of the sea, sustained her during the autumn and winter months. She knew she couldn't stay at home forever, that she must find another position; in the meantime, the fact that Tabby had become too old and frail to do much, throwing most of the housework onto Charlotte and Emily, assuaged her conscience. Hard menial work was no degradation; after the humiliations and thankless drudgery of Stone Gappe, Charlotte found chores like blackleading, sweeping, bed-making and baking positively congenial.

Her head was so full of the joys of freedom and memories of the ocean that she was sometimes careless. One day Aunt set her to ironing, something new to her. The bubbling of her spit upon the hot iron so reminded her of the swish of the waves upon shingle that she stood there entranced until a brown triangle had been burned in Aunt's petticoat. She was scolded like a child; but it was so different from being scolded by some snobbish stranger, that Charlotte hardly minded.

The only blot upon her—and Emily's—happiness was Anne. She was still at the Inghams', and nothing had improved; nothing could, for the children seemed hardened beyond the reach of love and gentleness. Indeed they grew more cruel and intractable the more they saw how their callous ways affected their governess.

Perhaps the worst thing that happened—even more scarring than the final disaster—was the incident of the fledglings.

It was Joshua who found the nest. Anne always dreaded his finding any living creatures, and was grateful that he usually preferred whacking the heads off flowers or throwing stones fruitlessly at birds to doing any serious climbing or exploring. But on this occasion he came running to show Mary what he had found in the shrubbery—not just a nest of eggs, but of baby birds, newly hatched, naked and helpless.

"Six of them!" gloated Joshua. "You can kill one, and I will do the other five."

"Ugh!" said Mary. "Look at their bulgy eyes and nasty thin skins! I'll take mine up to my bedroom and drop it through the window. How will you kill yours?"

Joshua pointed to his victims one by one, appointing their separate dooms.

"This one I shall pull the head off. This one I shall cut in half with my penknife. This one I shall drop in the pond, and this one I shall feed to the cat—"

Anne had stood by thus long out of a sort of paralysis. The depravity of these children was known to her, but somehow she had never quite allowed herself to accept it. Children might be thoughtless, wild, perverse; but that they actually delighted in causing suffering was too horrible for Anne to believe. But now as Joshua reached for the first bird, something snapped in her, and she rushed at the pair of them in fury, pushing them both over backward.

"No!" she cried. "You shall not! You shall not!"

"And how will you stop me?" shouted the chief executioner from the ground.

"By killing them myself, swiftly and mercifully!"

With that she picked up a big piece of loose paving, and without daring to give herself time to think—either of the horror of the deed or of its likely repercussions—she dropped it flat upon the nest as it lay on the path. Then she burst into tears and began trembling all over.

"I'll tell Mama! I'll tell Papa!" screamed Joshua in a perfect passion.

Anne, harnessing the spirit and energy generated by anger, raced him to Mrs. Ingham's study. Joshua pushed past her in the doorway and began to bawl out his grievance before Anne could speak.

"She killed my birds, Mama—she killed them all with a stone."

"Miss Brontë! Did you do so?"

"Yes, I did! And I would again! Was I to stand by smiling while he tortured them to death for his amusement?"

"They were but dumb brutes, after all—such a fuss! I'm surprised you thought it necessary to destroy them yourself if you are so concerned for their lives."

"I killed them to save them from your son's cruelty!"

"Calm yourself at once, Miss Brontë This is undignified. Boys often speak roughly, but I'm confident my Joshua would not really have harmed them."

Joshua turned his back on his mother and smirked his triumph at Anne's tear-streaked face.

"He was about to pull the head off one when I intervened. That is how little he meant to harm them!"

"Nonsense, he was teasing his sister no doubt. In any case you are behaving as if he had injured a fellow human being."

Anne's blood was now thoroughly up, and she retorted, "He is quite capable of that too, Mrs. Ingham! Do you wish to see the bruises on my legs?" And she laid hold of her skirt.

Mrs. Ingham rolled her eyes and raised her hands in wordless protest against this indecorous display.

"Miss Brontë, I have said before, if your powers are not equal to your task, you may speak to me. I think I know how to deal with my own children. Joshua, you must be a good boy and a little gentleman. You will, won't you?"

"Yes, Mama."

After this incident it was impossible to pretend even to herself that she could love these children. She was now forced to the conclusion, inimical to her whole philosophy, that the dark side of human nature could manifest itself even in childhood to the exclusion of all that makes man akin to God. To live on under the Ingham roof in these circumstances was the severest possible test of Anne's determination. She felt soiled by the experience of looking after children she had come to detest. Yet she hung on grimly, until one fatal morning in December.

Mary was a big, heavy girl for her age. Her chief delight was to lie on the floor and sing discordantly in order to drive Anne to distraction. When it was her turn to be put to her books, Anne often had to lift the child up bodily and support her lolling trunk, while holding the book before her eyes with her free hand. On this particular morning Mary was quite determined to read nothing, repeat nothing and, in fact, do nothing other than flop about and squawk out her songs. Anne, weary and exasperated beyond bearing, eventually lost patience.

"Very well, Mary. You have tired my arm enough for today. You shall sit on your chair in the corner until you have completed your lesson."

"I shan't sit there for even one minute," retorted Mary.

"Then I shall be obliged to tie you!"

Taking up the threshing, kicking child in her arms, she sat her in her chair and, pinning her there with her elbow, bound her to the back of the chair with a scarf. While she was doing it she realized that Mary's shrieks might easily bring her mother upstairs. But her brain was inflamed with anger and she could not reverse her actions now.

Suddenly something landed on her back, clawing and pummeling. It was Joshua, eager to join the fray. She flung him off— once, twice. Then he had a fresh idea, and running to her desk, cried out:

"I have got your workbag, you beast! I am spitting in it— there—there! Now I shall throw all your things through the window!"

Anne jumped up and ran to the window, but too late: the entire contents of her bag was at that moment falling in a miscellaneous shower toward the paving stones below.

"Oh, you horrid boy! You horrid, awful boy!" she cried, almost ready to throw him down after them. And just then Mrs. Ingham appeared in the doorway.

"*What* is going on here?"

Her eyes fell on Mary, whose chair, with her attached to it, had fallen over sideways. Crouching at her side, Mrs. Ingham threw up at Anne such a look of unequivocal outrage that Anne knew it was the end. It was a relief. And yet, as she packed her box, sobbing bitterly, she felt the disgrace and injustice of her dismissal would kill her. She had failed ignominiously, been "sent home crying," just as Joshua had predicted.

But her homecoming did not turn out as she had imagined. Something had happened at the parsonage during her absence that put the reason for her return quite in the shade.

In August Emily had written to tell her that Papa had a new curate and that he was "quite lively, not the usual thing." Charlotte, too, in her letters had frequently commented on this reverend young gentleman, called William Weightman, whom she was pleased to dub "Celia Amelia"—because of his curly hair, she *said*, but Anne had vaguely supposed there must be something effeminate about him. She really hadn't registered him particularly as a semiaddition to the parsonage household.

She was therefore not prepared for the door to be opened to her by a tall, fair young man with fresh skin and merry eyes.

"Good afternoon, ma'am! And whom have I the honor to address?" He looked more closely, and then gave a sudden, rather theatrical start. "Why—need I ask? It can only be Miss Anne, home from the wars!"

Anne, taken aback, countered with, "And who are you?"

"The Reverend Willie Weightman, at your service!" And this curate among curates swept her a courtly bow.

By this time the others were pouring down the stairs and out of the kitchen, and for a while all was tumult. But because of the stranger—as he still was to Anne—she was constrained in her explanations, and because of him also, nobody bothered much even with these. They were all too eager to introduce Anne to Willie and Willie to Anne. So it was not until some time later that Anne timidly told Emily of her humiliation and defeat. Emily brushed the whole matter aside.

"Oh, stuff, Anne! No one thinks a pin the worse of you for it—how should we? You did far better than any of us. For my part I couldn't be happier that you are out of it. Now tell me what you think of our Miss Weightman?"

"Miss? Why on earth do you call him that? He's not at all girlish."

"Oh, he is quite vain about his good looks. Charlotte teases him unmercifully, saying his best friend is his mirror. But she likes him—we all do. What a contrast to all those dreary clerics who have passed through our lives virtually unnoticed. The day he arrived, he kissed all our hands, if you please—even Aunt's—and within the hour had us seated around him in the garden listening to his tale of star-crossed love—"

"Is he in love?"

"We heard no more of his adored Agnes after the first week or so. By that time he had taken the measure of our local maidens and they of him, and nowadays it is all Liza and Sophie and Susan. Whoever is nearest at hand is nearest at heart."

"In other words," said Charlotte, who had just come in, "our curate is a thoroughgoing male flirt, quite unworthy of all the attention we lavish on him."

"At least he livens us all up," said Emily.

"Indeed! And since his heart is forever engaged elsewhere, *we* may flirt with him a little ourselves."

"Charlotte!"

"Why not? It will do us good, and is perfectly harmless in his case."

Anne was not convinced there was no harm in it and was shocked at Charlotte. But when they were all together with Mr. Weightman she quite saw how hard it was not to flirt with him a little. It was extraordinary to see even Emily—usually so sour and remote with young men—relaxed and laughing when Willie teased her, teasing him back and offering to chase him out of the kitchen when he pestered her. As for Charlotte, she was beyond everything, calling him "Celia Amelia" to his face and positively provoking him. Branwell said openly that she must be in love with him to torment him so sorely, to which Charlotte responded with hoots of laughter.

"I would as soon fall in love with a cherub!"

But Anne's idea of a romantic partner had always been radically different from Charlotte's. She had not shared her soul-shaping devotion to Byron, nor been swayed into her darker proclivities for domineering, flawed, Plutolike men.

Her hopes of love, not very clearly formulated, tended toward a male equivalent of her own basically sunny nature. Though Calvinism had thrown its shadow over her spirit, all her true inclinations were toward happiness, humor, optimism. And these the young curate personified, even in appearance. He looked so healthy it gladdened her heart to see him with his ruddy lips and cheeks, his bright curly hair and boyish vigor and charm. What if he wasn't very "grown-up"? Anne liked him the better for that. Even his rather flippant attitude to his calling failed to put her off. She had suffered much through taking her religion so seriously.

In a word, she began to love him. But it was a love that must at all costs be kept hidden. The whole household was in such a "daft" state about him that it would be disastrous even to take his part when they mocked him. To let *him* have a hint of it would be worse; then the joyous, carefree atmosphere his presence generated would become tense and strained. Fickle as he was, he was kind, and would be appalled to think he was causing her heartache. He would come less often, behave more soberly, and altogether cease to be the person she delighted in.

So she mantled herself in a protective veil of complete self-control. When Willie sat with them around the parlor fire, she laughed and joked with him just like the others and never let them see how her blood fired up when he came near her. When several days passed without a visit from him, and then she heard his step outside, she held all her natural excitement within her. She flattered herself she could even control the blushes that had always been the telltale curse of her fair skin.

In January, Branwell finally got a situation as tutor.

Its chief attraction for him, apart from putting some money in his pockets again, was that the family he was going to lived in the Lake Country. In his childhood Branwell had fallen in love with the lakeland poetry of Wordsworth, Southey and Coleridge. Now he would not only see for himself—a prospect as thrilling to him as the sea had been to Charlotte—but would be privileged actually to live and work in the midst of all this beauty and inspiration.

On his last night at home John Brown came to fetch him and take him down to the Bull for a farewell cup. John was now getting on toward forty. He was married, with a large family, and was to all intents and purposes a settled and respectable member of the community. But Branwell perceived there was much of Old Nick left in the supposedly sobersided sexton. A few drinks, a sly nudge, a doubtful story or two, and this imprisoned per-sonage would first peep through the rather pouchy eyes and then come bounding out on a limited—but for the time unbridled—parole. Some of John's doings that Branwell had had wind of would have scandalized Patrick, had he ever heard of them. But they fascinated Branwell. John was a far cry from Northangerland; but he was the best local rakehell available, and Branwell made great efforts, in his company, to distort his own innocuous proceedings to match John's goings-on.

Now, as they toasted each other, Branwell joked freely about how he was to disguise from his new employer, Mr. Postlethwaite ("What a name! It fairly reeks of pomposity!"), his natural bent for dissipation. But even as John was egging him on, Branwell was secretly swearing new oaths of resolution to himself. "I shall enjoy a last fling on the way," he thought. "But from the moment I arrive I shall be virtue its very self. Such heavenly surroundings will bring out the noblest and best in me."

His "fling," at the overnight stop at Kendal, was pretty tame by any standards. Tired out after the long coach trip, he barely had the heart for a few lonely drinks in the taproom of the inn before stumbling up to bed. Once there, he lay awake, disappointed with his failure to indulge in the Percylike debauch he had outlined to John. The bedroom was icy cold, the wind was blowing snow flurries around the inn, and the sounds of revelry below did nothing to cheer him. He was apprehensive about the two preadolescent boys he was to teach; they gibbered at him in imagination like demons waiting eagerly to sink their pitchforks into him. But there was another cause for depression. On his journey he had had to pass the former site of Cowan Bridge, that hated school which had killed Maria and deformed his life. The memory of those grim walls returned now to harrow him, so poignantly that he felt like weeping.

However, his gloomy thoughts were banished by the beauties of the scenery on the remainder of his journey to Broughton. His strength of purpose grew: the whiskeys he had swallowed the night before should be his last until summer. His liquor would be these snowy mountains and pewter lakes, these rich-textured

forests and tender water meadows. Here he would be near to
flesh-and-blood idols, far more akin to his true nature than the
seductive but depraved Percy. Perhaps he could get in touch with
one of them while he was hereabouts. The lakeland poet who
appealed to him most was Hartley Coleridge, son of the great
Samuel. Branwell had heard a lot about him and even glimpsed
him once in Leeds. He was a strange-looking man; white-haired
but young-faced, very small in stature—even shorter than Branwell. And brilliant! Yes, Branwell would write to him. But first
he would advance further with his new project so as to have something to show him—the translation of Horace's *Odes*.

In every position Branwell began well. The Postlethwaites liked
him at once and he them. The two boys, called John and William
like the Browns, were high-spirited and sufficiently intelligent to
make them a pleasure to teach. Branwell was comfortably lodged
in town with a surgeon's family, where the wife took a great fancy
to him and mothered him unmercifully. The surgeon unwittingly
made another sort of contribution to Branwell's well-being. He
drank heavily, and was so unattractive when drunk that he helped
to keep Branwell sober.

Branwell loved to act, and now he acted to perfection the part
of a rather prudish and proper young man, one who might have
been destined for the cloth. The very quintessential correct little
tutor they all thought him, sedate, good-natured, a touch priggish.
He took to wearing black and standing with one hand folded over
the other in front of him, rocking a little on his heels with a prim
but watchful smile pursing his lips, as he had seen some of his
father's more mannered young curates do. This made the good
people of Broughton highly respectful and a little nervous of him.
The surgeon, his landlord, would cough loudly and hide his bottle
when he heard Branwell's step, and Mr. Postlethwaite refrained
from playing cards when he was in the house for fear of scandaliz-
ing him.

After a few weeks, he received a note from John Brown asking
how he was conducting himself. Gleefully Branwell wrote him a
long letter, not only outlining his present role, but describing in

torrid detail the fling he had *not* had in Kendal, inventing a drunken brawl which would have done no discredit to Patrick Benjamin Wiggins, or indeed to Northangerland himself.

He dashed off this highly-colored fiction in an idle half hour and mailed it with no precaution other than a request to John to blot out certain lines and to show it to no one—rather contradictory advice. John did the first all right, but the temptation to show the letter around, at least at the Three Graces Lodge, where all Branwell's brother masons clamored for gossip, was far too strong. Before the week was out most of Haworth had seen the letter, and somewhat garbled hints had reached Patrick's ears —hints that filled him with foreboding. He lay awake at night wondering if he should write to Branwell and tell him to come home. But the boy's letters to him were of quite another temper and spoke of nothing but satisfaction in his work and the good opinion of his employer. Patrick did not know what to believe or what steps to take.

"I am getting too old for all this," he thought fretfully. "The boy should be quite off my hands by now. It is time for me to be released from all these fears and tensions, it is time for me to reap my harvest of pride in him." But there were no harvests, and the anxiety made Patrick's stomach trouble worse. In vain he pursued his old ritual of solitary meals, simple food, adequate rest. Several times a day indigestion punished his vitals with harsh spasms.

A doctor he'd consulted several years before had suggested he take a little wine with his meals as a palliative. It had worked as well as anything, but he had not felt comfortable in bringing alcohol into the house while Branwell was at home. Now that he was not, Patrick began to apply this pleasant remedy once again. So soothingly did it work upon him—calming his anxieties as well as his digestion—that he gradually increased the dose. Since his purpose in taking a glass or two was entirely innocent, he was quite open in his orders to the local wine merchant. Unfortunately, such things have a way of getting around in a small village. Soon it was rumored that the parson was going the same way as his son, driven to it no doubt by that ne'er-do-well now freely brawling and tippling away in Lancashire.

The ironic fact was, however, that Branwell had stuck to his resolves and was living more abstemiously than his father! The months of abstinence, healthy walks and rides, and the inner satisfactions of good conduct had worked radical improvement. His hand no longer shook; his head and eyes were clear; he was sleeping soundly and writing better than ever. He was truly proud of his work on the *Odes*, and for once with reason. Now he felt he had really earned an acquaintance with Hartley Coleridge.

From a point of sober equilibrium, he wrote a good letter, modest and sincere, a letter deserving of a fair answer. And it received one. Hartley Coleridge invited Branwell to visit him in his cottage on Rydal Water on the first of May.

It was a day to cherish in memory. Branwell had met literary men before but never one who had truly achieved fame; had his talent ratified by general acclaim. Hartley Coleridge stood for all that Branwell had anticipated for himself and failed to reach; and yet when they were together Branwell found they could talk as equals. The exaggerated humility with which he was used to speaking to men whom he considered great, somehow seemed unacceptable with this really great man, who was simple, straightforward and unexalted in his own eyes. Then, too, he was small; his gait was shuffling and strange; he was as timid as a fawn, jumping at the slightest unexpected sound. Branwell, who for years had been subconsciously aware of his physical disadvantages, saw suddenly that they were no impediment to success.

At the same time, he was deeply envious of this man. His father's renown had opened all doors to him, some of the very same doors that to Branwell had remained hermetically sealed. Christopher North would not have dared to leave unanswered any letter signed Coleridge! Then there was the cottage, a paradise set into a paradise, redolent of peace and inspiration and the total absence of financial constraint. Hartley's father had attended to all that.

"He saw that I was wholly unfitted for the world," Branwell's host explained. "His will set up a trust to ensure that I never need trouble myself with practical matters. I can't cope with people! I am too much a prey to nerves and ill-temper. I swear if I had to rely on myself as you do I should never write a word."

Ah, yes, thought Branwell. *For you it's easy!* But though he knew that this man was worthier than he of such a benign dispensation, he couldn't help feeling that their temperaments, their needs, even their inadequacies were much the same; that it was tragically unfair that he, Branwell, must struggle fruitlessly in the cold world while Hartley Coleridge reclined, as it were, protected and privileged in his beautiful retreat.

After they had spent some hours in stimulating talk, Branwell mustered the courage to ask if Coleridge had read the *Odes* he had sent for his opinion.

"Indeed, of course I have read them! I was greatly impressed. You are most gifted."

These intoxicating words were thrown away almost casually, as if the speaker had no idea of how vitally important they were to the hearer. Branwell had not confided in him the trials and errors that had made such heavy weather of his life so far. Hartley Coleridge assumed him to be an eager, talented young man, in less happy circumstances than himself, but with his way open before him and every chance of success. Of course the boy must know he had talent—the translations were excellent. It never occurred to Coleridge that such a statement of the obvious would have so radical an effect on Branwell's future.

He arrived back at his lodgings in Broughton that evening drunk, but not with whiskey. He was simply drunk with new hope. If such a man as Coleridge praised him and offered to help him find a publisher for his completed *Odes,* what was he doing wasting himself as a tutor in a little lakeside town? His head was reeling with pride and excitement. For hours that night he paced his small room in the doctor's house, reading Homer aloud in the original and noting the rich, well-turned English lines that formed like magic in his head. He wrote nothing down; there was no need, for it was all there—all there! He might transcribe it at his leisure. He was a writer—he *was*—Hartley Coleridge had said so!

Next morning he overslept, swept far from reality on a tide of ecstatic dreams, and even when the doctor's wife knocked on his door and woke him, he was in no hurry to rise. He lay there reveling in the return of his happiness, which had always been bonded to his conviction of greatness in himself. The routine in the schoolroom that awaited him on this morning of mornings seemed too dismal, too petty to be borne. He burned to get on with his *real*, his destined, task. Hartley Coleridge had ratified it as such. What more was needed to justify Branwell in abandoning everything else?

In the end, of course, he did have to go to the Postlethwaites and attend to John and William as usual. But all was changed. His heart and mind were not in it. The sound and wholesome resolves that had kept him steady till now had been swept away at a stroke. His attention strayed to Homer, to Coleridge and further: to Charlotte and Papa, overwhelmed with pride in him as he laid the first bound copy of his *Odes* in their hands; to a letter from Wordsworth, congratulating him and begging pardon for his former neglect; to Christopher North, imploring him to contribute some trifle, however short, to *Blackwood's*. In the end, hopelessly restive, he assigned tasks to his pupils and went out for a walk.

This became the pattern of his days. He gave brief, ill-prepared lessons, assigned work and then settled down to his own writing while John and William shuffled and whispered at their desks. If they interrupted him to ask a question, he gave them short shrift, for they broke his concentration.

His efforts with Homer grew so intensive that he became wrought-up and was shocked to feel the old sensations returning—those fearful harbingers of *petit mal* he had suffered from in his teens which had so terrified his family. The condition had lapsed of late and he had all but forgotten its horrors, but now, as he felt his brain beginning to burn and his limbs to shake, he knew

he must take the old remedy for all "inflammation of the brain"
—either drink or opium. Opium was better, for drink was de-
tectable; so at last he went to a chemist and thus entered again
into the thralldom he thought he had left behind.

The drug at once calmed and inspired him, but it did nothing
to pull him back onto the straight-and-narrow way to adulthood.
His employer became increasingly dissatisfied with his work, and
Branwell sensed that the moment was not far off when he would
face ignominious dismissal. It was not the dismissal he feared—
he longed to get home and be free to write—but the ignominy.
He refused to allow even a technical failure to overtake him at
this stage.

So he wrote to his father and asked him to send for him. Life
at the Postlethwaites was impossible, he said, and hinted that a
literary career had again opened before him, but that he would
have to devote himself wholly to it. Patrick, who had dreaded
far worse than this, complied at once.

6

NEW
ENTERPRISES

I T WAS MIDSUMMER WHEN BRAN-
well returned to the parsonage. Far from having his tail between
his legs, he behaved like the favored of fortune and settled down
immediately to finish his translation.

The family, as always, greeted him rapturously and uncritically
—all except Charlotte. She was beginning to have serious and
painful doubts about him, yet she despised her cynicism and
longed to believe that a bright future could still lie before him.
She refrained from prying about why he had left the Postlethwaites. Her own experience in strange houses had shown her
that no excuse was necessary for leaving them; the need to maintain self-respect was enough. At the same time she was miserably
aware that the oneness of soul that had existed between them was
getting lost. She could not help seeming critical, doubting; the
old adoration had been undermined. Branwell sensed this and
resented it, so that the least word from her could provoke a
quarrel. And quarrels with Branwell were something to be
avoided, now more than ever. Not only was he still liable to be
seized by something like a fit if his temper rose too high, but

before that stage was reached his speech would deteriorate to a degree that shocked Charlotte profoundly. In a rage, he employed the language of the taproom, even to her. Afterward he would apologize, but that did not soothe her secret fear that he was becoming degraded.

Sometimes, however, they could still laugh and be happy together. Oddly enough, when the name of William Weightman came up all the gaiety of their childhood was revived.

"You will never believe, Branwell, what he did in February. He asked us casually how many valentines we each expected to receive. Of course we said none, and when Emily added that we never received any he affected horror. 'Disgraceful!' he exclaimed. 'All your suitors must be boobies.' We thought no more of it, but on the fourteenth the postman brought us each a valentine! Imagine! Of course he denied they came from him, but in the end we forced the truth out of him. Anne turned red and white by turns, and Emily nearly wept from laughing. Really, he is beyond everything! He should never have been a parson—never. He has not a serious bone in his entire body."

Branwell was very much drawn to Willie, and often, when they were together, would stare at him, admiring his good looks and frank, outgoing manner. He was a good listener, always an advantage with Branwell. During the summer they often went out shooting together, and they spent some very happy hours striding the moors arm in arm. Willie enjoyed contact with those he liked, and somehow Branwell, who always shrank from being touched, did not mind at all when Willie threw an arm around his shoulder.

But before long this cheerful influence was removed, for Willie was off to Ripon to prepare for his ordination. Branwell was dismayed at the difference his absence made. Though all the inhabitants of the parsonage were busy and contented at that time, a pall fell over the place after Willie's departure. Even Emily remarked that things weren't the same without him, and for Anne, still nursing her love in secret, the summer days seemed suddenly endless.

Charlotte and Branwell threw themselves into their writing,

and soon the *Odes* were ready to go off to Coleridge. Branwell sat up half the night composing a letter to accompany them.

"Let me read it," Charlotte begged.

"No."

"Please, Bany. You know you sometimes express yourself unwisely."

Branwell looked at her, his eyes narrowing dangerously.

"Unwisely?"

Charlotte read the warning signals, but this was so important that she ignored them.

"Yes. I must say it. You veer between exaggerated humility and exaggerated conceit. If Coleridge is a simple, honest man, as you described him to me, anything extreme or overblown will turn him off you. Surely I needn't remind you that in the past—"

"Ah! I knew it! Past reverses never die in your memory, do they? And naturally you blame me for them all! So much for your sisterly loyalty—so much for your faith in me. Devil take you, Charlotte! I'd rather head for hell than spend five minutes with a whey-faced prig like you, for you understand nothing about me!"

With that he rushed out of the house and straight down to the post office, where he sent the package on its way without giving his letter a second look as he had intended. Then he suffered agonies of doubt for days and nights, agonies for which he cursed Charlotte. Had he done wrong to offer Coleridge a half share in sales if he managed to secure a publisher? Would that act as an inducement, or might it—God forbid!—insult him? Charlotte would have known . . . If only she had not challenged him, maddened him, he might—no, he definitely *would* have asked her. Why, why, *why* did none of them understand his impulsive nature? Why could none of them treat him tactfully? His head began to throb with frustration and anger; he ground his teeth. After a while he went down to the chemist.

Charlotte saw how she had upset him and was sorry. She had sent some of her own work secretly to Wordsworth and fully understood her brother's anguish of mind while waiting for a response. But one thing cheered her. Mary was coming for a visit. Surely that would distract Branwell and—who knew? Unlikely as it seemed, they had got on so well together last time that she had faint, quixotic hopes of a match between them.

The intervening months had done nothing to dim Mary's interest in Branwell—quite the reverse. Sensing his nervousness of her sex, she had decided to show her admiration more plainly, to overcome his shyness. But her approach proved totally wrong.

Before a week of the visit had passed Branwell was complaining to Charlotte, "What ails this friend of yours? She's changed. She used to be amusing and comradely. Now she's turned flirt. I can't bear forwardness in girls—at least, not of my own class."

"Branwell, for heaven's sake!" cried Charlotte in distress. "You mistake her! She is not forward! It's just that she has no silly wiles, no hypocritical concealment in her nature. She likes you and in her honest fashion she has let you see it. Is that a reason to speak so slightingly of her, as if you despised her?"

"She looks boldly in my face like a tavern-maid. It's unseemly."

Charlotte stared at him, aghast at his lack of perception as much as at his coarseness.

"Well, at least have the goodness not to let her see what you feel. She is sensitive and you will hurt her."

The truth was, Branwell had liked Mary; he had liked her very much—until he saw that she liked him. Deep down, he reasoned thus: "How can this pretty, intelligent, forthright girl be attracted to me? She must be other than she seems or her choice would fall on a better man than I." So he began to despise her, and to show it plainly. He would leave a room hastily when she entered it, ignore her when she tried to talk to him, and even make remarks that were intended as rebuffs. Charlotte watched this wretchedly, for Mary's bright spirit was wilting. At last Charlotte came upon her weeping, a very rare thing indeed.

"What have I done, Charlotte? Why does he treat me so woundingly?"

"Oh, Mary dear, what does it matter? Don't mind it."

"But I can't help minding! I have thought of him so much, so wanted to renew acquaintance. But now it is all different!"

Charlotte stroked her hair.

"Mary, you and I have no guile in these matters. Anyway, Branwell is so strange about girls; I love him, but I don't think him a fit partner for you, Mary. You deserve a man who will not run away from the first frank meeting of eyes."

So for the remainder of the visit Mary left Branwell severely alone. And this apparent change from affection (howsoever unwanted) to aloofness perversely piqued Branwell, so that he sulked, and the atmosphere became strained. Usually he flounced off straight after supper, either down to the Bull (which he had again begun to frequent) or up to his "studio." This left the four girls alone in the parlor, for Papa still kept to his habit of retiring sharp at nine.

At first Mary was puzzled, then amused, by the girls' habit of walking around and around the table while they talked. Charlotte took her arm and insisted on her joining them. The talk was desultory, for this was the hour when they normally read their work to each other and discussed their creations, and they could not do this before Mary. But of course she knew nothing of this and began to grow impatient at the lack of positive purpose in their conversation.

"It seems to me that none of you is very practical," she observed one evening. "You all know what you want and what you don't, but you can't seem to put the two together for a solution. Listen. You all hate being governesses. True?"

"True!" they cried with one voice.

"Yet since you would regard any sensible work as degrading, there is nothing you can gainfully do except teach. Another of your mutual dislikes is leaving home. So what have we? Governessing—out. Teaching, though—in. Leaving home—out. Staying here—in. Put together, these permutations leave us with one clear possibility." She looked around them triumphantly. "You must teach school *here*."

The three sisters gazed at each other. After a moment's silence, the idea took fire.

"Teach school—here? How could we?"

"The house is too small!"

"Papa would never agree—"

"How many pupils could we take?"

"Four at most—"

"Yet if you were to extend the house a trifle—" put in Mary.

"What, add to the structure? But the cost—!"

"Aunt might—"

"Never!"

"She *might*. If it meant we would be permanently at home and keeping ourselves."

"Just think!" cried Emily, unwontedly roused. "You two could do most of the teaching while I ran the house and cooked. With an extra room built on as a dormitory, we might house six or eight girls! Let's get pencil and paper and work out how much it would cost."

With Emily and Mary in charge of the practical side, they sat around the table nightly, figuring and dreaming. They did not speak of it to Papa, nor yet to Aunt, for they wanted all the sums to be done in a businesslike way first.

Branwell was also left out, much to his chagrin, for he soon realized something was afoot. He took to hanging around after supper, knowing they did not want him and that he was keeping them from their secret discussions.

At last Mary went home, reluctantly, ordering them to keep her informed. Her leave-taking from Branwell was markedly chilly on both sides. Branwell's hauteur was overdone, Charlotte thought, and this was borne out when he remarked later, "She'll be sorry when I'm famous."

"And when will that be?" asked Charlotte caustically.

"Sooner than any of you think," retorted Branwell.

He meant, of course, when the *Odes* were published and acclaimed. But already the familiar, and so doubly terrible, trickle of doubt and fear was crawling through him as the days passed and no message came from Coleridge. Meanwhile, to make matters worse, Charlotte had an answer from Wordsworth. Again it was not wholehearted encouragement, but at least he had not ignored her altogether, and a little correspondence was struck up. Branwell watched in a thickening haze of jealousy and bewilderment. Why didn't Coleridge write? What had Branwell done that had so effectively destroyed that inspiring, bolstering, vista-opening friendship? Alone in his room, he paced about, striking his forehead repeatedly with his fist, cursing, and even weeping. Now, indeed, the laudanum he had hitherto used as a booster or a palliative became a necessity, for without it it was hard to get through the nights, spent agonizingly anticipating the next day's post, and the days, spent wallowing in disappointment.

It was Emily who came to his rescue. She found out about the laudanum by accident, when the chemist, to whom she applied on Aunt's behalf for a laxative, mistakenly thought she had come for Branwell's "dose," and unwittingly betrayed him by giving it to her. At first she was stunned. Then she rallied. At all costs this must be kept secret from Papa—and from Charlotte, whose increasingly critical attitude toward Branwell, Emily had long felt, was making his general condition worse. If she knew of *this*—! But Emily was more tolerant. Of course it was dreadful and dangerous, but not so much morally as physically. She lured Branwell out for a moorland walk and tackled him, as always, head on.

"Branwell, you'll have to stop taking opium. Yes, I know all about it. Don't say anything. I'm not criticizing, I don't judge you, but you must stop before it's too late."

She stopped talking to give this a chance to sink in. Branwell said nothing, but dropped down on the turf and buried his face in his hands. Emily sat beside him without touching him and turned her face up to the bright, windy sky, unable to prevent herself, even for the space of this bad moment, from reveling in the beauty of all that she loved.

"I want to suggest something. As long as you're at home you

won't be able to give it up, I realize that. So you must get away. Find yourself a sensible, honest job and make a fresh start. It doesn't mean giving up your writing and painting."

Branwell uncovered his face abruptly.

"I have been thinking," continued Emily. "The railway is evidently the thing of the future. Had I any money of my own to invest, that's what I would put it into. By the same token, if I were a young man (as I often think I should have been), I would go for a position with the railway, no matter how humble to start with. A niche carved in that enterprise can hardly help being the start of a good career for anyone who is honest, intelligent and ambitious—and you are all those."

Branwell stared at her, his brain working feverishly. A job with the Manchester-Leeds railway! New lines were opening all the time. He'd seen positions advertised in the local paper. "Clerk-in-charge" . . . "Clerk" sounded worse than "tutor," but the "in-charge" part rang well enough. Perhaps it would not hurt to try. Besides, if he did not, what was left for him at home? Now Emily knew of his habit, it would be almost impossible to continue with it, which meant going back to a reliance on rum and whiskey, which in turn would lead to more rows with his father. There was no longer any joy to be had from being close to Charlotte; in fact, he felt bitterly that in some strange way she was driving him away with her sarcasm and her sharp looks.

"Well, I'll try," he said slowly.

"Good," said Emily, her hand gently stroking the grass.

Rather to his surprise—and somewhat to his alarm—Branwell got the first post he applied for. It was as assistant clerk at the newly-opening station of Sowerby Bridge, two miles from Halifax. The salary seemed princely—seventy-five pounds a year, payable quarterly in arrears. The prospects were excellent—promotion was promised after a six-month trial.

The family's reactions were mixed. Patrick's hopes for his son were at such a low ebb that *any* respectable job would have raised them, even though it was hard for him to hide his disappointment at its mundane character. Aunt patted his hand, dabbed her eyes and lips with her handkerchief and kept her thoughts to herself, while Anne kissed Branwell heartily and said that with such a salary they could all now take their ease.

And Charlotte? Charlotte was too outraged to speak. She shut herself in her room and stifled baffled sobs. How, how, *how* had Branwell come to this? Chief Genius Brannii—clerk at a railway station! She would have scrubbed steps herself rather than see Branwell so reduced. If a woman did not rise in the world, that was only to be expected; but if a man of Branwell's talents failed to do so, it could only—in the final analysis—be his own fault.

But she took hold of herself and put a good face on it when the time came in September to bid Branwell good-bye and good fortune. To no avail—he still had only to look into her eyes to know what she truly felt, and both his face and his spirits froze as he turned from her and walked in furious silence away from the parsonage.

Nor did Sowerby Bridge and its environs do anything to cheer him. No one had thought to warn him that his "office" would consist of a shed made of wood and corrugated iron, in default of the new one that had not yet been built. The place itself was a backwater. His immediate superior, one George Duncan, was also new, and unable to reassure Branwell that the prospects made up for the appearances.

"What've we coom to, eh, lad? We're at back o' beyond and no mistake."

In no respect whatever was Duncan a man whom Branwell could look up to. Here was clerk material, if you like! A simple, stolid fellow with a grasp of figures and a passion for engines, his position rested on diligence rather than on any quickness of mind. Branwell tried out a few Latin tags on him and was rewarded by blank stares and a consequent pleasant feeling of superiority. In the long run, however, this was poor compensation for a complete lack of companionship.

Small wonder that Branwell's chief relaxation was to walk two miles down the steep road to Halifax, to restore his sense of his true self in conversation with Joseph Leyland. The sculptor was working on a commission of five warriors for a Manchester gallery, and there were other half-finished pieces scattered about. Branwell noticed that Leyland didn't seem to be concentrating very hard on any of them. He was fretting to get back to London; but money was always tight, mainly because as fast as he came by it he either drank it or gave it away to friends. Branwell was not the only one in his debt.

"In December I'll pay you every penny, never fear."

"Don't trouble yourself about it, my dear fellow! What's money for? Come, I've exhausted my muse for today. Let's go to the Talbot and have a glass together. Your way back to your labors lies all up hill."

This was true. The way *to* Halifax was joyful and easy; one could run most of it, and Branwell often did. The way *back* was a long slog, often made with an aching head and always with a reluctant spirit. In Halifax Branwell could still think of himself as an artist. In Sowerby Bridge, wretched godforsaken spot, he was nothing but a clerk—an assistant clerk—chained to his ledger and to a bovine colleague with nothing in his soul but trains and numbers and pints of ale. He began to see his situation much as Charlotte had seen it from the outset.

In March he got his promotion. But it was not, as he'd expected, to some major station where he could have had a sense of real power and prestige. It was merely a few miles down the line, to a place called Luddenden Foot. True, he was in charge there. But it was such a miserable spot, and any sort of ego-building success seemed so far off that Branwell's determination began to break down once again.

At home something else was breaking down, or at least not moving forward: the school project.

The girls had presented Aunt with their plan, and humbly begged her to help them; but, though she showed some interest, when it actually came to advancing money, she hung back. Patrick, too, was not very keen. The fact was that he and his sister-in-law were getting on—Patrick was sixty-four—and at their age such enormous changes in their lives were fearful to contemplate. They didn't exactly condemn the idea, for they perceived its merits, but they prevaricated endlessly, throwing up all sorts of real and contrived impediments.

So with almost insurmountable reluctance Anne and Charlotte faced again the task of finding positions.

It took them the whole winter. Charlotte's chief recreation during the dark months was writing to Ellen. To her she was able to unburden herself of the dread she felt of being again among strangers. But all her letters were not gloomy. Willie Weightman was back, and his flirtations occupied quite a portion of them. There was a good reason for this. Ellen had met Willie the previous spring and had been the recipient of his most entrancing wiles. Charlotte, watching them together, had not altogether liked it. Not, she told herself, that *she* was the least interested in "Miss Weightman"; but the idea of Ellen falling a prey disquieted her.

So when Ellen went home, Charlotte took care to keep her posted—in the lightest vein not untainted by a sort of affectionate contempt—on Willie's amorous exploits in the neighborhood, so as to disillusion Ellen if she *had* mistakenly thought he meant anything special by his attentions to her. Sometimes her conscience troubled her, for there was more to Willie than vanity and flirting. Honesty made Charlotte report incidents of his kindness to the poor of the parish, which were the more impressive because, in the true spirit of the Gospels, he acted secretly, leaving Charlotte to find out his good deeds by report. Unthinkingly she also told Emily and Anne, little guessing how each incident of good-heartedness and Christian charity added to the painful burden of Anne's love.

By March, when Branwell moved stations, the girls had put the school scheme into mothballs for the time being, though they hadn't abandoned it. And both Anne and Charlotte found employment.

Their positions were widely separated, both geographically and financially. Charlotte left first, for Rawdon, near Bradford. Her family's name was White, and she accepted the situation because she believed they would treat her with more consideration and civility than she'd received from the Sidgwicks. This hope weighed so heavily with her that she accepted the wretched salary of twenty pounds a year, of which four was to be deducted to pay for her laundry.

Anne said nothing—it was Charlotte's decision—but she was determined not to sell her own sweated labor (for that's what she now knew it was) so cheap. Without telling anyone, she advertised her services: "Music, singing, drawing, French, Latin and German." And scarcely daring to believe her own boldness, she added: "Salary required, £50 per annum."

This was an enormous sum to ask for, and she was not surprised to receive only one reply. It was from a Reverend Mr. Robinson of Thorp Green Hall, Little Ouseburn—a matter of seventy miles from home, close to York.

There was the usual family uproar when Anne made her announcement, but once again she overrode it and set off at the end of March on the ten-hour journey by gig, coach, rail and finally by Mr. Robinson's phaeton. Her heart was high—fifty pounds a year! On that she could save for their school. The idea of setting something aside for her own dowry did briefly occur to her, but she banished it. If she could not have Willie she would not marry, and it was clear to her by now that Willie regarded her as a sister. It was good she was getting away—the further the better.

The few months until both sisters were released for the brief summer holidays passed not too unpleasantly on the whole. That is not to say that either was precisely happy, but in each case the situation was a vast improvement on the previous one.

The Robinsons of Thorp Green Hall were wealthy philistines, and too worldly for Anne's tastes. She thought it odd to see an ordained minister spending most of his time on the hunting field, and his forty-year-old helpmeet concerning herself almost exclusively with fashion and balls. Her two teenage daughters, Lydie and Eliza, struck Anne as being the inevitable product of their environment: they were lazy, feckless and trivial-minded to a degree, mirroring their mother's habits and standards. Neither seemed to have any moral principles worth the name, and all their ongoings were based upon a single consideration: Did one course of action hold out the prospect of more instant pleasure than another? If so, that was the one to follow. Lydie, at fifteen, was already a hardened little heartbreaker; and Eliza, a year younger, was a hoyden, coarse, foul-mouthed and boisterous.

The youngest daughter, Mary, not yet eleven, was as yet unspoiled by coquetry and worldliness. Anne felt that with her at least she might do some good. As for the only son, Edmund, whom she was expected to "cram" with Latin so that he could get into a public school, she found she could do nothing with him at all. He thought it beneath his dignity to have a governess, and declared he would learn only if he was given a tutor.

Of society or food for self-esteem, Anne received none. The Robinsons were as snobbish as the Sidgwicks and treated their servants with less warmth than their dogs and horses. Anne was confined to the nursery wing of the large hall, never venturing into the grander apartments. Her time was taken up with her duties, and apart from the uncongenial companionship of the girls, whose idle chatter she found wearying, she had no company at all. Nature was her only consolation. The children liked to have their lessons outdoors, and as spring advanced Anne was able to spend long hours in the noble grounds of the estate; but the land lay low, close to the river, and too much sitting out on damp lawns did nothing to improve her general health.

However, after the Inghams it was quite bearable, and when the loneliness and the humiliations grew too much, she would set her teeth and recite, like a litany, "Fifty pounds a year! Fifty pounds a year!" That was almost a pound a week. *Let them slight me, let them look through me as if I were not there*, she thought. *I know who I am. They cannot diminish me.*

Charlotte's lot was harder, in that all her toils barely sufficed to keep her; yet easier, in that her family was kinder to her than Anne's.

Mr. White was a most gentlemanly man who treated her very courteously, and if Mrs. White was not quite so pleasant, Charlotte was becoming accustomed to her general failure to get along with older women. Her pupils, a little girl and boy, were not the fiends she had had to deal with before, but ordinary if rather spoiled children, not too stupid to make some progress in lessons and not too steeped in class-consciousness to show her some affection.

Her partially successful struggles to clip her own ambitious wings were rudely assailed shortly after the brief holiday she was permitted to take in July. She had heard, of course, that Martha Taylor had been sent to finishing school near Brussels, and that Mary was having a glorious time traveling about Europe with her older brothers. In August, then, Charlotte got a letter from Mary, so filled with vivid word-pictures of European capitals (Brussels in particular), of their magnificent cathedrals and art collections, their splendid public buildings and stimulating society, that Charlotte's assumed mantle of humility and resignation was torn away as if by a hurricane of longing. To Ellen she wrote:

I hardly know what swelled to my throat as I read her letter—such a vehement impatience of restraint and steady work. Such a strong wish for wings—wings such as wealth can furnish—such an urgent thirst to see—to know—to learn—something internal seemed to expand boldly for a minute. I was tantalized with the consciousness of faculties unexercised—then all collapsed and I despaired.

She did not quite despair, however. The school project had revived; for Aunt, during the holiday, had suddenly announced that she had decided after all to open her purse somewhat to further the scheme, provided she could be convinced that it had some chance of success. And at about the same time, there came an offer from Miss Wooler to hand over the Dewsbury Moor school to Charlotte's management.

This was potentially very thrilling, and at first the girls allowed themselves to get excited. After the briefest of conferences, during which elation overcame practicality, Charlotte wrote off and accepted Miss Wooler's offer, which was to include all the furniture and equipment. The fact was, the school was running down, and Miss Wooler had hopes that Charlotte's "special qualities" would pull it out of the doldrums.

So Charlotte had returned to Rawdon in a mood of unwonted exhilaration. It was then that Mary's letter came and so disturbed her that the consoling and invigorating prospect of the school dwindled somewhat. Nevertheless, she did her best to crush down her greater ambitions and to concentrate on the lesser, more attainable ones, waiting eagerly for Miss Wooler's response to her acceptance. Only with the prospect of real independence held before her inner eye to steady her could she quell those wild hopes and dreams that Mary had, accidentally or deliberately, touched into flame with her letter.

Miss Wooler, however, was having second thoughts. Her sister Eliza, who had been running the school, and running it badly, had volunteered in a moment of despair to give it up. But when Miss Wooler gaily announced that she had found as a replacement none other than their old pupil Charlotte Brontë, Miss Eliza faced about abruptly.

"*That* nondescript little chit?" she cried, gathering her pride about her like a fichu. "You shall not do it, sister! To suggest that *she* might do what *I* cannot! I shall never agree to it."

So there was silence from Dewsbury Moor. But not from Brussels.

This time there could be no doubt about Mary's intentions. During the whole of their relationship she had been striving to get Charlotte out of her provincial rut, to harness her tormenting dreams and force her friend at least to try to realize them. Now that Mary had herself seen something of Europe, she could not endure the idea of Charlotte rotting away in perpetual servitude. "It is such a waste!" she thought, for she had always sensed something akin to greatness in Charlotte, which could easily become twisted into bitterness and despair if it was not allowed to stretch out and blossom.

So now she took a bold step, knowing that to hold out hope could, if it was not fulfilled, recoil against her deep wish to do her friend good. Having had some indication of how disturbing Charlotte had found her first letter, Mary now openly urged her to do everything possible to come to Brussels. It would not cost much; if her aunt was willing to finance a school, how much more sensible initially to pay for Charlotte to equip herself to teach in it? Polish was what she needed—qualifications. Without these she could not attract pupils. The Taylors would give her every assistance from that end. And, if she was reluctant to come by herself, what better than to include Emily in the scheme? At all events, she must try. She *must try*.

When Charlotte got this letter instead of the one she was expecting from Miss Wooler, it was as though some delicate scale in her soul that she had been straining to keep in balance tipped suddenly to one side, throwing all her endeavors and plans, her very being, into a tumult of excitement.

Ellen had gone down to Sussex to help run her brother's vicarage—*her* advice was not to be had. Seeing the great spires and limitless intellectual possibilities of Brussels suddenly opening before her, Charlotte rushed to the only responsible adults available, her employers, in a fever of longing and confusion.

"Advise me to be sensible! Advise me to take thought!" she begged them. "I feel as if against all reason I am being swept away! It cannot be, can it? Bring me back to earth with sound practical advice!"

Mr. and Mrs. White stared at her, dumbfounded. She no longer looked at all like their mousy little governess. Her face was alight, her movements were wide and unrestrained, her hair had tumbled down; her eyes, never less than beautiful when she opened them wide, were now luminous with longing, and her tight lips were parted in excitement. Mr. White was particularly taken with the sight of her. He saw what he had often suspected, that she was a woman of some attractiveness, and in her present mood he felt both admiration and fondness for her.

"My dear little lady," he said, "far be it from either of us to damp your spirits in this matter. You are a clever girl and you deserve a chance to improve yourself. By all means, go to Brussels if you can. Your prospects of success in a school of your own would undoubtedly be greatly enhanced by a spell at some establishment on the Continent. Nothing impresses more the ambitious mothers of daughters, I promise you!"

Charlotte turned those wild, shining eyes on him with a look of incredulous gratitude.

"You think it possible? Even desirable—from a *practical* point of view?"

"Certainly. There are so many seminaries for young ladies in England, all competing against each other—anyone venturing upon the field of education *must* equip herself with the highest advantages possible, especially foreign languages, or the hardest struggle would yet be likely to end in failure. What your friend proposes is not a wild scheme, but great good sense, and you should not be put off it by any perverse idea that it must be wrong just because you will enjoy it. The Devil is not hidden in every pleasure, Miss Brontë."

Charlotte needed no more than this. That night she expended an entire candle, writing and rewriting a long, long, diplomatic letter to Aunt Branwell.

7

DESPAIR
AND NEW HOPE

*B*RANWELL'S JOB AT LUDDENDEN
Foot was a bitter disappointment to him.

The location, first of all, was demoralizing. The station was not
a busy junction, as Sowerby Bridge had been; it was merely a stop
on the line, so that although he tried to convince himself (and
the family) that the change was a rung or two up on the ladder of
success, it felt more like a demotion. Then, the station itself was
hacked out of the base of a great black rock-face, which seemed
to lower over it, darkening the makeshift office and throwing a
dank pall over the whole enterprise. It was too far from Halifax
to allow Branwell his previous frequent exit into a less soul-
destroying environment. And he was much lonelier on the job,
for here there was not even a boozing George Duncan to keep
him company.

During the week he was all but overwhelmed by boredom and
isolation. He felt as if he had been shuffled away and forgotten.
Letters from home speaking of hopes and plans for a school, plans
from which he was excluded, added to this feeling. After a while
he became miserably obsessed with the idea that they hardly

cared for him, that all their hope in him had dwindled; he no longer went home every weekend and would have respected himself more if he could have stayed away altogether.

Fortunately his friends did not abandon him. If Mohammed was too strapped to come to the mountains, the mountains—in the shape of Joseph Leyland and his brother Francis—would come to him when they could. And Branwell met another Francis, Francis Grundy, who was an engineer with the railway. They met on one of his routine visits to Luddenden Foot. Branwell, who always rocketed into a state of ebullience whenever a congenial visitor interrupted the dismal monotony of his life, pounced on this young man, delighting in the discovery that he was well-educated.

"To meet someone in this wilderness who can understand a word of Latin! You can't think what it means. Look out there— see that fellow slouching along the platform, with his dull eyes and sheepish, champing jaws? That, my dear Grundy, is one Walton, the porter, my only companion here. I would as soon be shut up with an amiable chimpanzee! But you must meet my friend Leyland—the famous sculptor, you know—he's coming tomorrow to take me out of myself. We're going walking up on the Craggs. Stop over and come with us. We usually end up at some cheerful inn or other, dry from talking each other's heads off!"

Grundy turned out to hold a better card even than his familiarity with the dead tongues—he had a railway pass. Judicious use of this enabled the four friends to range farther afield on their Sunday outings, and taverns all over the district came to know them well. Branwell's hangovers after these hilarious evenings were exacerbated by a sense of guilt so strong that Leyland used to laugh at him.

"But, my boy, these are the common pleasures of mankind! Will you be forever abusing yourself for indulging in simple enjoyment? Thank God I'm not a parson's son, for my life would be spent doing penances!"

Not that his regular glimpses of hellfire had any real effect on

Branwell's behavior. He needed the escape; life was wholly unbearable without it, and so, even when friends of his own choos-
ing were not with him, he would go drinking locally.

His regular companions at first were the clientele of the Lord
Nelson in the village—young, hard-drinking sons of manufacturers
and tradesmen. Among them he met a lad called James Titterington. His father was a wealthy millowner, and James combined
exactly the qualities of wildness and intellect that appealed to
Branwell. On one hand, they would go to meetings of the local
Reading Society together, meetings at which rough language was
punished by a fine. On the other, when these finished, James
would bear Branwell off to a very different sort of gathering. For
this rich young man enjoyed slumming, and reveled in the extreme contrast to his own life provided by the poorest working-
men's taverns down by the canal basin where the barges moored.

"This is where the life of the place really is," he would say,
waving a well-suited arm around the sordid purlieus of the
Weaver's Arms. "These fellows don't live at one remove from
reality, as we do, Brontë. Their feet are rooted in the earth. To
us they seem simple, but we are fools if we call them dull. Only
in their company can we learn the true nature of the world and
its passions."

Titterington turned for his sexual pleasures to the women of
this district and urged Branwell to do the same. But although
Branwell could enjoy a drink and a jest in the company of these
cheerful sluts, the thought of a closer approach repelled him, on
aesthetic as well as moral grounds. It consoled him somehow for
his addiction to stimulants that he retained his chastity in the
face of what he chose to regard as extreme temptation, for Grundy
and Joseph Leyland also pressed him to patronize the local
"skirts."

There was another group of men frequenting these humble
drinking houses who were also set apart from the general company. These were the Irish immigrants who had been brought
over by the millowners as cheap labor. Most of them had left
their women behind in Ireland and lived in a cluster of squalid

shacks along the canal, in conditions that seemed to fascinate Titterington. He described to Branwell in the most avid fashion the dirt floors, the leaking roofs, the beds made of bundles of tarpaulin "borrowed" from the barges, the outdoor fires. He dwelt upon the way these hovels stank, of the hunger and degradation of the inmates, of the drunken brawling and debauchery that caused even the meanest of the local workmen to despise the Irishmen and shun them. It never occurred to this young man that his own father, among others, was a direct cause of all this misery. He would not have rectified it if he could have, for he reveled in its picturesque existence and loved to stroll with Branwell down past the shacks, discoursing upon the failure of Popery (the religion of all these Irish workers) with all its strict precepts to prevent its misguided adherents from wallowing in every type of vice.

It goes without saying that none of this really helped Branwell in his weakening attempts to reform himself. But the *coup de grâce* was delivered, all unwittingly, by Charlotte, when she wrote to him in intense excitement to tell him that Aunt had agreed to furnish both herself and Emily forth to Brussels to finishing school.

That this should have been a crippling blow was mainly due to a very minor point in the letter, one that Charlotte had put in without thinking for a moment how it might strike Branwell. She happened to mention that Mary and Martha were always chaperoned on their travels by one of their brothers, who would also help her and Emily. When Branwell read this, he knew for certain that his family had discarded him as an effectual male member. For there was not a hint that *he* might serve a like office for them. *Papa* was to accompany them to Brussels. Branwell evidently had no part to play in this exalted scheme—not even that of escort. He was not only to be left behind in his forgotten outpost, but they had not even thought of involving him. And the worst was, he saw the justice of it. He had had his chance when they sent him to London. He had had subsequent chances. Now it was his sisters' turn, and he was forever cast aside.

That night Branwell went down to the Weaver's Arms alone.

When he had first seen the Irish workers, half sullen, half bombastic, huddled by themselves in one corner of the taproom, he had felt an immediate kinship with them. They were, after all, his father's people. Their brogue was something Branwell had grown up with, and he could adopt it at will. Now he strolled over and, pretending to be an Irishman himself, set about ingratiating himself.

A few drinks dispensed among them, a few bawdy jokes, a touch of blasphemy—not too much, just enough to send a shiver down the spine—and they opened ranks. Branwell was drawn into their midst. Warm, slovenly drunken voices encouraged him; grimy hands fondled him; eyes hungry for fellowship, for approbation— so he imagined—fastened on his face and slithered down his body. They encircled him and he felt comforted by their quick, close acceptance of him.

But his appeal for them was not what he supposed. His slender, somewhat effeminate build, his dandified clothes and the elegance of manner he could not quite disguise, made him seem fair game to some of the sex-starved immigrants. His deliberate approach to them was not seen in the light of friendliness, or even patronage. While the locals smirked and nudged each other at the far side of the room, Branwell's new acquaintances set about filling him up with whiskey. He was a willing accomplice to his own downfall. The drunker he grew, the more at home he felt with this feckless, merry, affectionate crowd.

One man began to talk about his family, left behind in famine-stricken Ireland, and the tears coursing down his face woke all Branwell's own facile sentimentality. He wept with him, pouring out a garbled tale about his poor sisters slaving in the homes of the snobbish exploiters. But before long someone made a jest and they were all laughing again. It was just the kind of free and easy, overemotional atmosphere Branwell loved, and when arms encircled him or hands came to rest on his thighs he hardly noticed the warm currents of his blood; Willie Weightman's innocent caresses had destroyed his moral warning-system. In any case, he was almost totally ignorant of such things.

They persuaded him to come home with them. Branwell had never seen inside the shacks, and Titterington had made the life within them sound so warm, intense and earthy that Branwell had a kind of voluptuous curiosity to go there. Soon they were leading him, a frail, unsuspecting prey, out along the dark banks of the canal and onto a moored barge.

"Come, me lad, we can finish our bottles out in God's fresh air!" shouted one amid a roar of senseless laughter.

But their pious references did not prevent them from thoroughly debauching Branwell.

They left him at last, drowning under a deluge of undreamed-of sensuality, and numb before the onset of the most unmanageable guilt of all his guilt-ridden life.

After this searing episode, Branwell lay in bed for three days, overcome with self-disgust and horror at his new vision of the world and its wickedness, a wickedness in which, he was all too well aware, some warp in his own nature predisposed him to be a willing partner. He swore solemn oaths before God that he would never again lend himself to such dealings, and pleaded ignorance as his excuse for his lapse. But his guilt was so terrible that he could not bear it. He sent his landlady out for laudanum and drugged himself into insensibility with it. But he did not lose consciousness until, in the carnal visions induced by the drug, he had relived with embellishments the episode on the barge. Waking, he realized in horror that the very escape route he had chosen to carry him away from his remorse had treacherously renewed his reasons for it.

Degradation, sinfulness, lust, seemed to lie on all sides of him, like a bog he could not cross to safety without miring himself to the throat in it. When Maria appeared to him in dreams, he screamed in terror and fled from her. He could not bear to think about anyone he loved, especially his sisters, who now seemed to him beings from another existence, wholly alienated from him by his own disgusting moral fall.

Since no trace of goodness remained in him, since he could

never look in their faces again without deceit and concealment of what he really was, what did life hold for him now? Might he not just as well wallow in whatever pit of filth his debased nature had decreed for him? Might he not enjoy the road to an already inevitable damnation? Was that not what Northangerland had done, in his own way? And had Branwell, in creating Northangerland, not perhaps been guided by the Fates that had predestined him (oh, Calvin was right after all!) for the fire? In Percy he had foreshadowed his own story, his own moral doom. What use to struggle against it? That would be puling weakness. No. *Be* the great Northangerland. Jettison guilt—it was the only impediment. And it could only be escaped by heaping so much sin upon the soul that guilt itself was smothered.

So, thought Branwell, *I shall become Percy*. I shall submerge myself in that Satanic figure. I shall find out how far mind can carry body, until, having lost innocence, I lose the desire to regain it. If I am to go to hell, at least I shall not suffer here. Let me justify whatever malignant fate has cursed my life—I will let it carry me wherever it likes, and not struggle against it anymore.

So at last, for lack of alternative, he went back to work. But from that time on he forced himself to break down as many as he could of the ingrained habits of virtue he had grown up with. He never returned to the Weaver's Arms, but now he let his friends persuade him to accompany them on their pleasure-hunts. Coldly and deliberately, against his nature, he drove himself to sample the more "normal" sensual outlets. He loathed it, but *he was Northangerland*, and in this role he satisfied friends and whores alike.

When he ran short of money (having kept his word and repaid Leyland) he stood before the station till and commanded his hand to rifle a small sum from it. At first his hand would not obey, but a strange superstitious idea came to him. He had always been able to write equally well with either hand and had developed the trick of writing different things with each at the same time. Now it occurred to him that his left hand belonged to the Devil. He switched the command to this hand and it obeyed him, scooping a couple of half crowns from the drawer, and pocketing them. Later he used the same hand to falsify the books.

This duality persisted. Guilt did not prove so easy to smother. All his upbringing rose in protest after every petty theft, every false entry in his employers' books, every drunken debauch, every lying letter home. Sometimes when he was writing down cost entries in his ledger, relieved of his misery for a few moments by mental effort, the "Devil's hand" would stealthily pick up a pencil and cry out (as it were) in the margin, "Jesu—Jesu—Jesu!" Catching sight of these "cries," these manifestations of the need even of his black side for salvation, Branwell was assailed by nauseating waves of panic. Was he going insane? What was happening to him? Perhaps God was still in him somewhere; perhaps, despite all, there was still hope.

But no. That wasn't possible. He put his head down on the open ledger and wept, and now it was no mere sentiment but the uncontainable sign of the most profound wretchedness and moral confusion. For once, Branwell did not rail against his family for their failure to understand him. He truly believed himself to be beyond redemption. Although he fought desperately against the agony of his guilt, he no longer tried to shift the blame. For the first time, he accepted personal responsibility for himself. It was ironic that just at the moment when the graph of his life took this fatal downward plunge, he should have arrived at his first belated milestone on the way to maturity.

The family had no inkling of any of this, of course. They were, as Branwell had so painfully surmised, scarcely thinking of him at all in the unprecedented thrill of planning the trip to Brussels.

Charlotte had anticipated an almost insuperable reluctance on Emily's part to go with her. And Emily's first reaction did indeed seem unequivocal.

"I won't go unless Anne can come, too."

"Emily, you're older. You know you've got as far as you can by yourself with your French and German. As for Anne, she will have her turn. When our school is under way, we will send her abroad ourselves."

But it was Anne, in the end, who persuaded Emily to go. She herself did not want to go abroad. The idea of staying quietly at home, after the horrors of living with strangers, soothed her; and she had another reason. There would be a poignant joy in having Willie to herself.

But just as it was all arranged, a letter arrived from Thorp Green for Papa. He came into the dining room with it in his hands.

"My dear," he said to Anne, "I thought you said you did not get on well with the Robinsons?"

"The older girls thought me a nagging prig, the son, Edmund, ignored me and Mrs. Robinson found fault continually."

"How strange! She has written to me that even these few days without you have shown your value to her household. She begs me to use my influence to persuade you to return."

"But I am to stay here and look after you!"

"If that were not necessary, would you go back?"

Anne sighed. "I suppose so. I'm unlikely to earn so much elsewhere."

They all gazed at her. Her fortitude, her capacity for self-sacrifice, were a never-ending revelation to them.

"I'll not have you go back there if you are truly unhappy. But there's no denying the money is very important to us just now."

"But what about you, with Tabby so poorly again?"

"We have Martha Brown, and perhaps her sister Hannah can help her."

"Good heavens, Papa! Think of those two little girls doing all the heavy work! I can barely lift the wet sheets out of the copper myself! And who will feed Emily's pets? Martha is terrified of the hawk."

"My hawk must be cared for," said Emily sharply.

"I will undertake that task personally," said Patrick. "We'll manage somehow. But Branwell, you know, sends so little home— not half what you provide—"

"Well, but he must keep himself, Papa," said Anne quickly, seeing his sad eyes. "As to going back, there's one nice thing about it. When summer comes, Mr. Robinson may take us all to Scarborough again. You can't dream how beautiful it is there! I would go through almost anything for the promise of another walk along St. Nicholas Cliff as I saw it last summer. Really, I'll be glad to go back if you want me to—I do miss my little Mary. It's very satisfying to think I am some help," she added shyly.

Emily got up from where she was sitting and came around the table.

"You are the best of all of us," she said shortly, and kissed her.

Branwell had not been home for months. The absolute unavoidability of a brief visit in January to bid the girls Godspeed was weighing on him. Most of all he dreaded facing Charlotte. How much of what he had been through would she perceive, simply by looking at him? If only he could hide! If only he could run away—kill himself . . . There was no limit to the frantic escape-thoughts that preyed on him, awake and asleep, all over Christmas, a festival which he passed alone in utter terror, misery and despair.

In the end he was forced to resort to opium. He had recently become deeply afraid of the tyranny he knew it held over him, and had seriously tried to substitute alcohol, with some success. But now it was imperative to clear his yellow eyes, to still his shaking hands, to rid his face of the puffiness that whiskey had put on it; so he went back to his familiar demon, and with its treacherous help was able to get himself to Haworth on the appointed day. "Perhaps she will not notice . . . Perhaps she will not notice . . ." The pathetic refrain rattled in his head with the carriage wheels.

And extraordinarily enough, Charlotte did not. Aunt did, and Papa did, and Emily and Anne did, and they all, in their own ways, reacted to the change in him. But Charlotte herself was in the grip of something so absorbing that even the traces of ruin on the face of this twinlike brother could not reach down to the essential soul in her, which would once have leaped up in horror and dismay at the sight of him.

Patrick, his face as white as the silk with which he swathed his increasingly eccentric stock, drew her into his sanctum and muttered, "What ails him? He looks so ill!" But she merely stiffened her head in a sudden spasm and replied, "I cannot do anything about him just now, Papa." Her voice was shrill and tense, her eyes unwontedly hard and evasive. He let her go.

Anne it was, not Charlotte, who ventured up to sit with Branwell when he retreated to his studio to rake apathetically through his dust-covered canvases.

"What have you been doing to yourself?" she asked him.

He had no heart to reply, and only shook his head.

"I wish you would tell me."

"What use is it? You're going away soon. Oh, look. Here's the portrait Charlotte did of Willie in his silk gown. It's quite good . . . Good old Willie . . . at least he hasn't changed. . . ."

"Could you talk to *him*?"

Branwell shot her a quick, anguished glance, and shook his head in an almost shivering motion. The glance showed her again the depths of suffering in his eyes, and she got up and put her arms around him. "Bany . . ." she said, her voice dropping low with a sudden surge of warmth and pity. "Do not mind so much. There can always be new beginnings. There's always forgiveness. That's what religion really is. That's all guilt is for, to make us start again."

Branwell sat perfectly still in her embrace for a moment, then his hands tremblingly began turning over the canvases again. "Oh, look," he repeated dully, "here is the one I did of you three . . . It is a good profile of Emmy, but I haven't caught you or Charlotte. Remember how we laughed and joked while I did it—how happy—"

He choked and was silent. Anne held his head against her breast, watching while his slow tears fell onto the picture.

She spoke to Willie. Though the subject was so painful, it was pure delight to have a reason for a serious private talk with him.

They sat in the kitchen together and had a cup of tea while the bread "proved" in a big wooden bowl near the stove.

"I suppose you've noticed how awful Branwell is looking."

"I have. I'm very much afraid he has been drinking again."

"Yes. But it is worse than that, somehow. Something bad has happened to him—I feel sure of it. Heaven knows Branwell could not have found a situation more certain to send him to the bad than the one he has. He needs constructive activity and the right kind of company. I wish with all my heart that he were to stay here, where you might keep an eye on him and befriend him."

"I'd be glad to. I'm very fond of him. Yes, it's a pity he is stuck so far away from us."

"Perhaps he will not be there much longer. Every position he has had has ended prematurely," said Anne thoughtfully.

"If my business for your father around the parish did not make such demands on my time, I would gladly visit him at his station. Maybe I could find time anyway—if *you* request it," he added, with a meaningful emphasis that made her look up at him sharply.

It was not the first time he had paid her some small, gallant compliment; he did it with every girl. Yet now it seemed to her suddenly that he had his large, comely eyes fixed on her in a subtly different way.

"That's—very kind of you, Willie," she said, struggling to control the breathless quality in her voice.

"You are the kind one," he returned quietly. "And the brave one. I have been wanting to tell you how much I admire you for agreeing to return to Thorp Green Hall when you must have far preferred to stay at home. I don't like to think of you there. You, too, should be at home where . . . those who care for you can watch over you."

Anne had built up a fair degree of self-mastery in the matter of her love for Willie over the months, but this was too much. She felt the hot blood rising to her neck and her heart beginning to pound with a passionate elation that it was quite beyond her power to hide. She jumped up and ran out of the kitchen, leaving Willie sitting at the table.

That Sunday they all went to church together, except Branwell, who dealt his father a stunning blow by announcing that he no longer attended church.

"My boy! You can't mean that! Have you lost your faith?"

"Among other things. I can't be a hypocrite, Papa, even for your sake. It all means nothing to me anymore, less than nothing."

The shock of this was so great that Patrick found he was unable to conduct the service, and Willie, now fully ordained, had to take over for him. He gave a rousing sermon directed against Dissenters, a subject upon which he felt so strongly that he could speak extempore at any moment. But while he talked, he was aware of Anne, seated demurely in the congregation below. All eyes were turned up to him except hers, which were upon her muff; only her bonnet and the fair curls under it were visible. Yet it seemed to him that when he looked away her head came up again. She had changed somehow since she went away. She appealed to him strongly, for she was, he now perceived, not merely pretty and gentle, but also strong and good. Since their talk in the kitchen he had been thinking of her a good deal, and found himself very sorry indeed that she was not staying longer in Haworth.

"I saw you making eyes at Anne in church, you rogue," whispered Charlotte gaily as they walked home in a party. "Have you appointed her your next victim? If so, you would rob the cradle. Shall I invite Ellen back to tempt your fickle eyes away from my little sister?"

Once, Willie would have accepted all this teasing in the superficial way it was offered, but now he frowned and moved away from Charlotte. She had displeased him. Obscurely he felt that she should have reached out of her own preoccupations, however strong they were, to understand something about himself—about Anne—which was above banter. But he did not know what it was, or if it was really anything.

PART IV

The Passionate Years

1842–48

PROTESTANTS
ABROAD

*T*HE JOURNEY FROM HAWORTH TO Brussels was so exciting that even Emily forgot to pine for Anne, and Branwell was only a ghost at the back of Charlotte's mind; the soul mate for whom she would once have been storing up all these ecstatic impressions was for the moment forgotten.

Her first glimpse of London, unlike his, fulfilled all her childhood dreams. They had three glorious days there before they had to take ship to Belgium. The weather was cold—what of that? Mary, who was with them, and her brother Joe, seasoned and almost blasé travelers both, shivered and begged to remain indoors. But Charlotte was having none of that. As early as ever breakfast could be finished with the morning after their twelve-hour train journey, she was hustling them all out into the raw and blustery streets and shepherding them relentlessly off to see the sights.

For all the hours of daylight Charlotte forgot everything—including, to Joe's particular dismay, the dinner hour—in her delight at the beauties of the great city. St. Paul's had to be explored literally from top to bottom, and then, without so much as a five-minute sit-down in a pew, she had them almost running through the streets to the Royal Academy, the National Gallery and as many others, great and small, as she had time and strength for.

"Enough!" cried Mary, after two exhausting days of this. "I have seen so many pictures and statues and churches and views that my brain is stuffed to capacity. Not one more image will enter there. Tomorrow I shall stay in the inn with eyes closed, digesting all this rich fare, or I shall break out in a rash, and each pimple will spring up in the form of an Elgin Marble!"

Papa had fallen by the wayside the day before, and since he would not hear of his daughters wandering the streets of London unescorted, Joe, though begging for mercy, could not be let off. For one day more he trailed after the indefatigable sight-seers, listening to their gasps and exclamations, being called in to adjudicate their frequent differences of opinion about various works of art; he endured his rumbling stomach and aching feet and marveled at the stamina of these two frail-looking girls.

At last his ordeal was over. On Saturday morning, the 12th of February, they boarded the Ostend packet. The girls were at first delighted with all the novel sights and sensations of sea-travel; but before the long voyage was over, Charlotte was prostrated with seasickness and Emily with the first onset of homesickness. Both arrived in Belgium in a state of depression quite as low as their former spirits had been high.

Seasickness departs and leaves no trace. But what Emily had felt had reminded her all too sharply of those crippling pangs that had beset her at Roe Head. That mustn't happen here. No disabling anguish could be tolerated. She had set herself a task—to learn. Learn she would, and nothing would stop her, certainly nothing that her will could stave off. She thought of Anne, left behind in her hated post at Thorp Green. Would Emily be weak when Anne was so strong? Whenever she felt her spirits sinking she would give herself a good shake, as her latest dog, Keeper, shook himself when emerging from a cold dip in the brook.

The school that they had settled on only after many anxious

letters of inquiry was called the Pensionnat Héger. It was under the direction of a married woman of that name whose husband was a professor at the adjacent boys' academy. They would only meet him at the end of the day.

Mme Héger, a plump, efficient, brisk little woman, handsome and well-groomed, was in the hall to greet them. She "took them over" from Papa, Mary and Joe (who bid them tender and encouraging farewells) and at once led them up to the dormitory, chatting brightly to enable them to get over their tears.

"I thought you would like to be together, and not too much mingled with the other girls," she said, indicating two curtained-off beds at the far end of the long room. "You are the eldest pupils in our school, and—may I mention it?—the only Protestants. Naturally this does not concern me, but you may find it adds a trifle to the inevitable difficulties of adjustment. Of course you need not attend mass or take any part in our religious life if you don't wish, but this might set you further apart from the others. It is to be considered."

Charlotte and Emily glanced at each other, and Charlotte spoke for both.

"We will not attend mass," she said. "But it would help our French to hear the ordinary religious instruction."

"Excellent. Well! You may have today to settle yourselves. You will meet my husband tonight. And tomorrow you will begin lessons." She smiled at them and touched their hands. "It is my hope you will be happy here and profit from our school."

After a few more friendly remarks, Mme Héger left them.

"It seems so strange, having a married woman running the school instead of maiden ladies," said Charlotte. "Did you notice that she is *enceinte*? It will make the atmosphere very different, to have a family at the heart of the establishment."

"It's healthier," said Emily. "Unmarried women grow strange. We'll find that out for ourselves, no doubt," she added drily.

"Nonsense," retorted Charlotte. "*I* shall not 'grow strange,' as you call it, because I'm not spending my youth sitting about longing to be married. That is what causes the strangeness—

disappointed expectations. We shall fill our minds with tasks and accomplishments, and not strain after the impossible." She looked about her. "To think! In a little while this room, the school, and the whole city will be as familiar to us as home! It's like a miracle . . ."

Emily paused in her methodical unpacking. "What's that uproar downstairs?"

They both listened. The long, low building, which had been gently vibrating with the muted murmur of study when they first arrived, was now resounding with noise. They hurried down. The hall, formerly quiet and empty, was filled with a turbulent mass of girls, all seemingly shouting at the tops of their voices, running about, waving their arms and uttering raucous yells of laughter. The contrast between this unbridled scene and the decorous conduct taken for granted at Roe Head and Law Hill was stunning to the newcomers. These wild creatures seemed to know no rule, no restraint; dinner was ready, they were hungry and they romped tableward like a herd of newly-liberated wild ponies.

Suddenly, above the commotion there was a roar. In the ensuing silence, all eyes swung to the garden door, where a short, stocky, black-haired, red-faced man was standing with both fists raised to shoulder height. The roar had emanated from him, and was now succeeded by another.

"*Silence, mes élèves!* Have you all lost your faculties of self-control? You are not starving! Your food will not vanish before you can reach the *réfectoire!* Calm. Order. Discipline. Form pairs! SILENCE! That is better. Now. In ABSOLUTE QUIET—NOT ONE SOUND, not even a footfall—forward!"

A long, subdued line wound through into the dining room. A few stifled giggles and mischievous looks were exchanged, but otherwise the sturdy little figure, now with its arms sternly folded, was given no cause for a further tirade. When the last pair had gone, he unfolded his arms, the frown vanishing from his face as he turned to greet the newcomers, who had been standing open-mouthed on the stairs before these uninhibited proceedings.

"Mesdemoiselles," he said, greeting them with a slight bow and, to the astonishment of each, a kiss on the fingertips. "You are welcome. Excuse my outburst. Pardon our unruly tribe. Could such an uproar occur in any seminary in England? Do not shame us by answering. Perhaps your sedate and dignified presence may have a subduing influence upon our little Belgian savages. Come, you must be hungry."

With that M. Héger—for it was he, having come back at the dinner hour to meet them—led them into the dining room and onto a dais from which, after roaring again for silence, he addressed the school in his rapid French.

"I present our new young ladies from England. Their French is as yet negligible. You will treat them with kindness but you will not reduce the rate of your speech with them, or they will never learn to comprehend normal conversation. Miss Charlotte and Miss Emily Brontë."

Being the captive focus of so much unwanted attention reduced both of them to a state of shyness painful beyond belief. Their hands met and gripped and they shrank into themselves. Several of the Belgian girls sniggered openly.

"*Chut! Déportement!* You may continue your meal."

Later, the sisters attended their first *lecture pieuse.* This lengthy reading from a religious work was a regular feature of the evening routine. Charlotte had been stung by M. Héger's dismissive remarks about her French. Yet now she began to realize, as the quick flow of foreign sentences flooded her ears, what a long, hard road she had to travel. The thought invigorated her, and she sat motionless, straining every faculty. She was concentrating so hard that she jumped when Emily touched her at the end and whispered, "The basis of this popish doctrine of confession seems to be that you can do what you like providing you are penitent afterward. Just imagine emptying your heart to some greasy, garlic-breathing old priest! I shall have hard work to keep my countenance if we have to hear too much of this sort."

"We shouldn't form judgments too quickly," Charlotte whispered back primly. But she was taken aback. Alone, without a teacher, her book propped before her while her hands pounded bread dough in the parsonage kitchen, this extraordinary sister of hers had achieved a higher standard of French than she had herself.

Charlotte's laudable intention of reserving judgment on Catholicism lasted less than a week.

They had arrived on a Tuesday. By Sunday Charlotte had determined that she would not avoid mass or any other opportunity of improving her French. A girl coming to England to study English, she felt, could do no better than listen to her own father's sermons, or follow, however imperfectly, the exquisite liturgical language of the church service. Leaving Emily, who would have none of it, Charlotte repaired to the glorious church of St. Michel and Ste. Gudule; its warm, sonorous bell had awakened her that morning and helped overcome her Protestant scruples.

Seated with the other pupils, Charlotte covertly watched the remote, grandly-dressed priest perform his office. To her eyes, accustomed to a simple white surplice worn over plain black clerical garb, not to mention the humble interior of Haworth church, whose stained windows and vases of fresh flowers on festivals were its only adornments, the priest looked like a gaudily-carapaced beetle and the great church itself like a cave of idols. She was shocked to notice that the priest seemed unaware of the existence of his flock, and when (after several minutes of wondering if her ears were deceiving her) she realized that the entire mass was in Latin, she was ready to get up and walk out in disgust. However, inhibition held her till the end.

"Well?" asked Emily, looking up as her sister returned. Charlotte was still red-faced from indignation and the feeling that she had betrayed her faith for nothing.

"Never again," she said shortly.

Emily grunted and returned to her studies.

Emily was homesick, but she did not allow it to lay her low as before. She knew it was out of the question to return home; this would not only throw Aunt's generosity in her face, but would render Emily unfit to contribute to the project of their school. So she suppressed her feelings as far as she could, by imposing on herself a regime of continual hard labor.

One negative result of the suppression Emily exercised over her longing for home was that it tended to make her more contentious and intolerant than usual. Even more than Charlotte, she had conceived a detestation of Catholicism that she took no trouble to hide, uttering snorts of contempt during the more outrageous passages in divinity classes or the *lectures pieuses.*

"To think of believing that if you pay enough to the priest, your loved ones will escape the sooner from purgatory! Can God be bribed? Is He mollified to see his priests living in luxury, swathed in embroidered silks and reeking of pagan incense? What became of the concept of Jesus as a man of the poor, not to mention St. Francis and St. Clare? They see no inconsistency in holding these up as ideals, while accepting a creed whose whole basis is mercenary."

Many of the teachers, especially the women, came in for Emily's private scorn. But there was one teacher whom she did respect, and that was M. Héger. Most of his days were spent across the gardens in the boys' school, but for several periods a week he would return to teach French in his wife's establishment. Then the entire school would stiffen, catch its breath and prepare, on pain of frightful consequences, to give its best.

The lessons taught by this fierce-faced little dark man, with his thunderous frown, wild sudden movements and drill-sergeant bellow, were the most exciting and rewarding to both Emily and Charlotte—and not only because during them there were no inattentive fellow pupils to distract them. They enjoyed these sessions because the man was a born teacher; because he demanded their utmost and gave the like to them; and last but not least, because despite his unprepossessing appearance he was very much a man, and every girl in the school knew it.

Though he saw relatively little of his wife's pupils, and appeared to take no special notice of any, in reality he knew each of them: her potential, her personality, her performance had all been assessed, and in truth very few of them seemed to him worth bothering about. But it was not many weeks before he realized that these two English pupils, Protestants or not, were something special. He was particularly impressed with Emily. The efforts she was making would have gained his admiration even if they had not shown exceptional results, for he put a high premium on sheer dynamic energy and discipline—these were his own specialties.

Perversely, he would tease her.

"Why do you work so hard, Mees Emily? Why can you never be lazy like your fellows? Are not ignorance and idleness natural to young girls? I appeal to you! Do not disturb my fixed idea of the proper order of things! Horses work. Girls do not. Perhaps you are a horse in disguise?" And he would stoop to peer into the face she had bent over her book to hide her tight, cryptic smile.

But they did not always get on.

After a short time, M. Héger saw that for once he had high-quality minds entrusted to him, and he grew excited by the possibility of doing some real teaching. He began to give the Brontë sisters private lessons. For these he devised a new system. He would not oblige them to memorize grammatical rules or vocabulary lists—that was for children. Instead he proposed to read them excerpts from the writings of great French men of letters, lecture them on style and content (in French, of course) and then demand of them original compositions in the same style, forbidding them—a demonic twist, this—the use of grammar texts or dictionaries.

When, rubbing his hands and chuckling with pleasure at his own cleverness, he had outlined this plan to them, he asked them quite rhetorically how it struck them.

Charlotte opened her mouth to give her accord—she was so much in thrall to the man as a teacher that she automatically agreed with him on everything—when Emily at her side said flatly, "I see no good in it at all."

The little man's smile slid off his face. He gazed at Emily for a moment in blank amazement, and then his black brows slowly and ominously drew together.

"And what, pray, do you find to object to in it?"

"If we are to copy other people's style, how shall we form our own? At best we can only achieve the status of mediocre imitations. It is far better to study how we may express our own original thoughts and concepts in good French."

There was a moment's deathly silence. Then the strong, short arms rose slowly to shoulder height, fists clenched. The sallow face turned a choleric crimson, and the lips, rich with Gallic sensuality, curled back from the little white doggy teeth.

"So! You know better, do you? You are too proud to follow in the footsteps of French masters! You must needs pursue an *original* course! Original, indeed! And what great 'thoughts and concepts' may we look to see from a young woman who until five weeks ago had never set foot outside her native village, never been exposed to greatness in any form? So soon she has decided she can do without models, models which the greatest writers of our times are not ashamed to pattern themselves upon? In your execrable French you dare to wish to express your stupid, uncultivated *little, little, little* thoughts—" With every repetition he hammered on her desk with his fist, bending over her with his furious face thrust right into hers.

Emily for her part sat straight and still, staring ahead of her unblinkingly. Only Charlotte saw from the tenseness of her jaw how she was clenching her teeth to hold herself in her posture of apparent indifference. They had very often seen M. Héger in a rage before—he raged daily, as other men take regular physical exercise—but his fury had never before been directed at either of them. Charlotte was so upset she burst into tears, and this brought the furious little man up short.

Crouched over Emily, his head swiveled on his neck toward Charlotte.

"*Ciel!* What might be the matter with this one? Have you also something to say against my program?"

Charlotte, hiding her eyes, shook her head.

"She is upset on my account, Monsieur," said Emily calmly. "I believe she thought you were about to devour me."

He turned back to Emily, his color rising once again.

"And so I may, Mees! And so I may! I am not accustomed to have my teaching methods criticized! If you do not like my plan, you may go back to your Yorkshire with its peasants and its puddings and leave higher learning to those blessed with greater humility! Oh stop, stop, stop!" he added to Charlotte. "Have you no handkerchief? Take mine. Calm, calm, be calm, I cannot tolerate this loss of self-control!"

Of course in the end they followed M. Héger's plan, and although Emily sighed and groaned and gave other tacit indications of rebellion—enough to keep the professor perpetually on the brink of fury and herself satisfied in her own *amour propre*— the improvement that shortly appeared in their *devoirs* was enough to justify his unorthodox methods. At the same time, he was forced to acknowledge that a certain style of her own *was* apparent in Emily's writing, and in Charlotte's as well.

"They are extraordinary, these English girls," he said to his wife as they sat outside in the sunny gardens behind the school on a Sunday with their little brood of children playing around them. Madame expected her confinement at any time and consequently had not seen much of the new pupils. "They have something. They have what is very rare, ideas, a vision entirely their own. When I assign a *devoir* with freedom of subject, they choose, not the easiest like all the others, but something—some new approach, some unusual view. The mistakes in language become all the more galling because they break the flow, the enjoyment of reading. Such imagination! Such fire! We did well when we made financial concessions to accept them. I predict they will do more credit to our school than all the rest put together."

"And do you tell them anything of this?" asked his wife with a smile.

"Tell them? That would be madness! To fill their heads with conceit? Why, my dearest, will you believe that even Charlotte, who seems so modest, so humble and grateful for any help I give her, even she has buried inside her an opinion of her talents that I suspect needs no praise from me to inflate it? No. Rather I abuse and drive them. Charlotte no longer breaks into tears when I am stern with her. I understand her. And by now she begins to understand me."

"And is she in love with you, like all the others?"

" 'The others' are little, silly, frivolous children, with nothing in their heads but romance and nonsense. These are young women with intellectual ambition. They have no more time for such idiocies than I have."

"Well, I am glad. They are nice girls. I would not want to see their hearts broken by my bullying but very magnetic husband," said Madame fondly, stroking his small hirsute hand.

At the beginning of April, the girls received a shock.

It came in a letter from Papa that was couched in such evasive terms that Charlotte had to read it twice before she hurried to find Emily.

"Emily! I fear something bad has happened with Branwell. Papa does not precisely say why, but he is home again, and in a sad state, apparently. Why should he have left his post? Can he have been dismissed?"

"Very likely," said Emily shortly. She took the letter from Charlotte and read it. "I fear he has really done something disgraceful this time."

"But you are not shocked."

"What's the use? Nothing people do really shocks me. Of course it's painful, but—"

"Painful!" Charlotte felt abruptly washed with pain. Branwell's suffering face as she had last seen it returned to her, and in guilty anguish she marveled how she had managed to turn her back on the evidence of his misery to pursue her own course so selfishly. Had she been able to forget how much she loved him? If so, she remembered now. All their closeness, all their intimate sharing, their creative adventures together and their unfailing support for each other rushed back upon her so that her behavior during his last visit seemed wholly incomprehensible to her. Perhaps her lack of sympathy had been responsible for pushing him— or allowing him to slip—into whatever ugly scrape had now resulted in his dismissal from his post? Emily was watching her.

"Now don't you begin abusing yourself; that won't help," she said. "Branwell's nearly twenty-five, you know, you can't be his nursemaid forever. If he's destined to fail, he'll fail, and all we can do is not make things worse for him by being his judges. Write him a nice letter to cheer him up, and then you must put his problems aside for the moment and get on with matters here."

But Charlotte couldn't write "a nice letter." When she tried, something fundamental in her character got in the way. The letter became critical; questions crept in and priggish urgings to amend. She felt it was wrong to pander to his vanity, to let him feel that no matter how he behaved or what he did he would be rewarded by the same love and devotion that would be his due if he did well. She *did* love him, and yet the thought of what his dismissal must have meant to Papa gnawed at that love and left ragged holes in it. In the end she threw the letter away and said to Emily:

"You must write. I cannot."

Emily sighed. "Poor Branwell," she said.

2

BACK FROM
THE DARK

ILLIE WEIGHTMAN KEPT HIS word to Anne. When Branwell came crawling back from Luddenden Foot in a state of nervous and emotional collapse, he came almost daily to visit and talk to him. But it was Aunt Branwell who really took him in hand, who bore the heaviest burden of nursing him, body, soul and ego, back to something like health.

Patrick felt powerless under the crushing weight of his shame and disappointment. He kept away as much as he decently could from the bedroom in which his son lay, a flaccid, white-faced wreck, and to salve his conscience redoubled his work among his parishioners.

But Aunt, equally old, equally—or almost equally—disillusioned, and by no means in perfect health herself, now called upon the full reserve of spiritual power she had built up in herself through a life of quiet discipline, self-denial and good works. Without fuss, without visible signs of distress, and without ever once uttering a word of reproach, the old lady set to work to mend her nephew.

At first he would moan endlessly whenever she entered his room:

"Aunt—how can you trouble yourself about me—why don't you cast me off like the rest—you are so good—don't soil your hands with such a wretch as I am . . ."

In truth he both longed for and dreaded her strictures, but they never came. Instead she treated him more tenderly and less severely than ever she had when he was a child.

"Come, my dear, drink up this beef tea, it will bring back your strength."

Pettishly he would turn his head away. "I don't want it. Let me just waste away and die, that's what I deserve . . ."

"My dear boy, you wouldn't distress me by dying! Come. To please Aunt."

She never offered to pray with him, and her prayers *for* him were said upon her knees in the privacy of her own room. If he had not learned lessons from life, she had.

"You've changed, Aunt. You used to be so strict. Now when I have been really wicked, you don't abuse me."

"Don't you think I can see that you are getting enough abuse from yourself? You are not lost yet, Branwell. There now! Do you hear Mr. Weightman knocking at the door? Would he come to see you so often if he thought you beyond hope? Come, sit yourself up, there's a good boy, and try to put a smile on to match his."

And somehow Willie's smiles were indeed so nourishing in their warmth that Branwell could not stay wholly swamped in misery while his visits lasted. But when he had gone and Branwell lay alone, the pressure of guilt was renewed. Would Willie treat him so kindly, so matter-of-factly, if he knew—? At last, after a month, when Branwell, thanks to total enforced abstinence, and to Aunt's practical ministrations, was becoming stronger, he resolved to test Willie.

"You're my dearest friend at present," he began, "but you're also a minister. Usually you let me forget that side of you. Now I would have you forget the friendship and look upon me as a—a sinner."

Willie said nothing, but gazed at him with his large, gentle eyes.

"You know why I was dismissed from the railway?"

"Some trouble over money, wasn't it?"

"I know Papa must have told you."

"He has been vague. I gathered only that you were taken to task for absenting yourself too often from your post, allowing your porter occasion to help himself from the till."

Tears came into Branwell's eyes. After a lengthy struggle with himself he muttered shakily, "I took most of it."

If Willie was shocked, he did not show it. After a moment he took Branwell's hand in both his, as kindly as a father.

"Why then you must pay it back."

"It is paid back. They took it out of my salary."

"Why did you need it?"

"To drink. To escape." His voice dropped to a whisper. "To buy drugs."

"Was it so bad for you there?"

Branwell looked up almost eagerly. "Awful, Willie! You can't conceive of it. I was separated from all that mattered to me, condemned to a life of boredom and drudgery, with such a sense of failure as can't be described. I was never meant for such an existence, nothing had prepared me for it! Oh, if you knew what expectations I grew up with, what convictions of my own bright future were implanted in me! Sometimes I prayed that the great black cliff-brow overhanging the station would fall and crush me to dust, I was so unhappy."

"Branwell, you've paid your debt. As to the sinfulness, God forgives all who are truly penitent, as anyone can see you are. Tell me, is it hard for you to be without the stimulants you are used to?"

"It was at first. Now I must say I feel better for it."

"Then you must not on any account go back to them. You must start afresh. I'll help you."

Branwell clutched Willie's hand and sobbed.

"You're too good to me—"

"Nonsense. I'm very fond of you, old fellow. We all are."

Branwell was silent, trying to get control of himself. But after a while he choked out, "Charlotte—no longer loves me."

"What makes you say so?"

"I know it. She has lost faith in me."

"Then we must work to give it back to her."

Five weeks after his return home, Branwell was up and about again. He found it just possible to face out his disgrace in the village, since no one but Willie knew the true depths of it. At Willie's urging he began to do a bit of "scribbling," and as usual, lost some of his grief by losing himself briefly in creativeness. This, he told himself, was the better escape. He mustered strength to renew his pledges to himself, reinforced by repeating them solemnly to his friend, that he would lead a new life, with no more backsliding.

A small, long-desired triumph went a long way to help him in his resolve. He had two sonnets accepted and published in a Halifax newspaper. His elation at seeing his poetry printed was so great that his family and friends were reminded of the old Branwell as he rushed around the house and village, almost crowing with childlike pleasure.

In the evening he visited Willie in his lodgings, and showed him the first sonnet. Willie read it attentively, and then looked up with his warmest smile.

"Well done, Branwell! It's first-class. You see? And this is just the beginning, of that I'm certain."

Branwell stood before him breathing fast, his hands on his hips and his bright hair on end, the picture of untrammeled youthful exuberance.

"Just the beginning!" he echoed. "Do you see that I have signed it 'Northangerland'? That is my *nom de plume*; it will carry me to fortune! I always knew the old devil would bring me luck one day!"

In June, Anne came home for a short holiday.

She was bearing up very well under the trials of working for the Robinsons. She still disapproved of her employers, but she felt she was making some headway into the respect and even affections of all three of their daughters, especially Mary, who was devoted to her. Lydie was more flighty and callous than ever, and Eliza was only reluctantly modifying from tomboy into something recognizable as a young lady of fashion, but they were both fond of their governess in a careless way and she could occasionally influence them.

"The main trouble," she confided to Branwell, "is Edmund. His parents still insist that I must somehow bludgeon some Latin into his head, but when I try he sits there, mute and mutinous, and will have none of me. He wants a tutor."

Branwell pricked up his ears.

"Is it very awful, living there?"

"Oh, no, not really, now I'm used to it."

"Does one feel like their slave? Do they degrade one with their snobbery?"

"A little, at times. One has to have other resources. I am writing a lot, and that helps."

"What are you writing?"

"Oh . . . I call it *Passages in the Life of an Individual*. It's about myself really. When Emily's with me we always play at Gondal, but when she's not I confess I take a rest from all our rascals and treat of subjects closer to home." Anne's "journal" was more than simply a diary of day-to-day events. She hoped, sometime, to fashion it into some particular shape—perhaps even a novel.

A few days later, Branwell said casually, "You know, I might be persuaded to become tutor to that young scoundrel."

"Might you, Branwell? Well! It's worth considering."

"Do you think they would have me?" he asked, his voice betraying anxiety.

"I could write and ask them."

"Would you?" And now it was plain that he had been thinking about little else and was extremely eager. Anne smiled to herself. So far all was going according to plan . . . a plan she'd been hatching ever since he had lost his position. She longed to help him; but she had waited to see how he looked and behaved, for she was not prepared to risk her own situation by putting forward a brother who was dissolute or unreliable. But Branwell looked better than he had for some time, and she thought it might answer.

After due discussion, she wrote to Mrs. Robinson. Her letter was nicely balanced between a reasoned setting-out of his qualifications, and a desire to help spare Mrs. Robinson the tiresome task of looking for a tutor. Branwell was speedily engaged. But the family was going on holiday to Scarborough as usual, and he would not be wanted till late autumn. So Anne had to leave home first.

Willie came to say good-bye to her. She was in the kitchen kissing Martha and Hannah Brown when she heard his knock.

"Martha, that is Mr. Weightman. Run and ask him to step through."

"To the kitchen, miss?"

"He's not the sort to mind, Martha."

Willie came in, ducking his head under the lintel. His hat was in his hand and his curls were windblown.

"You'll have a blowy ride of it to the station," he said.

"If my hair curled as yours does, it would not matter," she said with forced gaiety.

"Don't *you* tease me, Miss Anne! I put up with it from your sister, but from your lips I expect only serious remarks."

"Then I will make one," she said, her heart thundering. "Your goodness to Branwell exceeds everything. I believe you've saved his life, or helped to do so, and if his luck turns now we shall have you to thank."

He seemed about to protest, then took a different tack. He bowed and said lightly, "I can't imagine saving a life I like better. Unless it should ever be my good fortune to save yours."

Martha had already taken herself off into the back kitchen. Now Hannah broke into giggles and ran out there, too. Tabby alone sat on in her rocking chair. The two young people stood for a moment in silence, and then Anne put out her hand to him.

"I must go."

"I have missed you. And now I must miss you again."

He held her small hand in both his and suddenly kissed it.

"Till Christmas," he said.

She smiled as he let her go. *Good-bye, my heart's own love,* she thought. And as she drove away, turning back to wave to them all as they stood in the lane, she felt a happiness, a hope as sharp as pain. *It could happen. It could!*

Branwell redeemed; Scarborough—beautiful, revivifying Scarborough—just ahead; Charlotte and Emily due home soon, and the prospect of starting their school growing brighter. And now this: this jeweled moment to carry away with her to shine through any incidental hour of loneliness.

No wonder that when she arrived at Thorp Green late that night, Lydie remarked "Just look at our Miss Brontë! I declare she looks almost pretty with those bright eyes!" But nothing mattered to Anne, who went to bed as happy as she had ever been in her life.

3
BAD NEWS

CHARLOTTE AND EMILY WERE due home at the end of the summer when their half was over. But M. Héger was not prepared to part so soon with these two most rewarding pupils.

The progress they had made was astonishing, and his satisfaction commensurate with it. True, Emily was troublesome; but in a way this was no great disadvantage—the fiery little professor rather enjoyed the battles with such a worthy adversary. Charlotte, by contrast, was gentle and compliant, and he grew extremely fond of her, even softening to the extent of occasionally praising her work for the pleasure of seeing her austere little face break into one of its redeeming smiles. To both girls he freely gave of his time and of his very considerable didactic talent. In a word, he had invested in them. There must, he decided, be no question of their leaving so soon.

He said as much to his wife. She, having recently produced her first son, was in such a euphoric state that she would have agreed to anything; she cheerfully proposed to Charlotte and Emily that they write to their father and request an extension to the end of the year. If money was a problem, Madame would dismiss her English teacher and Charlotte could take his place as payment for lodging and tuition, while Emily could give piano lessons.

Charlotte was overjoyed. Six months of intellectual fulfillment and a quite extraordinary happiness had made the thought of leaving Brussels intolerable. Now she saw that she would not have to go, her exultation could barely be restrained until she had Emily alone.

As a mark of favor, the *"allée défendue,"* an avenue of trees on the grounds, had been put in bounds to them, and it had become their favorite place. They often strolled there under the arch of acadia leaves, or sat in the little arbors formed around benches by the trimmed hedge, which gave them a feeling of privacy. Now Charlotte lost no time in dragging Emily off there to pour out her delight that M. Héger (she knew the idea must originate with him) wanted to keep them on. This aspect was by no means the least important to her.

It took her some time to notice how unresponsive Emily was.

"What is it, Emily? Surely you are pleased!"

"Pleased!" Emily burst out. "I have had nothing to keep me going for these months but the thought of going home at the end of them."

"But—you've never said a word!"

"Did you think I *liked* it here? Among all these barbarians and heretics? Studying in a class of undisciplined hoydens, going to church with those overblown roses from the English community, being shouted and screamed at by that little male virago, that hysterical hyena, that—that—"

"Emily—!"

"Oh, the man can teach, I won't deny it. But he is abominable for all that—foul-tempered, ill-mannered—and furthermore his breath reeks of garlic and French cigars. I've had quite enough of him, and of Madame, too."

"Madame? But she's been so kind to us!"

"And will continue to be so, no doubt, as long as we keep her lord shouting at us, leaving no spleen over for her. But I wouldn't care to get on the wrong side of her, nor have her jealous of me. If we stay on, and Monsieur continues to devote so much of his free time to us, I think a quite different side of her character may show itself."

"You can't mean she might think that he—"

"Oh, not that, of course not—though these Belgian women with their prurient Catholic mentalities might sink to any evil thoughts. But we are his favorites. The other girls detest us for it already, and even the female teachers sniff and whisper about us. Really, their behavior in general is disgusting! No English-woman could lower herself to show her baser feelings so un-ashamedly. If you ask me, they are one and all in love with the mad little black monster, and would eat us alive if they could, just because he spends time with us." She heaved a huge sigh. "Oh, never mind! If we must stay another half, then we must. I shall put on my horse mask and toil on—I dare say I shall survive somehow. But do *not* expect me to share your rapture that we shall not see our family or the moors, or my hawk or my dog, nor do anything that counts, for six more months to come."

Martha and Mary took Charlotte's part, of course. Martha was at school just outside Brussels, in a much grander establishment called the Château Koekelberg, and Mary often stayed there with her. They were almost the only friends Charlotte and Emily had in Brussels. Other English families had done their best to be-friend them, but it was such agony trying to break through their shyness that the attempt was generally given up.

But alone with Mary and Martha in the spacious, peaceful grounds of the Château, they could relax and be themselves. There they fought out their battle all over again while the Taylor sisters sat by, urging Charlotte on and heaping derision on poor Emily.

"Of *course* you must stay, what folly to think of any other course!" exclaimed Mary. "What does it *matter* how Monsieur shouts or what noxious fumes he breathes over you? Why should you care how badly our expatriate countrywomen dress at church, or whether the teachers lack principle and dignity? You are *learn-ing*, Emily—learning from a truly great teacher! And you are seeing life. How can you talk of burying yourself in heather one moment before you must?"

Emily was silent for a while. Then she said:

"All these irritations are petty, I don't really care about them. But you don't know how I long for home. When you mention heather, at once I'm overcome by such a gnawing hunger for the moors that I am struck breathless." To lie on her back in the heather and watch the racing clouds through the stiff, budding strands, to taste the ling berries, to hear the rustle of Keeper leaping through the grass . . . "Oh God! I mustn't think of it. I shall go mad from wanting it—"

She hid her suddenly overflowing eyes in her hands. The other three exchanged looks of awe and anxiety. It was Martha who scrambled to hug her, saying:

"Now, Emily darling, don't cry. Oh, we are wretches to upset you! Nevertheless, you must stay. How would Charlotte go on among the barbarians without you?"

So they wrote to Papa and explained, and he readily agreed to their staying on, though he felt himself aging and it was a sacrifice to go on doing without them. Still, it was amazing how Elizabeth still ran the house to his satisfaction with so little help. Tabby was back, but the poor old woman was very lame and going deaf as well. Miss Branwell had another virtue in Patrick's eyes: she could manage Branwell. These two were now close as never before, and Patrick watched in some amazement as the boy sat and read to his aunt in the long summer evenings, even after tramping the moors with Willie, Keeper and the guns.

One day he returned hangdog from such an expedition. Two fat rabbits and a brace of partridge dangled from his hands, but from his expression Patrick knew at once that something had happened.

"I have lost Hero, Papa," he muttered at last. Hero was Emily's hawk.

"You have *what*?" cried the old man in dismay.

"I wanted to see if he could be trained to hunt like a falcon, and—"

"Oh, Branwell! How could you be so foolish! What are we to tell Emily?"

"Thank the Lord she is not returning yet after all. Perhaps she will have forgotten him by Christmas."

Patrick shook his head. Even in small ways, Branwell continually let him down. He had no way of knowing that it was Northangerland who had gone "hawking" and needed a live prop for his noble sport.

Willie had not been with him or it would never have happened. Branwell blamed his friend in his heart for having considered his parish duties more important that day than accompanying him, and hence allowing this disaster to overtake him— just when his conscience was beginning to quiet down a little. That evening Branwell walked over to Willie's lodgings, meaning to confess to him, at the same time laying some of the blame at his door. But his landlady met him on the stairs and gripped his arm.

"Oh, Mr. Brontë, I'm glad tha's come! Mr. Weightman is took that poorly, I'm afeard for him! I sent for t' doctor an hour since, but he's never come yet—perhaps you'd run and tell him fever's higher and would he please to make haste? There's cholera going round t' village, tha knows, and Mr. Weightman never troubles about his own safety when he's visitin' the sick . . ."

Anne went about her business the whole of that September day, with the letter unopened in her pocket.

She often did this, unwilling to spoil, by the annoyance of Lydie's teasing or Eliza's peeping over her shoulder, the pleasure of news from home. It was better to save it up for evening, and then, when her work was done and the girls gone off to some party, to slip out onto the twilit lawn and read and reread at leisure, surrounded by the sweet-scented garden and the last bursts of birdsong.

Thus she held onto her hopes and her happiness for some eight or ten hours longer than she might have done.

When she read, in the opening words of Branwell's letter, that Willie was dead, her eyes went on following the meaningless pattern of ink on the paper for several seconds. Then they stopped, and she sat still, enveloped in a merciful but temporary numbness. After some time she looked up. Nothing had changed yet. The green lawn, smooth-cut as richly napped cloth, stretched away toward the river; the treetops rustled gently; the red brick of the great house glowed in the last of the sunset. Quite soon it would be dark. All this would gradually disappear, and by the time the sun rose again tomorrow morning, Anne knew that none of it would look the same to her. Its peaceful beauty—her one solace and delight during all the weary months she had labored in this place—would be forever marred and spoiled. She would never look at it again without remembering this moment when all her hopes ended. She sat there without moving until the darkness and silence closed in on her, holding the letter in her hands, waiting for the misery to begin. A misery that could not be shared with anyone. Ever.

The news came as a blow to Charlotte and Emily, too, when it reached them later in the month. They gave no special thought to its effect on Anne. They assumed that she and Branwell would be as grieved as they were, no more, no less.

They carried their sorrow to Koekelberg to share with the Taylors.

"*Willie* dead?" was Martha's incredulous reaction. "If Willie can die, then we are none of us safe!"

Both schools had restarted for the autumn term, and the Brontës didn't visit the Taylors again for several weeks.

One evening in early October, Charlotte, studying in the long *salle de classe* overlooking the garden of the Pensionnat, was interrupted by one of the servants.

"*Un message vient d'arriver pour vous.*"

It was from Mary, a brief scrawl. Martha was ill—would they come?

They could not go that evening. Madame never gave permission to leave the school at night. In any case, neither of them thought there was any special hurry. The next day was Thursday, their weekly half-holiday. They would walk over to Koekelberg after lunch and take Martha some flowers to cheer her up.

They arrived at the *pension* where the English girls lived just after two. The place was very quiet, as always at that hour; but as soon as Emily stepped inside and felt the cool darkness of the stone hall, she said at once:

"Something has happened."

They went straight up to Martha's room, which Mary shared when she was in Brussels. They knocked, and Mary's voice said clearly, "Come in."

Charlotte noticed nothing strange about the voice and put her hand on the latch, but Emily said in a sharp undertone:

"Martha's dead."

"*What?*"

"She's dead. Prepare yourself."

Charlotte stared at her, aghast. The door of the room opened and Mary stood there. Charlotte turned to look at her, and at once the apprehension changed into ghastly certainty.

"Martha died last night at ten o'clock, two hours after I wrote to you. She'd been ill for over a week. They didn't know what it was at first. They said it was just a mild attack of low fever. Then she took a turn for the worse yesterday, and they told me it was cholera."

"Cholera! The same that killed—"

"Yes, I thought of that, after what she said . . . Come in and look at her—otherwise you will never be able to believe it . . . ."

They stared down at Martha's corpse, clumsily laid out by Mary but with a strange rictus on the lips that she had not been able to make smooth. It didn't look like Martha, so the sight hardly helped lessen Charlotte's absolute incredulity.

"Was it a—did she die—peacefully?"

For the first time, Mary's voice betrayed her.

"No."

Charlotte turned to her in horror.

"You can't mean she suffered? *Martha suffered?*"

"She suffered so much that I was glad when she died."

Charlotte began to tremble and cry. "Oh, my God—my God—"

"*God?*" exclaimed Emily harshly. "What's the use of calling upon Him? If He would not ease her pain, why should He comfort yours?"

They buried Martha in the Protestant cemetery beyond the bounds of the city. It was a long way. They walked together, the three of them, Charlotte weeping all the way, Emily stony-faced but leaning on Charlotte's shoulder as she often did, and Mary walking along quietly on her other side. Her eyes were fixed on the rough road over which, just ahead of them, the wheels of the funeral carriage creaked and grated.

The cemetery might have seemed a pleasant one in Belgian eyes, but to those accustomed to the rank grasses of an English churchyard, with its unflamboyant ivy trails and guardian yews, this sunny spot enlivened by wreaths of everlasting flowers and garish beaded bouquets could only seem alien.

"It seems so dreadful to leave her here, in this foreign place," Charlotte whispered. "I wish we could take her home!"

Mary watched the coffin being lowered into the ground. Charlotte clutched her hand convulsively, half expecting a sudden outburst of wild grief. But none came, then or later.

"She is better where she is," said Mary enigmatically.

They had barely accustomed themselves to their mourning clothes when a letter arrived from Papa to tell them Aunt had been taken very ill and they should return home immediately.

Charlotte was thrown into a state of hopeless confusion by this third blow within a month, but Emily took charge. She went directly to Mme Héger and told her that they would be setting off for England the next day. She packed for both of them. Charlotte, lying on her bed watching listlessly, was suddenly roused to say, "Why are you packing everything? Surely we shall be coming back!"

"You may be. I'm not."

The next day, just as they were preparing to leave, another letter arrived. Aunt was dead.

Charlotte uttered a cry, in which sorrow and relief were strangely mingled. "Perhaps now it is pointless to go at all!"

Emily looked at her, her eyes narrowed.

"Can you be serious?"

"The funeral must be already over! What is the sense—"

"You don't think Papa may need us?"

Charlotte was silent. "Anne will be there," she muttered at last.

"And so will we, just as soon as the packet can carry us. Afterward you may do as you please. For my part—" She looked about her, her scornful glance taking in the building, the grounds, the inmates, in fact the whole of Brussels. "I say good-bye to all this with a heart so light that even poor Aunt's death cannot wholly drag it down."

Charlotte went to Mme Héger's private quarters to bid good-bye to her and to the children. Monsieur was not there—he was teaching at the Athénée. As Charlotte kissed the three little girls, she felt a dragging ache begin, as if she were tied to this spot and would have to tear something within her to leave it.

"Will you bid your husband good-bye for us, Madame?"

"*Au revoir* only, *ma petite*, I trust. We don't want to lose you. He is most upset that you are leaving. Here is a letter he has written to your papa—such a letter as I think he will be proud to receive."

This was some comfort, but not much. Charlotte glanced around the little sitting room despairingly. If only he would appear! Just to take her hand and say a kind word to her, a word for her to carry on her unwilling journey. Oh, it was hard that Emily and she were so divided in this! How could she explain her deep reluctance to leave? She knew her duty to Papa demanded her return, and yet . . . Might not two of his daughters have been sufficient?

Anne had not gotten home in time for the funeral either. Mrs. Robinson had not let her go. Branwell had borne the brunt of it alone. With Charlotte he broke down and confided something of his ordeal.

"If anyone ever deserved an easy death, it was Aunt! Was there ever such a *good* woman? As I watched her sufferings, and heard her—not praying, not looking forward to her reward, only crying out for relief from pain—I kept asking myself, 'Where is God?' *Her* God, the one she put all her trust in, the one she sacrificed everything for. She died speechless, panting with agony . . ." He passed his hand briefly over his eyes, and then reached it out, wet, for Charlotte to take. "I went to church for the last time when we buried Willie. I shall never set foot there again."

Patrick sat in his study with his four children, apparently considering the proposition in M. Héger's letter which Charlotte had just translated for him, but inwardly in a state bordering on panic.

Elizabeth was dead. Willie, whom he had loved like a son and who, moreover, was the best curate he had ever had—dead. Anne was to return to Thorp Green immediately, and Branwell must follow in a few weeks. And here was this foreign professor urging him to yield up the other two for a further six months or a year. Old, going blind, in the poorest health, could he expect to live that long, abandoned by them all? He looked around at their misty shapes, and though he had endured much with patience and firmness, tears of self-pity and despair rose to his cataracted eyes.

"Well, my dears," he said shakily, groping for a handkerchief. "Do you hear? You must make your own decision."

Emily spoke up promptly.

"Charlotte may go when she wishes, Papa. I am determined to stay here."

In the act of wiping his eyes, all inclination to weep left him. He rose and embraced her. She could feel his trembling.

"My dear child! Are you sure?"

"Quite sure, Papa. Nothing would induce me to go back."

The others exchanged relieved looks. Charlotte, especially, had to subdue a sudden heart-leap of elation. Patrick was smiling broadly as if death and trouble had not touched them.

"Why, then all is settled! Things are not so bad after all. Charlotte must stay with us over Christmas, and then we go our ways. Emily, my dearest, we all thank you—"

"Never mind about that," said Emily. "I have something far more serious to speak of." She withdrew herself from her father's arms, stood up and glared around at them all.

"Where," she asked sternly, "is my hawk?"

4
CHARLOTTE
IN BRUSSELS

FTER A CHRISTMAS WHICH
under the shadow of still-fresh sorrows was as happy as could be
expected, they "went their ways."

Branwell set off to join Anne at Thorp Green, full of new courage and high determination to justify Anne's—and Aunt's—faith
in him. As ever, when under such an influence, he made a splendid impression. Any qualms Anne had felt about the wisdom of
getting him the post quickly faded.

He got on well with the recalcitrant Edmund, rejoiced in Mr.
Robinson's unclerical sporting pursuits, and charmed every female in the household. Mrs. Robinson took to him particularly,
and from the outset he was treated far more as one of the family
than the somewhat superior sort of servant that Anne was. Because of this, *her* status in the house improved. They couldn't
very well include Branwell, with his entertaining manners, in
their family gatherings or even invite him to their less grandiose
parties, without Anne; and to their ill-concealed amazement they
discovered that their quiet little governess did them no discredit.

At home, Emily settled down—like a homing bird on its roost

—to run the parsonage for her father. She was utterly happy and occupied, free as air to arrange her days as she wished without interference or restriction. Patrick even let her off teaching Sunday school when he saw she didn't want to.

Father and daughter got on together beautifully. She had all the domestic talents needed for his comfort, and although she was so reserved, with none of Charlotte's impulsive affection or Anne's willingness to put his wishes before her own, Patrick came to feel that Emily was more kin to him than any of them. She required privacy and thus respected his, never intruding on him, making no demands; yet she loved him, and could be companionable when he felt lonely. She even let him teach her to shoot, something he could hardly imagine doing with the others! She would drop everything to join him in a bout of pistol practice on the lawn, and with her steady aim and unblemished sight became a far better shot than he was, for he could hardly make out the target anymore.

"Not for nothing did poor Willie dub you 'The Major'!" the old man would exult, when she brought him the target for inspection.

So the three youngest Brontës passed that year in unusual tranquility. And Charlotte went back to Brussels.

On her journey she had a strange little adventure. She reached London so late at night that she felt it somehow impossible to present herself at an inn. Since she was due to sail the next morning, she took a cab from Euston Square straight to the dockside, and inquired where the packet lay. It was pointed out to her, lying off the quay, its lights reflected in bars on the oily water. The men she had spoken to were watching her, smirking. She turned to one of them, quivering but determined.

"I wish to go on board that packet. Can one of you row me out there?"

They exchanged looks, and one man laughed aloud. Charlotte went hot and cold. Was she mad? Why hadn't she gone to the inn? However embarrassing, nothing could be worse than this!

" 'Ow much?"

"Three shillings," she answered recklessly.

There was a scramble to oblige her after that, and soon she was seated in a rowboat being conveyed out across the inky river. She sat primly in the stern, her luggage at her feet, listening to the dip and splash of the oars. There was a numbness upon her, as if some outside force were compelling her; she was terrified, estranged from all she knew of herself—yet she was obliged to act out this impulse now to the end.

They came under the side of the vessel, and a voice from the blackness above shouted down, "What do you want?"

Charlotte stood up in the boat. "I am a passenger. I want to pass the night on board."

"We don't take no overnight passengers. Come back tomorrow."

"I have nowhere else to stay. Kindly call an officer."

After a lot of argument, they let her come aboard. She mounted a swaying ladder and was helped over the rail by grinning sailors. The officer led her to a stateroom below, and a steward brought her tea, which she was too tired to drink. She undressed and lay down on the hard, musty-smelling bunk.

But she was also, it seemed, too tired to sleep. Her restless mind began to prick her with questions. "Why did I do that? I've never done such a thing before—being so boldly insistent, obliging them to break their rules for me—it is most unlike me."

And then, and not till then, the voice of conscience suddenly spoke to her quite clearly:

"What are you about? Why haven't you inquired of yourself why you are so eager to return? Your duty lies behind you. Haven't you learned that an impulse such as you followed just now—an impulse so strong that you couldn't even wait till morning to advance your journey—is suspect? Yet you have not questioned it."

"I'm following my destined course. There is no wrong in it."

Nevertheless she passed a troubled night. But the next day was fully occupied with seasickness, through the torments of which no conscience, however alert, could inflict much punishment. And by nightfall she was back in the Pensionnat Héger.

Her welcome was so warm that all doubts fled. Madame em-

braced her and Monsieur almost did so, too. Even the despised
teachers gathered around to greet her, and one in particular, Mlle
Sophie, kissed her soundly and said, "Our school is itself again,
now we have our Charlotte back!"

"She is not 'our Charlotte' any longer," said M. Héger sternly.
"She returns to us on a new footing. Henceforth she will be
known as Mees or Mademoiselle Charlotte, since she is now a
mistress and not a pupil."

"Monsieur! But you will continue to teach me?" she cried in
dismay.

"No, Mees. *You* will teach *me*."

"I? You?"

"*Oui*. I and my brother-in-law, Monsieur Chapelle, wish to learn
English from you."

"And now that you are a fully-fledged member of the staff,
you must force yourself to take some liberties," said Madame
gaily. "You will sit with us at meals, of course, and in the evenings when you are at leisure you will use our sitting room so
that you shall not feel lonely, now your sister is no longer here
to keep you company."

Charlotte felt her soul expand with pleasure. They did like
her—they did appreciate her! *That is all I want! It is worth ten
times fifty pounds a year to be treated as an equal by such a man
and woman as this*, she thought joyfully.

The first weeks brought bitterly cold weather outside but much
warmth and comfort within. The Hégers showed Charlotte great
kindness. It was a joy to her to enter their family circle in the
evenings and sit by their fire, sewing and listening to their conversation. When one of their little daughters would climb on
her knee to beg a story, she was enchanted. She had never got
on well with young children; yet these seemed to catch their parents' fondness for her. She even loved to hold the baby, Prospère,
and once boldly set her spectacles on his tiny nose to show his
father how closely his son resembled him.

But she detested her regular lessons. The Belgian girls seemed
to her as coarse, boisterous and unbiddable as ever, and their

two-faced attitudes brought out the most lively contempt in her, for they were prim and pious at their devotions; worldly and selfish at all other times.

Her loathing of Romanism grew. It was a heavy item on the negative side of life in this place. The worst of it was that she could not reconcile M. Héger and his Catholicism. How could a man of intellectual integrity, who scorned bias, hypocrisy, and cant, still sink his soul in such a mire?

The English lessons she gave to him and M. Chapelle were the climax of her week, the hour she looked forward to and prepared for more carefully than for any other. At first she was overawed and could hardly teach for nervousness. Monsieur teased her unmercifully, calling her his cruel task-mistress, affecting terror and even, if she ventured to correct his shocking pronunciation, pretending to burst into tears as she had used to do.

"Now you can see how you discommoded me," he would say. "Come! Make me weep! Be angry if I am stupid! It is the only way."

At last she grew bolder and began to assert herself. And as soon as she saw that the heavens did not fall on her, that in fact his respect for her grew, she felt confident enough to cross swords with him even in the matter of his religion. It gave her a curious thrill of intimacy to argue with him. One evening, however, she went too far.

"Monsieur," she said, as they sat *en famille*, as it were, in the Hégers' sitting room, "I see you write here in your *devoir* that the Pope is infallible. That is to say, that God acts directly through him. Is that what you seriously believe?"

Monsieur looked up from fondling Prospère, who was lying on his knee, and said, "Most seriously I believe all that concerns my faith."

"You are obliged to believe it, or you could no longer call yourself a Catholic?"

"You have it."

"Yet popes have made errors—terrible errors that history has condemned. There have been wicked popes."

Madame, beyond the fire, looked up from her sewing.

"Ah! You go so far? Wicked?" said Monsieur mildly.

"Well. The pope at the time of the Borgias was quite corrupt. I believe he sired several of them."

"H'm," said Monsieur with a smile. "It would certainly seem that God allowed his vicar's baser clay to show through his sacred raiment on some occasions. But it is not claimed that the Pope *is* God, you know, merely that he is God's representative on earth. And as such he may err, like any other servant, when the Master's back is turned."

"But how may God turn His back upon a man through whom He guides the lives of millions of His children? Now, *we* do not believe any man is infallible, but rather that God acts through each of us. We are all the keepers of our own consciences, the makers of our own decisions, the judges of our own actions, and on that basis we shall be called to account. I fail to see," she continued, ignoring Madame's disapproving frown in the delight of having Monsieur's quizzical eyes so firmly fixed on hers, "I fail to see why any Catholic need fear hell, or indeed trouble himself about matters of personal responsibility at all. All he need do is obey his priest unthinkingly, or at worst confess his sins weekly. Obedience and mental subjugation must soon become habitual as the mind loses its capacity for independent thought. What puzzles me is why, if this is the true religion and divinely inspired, so many who are safely within it seem to receive so little help in controlling their bad impulses."

Monsieur's arms were growing agitated. Madame rose hastily and removed Prospère to safety.

"To whom do you refer?" he asked with dangerous politeness.

"Oh, need I say, not to you, Monsieur! But take my pupils. Our Protestant girls don't allow themselves such freedoms as I witness every day in my classes."

Madame interjected, with the least hint of chilliness, "Do our girls prove too much for you? You remember, I offered to stay in class with you, but you refused."

"I must manage on my own, Madame, sooner or later. And I

do, more or less, I believe. I don't speak of their bad behavior to invite sympathy or help, but only to illustrate my point."

"Which is, to boil it down, that Belgian girls behave worse than English ones, or rather that Catholics behave worse than Protestants!" exclaimed M. Héger, his voice rising. "You over-simplify. I believe worse of you—that you willfully misconstrue what you see to reinforce your insular prejudices! Was teaching so easy for you in England? I think you once told me otherwise."

"I was younger then. And at least I never had to lock an English girl in a cupboard before I could restore sufficient order to make myself heard!"

Monsieur seemed outfaced, but only for a moment.

"And you are foolish enough to blame this on her religion? I know to whom you refer. Undeniably the girl is unruly, but it is her mother's fault, not that of her Mother Church!" Jumping up, he began to stamp about the room. "Thus functions the mind of even the most intelligent woman! Determined to find fault with a faith you have been taught to despise, you see evidence in every human weakness of that faith's failure. You discourage me, Mees! You severely discourage me!"

His voice was now so loud that Prospère broke into a wail. Charlotte, glancing his way, had her bubble of excited contentiousness pricked when she saw in alarm that she had seriously displeased Madame, who carried the baby to bed without a word. Charlotte was instantly contrite.

"Have I annoyed her, Monsieur?" she asked anxiously.

M. Héger chuckled grimly. "You have, by annoying me. My wife protects me devotedly and does not like to see me roused."

"But surely one may argue—"

"The classroom is the proper place for arguments, not the sitting room."

Charlotte could now stand up to almost anything Monsieur might throw at her during an intellectual exchange. But this implied rebuke, spoken so quietly, went straight to her heart like a dagger. Tears sprang to her eyes. Seeing them, Monsieur hurried to her side.

"*Tiens, tiens!* Don't weep, it is not so serious. Do—not—cry," he said forcefully in English, trying not to roll the "r" in a French manner. It sounded so quaint that she could not help smiling. "Good. Now cheer up, and we will discuss something less explosive. Do tell me the full history of the incarceration of Mademoiselle Hortense in the cupboard—that should put an end to all gloom."

He was bending over her, proferring his handkerchief, when Madame suddenly reopened the door.

"Constantin, the girls wish you to come and—"

She stopped, her eyes fixed on the tableau before the fire. Then she at once continued, "bid them good-night." She withdrew without looking at Charlotte. As Monsieur straightened up in leisurely fashion, leaving his handkerchief in Charlotte's lap, she felt a sudden chill pass over her. She did not allow herself to contemplate the scene as it might have appeared in Mme Héger's eyes—but something had happened. Something had changed. She clutched the handkerchief as Monsieur absently patted her shoulder.

"*Excusez-moi.*"

"Of course, Monsieur."

He walked away from her and closed the door behind him, leaving her alone.

She laundered the handkerchief herself, and instead of simply handing it back, she sneaked it into his desk, a white, folded oblong, like an envelope. She had no contact with him for several days afterward, and she did not go back to the sitting room, but sat up in her own little room in the evenings and worked, and wept, and wondered why she wept. She felt strange, as if the inner strength that had come of her happiness and her sense of being liked and accepted were crumbling away. Yet there was no real cause to think so. Madame spoke to her as usual, or almost as usual. Perhaps the slight chilling of her manner was only in Charlotte's imagination. She prayed it was only that. The evenings were very long. If only it were summer, she would be able to stroll out into the *allée défendue,* her favorite spot, with its little arbor sheltering the seat where she and Emily had used to sit. At the thought of Emily, Charlotte cried afresh, as a sudden unwonted wave of homesickness swept over her. She had not been homesick at all until now.

The evening before she was due to give Monsieur and his brother-in-law their next lesson, she sat up late preparing it with extra care. When all the school was asleep, she decided she needed a book from her desk downstairs. Taking a candle, she slipped down to the long dark classroom. As she entered, she thought she caught a whiff of the cigars Monsieur always smoked; but then that aroma permeated the air of the whole school. There was no reason why it should hover especially around her desk. Opening it, however, she saw at once that there were two books there that were strange to her. She picked them up. One was a book of French essays, the other a slim volume of German verse. Charlotte, trembling, turned back each cover, looking in vain for an inscription. The gifts—if they were gifts and not loans—were to be, at least theoretically, anonymous. Yet there was no doubt at all where they came from. Only a week ago Monsieur had urged her to give her serious attention now to the study of German. Less than a week ago he had mentioned these particular essays.

Her spirits, so low a moment before that the dark, sleeping school had depressed them to the point of fear, now shot up like a firework in showers of colored sparks. She forgot the book she had come down for. Unable to wait till she got upstairs, she sat down then and there and began to read an essay by candlelight. She read till the candle burned away, and she had to grope her way up to bed. She slept that night the sleep of the totally happy who do not question their happiness.

One of the female teachers, a Mlle Justine, made determined efforts to befriend Charlotte. She chattered unceasingly about her dwindling hopes of matrimony, and quite shocked away any possibility of sympathy in Charlotte by revealing that these hopes were based on the device of persuading her brother to distribute wistful letters from her among his masculine acquaintances.

"But how can you humble yourself to do so?" Charlotte had exclaimed.

"My dear, when you reach my age, pride seems a most dispensable luxury when weighed in the balance against the prospect of being forever unloved and alone," replied her would-be friend.

These words, despicable as they were, stuck in Charlotte's memory. The carelessness with which she disposed of the subject in conversation with Emily, Mary and Ellen, as if she cared nothing one way or the other about spinsterhood, was only a front. At heart the thought of eternal loneliness rankled more and more. It was this that caused her to be so censorious with pupils who were the Flemish equivalent of Amelia Walker—budding, or even fully-blossoming, coquettes—whose manners were vain and whose hearts were hard and shallow and greedy for conquest. *These* would not have to face loneliness—they would find havens aplenty offered them, not through spiritual and moral desert, but by virtue (if that was the word!) of their physical charms. The cruel injustice of this fact of life confronted Charlotte continually as she looked about her. Emily, Mary, perhaps even Ellen, and certainly she herself, would never marry, not because they would not make worthy wives, but because they were not pretty enough, heartless enough, sufficiently wily and deceitful. Because, in short, they had not the readiness to obey the dishonorable rules of the husband-getting game. So inevitably life's prizes would go to the Amelia Walkers and the Lydie Robinsons, the Hortenses and the Virginies—pretty, unprincipled, trivial, scheming, cruel girls. It was all wrong. All, all wrong.

She had never thought of Mme Héger in the light of one of these undeserving prizewinners, but now it began to dawn on her that she had indeed been blessed with more than her due.

The husband she had might not be every woman's· choice, yet he had "a mind that envy could not but call fair," the finest masculine mind that Charlotte had ever met with, which, she saw, to a discriminating woman could easily outweigh his physical shortcomings and even his violent and mercurial temperament. This husband, moreover, not merely respected her rights to her own profession; at the same time he repeatedly advertised, so to speak, his fundamental view of her as a woman worthy of devoted love. Four beautiful children already, and though she was far past her first youth, a fifth (rumor had it) on the way. To see her seated by her fireside with her little ones clustered around her full skirts, her youngest in yards of snowy linen on her knee, and Monsieur standing by her smiling with pride, was to Charlotte a kind of agonizing rapture. At first she had been able to subdue the agony and exaggerate the rapture, but as spring advanced it became impossible to do so. She stopped visiting the Hégers' sitting room altogether. The sights and sounds there were too painful. And besides, she became convinced that whatever Monsieur might feel, Madame no longer welcomed her there.

There was a fellow teacher, Mlle Blanche, whom Charlotte had always instinctively disliked, and one day as she was going into her room she met Mlle Blanche coming out. Was the woman spying on her? Or just prying about for material to feed her endless hunger for gossip? From then on, Charlotte locked everything up—everything she regarded as private. But her books were left on the open shelves, and one day Mme Héger remarked, "Oh, Charlotte, could you return the French essays my husband lent you some time ago? He needs them for the upper class."

Charlotte stood rooted to the floor, cold and speechless. Later, she left the book on his desk. But it filled her with pain, and a sort of helpless anger, to be forced to part with it.

So this much-blessed Mme Héger was as two-faced as her pupils, offering apparent kindness with one hand, while employing members of her staff to spy upon each other. "But why should she spy on me?" Charlotte asked herself. "What does she expect to find out?" She could think of no reason why Madame should have changed toward her, other than Charlotte's possibly having offended her with her frank opposition to Catholicism.

The weekly lesson continued to be her chief delight, contrasting ever more strongly with all her other work and with all the rest of her time. During this scant hour she enjoyed equality, even a kind of intimacy, with her former master; they could pit their brains against each other, to the mutually agreeable end of stimulation, growth and progress. But after it had ended, and another week lay before her with little hope of more than a passing word with Monsieur, Charlotte had to fight to avoid falling into a deep depression. For the lessons were like a rich banquet once a week: there was starvation in between.

"Why do you not come to sit with us anymore, Mees?" Monsieur asked one day at the end of a lesson. "The children ask for you in the evenings. My tales do not please them as yours do."

"I don't wish to intrude on you, Monsieur."

"Intrude! It is no intrusion. Mademoiselle Blanche often comes."

Charlotte stayed meaningfully silent.

"You do not care for Mademoiselle Blanche," said M. Héger sardonically.

No answer. Charlotte, her head proudly lifted, looked past him.

"And Mademoiselle Justine? She has also forfeited your esteem?" Silence. Monsieur flushed ominously. "You are hard to please, Mees. You prefer to hold yourself aloof in the presence of all we poor deluded papists. Or perhaps you fear contamination from too-close communion with these polluted souls that surround you? I must speak frankly to you. Your pride will be your undoing. There is such a virtue as universal benevolence, which is, alas, as unknown to you as religious toleration. Try to look upon your fellow beings as equals and partners in the trials of this world, not as your enemies or inferiors. Blanche is a loyal and goodhearted girl. Justine one must pity, and where one pities one should tenderly protect from hurt. Yes, Mees, you hurt people with your cold reserves. Benevolence—the wish to do good! Think on it."

Think on it! For days Charlotte "thought on" nothing else. She struggled to see how she might win back his approval—if she had lost it. But that was the trouble: she could never be sure with him if he was seriously displeased with her, whether a lecture or even a round rebuke was a sign of something lasting or something of the moment. She made a serious effort with Justine, but Blanche she could not endure, being more than ever sure that she was Madame's "creature."

With Sophie, the third female staff member, she was already tolerably friendly, if only because Sophie loathed Blanche as much as she did. One day, all unwittingly, she confirmed Charlotte's suspicions.

"Blanche is as thick as thieves with Madame," she remarked. "Never say to Blanche what you do not wish *her* to hear, for she repeats everything; and when she has nothing to repeat, she invents. And *you* must be especially wary."

"Why must *I* be wary?" Charlotte asked, startled.

"Monsieur pays attentions to you. Oh, I know there is nothing in it, but you know, women of Madame's age who are in a certain condition get strange fancies."

These words threw Charlotte into a turmoil. The idea of Madame, the favored of fortune, being jealous of her was at once horrifying 'and—but this was inadmissible—intoxicating. The amalgam of the two, reacting with some unacknowledged ingredient in Charlotte's own heart, turned into anger against Madame, outrage, bitter resentment.

"It is impossible that she should consider it for one moment," she kept repeating to herself, until her mind was inflamed with her own innocence and Madame's iniquity in doubting it. It turned her against Sophie, too, for having introduced this new anguish into her mind, and as for Justine's whimperings about her single state, these became altogether intolerable to her in her present distress. She withdrew entirely into her shell.

Then something far more terrible happened. Madame put a stop to the lessons.

Of course Monsieur did not admit that it was she who had stopped them. He said that he had examinations to prepare before the *grandes vacances* in August, and had she not known better, Charlotte might have accepted that—there was prize-giving,

parents' day, and his own *fête* to arrange as well, and he was
indeed exceedingly pressed. But Charlotte was beyond being
reasonable. She knew without having to ask that the lessons would
not be resumed in the autumn. She was now merely the English
teacher, as Sophie was the French teacher. She had nothing before
her except the infliction of those wretched Belgian girls, brought
under control now, but no more rewarding, no more inspiring to
teach, than clods of clay.

So what held her? Within a matter of a few weeks, she faced
the awful horror of the long summer break, when everyone else
would be going home and she would be left here alone and
friendless in the great hot alien city. She looked ahead to it as to
some endlessly protracted period in the Catholic purgatory she
had heard so much about in the *lectures pieuses,* a period both
timeless and hopeless, of gray heat, abandonment and utter
aridity of the soul.

"I will go home," she thought a thousand times a day. And
at the thought of it the heavy pain of dread bearing down on her
seemed momentarily to lift, as when a sufferer in that same
legendary penal colony dwells on the thought of heaven. Yet the
burden at once resettled itself, for she knew she would not go—
that it was beyond her power.

She had to have a reason to stay—for herself, as much as for
the family and for Mary and Ellen. So she decided it would be
a determination to perfect her German. (In the holidays? Without a teacher? Never mind.) Thus she gave it out to the family in
her increasingly lifeless letters. To Branwell she wrote that when
she was alone in the evenings the old fantasies returned to her
irresistibly; what she did not say was that now she had no sense
of guilt in indulging them. The idolatry she had tormented herself with at Roe Head now seemed the palest of gray little sins,
the merest peccadillo. Even "entertaining" Zamorna stabbed her
overwrought conscience no more than receiving into one's home
the black sheep of the family, long since purged of his vices.

The festivities at the end of the school year came, and Charlotte played her part in them dutifully. The only thing she had

really looked forward to was Monsieur's *fête*, during which, according to custom, he would sit up on a platform and receive a tribute from every pupil in the form of a bouquet or a little gift. Charlotte burned with longing to make something for him, some personal object that would shine out—not for its costliness (he despised show), but for the taste and care that had gone into its creation; she even began to crochet a silken pouch to hold his watch. But then she realized she would utterly lack courage to offer it to him under the eyes of Madame. Every way she turned, there stood Madame, precluding the most innocent gestures, the simplest exchanges, the most ordinary intercourse between Charlotte and Monsieur.

In the end she went into the *allée défendue*, where occasionally in the early spring he had strolled with her, talking of his past life, of his blighted hopes of a legal career, even of his first wife and child, who had both died. Oh, happy, innocent intimacy! Tears—so frequent with Charlotte now in her increasing wretchedness and weakness—poured down her cheeks as she gathered a small posy of colored leaves. At least her offering should be unorthodox in some particular! In the heart of the leaves she concealed a single red rosebud, and bound the stems with silk.

As the whole school assembled for the ceremony, Blanche, peeping about to see who was giving what, caught sight of Charlotte's leaf-posy.

"Leaves only, Mees Charlotte? Monsieur will not like that! See mine!" She flashed under Charlotte's nose a gorgeous posy of hothouse flowers she had bought in the town. Their exotic scent ravished the air. *Oh, yes*, thought Charlotte, tasting wormwood. You are free to display your admiration, you are not too reticent to sit with them evening after evening, you may talk to him when you wish, and Madame thinks nothing of it. Yet I, whose mind is fit to challenge his, who have so much to gain and even give in conversation with him, *I* am banished, *I* am suspect, *I* must be curbed and held in! In an impulse of the strongest bitterness, she threw her posy away into a bush, and sat stiff and motionless throughout the ceremony, the only member of the school who made no offering at all. Her reward was raised eyebrows from Madame, and a brief, heart-stabbing look from Monsieur of child-like disappointment. She felt she had spoiled his *fête*. Her misery was complete.

The holiday came. Pupils and teachers joyfully packed and joy-fully departed. Monsieur and Madame took their children to the seaside and Charlotte was left alone in the big deserted school.

As Madame had said, Charlotte had been solitary even amid numbers when the school was full. But now it was not, solitude felt quite different. The school echoed with emptiness. The long rows of white-curtained beds down the dormitories were like shrouded figures as she roamed among them, much like a ghost herself in her plain gray dress, silent on her tiny soft-shod feet. The cook-housekeeper made her meals for her and served them wordlessly in the great *réfectoire*, where Charlotte sat alone at the head of the top table. During the hot days she would try to escape by wandering around the town, often walking far afield to tire herself out. The beauties of the *haute-ville* no longer gratified her senses—the grander the spectacle, the more splendid the crowds, the smaller, the more lonely, the more diminished she felt by comparison. In the *basse-ville*, the older, poorer part of Brussels, she felt no less alone. The very poverty of the dwellings gave a sense of the closeness of the family life she could see and sense in the streets and houses she passed; everywhere there were children, everywhere there were signs of a *shared* struggle for sur-vival that exuded its own peculiar warmth. It sometimes seemed to Charlotte that there was not one person she had encountered in either section of the town for whom she need feel sorry, or rather, whom she did not need to envy, for everyone seemed to have someone.

Perversely, there were only two places where Charlotte's misery was eased. One was the cemetery beyond the city where Martha lay; there it was peaceful, not simply emptily silent, and she could sit on a bench near the grave, contemplate the insentient dead and try to believe that she was at least luckier than they. The other place was the Church of Ste. Gudule.

The first time she had gone in there, Charlotte had recoiled. It had seemed to her then something worse than a temple of idolatry, with its vulgar, gaudy statues and its air of false mystery: it had seemed morbid, oppressive with error, almost evil. Yet now it suited her. How was this? She stood in the nave under the soaring roof. It was twilight outside, and the last rays of the summer sun were streaming through a magnificent stained-glass window, littering the flag floor with jewels of light. Still the high altar and the corners of the building were gloomy; no natural light ever brightened or warmed them, only the pitiful flames of candles lit in misguided trust, to placate or entreat the unmovable plaster forms of saints.

Charlotte ignored these, and savored the irresistible grandeur of the place. Seen like this, it had all the fabled glories of Verdopolis, and all its vileness, too; it suited her. She was part of all that this place represented: the soaring vision held down to earth by mortal proclivities, the preoccupation with sin and damnation. Yes! That was it. It was as a *sinner* that she felt at home in this place, where evil, recognized and unrecognized, lay at the very foundations. They understood sin here. They catered to it.

She went into a pew and sat motionless until the candles were the sole source of light. She noticed some activity going on in one corner where a sort of fretted cupboard stood. A number of people, mostly women, soberly dressed and with their heads veiled, went to this box and hid themselves in it for some minutes. They emerged with eyes lowered, and crossing themselves, they crept away. A woman kneeling near Charlotte suddenly turned to her and whispered:

"*C'est vous au prochain tour.*"

"*Moi? Pourquoi?*"

"*Ne voulez-vous donc pas vous confesser?*"

Charlotte understood then, and she was about to answer no and let the woman go next, when an extraordinary impulse took hold of her. Almost as if something else were guiding her, she rose, drew her shawl forward to shield her face and walked to the confessional. Inside, she knelt mechanically. It was only when she saw the side of the priest's head through a sort of grating that panic seized her. But just as when she had stood in the rocking boat on the Thames and opened her lips to call up to the sailor, she felt there was no way back. She must now go through with it, whatever it brought.

But she did not know the formula—how to begin.

"Well, daughter?" murmured the priest beyond the grill.

"Father, I—I am a Protestant," Charlotte blurted out.

The man turned his face, and now she could just see his dark eyes peering at her in amazement.

"Then why do you come to me?"

"I am alone. I'm all alone, Father! I must speak to someone. I have been alone for three weeks. My nights are torture—I dream most terribly—I seem to look down into the pit of hell . . ."

She looked into that pit now, in recollection; it came back to her so clearly that she gasped. In her dream, she had felt hands, strong, warm, hirsute hands, pushing her in. She had reached behind her, clutching them, pleading, but knowing all the time that if she could hold him so that they fell down there together she would not mind.

"Father, I have sinned!" she cried out suddenly.

"Shhh . . . We have all sinned. I cannot confess you. You are not of our faith."

"Please, don't deny me! If it's any comfort, if it offers any strength to go on living, to draw back from that brink that I see in my dreams, please help me, don't turn me away!" she whispered frantically, tears choking her.

He was silent for some time. "I have not met with such a case before," he said. "Perhaps you had better return tomorrow when I have consulted a brother-priest with more experience. Yet I don't like to refuse you . . . You will not do anything foolish?"

Charlotte did not know what he meant. "My sin is not a sin of action, but one of feeling," she said. "I have feelings that are wicked and forbidden—I can't explain them to you—I wish I could tell you, 'I have done this and that, I want to do penance and be forgiven.' It is not so simple. I only know I live in torment. You will tell me to struggle against these wicked longings, but I can't—I can't! I can't even go away, I can't leave here, I am doomed to stay forever, to suffer and sin and suffer more . . . Oh, what's the matter with me? I feel I shall lose my reason!"

The priest was getting very agitated. "Hush, poor child, don't distress yourself so! Listen. I must think about this. Perhaps all this pain is being sent to drive you back to the True Church. Those who suffer as you are suffering often have a vocation to ease the anguish of others. Come to my house tomorrow morning, and we will talk. Here is my address." A slip of paper was passed through the grill. "Will you promise to come?"

Charlotte, feeling suddenly wholly exhausted, whispered dully, "I promise."

But when she left the church she fled back to the Pensionnat as if the Devil were chasing her. Her heart beat so wildly that by the time she had climbed the stairs to the dormitory she could scarcely stand upright. She flung herself down on her bed and lay there in the profound silence until her body was calmer. But her mind was in bedlam.

Perhaps she truly was going insane! She had delivered herself into the hands of that simple French priest, confiding in him the terrible secret that she had never before allowed herself to know. She could no longer delude herself. In telling it, reliving it before another person, she had uncovered the mystery. She knew now, inescapably, to whom those beloved, damning hands belonged.

5

PARTING

BY THE TIME THE SCHOOL RE-
assembled in early October, Charlotte was in a state of complete
moral and physical exhaustion. She was under strong pressure
from Emily and Ellen to return home, and she thought she had
summoned the resolution to do so—until she saw M. Héger again.

She heard his carriage draw up in the Rue d'Isabelle outside
the front gate and the commotion as children and luggage were
unloaded. Madame came bustling in first. Her pregnancy was
obvious now, even under her flowing manteau; Charlotte, unnoticed in the shadows by the garden door, observed her with a
cold feeling of fear, as if this blooming personification of cherished
womanhood were a poniard advancing toward her breast.

The children rushed in, followed by servants loaded with luggage. Then came Monsieur with Prospère in his arms. Father
and son were bronzed by the sun; each in his own way was a
picture of health and vigor.

Monsieur, his eyes bright and sharp behind their lenses, gazed
about him happily, and then he spotted her.

"Mees! You have come to welcome us! How good. I see you
have taken my words to heart after all."

Charlotte, struggling to contain her joy, came forward shyly.
"Which words, Monsieur?"

"Benevolence! Benevolence! Did you have a good holiday?"

"Did you, Monsieur?"

"Excellent! The sea was superb. You should have been with us," he added with thoughtless bonhomie. "I am a giant refreshed with wine! A very little giant, *n'est-ce pas?* Come, tell me all the news."

"There is none."

He started back, as if appalled. *"None?"*

"None at all, Monsieur."

"Has Mademoiselle Justine then not found a husband?"

"Monsieur, is *that* a benevolent question?"

He chuckled and patted her shoulder, unaware of the tumult he was causing. "Perhaps not, perhaps not. *Ma foi,* how I require some coffee!"

And he strutted away.

Charlotte went out into the garden and sat alone in the *allée défendue*. The situation was clearly unbearable. She *would* give her notice. Perhaps then at least she could be sure, from his reaction, whether she had forfeited his interest and friendship. If not, she could withdraw her notice and stay on. But no. That was part of her—her moral sickness. She must go—she must go!

Yet she stayed. She told herself, and wrote to Emily, that it was because she could not face a return to Haworth with such an uncertain prospect awaiting her—the prospect, not of another dreary term as governess, but of their school. How such a prospect was to arise without her being at home to bring it about, she did not ask. Meanwhile, she stayed and taught "*les mauvaises animaux*" and struggled with her rampaging emotions.

If she was not even now ready to identify the precise nature of her feelings for Monsieur, she was very clear about her view of Madame. It was hostile. She saw her now as a cold, deceitful, self-interested woman, utterly ruthless and utterly untrustworthy. Her mind, outwardly so pure, concealed a seething brew of prurience, just as Emily had said. Charlotte's manner to her became ever more distant and cold; her eyes narrowed and averted themselves in her presence; she scarcely spoke to her if it could be avoided.

About two weeks after the beginning of term, things came to a head.

Charlotte had been sitting alone in the dormitory for two hours. It was raining outside—summer was ending—and the long, cold, dismal winter threatened. Listening to the moaning of the wind, Charlotte seemed to hear her own inner cries. She thought of the kitchen at Haworth, with Emily and Tabby and the dog. She imagined herself cutting up mutton for a hash, with Keeper gazing at her passionately and Emily saying, "Save the best bits for him, mind." Tabby was boiling potatoes to a glue on the stove, and Papa was in his study, where at any moment Charlotte might go to him. *At any time* she might go! What, oh what was she waiting for?

She stood up abruptly. Minutes later, she was knocking on the door of the private sitting room, so long abjured.

"*Entrez.*"

It was Madame's voice, and she was alone. She looked up from her embroidery. No smile warmed her face when she saw who it was.

"*Alors*—it's a long time since we saw you in here, Charlotte."

"Madame, I wish to speak to you."

"Sit down."

Charlotte obeyed. Madame, her eyes now lowered, stitched on in silence. At last Charlotte said:

"I want to go home, Madame."

It came out so gauchely that she blushed and clenched her fists. She thought she saw Madame smile *now*. But she did not look up.

"Indeed! And when will you be leaving?"

In a flash, Charlotte realized that her notice was going to be accepted without one word even of token protest. She became suddenly dizzy. It was not just the proof that all her suspicions were correct—that Madame did want to get rid of her. She was abruptly faced with the knowledge that she would actually have to go; there would be no chance to change her mind.

She mustered her pride and said shrilly, "As soon as possible."

After a few moments of silent sewing, Madame, having calculated coolly, remarked, "I believe I can replace you in a week or so. Will that suit?"

"Admirably." Charlotte rose stiffly and went to the door. There she suddenly turned. "What have I done?" she heard herself ask.

Madame looked up sharply. "What do you mean?"

"I mean what I say. What have I done? Why do you now detest me?"

"My dear! I can't imagine what you're talking about! I have no criticism of you, unless it be that you do not get along with the other teachers as I would like. A school is much like a family. The atmosphere can't be good unless everyone is friendly and gets on well with the others. But I assure you I have nothing against you."

"You deny then that your manner to me has changed? That you have had bad thoughts about me? That you have set Blanche to go through my things, looking for heaven knows what?"

Her adversary's face changed. She rose in dignity.

"Mademoiselle! You forget yourself! Do you dare suggest I have spied on you?"

"I know you have."

"Outrageous! You shall depart tomorrow."

Charlotte's blood was up. She had curbed her passions too long. White-faced and gasping, she faced her enemy. She cared for nothing any longer, and cried in her anger, "And who shall tell Monsieur why? You, or me?"

Madame, herself on the brink of fury but not yet over it, instantly put rein to her temper as the scene suggested by these words rose in her mind's eye. A quarrel between her and Constantin about this girl? That was the very last thing she wanted.

"I, naturally, shall tell him you are leaving. But you shall have your week, or rather, I shall have mine, for I must find another teacher. Now you had better go."

Charlotte stared at her wildly for a moment, and then rushed out. In her room, something like a fainting fit overtook her. She lay across her bed as limp as an empty garment, yet with the blood pounding through her body. She eventually fell into a weird mockery of sleep without undressing.

The following morning, iron self-control, achieved through years of practice, enabled her to tidy herself and go about her routine as usual. But the scene with Madame was constantly replaying itself with variations in her head, and several times during her lessons she lost the sense of where she was and what she was doing. The thought of meeting Madame filled her with terror. Eventually they met in the hall. They walked past each other without a glance, each woman stiff-jawed and white-faced. Somehow after that, Charlotte felt better. It was clear her enemy was suffering as much as she.

Had she known it, Madame was suffering even more. The scene when she had told her husband of Charlotte's intention to leave had been far more violent than she'd expected. His rage was so excessive that she was quite thrown off balance. In all the months during which she had been quietly machinating toward getting Charlotte out, she had never supposed that her husband might *seriously* object. Why was he so upset?

Madame had perceived the situation long before, and, seeing also that Charlotte was *une hystérique,* feared some unseemly demonstration that would cause a scandal in the school. It was not the first time she had got rid of a female teacher, or indeed a pupil, for a similar cause. But it *was* the first time she had intervened, albeit subtly, between her husband and a favorite. Her influence over him had been strong enough to wean him, first from teaching her, then from learning with her, and by stealth and persistence eventually from anything more than casual communication with her. She had thought in this way to make the final break, to which she avidly looked forward, virtually painless to him. And now this—this passionate explosion that had left her cold and shaken.

"She shall not leave!" he had shouted at last. "Mark that, Zoë!

She *shall not leave* this school!" It was with the utmost difficulty that she had prevailed on him not to send a servant that instant to wake Charlotte up and bring her down, to reverse her decision by force then and there.

But this morning Madame was living through torment. She knew her husband well enough to be sure that, though his temper cooled quickly, his deepest determinations were not to be modified. She knew she had lost the campaign, that Charlotte would stay, at least for the time being; her only desire now was to make certain that Constantin and Charlotte were not alone when he confronted her. To that end she kept her eye on Charlotte's movements all day, even though the professor was teaching at the Athénée till four o'clock.

When that hour came, she took up her stand at a window overlooking the garden he must cross to return home; and soon she saw him, his little black figure striding through the trees, head down, hands clasped behind him, like a small, angry bull. She saw that he was heading for the long classroom in which Charlotte usually stayed alone to work after classes ended, and which gave straight onto the garden. With all speed she hastened down and stood outside the main door to the room, her head bent.

Charlotte's few murmured words were inaudible through the door, but Constantin's voice reached her intermittently.

". . . Outrageous ingratitude . . . must instantly reverse this wholly reprehensible decision . . . impossible to understand how a mind works that can . . . without any justification whatever . . ."

Mme Héger straightened up with a sigh of relief. She need not lose face by going in after all. This battle might be lost; but the war could safely go on with the same undercover tactics as before. In the end she would win. And in the meantime, the irrational, insidious fear that had laid hold on her last night was dissipated. How stupid she had been to imagine for a moment— After all, a man does not fall in love with a woman's *mind*. And what else did this strange, stunted little English miss have to offer?

So Charlotte lived out another few dreary months in Brussels, ever more wretched, ever more guilty, ever more homesick and heartsick. True, Monsieur made occasion now to speak to her, and these moments filled her momentarily with ecstatic joy; but it was a false joy, a joy for which she paid afterward with anguish. It was like having the sun shine on her briefly, showing her a vision of a warm, natural, beautiful world—but it was a world that was not for her, and immediately the beneficent light was turned away, she was again engulfed in hideous cold and darkness. And sometimes these flashes of painful happiness seemed to her a kind of cruelty on his part, as if he apportioned her a misery dole just in order to retain her devotion, to keep her from escaping him.

It was Mary Taylor who rescued her at last from this loving paralysis of the will. Mary was far away in Germany, and had even been talking about a wild plan she had of emigrating to New Zealand with her brother. Possibly she would never return to England, never see Charlotte again. This was terrible of course; yet it had its advantages. It made it possible for Charlotte to open her heart to Mary at least a little. And that proved enough for the perspicacious and uncensorious Mary to grasp the whole dangerous situation.

In December she wrote to Charlotte, advising her in the strongest terms to go home, come to her in Germany, do anything, in fact, so long as she got out of Brussels. She even urged her to throw in her lot with the New Zealand scheme! Anything would be preferable to rotting in hopeless misery where she was.

"If you do not go now, you will lose all energy to move—I know you," she wrote roundly. "If you don't bestir yourself, I shall come and drag you away, or you might as well bid good-bye to life. You'll be finished."

And Charlotte heeded her. She went straight to Monsieur, who was working in his study. She was so worn out that she could feel very little emotion when she confronted him. She leaned upon his desk as if her legs could hardly hold her, and with a deep sigh said, "I must leave you, Monsieur."

He started up, coloring, and opening his mouth to offer loud objections. But the sight of her suffering face silenced him. It was a long time since he had let himself take a proper, "seeing" look at her. Now he looked, and saw in a flash what had been going on. Zoë's strange behavior, Charlotte's deterioration—it was all suddenly spread out before him like a decoded message. All choler died in him. He rose and looked down at her, for, short as he was, she barely came to his shoulder, and after a long moment he said quietly:

"Fool that I am. Of course you must."

"Monsieur will allow me to go?" she asked piteously.

"I will," he replied, as tenderly as to one of his own children whom he had, through self-preoccupation, allowed to hurt itself. "I will help you to go."

He knows! He knows! thought Charlotte, rejoicing in spite of the scalding shame, for he was not angry or scornful or even embarrassed. Her acknowledgment of her love burst upon her, opened within her, like a blinding, burning white light. She swayed before him. He caught her, thinking she was going to fall, and for one unforgettable instant she felt his arms around her.

Then, as if from nowhere, Madame—an avenging demon in disguise—materialized at their side. "Seat her here. I will attend to her while you fetch the smelling salts," she said briskly.

The atmosphere changed. Madame became all kindness, all smiles, all consideration. Charlotte was not left alone for a moment, or so it seemed to her. Madame herself could not always be her companion; apart from other duties, she had a newborn daughter. But Mlle Blanche made a scrupulous deputy. Charlotte was aware of the unremitting surveillance, and was in no doubt as to the reason for it: now she was leaving, Madame was prepared to be magnanimous in victory—but not so magnanimous as to allow her one moment alone with Monsieur.

He was good to her, though, within the limits imposed by his wife. He gave her books; he drew her willy-nilly once more into the family circle; he promised to write to her—all this while Madame looked on, benevolently smiling.

That Christmas was the most punishing of Charlotte's life. She had to watch the joy and gaiety of the family celebration and pretend to share in it while her very soul seemed to be dying.

Then there were only days before she had to leave. Charlotte became inwardly frantic. At last she contrived an opportunity to come upon Monsieur alone while Madame was in the nursery and Mlle Blanche was out. A moment she must have—just one moment to say good-bye—otherwise her heart would break once and for all, leaving her no hope of recovery.

"Monsieur?"

He raised his head from his work. It was early evening. The lamp on the desk shone out against the encroaching gloom of the familiar *salle de classe*, while outside the winter rain lashed the long windows.

"Yes, Charlotte?" he said gently. He was always gentle with her now.

"You know I leave tomorrow. I've come to say good-bye."

"We will say good-bye only on the dockside. I am going to accompany you to Ostend."

For a moment her tired heart leaped with false hope. A half day's journey with him, alone, seated at his side, her arm against his arm; time to talk, time to make her peace with herself, to draw gradually away from him instead of being wrenched and torn! But no. Hope was senseless. She spoke more firmly:

"That cannot happen, Monsieur. Madame will not spare you."

Their eyes met. His dropped first.

"Well . . . In case . . . Let us say good-bye now."

He came around the desk, took her hand and held it in both of his. His back was to the light and she stood in his shadow. They looked at each other—two small, bespectacled, unprepossessing people; she trembling with love, he also filled with some emotion he could not name, compounded of pity, tenderness, admiration and anxiety—for suffering, especially if he had caused it, always pained him unbearably. If he could have done anything to ease her pain, he would have done it gladly; as it was, he felt the best way was to stifle all reciprocal warmth in himself, for her own good. It was hard for him; he felt her need for love crying out to him, and he was the kind of man who responds almost automatically to any cry of need.

"All partings are hard," he said at last, "but this one need not be final. When your school is well established, and you are prosperous and successful, you will return to us for a visit, and perhaps to steal pupils from us—yes? I would not be surprised if we sent you Claire or Louise one of these days. That will be a link between us."

"But meanwhile—you will write, Monsieur?"

He hesitated. He often kept up a correspondence with old pupils, it would be nothing unusual; yet the passion in her voice checked his ready assent. Letters . . . Letters could be dangerous. He said, "Yes, I will write. But not too often. Let us limit ourselves to two letters a year."

"*Two a year!*" It was a cry of pain.

"Charlotte, trust me. It is better."

Her head dropped; she withdrew her hand. "As you wish," she said in a low, beaten voice. "Good-bye, Monsieur." And she turned and walked away from him into the darkened hall.

6
THE FIXED
IDEA

CHARLOTTE DID NOT KNOW AT first how bad it was going to be.

The parting had wrenched her and left her inwardly bruised and aching. But as he had said, it was not final. And he would write. He had promised. Communication between them—a sustained, perfectly proper and legitimate contact, without guilt, without the anguish of proximity—was better. Wise, kind omniscient Monsieur! He had said so, and he was right.

Besides, a palliative was at hand. Charlotte had every intention of throwing her full energies into the school project. She was equipped now. Monsieur had given her a diploma, ratified by the seal of the Athénée Royale where he principally taught, certifying her competence to teach French and German. Armed with this she was certain that doors would open, paths be straightened before her and, incidentally, that the boon of an interesting, absorbing occupation would help her recover from the sickness she had fallen into in Brussels.

But almost immediately on her return home, Emily took her aside.

"I couldn't dream of leaving Papa, even to come and help you start a school. As for having it here, as we once hoped, with Papa in such poor health and his sight virtually gone, I can't see how we could inflict it on him."

This abrupt scotching of all her hopes and plans struck Charlotte into blank dismay.

"But—but what has it all been for? What shall I do with my life? I can't start anything without you! We must, we *must* do *something*, otherwise how can I live?"

Emily was startled by her vehemence and seemingly exaggerated expressions.

"What are you complaining about? You've had nearly two years of study and pleasure—well, perhaps not all pleasure lately, but surely we've got beyond expecting life to offer us an unmixed cup of happiness? You've been very lucky. Now you're back, having done what you wanted, you'll just have to settle down to workaday existence again. At least you won't have to go out to work, thanks to Aunt's legacy. Why don't you do some writing?"

"Writing?" exclaimed Charlotte. "I can't. I can't write anymore. I must be active, I must occupy myself physically, I must have a goal and a routine!" But Emily just shrugged and went back to her housework.

A new despair crept into Charlotte's mind, a despair so dark that all pleasure in her homecoming was spoiled. Was the nightmare of idleness and uselessness to be her reward for all the effort and suffering she had invested in herself? Her new acquirements seethed in her brain for employment, for outlet. But she could see no possibility as long as Anne was employed at Thorp Green.

But wait—Anne was not happy in her position, or had not been, once. There might be hope there. When she and Branwell came home for a brief holiday later in January, Charlotte virtually pounced on her.

"Anne, why don't you leave your post and come home? Then you could look after Papa, and Emily and I could go off and start our school somewhere. I'm desperately anxious to get started. What do you say?"

Anne looked at her strangely and shook her head.

"I don't think that's wise just now. I think I ought to stay as long as Branwell does."

"Branwell! What's Branwell got to do with it?"

"Charlotte, we have been brought up in innocence—markedly so. I didn't realize it until just recently. But we are not *ignorant*, are we? I mean, some girls know nothing about—passion; but we imbibed much knowledge of the world from our reading, and I thought nothing could startle me. Yet when one sees with one's own eyes the worldliness, the lengths to which vanity and—and instinct will drive people, women as well as men, it can't help coming as something of a shock. Mrs. Robinson and Lydie are of this kind. They have ways with men that I could not believe at first, but now I do believe it, and—and I've sometimes wondered, in this year while you've been away, whether I was doing right to let Branwell stay."

"Are you saying that Lydie has designs on him?"

Anne hesitated.

"Charlotte, let's drop the subject. Truly, I'd rather not say any more. But I'm afraid I can't come home. Much as I often long to. Branwell must keep this job—another failure, another retreat, would kill him. It's my duty to watch over him."

So that hope ended too. And as January passed into the bleak, cruel months of February and March, and deep stormy winter with its inevitable train of illnesses and deaths held Haworth in its vise, the dreaded scourges of idleness, loneliness and discontent laid themselves on Charlotte.

From the stale prison that her home had become, she wrote her first letter to Monsieur. It was not a wise or temperate letter, and when the reply—unspeakably longed for—came at last, it was a "mixed cup" indeed. It did contain friendly advice upon her school and upon the best way of keeping up her French, et cetera; it was even affectionate, in a way. Yet it held also a well-meant but poignant rebuke. She had always tended to let her feelings run away with her. Her letter had been marred by a degree of hysteria that distressed him. She must try to modify her feelings, for he admired temperance and deplored excesses.

If he had spoken the words, his own peculiar tone and manner might have sent the shaft home without pain. But to see them written vitiated all the kindness of the rest, leaving only hurt and unappeased hunger. Was this what she must subsist on for six long months to come? She would starve! But she had given her word.

She strove to keep it, and had she had more to distract and occupy her, might have succeeded. As it was, she broke down after a few weeks and wrote to him again.

This time she restrained herself, and the letter she got back rewarded her. It contained no reproaches, and afforded the un-alloyed delight of a conversation with him. For weeks afterward she lived in bliss, as if the letter had provided her with a limited supply of some heavenly food; but there was one sting in it, for he reminded her of their agreement to exchange letters only once in six months. And the manna did not suffice for so long under those dismal conditions of bitter cold, loneliness and inactivity.

Charlotte's only resource was writing long letters to Mary in Germany. These invariably concluded with instructions to burn the letters. She need not have worried on that score—Mary was no hoarder: she meant to travel far, and for that she must travel light. But reading of Charlotte's misery, she abruptly decided to return home early. In May she was back in England, organizing a reunion between Ellen and Charlotte and herself at her brothers' new home in Cleckheaton.

"So you've given your heart to your little professor, Charlotte," she said with characteristic bluntness when they were pacing the garden waiting for Ellen to arrive. "I might have known you'd fall in love 'not wisely but too well'! And of course your overworked conscience is giving you no rest. But you know, you couldn't help it. I know from the first time you described him to me that there was enough of Byron's intellect and Wellington's dominance in him to be dangerous for you. Heaven help the man who shouted at and bullied *me*! But you love being lorded over. Submission suits you far better than command; that's why you prefer being taught to teaching."

"Well, you're right. But I've succeeded in leaving him; all I ask is a letter now and then and I'm satisfied."

"Oh-ho! You think so—seriously? Can the hungry heart be satisfied with crumbs? Crumbs of paper, to boot? Listen, Charlotte. You're deceiving yourself. Those crumbs will merely prolong your suffering. It would be better to cut yourself off at once and forever, famine and wither for a while, and then—either die at once, or recover. And as no one really dies for love, you *will* recover."

"You don't know," said Charlotte. "You don't understand. I would die in good earnest if I never heard from him again."

"Rubbish! However . . . it's not for me to say. I wept for love once, just once, and I hope not to do so again. I found a measure of my precious self-respect leaked out with each tear and I did not care for it. I tell you what, though, Charlotte. I think your miseries are the fault of our times. This upbringing that teaches women to curtail their abilities and ambitions into narrow channels with high, imprisoning walls. Now, if you could face New Zealand, I would make a new woman of you. Monsieur Héger would fade like a wraith in the sunshine, not only of the Antipodes, but of healthy exertion and new experience."

Charlotte shook her head, shivered, and took Mary's arm. "I couldn't go so far away from him," she said. "From here, I could reach him in three days . . ."

"But, Charlotte, wouldn't it be better to renounce any idea of seeing him again?"

"Better? Of course it would be better! But I want my life, and I know it would kill me to renounce him. No. I shall remain quietly here until I have some achievement to carry to him; then I shall visit him, full of self-possession, and he will praise and be proud of me. That is all I think about. And letters are my bridge between this time and that. Without them I can't set one foot before another these days. It's as if he had taken over my will. Without his direction, even from a distance, I am powerless."

"Dear heaven, Charlotte!" said Mary, truly shocked for the first time.

"Yes, it is terrible. But that's my nature. I am never more completely myself than when I am in thrall—to some idea, some purpose or some person."

"I can't believe that is any woman's nature. You've been brought up wrong, Charlotte! Yet I don't know. Emily is nobody's slave . . . Perhaps there is a warp in you somewhere. Oh, how I wish I could take you with me!"

"Are you really going?" Charlotte asked incredulously. "You don't even know what it is like there."

"That's the thrill of it! I told Ellen, I shan't be sorry to leave England; and if I ever do return, and any single thing looks at me with its old face, I shall kick its teeth down its throat!"

Emily could not go on indefinitely ignoring Charlotte's misery, hoping it would go away. She began at last to force herself out of her own self-sufficiency, and when she saw how ill Charlotte looked she grew belatedly concerned. And almost as soon as she had, as it were, put her antennae out again, the truth flashed upon her. They were sitting one June day by the brook, throwing clods of ling roots for Keeper to chase, when Emily suddenly turned to her and said, "Why didn't you tell me you were in love with Monsieur Héger?"

Charlotte said nothing, but looked at her with wide, piteous eyes.

"Oh, there's no need to give me that don't-abuse-me look! I told you, I don't judge people. It's inconceivable to me, but yet it makes sense . . . I should have known it. I've been too busy . . . I'm sorry." She lay back in the grass and stared up at the sky. "Now then, what to do? The school, of course. Papa's comforts must take second place to *this*, obviously. The others'll be home for their so-called summer holiday next week. We'll discuss the whole thing with Anne. It'll have to be at home, I can't leave

Papa, but we can do what we always said—enlarge the house a little. I'll arrange that, and you can draw up the prospectuses. Let's invite Ellen over. She knows so many wealthy people. Five or six pupils would be enough to get us started . . ."

Charlotte was gazing at her, awestruck by the change in her.

"You're a tower of strength, Emily."

"H'm. When I come out of my ivory one," Emily returned drily.

They had expected Branwell to help in the plans, at least to the extent of showing enthusiasm. But instead he seemed restive and irritable to a degree, and got on all their nerves.

"What on earth is the matter with you, Branwell?" Charlotte asked at last, when he had interrupted their meeting for the fourth time with some irksome remark or demand.

Anne answered for him. "Oh, don't mind him. He is anxious to get back to Thorp Green, that's all." There was a nervous edge to her voice that swung her sisters' eyes sharply onto her, for it was quite unlike her usual gentle tone.

"What is the attraction?" asked Emily drily.

"You should rather ask *who*," said Anne meaningfully, looking at her brother with oddly pinched lips.

"Be quiet, you," said Branwell, and flounced out of the room. But instantly he put his head back. "I am leaving because you all annoy me. But mind, I shall leave the door open and you shall not know if I am within earshot, so discuss me if you dare, you wretched little talebearer!"

By the time Anne and Branwell went off to join the Robinsons in Scarborough (Anne's particular heaven), plans for the school were well advanced. Charlotte had the prospectuses printed and sent them off to everyone she knew. Ellen received a whole batch, which she faithfully doled out among every daughtered family of her acquaintance. They had decided not to go to the expense of adding to the parsonage until they had made sure of getting pupils; but they were convinced they would find at least a few to start them off. Charlotte threw herself heart and soul into the business; she felt that here, at last, with Emily's support, was a prospect of salvation for her. Emily became very important to Charlotte again. She was greatly eased by being able to talk of M. Héger to her. Though Emily was by no means wholly sympathetic to Charlotte's obsession, and often damped her with sardonic remarks, it was still balm to her pent-up feelings to have a confidante close at hand.

The school project reached its zenith at the end of summer, when hope and enthusiasm was at its height at the sending-out of prospectuses. By September, hope was fading; by October, when not a single pupil had come forward, it was dying with the dying year.

Emily was not at all dismayed by their failure; in fact, she was almost relieved. She'd mainly entered into it on Charlotte's account, and now her only concern was that the disappointment should not cast Charlotte back into depression and despair. But at first Charlotte bore up well, writing quite hardily to Ellen that she regretted nothing and was not "mortified at defeat." But it was false buoyancy, the temporary uplift of defiance.

Mary had gone back to Brussels to teach for a while in a boys' school until her plans for emigration ripened. Charlotte's thoughts followed her; in her letters she poured out all the hopeless hunger for news of M. Héger that she dared not confide even to Emily for fear of her tacit disapproval. Endlessly she waited for a letter from him. When none came, she began to entertain awful fears— first, for his health; then when she was reassured about this by a cheerful letter from one of her old pupils, still at the school, she began to nurse suspicions of the most painful kind. Was Madame intercepting her letters? If the long one she had written in July had reached him, surely, *surely* he would have replied, however briefly, however tardily. How could he have failed her? It was *his turn*, and the six months were up and passed.

When she heard that Joe Taylor was going over to see Mary, she could bear it no longer. Without telling Emily, she wrote another letter, shorter this time and very, very circumspect. She reread it several times, even though Joe was waiting to go—she had to be sure that even if Madame did intercept and read it first, she would not find anything exceptionable in it to prevent her handing it to him. Oh, how it galled Charlotte to think of it! But so long as it reached him at last . . .

As she gave it to Joe she said, as casually as she could, "Joe, be sure you give this into Monsieur Héger's own hand, won't you?"

"If I can," he said, and later Mary wrote to say he had done so. Charlotte experienced all the guilty relief of a spy whose vital message has safely reached headquarters, but far more than this—the relief of a total conviction that, on Joe's return, or Mary's, whichever should be sooner, the letter she had burned for for seven long months would come to her.

In the meantime she pacified herself as well as she could. Even the sight of French in a book or newspaper, let alone the sound of it, was like a contact with her master. She set herself to memorizing half a page of French a day, and this gave her satisfaction bordering on the sensual. She wrote an occasional love poem. And she wrote regularly to Mary. But her sight seemed very bad of late. One letter a day was all she could manage, and she gave herself this excuse for not doing more creative writing. Was she, like Papa, going blind? It frightened her sometimes, but at other times, when her spirits fell very low, she felt it hardly mattered; the world was such a dark, dreary place anyway, she didn't care much if she lost sight of its miseries.

The Taylors' return was delayed, and while they were traveling around Europe Mary didn't write, so Charlotte received no direct news of the letter that she *must* be carrying in her luggage. Would she come home for Christmas? Charlotte, thinking it possible, refused an invitation to Ellen's new home at Brookroyd for fear of missing Mary. She passed a dreadful Christmas; her nerves were wrought up to a tight knot of tension, which made it all but impossible to behave normally and show nothing to those around her. Whenever she could be alone she paced the floor agitatedly, wringing her hands and pressing her knuckles to her teeth. Sometimes she would stare at herself in the mirror. She hated her face; it was so plain, even ugly, with its overhanging forehead and oddly formed nose and reddened skin . . . And she was aging, it seemed to her, every day. There were lines around her eyes, on her brow, lines of tension and bitterness. She would force herself to gaze and gaze at her own unattractiveness as long as any beauty gazes at herself for pleasure, but at last she would turn away with a stifled cry of despair to pace the room once more. *He must write . . . He must write . . .* The letter was in Joe's pocket, in Mary's reticule. *Be calm. It is there. He will not fail me. Be patient.* But the waiting devastated her.

At last she heard that Joe had returned. She sent a letter to him at Cleckheaton—had he something for her? And the message came back—nothing. But Mary was due back in a day or two. Charlotte wrote again: would she come immediately to Haworth?

On the fifth of January, Mary knocked on the door. Charlotte flew to welcome her, her hopes naked and shameless and desperate on her face. One look at Mary, standing there on the doorstep, told her the truth. He had not written. He had not sent a word.

Mary, the only witness to that moment when hope turned—not to despair, for that had been an element in it from the beginning, but to bitter outrage—never forgot the hard, wild, furious look of desolation on Charlotte's face. She could not bear it. She pulled her friend into her arms and held her there, all stiff and unyielding, and whispered:

"No Charlotte. Don't. He is right to do this, it had to be so. When I saw him with—*her*—I knew it would be very wrong of him to write to you. He is a good and honorable man. He doesn't want—"

Charlotte wrenched herself away. "It would not be wrong!" she cried out in a harsh, loud voice. "There is not a scrap of wrong in it! I want nothing that is dishonorable, only his friendship, and of that but a morsel. Out of all her great store of happiness in him, can she not spare me that? Out of his great overflowing kindness, poured out on the least of his pupils, can he not spare me one word to keep my heart from breaking?" She began to run frantically to and fro in the snowy garden, looking like some demented bird fluttering against the bars of a cage. Mary watched, aghast.

"What shall I do? Where shall I go?" Charlotte cried. "I cannot wait any longer. I cannot bear any more. Oh, he is cruel! He is granite! Is this not the worst of all, that he is not what I thought him?"

In the end, Mary ran into the house and fetched Emily, and together they helped Charlotte to her room. Mary sat with her, holding her hand and trying to calm her while she tossed and wept on the bed. She spoke of many small things in an effort to distract Charlotte's mind, and at last she said, "Have you heard about Ellen's poor brother George?"

Charlotte stared at her dully. Her eyes were red from weeping, but for the present she had stopped.

"He is quite broken down," Mary went on. "I'm afraid they will have to put him away."

"Broken down?" Charlotte asked tonelessly after some moments. "Do you mean he has gone mad?"

"It seems so, poor lad."

Charlotte sat up slowly. "George . . . He always reminded me of Branwell . . ." Another sob dragged at her breath. She sat there limply, her hand still in Mary's. Then she seemed to brace herself a little.

"The family must be very—distressed," she said. "I will write to Ellen at once."

"Yes," said Mary. "That would be a very good thing."

7

DISGRACE

RANWELL SEEMED MUCH
calmer when he came home that January. They all noticed it. He
had a new confidence, an air of what Patrick (in whom hope
sprang eternal) was pleased to call "maturity." But when Emily
commented on it privately to Anne, Anne was as enigmatic as
ever.

"One should never take Branwell at face value," she said. "Yes,
he is in a confident mood, but we have seen him confident before."

"*You* have no air of tranquility, however," remarked Emily.
"You're looking decidedly pale and jumpy. I wish you would tell
me what's going on. Is he drinking, or—anything of that sort?"

"No."

"Is his work falling off? Are the Robinsons dissatisfied?"

"No. On the contrary."

"They *are* satisfied?"

After a pause, Anne said, in a grim tone quite unlike her, "*Mrs.*
Robinson is excessively satisfied."

A look of incredulity came over Emily's face. "What in heaven's
name do you mean by that?"

Anne looked at her steadily and said nothing.

"But she must be twenty years older than he is!"

"Seventeen, to be exact."

"How far has it gone?"

Anne was suddenly angry.

"How can I answer that? Do you suppose they make love before me? I know there is something between them, and if I hadn't seen it for myself, almost from the beginning, Lydie would have left me in no doubt. She says quite blatantly that if she is not let do as she pleases, she will tell her Papa about 'how Mama goes on with Mr. Brontë.' Oh, they're a fine crew, I can tell you! Lydie herself is in love with a penniless actor she met at Scarborough. Her father's forbidden her to see him, but her mother is clay in her hands since she has this—hold over her. Lydie tried to involve me in her schemes to meet him, and it was when I would have none of it that she threw up this affair of Branwell's to distress me."

"But who began it?"

"Oh, she did, of course—Mrs. Robinson. I'm certain of that. Branwell would not have dared, however he might admire her. The trouble is that Mr. Robinson is in poor health, and although he adores his wife he is not with her enough. And she is too idle. You know what an impression Branwell makes when he reads aloud, or discourses on one of his pet themes—he becomes impassioned, and I guess she was taken with him, encouraged him to read to her, sit at her feet and so on. Then perhaps he wrote some poetry to her and she was flattered—oh, Emily, how easy it is to flatter such women! The most shamelessly false compliments turn their silly heads in a moment. He would only have to tell her that she inspired him, or affect to think her still in her thirties, and she would melt like dew. From then on, her hungry vanity could lead her into any folly."

"Have you talked to Branwell?"

"I tried once, but he was so furious and spiteful I gave it up. You remember how he was last summer? My guess is, things were not settled between them and he was on tenterhooks to get back to her. But now—"

"Now?"

Anne looked at her. "I believe Branwell expects to marry her."

"*Marry* her? How?"

"When her husband dies."

Emily stared at her, speechless.

"She will be a very rich woman—that's another thing. Branwell has often spoken to me of Hartley Coleridge, whose father so arranged matters that he need never worry about money or any practical consideration. Branwell is deeply convinced that his own genius can only flower under some similar dispensation. By marrying a wealthy widow who would take care of him, he—"

Emily turned away with an exclamation of anger and impatience. But after a moment she turned back.

"Well, well. Let me be my usual phlegmatic self, and think. What's to be done about this?"

"Nothing. Emily, he is grown up! Besides, I see little likelihood of her becoming a widow yet, though her husband is so poorly, and if she *should* ever be free, she will have more advantageous suitors than Branwell at her door, that I can tell you. Oh, I have learned some things during these four long years! I am not the life-sized lump of naïveté I was when I left home. I have seen drunkenness and lechery and corruption of youth displayed before my eyes, and although I know a writer must not shrink from real life, I cannot feel I am any the better for it! Sometimes humanity and their ways disgust me utterly. It's only when I am at home—or occasionally when I walk the sands alone at Scarborough—that I can recover *any* of that optimistic outlook that I used to have. Nowadays, I'm often as hard put to believe that any purity or goodness exists in man, as I used to be to credit any foulness."

"Don't cry, love."

"Oh, I am not crying!" Anne exclaimed. "Believe me, I cry very seldom now. I *have* cried—how I've cried! But tears don't help. Strength like yours is what helps, strength and the honesty to look at people straight and accept all they do without shock. Yet at the same time one must keep oneself aloof. How I wish I hadn't to go back there, and could stay here with you!"

"Then why don't you? If in any case there is nothing to be done."

"Because it was I who took him to that place. And things cannot stand as he imagines. When he finds out that she is only amusing herself with him, there will be some dreadful catastrophe. Then I must be there to help him."

Emily sighed sharply. "If it gets too unbearable, leave him to it. You can't save a fool from his folly."

Anne was quite determined not to "leave him to it," however painful her position became. But by early summer, matters were getting "beyond enough," as Tabby would say. Branwell's bearing was so overweening that he resembled a bantam cock, struting about Thorp Green Hall, constantly and with obvious difficulty suppressing loud crows. Mrs. Robinson appeared to go placidly enough about her legitimate concerns; yet Anne was not oblivious to the tender looks she flashed to Branwell, nor to the little surreptitious gestures of affection she continually made toward him.

One evening, Anne was sitting after supper as she often did in the great drawing room, sewing in a corner while Mrs. Robinson and Branwell flirted discreetly and the two older girls smirked and nudged and whispered over their game of cards. Suddenly Anne could stand it no longer. To have to witness these ignoble proceedings, with Mr. Robinson and two innocent children upstairs, simply sickened her. She stood up, and said, more loudly than she had intended:

"I am going up now, Mrs. Robinson. Branwell, please come with me. I want to show you a letter—"

Branwell threw a nervous glance at Mrs. Robinson, and the girls put their heads together in a burst of tittering. Anne stood like a rock at the door, commanding Branwell with her eyes. He

came, swaggering to cover his reluctance, and went ahead of her
to his own room. There he turned on her.

"Well?" he said arrogantly.

"Branwell, you must stop! It's too shameful, I cannot watch
it any longer."

"Go home then."

She gasped. She had hoped he might at least have the grace
to dissemble, but he was brazen.

"Don't you know you are committing the most awful sin?"

"That's no affair of yours."

"How can you say that! Surely you realize I've only suffered
the whole disgusting situation this long on your account? Does
that not make it my affair?"

"No. No one asked you to stay. I wish you had gone. You make
me uncomfortable with your great cow's eyes staring at me in
silent reproach every minute."

Anne struggled with her own outrage. To lose her temper
would achieve nothing. She must reason with him now; there
was no other hope.

"Branwell, what has she said to you?"

He turned his back on her and stood stubbornly silent.

"Whatever it is," went on Anne, "you must not imagine she
will ever take the matter further than it has gone now. She will
not make herself ridiculous." Branwell turned around fiercely,
but Anne raised her voice.

"She won't, Branwell! She is a very wicked woman if she has
led you to believe you have anything to hope for from her."

He stood back from her, panting.

"Say no more!" he gasped. "You must not make me so angry—
it is bad for me—you are tormenting me on purpose to try to kill
me—you are all the same, all of you; none of you understand
me or know what my needs are—only *she*—my beautiful, my
beloved—"

"Branwell! Stop, stop it! You are mad!"

"Oh, am I indeed? And if you think that when I am master

of this great estate and have the dearest, finest woman on earth as my wife, *you* will be invited to share in my good fortune, you are sadly mistaken! Now get out of my room! You make me ill, ill, *ill* with your foul-minded, spinsterish accusations!"

Anne stood before him, stricken. He looked quite beyond himself. His eyes were wild, a little froth flecked the corners of his lips; she understood now why Papa had always given way to him. Tears of shame and anger choked her, but she dared to assail him once more before retreating.

"It is a dream, Branwell, a wicked, irresponsible, corrupt dream. And it is she who has fed you with it—can't you see how ignobly she has treated you? Oh, Bany, come away, pray do come home with me before it's too late!" Again she came close to him, clutching his limp, cold hand in both of hers, urging him with all the power of her will to obey her.

Suddenly all anger and arrogance seemed to leave him. He swayed before her and put his free hand on her shoulder to steady himself, staring blankly at her. After a few moments he said indistinctly, "Go to bed, Anne. I cannot think about it now."

The next day Branwell lay in bed and declared himself at death's door. He tossed and groaned, and when Anne went to his room he raised himself in bed and shouted at her as if in a delirium.

"Out! Out, you harpie! Begone and torment me no more!"

The doctor was summoned, diagnosed overwrought nerves and prescribed complete rest. Mrs. Robinson appeared in great distress. She sat beside Branwell's bed, ministering to him, bathing his face, holding his hand. Anne waited her opportunity, and at last, overcoming a deep reluctance which was evidently mutual, spoke to her mistress.

"Mrs. Robinson, I think I had better take Branwell home, at least for the present. With Mr. Robinson ill, too, you cannot spare the time to nurse Branwell. And he will not let me do it."

"No—I am most puzzled by his attitude to you—his own sister! It is very strange and unexpected."

The two women eyed each other with bitter coldness masked by civility.

"So will you arrange a conveyance for us? We will leave for Haworth as soon as my brother is fit to travel."

It was clear Mrs. Robinson was put out by this firmness. The truth was, she enjoyed fussing over Branwell; yet she realized she could not keep it up. Sick people soon grew tiresome.

"Well, if you wish. But you will bring him back, will you not, as soon as possible? You know we are off to Scarborough shortly, and my husband desires your brother to stay here with Edmund to help him catch up with his studies."

"I will not bring him back, Mrs. Robinson. I shall not be returning."

Mrs. Robinson was startled. This was very inconvenient.

"Oh? You have not given warning, Miss Brontë! How inconsiderate of you."

"I'm sorry," said Anne shortly. She noticed Mrs. Robinson did not dare ask for her reasons.

Anne packed her box and prepared to leave Thorp Green Hall for the last time. She was too upset to want to say good-bye to anyone, but as she was waiting in the hall for the gig to come around from the stables Mary came rushing down the stairs.

"Oh, Miss Brontë! Mama told me you are leaving for good! Pray—pray don't—I can't bear it!"

She flung herself into Anne's arms, crying stormily, and held her around the waist as if she would not let her go.

"My darling, I must. I am—I am needed at home."

"Not half so much as here!" Mary cried. She turned her wet, anguished face up and whispered passionately:

"You are the only good person in this house! Who will teach me to be good when you are gone?"

A further movement on the stairs caught Anne's eye. Looking up, she was astonished to see Lydie and Eliza lurking above, both with handkerchiefs to their eyes; hardhearted, flippant and selfish as they were, they, too, were weeping over having to lose her.

"Yes, do stay, dear Miss B.—forgive us if we've teased you—"

"We're sorry we've been wayward. It's not our fault you are too good for us. Don't go."

For a moment, Anne hesitated. She had not realized . . . But no. Not even for Mary could she stand any more; and besides, it was imperative she take Branwell away.

"I must," she said firmly, putting Mary from her.

"Well then, at least take Flossy." Flossy was a spaniel puppy that Mary had recently acquired and was very attached to.

"Mary! I couldn't take Flossy!"

"I want you to have him. He is a bit of me that you will carry away to your home and keep to remind you of me."

At home, Branwell sank into a morose mood of resentment that nothing prevailed upon. Papa tried to breach it; Tabby tried; Emily tried. Charlotte alone did not approach him. As soon as Anne announced that she had left Thorp Green for good, Charlotte began making plans for a visit to Ellen.

Anne made one last effort at the end of the week, when she saw Branwell packing.

"You are going back, then?"

"Yes," said Branwell defiantly.

"Will nothing persuade you to stay here?"

"Nothing. And no one—least of all you. You alone know her, you alone should be able to judge her rightly and appreciate her. But you are incapable of understanding any great soul—you're too petty and narrow. I am done with you."

Anne shrugged and turned away. She had tried her best.

Branwell traveled the seventy miles back to Little Ouseburn in a renewed ferment of excitement. The week's separation from his beloved Lydia (he only called her that in moments of complete privacy of course, but he never thought of her by any other name now) had whetted his longing for her. As the gig entered the lordly drive and the great house came in sight, Branwell felt like the master of the house returning home.

He half expected Lydia to be waiting for him on the doorstep, and when he had to go looking for her in the garden he felt a little piqued. But her handsome, full figure in her splendid gown, the coquettish tilt of her head beneath its lace cap when she saw him striding toward her, transformed that pique into a spasm of desire so poignant that it was all he could do not to seize her in his arms there on the lawn, in full view of Mr. Robinson's sick-room windows.

"Ah! You are back!" she exclaimed, crinkling her eyes at him in a way that said, "I love you, but beware—we are observed."

He took her hand notwithstanding, and bent over it, pressing it ardently to his lips and murmuring:

"My treasure—I have never passed such an endless week. Tell me you have missed me half as much as I you, and I am repaid for my pain."

Her fine eyes flickered toward the house. Then she slipped a rose from the basket she was carrying on her arm and tossed it to him. Catching it, he jabbed his fingers on the thorns. She laughed gaily.

"Beware then, how you would clasp *me*! For my thorns are sharper yet. Make up a poem on *that* theme, seductive flatterer!"

Laughing back over her shoulder at him, she crossed the lawn to the house.

Branwell trailed after her, his thwarted body aching as if she had flogged him but his heart alight with joy. Any treacherous doubts that Anne had managed to infiltrate into his mind were dispelled. Would she treat him thus unless she loved him, truly loved him? As they passed into the house, Branwell threw a glance upward toward the room where his employer lay ill. Lydia had often told him (but so patiently, so uncomplainingly!) that her husband was no husband to her now, that her life was barren of affection and care. No, it was not wicked to wish him dead, it was natural! He longed for the right to fill her heart and her life.

However, his hopes seemed to be further from fulfillment than he had supposed. The prospect of the annual holiday in Scarborough had a tonic effect on Mr. Robinson, who was up and about again in time to supervise the arrangements. Branwell had to face the imminent departure of the family at the beginning of July when he was to be left behind with Edmund. The thought of this obscurely frightened him. It had never happened before that he and the boy had been left alone.

The nearer the date came, the more upset Branwell grew. His lady bustled about the house, arranging the packing and seeming quite unaware of Branwell's misery. Of course he knew that she must busy herself at such a time, but nevertheless her apparent cheerfulness in the face of several more weeks of separation inflamed him. At last one day he accosted her in her study.

She was writing at her desk when he tiptoed in and put his hands across her eyes. She started violently and turned, pushing his hands away and looking up with an expression of annoyance.

"Don't do that again, there's a good boy. I hate it."

"I'm sorry," said Branwell, abashed. He stared at her. Whenever they were alone together he could never take his eyes off her. Usually she liked it, but today she said, almost sharply, "Don't stare at me like that—you look like a spaniel waiting for a biscuit."

The hurt this gave would have been unbearable if Branwell had not learned to deafen himself to such chance remarks, knowing she would later soothe him with tender compliments.

"I've come," he began winningly, "to make a suggestion. I'm sure you'll like it. You know Edmund is in an uncooperative mood—I don't think I can manage him alone while you are all enjoying yourselves by the sea. Why can you not stay on with us here for a little while?"

Her face was blank, and there was such a long pause that his skin began to crawl.

"I don't understand. Do you mean that my husband and the girls should go to Scarborough *without me*?"

"Yes!" said Branwell eagerly. "Think! You could easily say it was because of Edmund, and so it would be—partly." He dropped to his knees beside her, and taking both her limp hands in his, gazed ardently up at her. It was a posture she had often responded to—the first time she had ever caressed him was when he had been kneeling beside her reading a poem—and for a moment he felt sure of success, so sure that he opened her two hands like a bowl and buried his face in them. While kissing their palms he murmured passionately:

"Lydia—I can't wait any longer—I am suffering desperately on your account. Please, please stay with me, if only for a week; I can't bear to be parted from you again."

She stood up abruptly, almost causing Branwell to fall over. Her morning gown swished with a strangely cold sound as she twitched it away from his outstretched hand and moved off across the room. At the window she stood for a moment, and then turned to him.

"My dear boy," she said, "you must not be importunate, or you will begin to be repugnant to me. There is absolutely no question of my remaining here. My dear Edmund is not well enough to travel alone, and even if he were, it is my duty to go with him. As for young Edmund, he must do as he is told, and if you cannot manage him, then we must find someone who can."

After a moment of terrible numbness, Branwell scrambled awkwardly to his feet. He felt dizzy. Some monstrous blow had fallen on him, or was about to fall. He looked up at her and saw again his peerless angel, his beloved mistress and wife-to-be. Yes, he had gone too far—she was right. He faced her, and now there was dignity in his bearing.

"I beg your pardon, Lydia. You are too beautiful, too—desirable. Don't be angry with me. I accept your decision. One day we shall be together for always. I shall be patient till then."

He bowed to her and started for the door. But she stopped him.

"Just a moment!"

He turned. Her face had changed.

"What can you mean, 'together for always'?"

"I mean, of course, when we are married."

Now it was her voice that went shrill. "*Married?*" And she

laughed outright. "Who ever dreamed of such a thing? Married? I—to you?" She looked his short figure up and down in unmistakable contempt.

"But—you told me—you would like me to belong to you—to endow me with everything that is yours—if only you were free!"

"But I am not free!"

"You will be! He cannot live long. That is the hope I survive on."

She started back from him as if in horror. "Do you dare to tell me you thought that the nonsense I spoke to amuse you, as a mother promises her child the moon and stars, has caused you to think I am looking forward to my darling Edmund's death?"

"You told me he cared nothing for you—"

"Never did I say such a thing! He adores me."

"—that he neglected you—"

"Fantastic nonsense! He worships me, he heaps me with tokens, he would do anything to please me! While he has been ill I may have felt a little lonely and ill-used, very naturally, but I have never said a word against my beloved Edmund, nor given you the least mandate to think these wild, wicked thoughts! As God is my judge, the day my Edmund dies will be the blackest day of my life. And as to you, you foolish boy, you are like a little spoiled poodle. Your appetite for sweets has grown too voracious. Now I have had enough of this absurd scene. Go back to the schoolroom and get on with your work. I don't wish to see you again before we leave."

How he got out of that room and into his own, Branwell could never remember afterward. When he recovered some perception of the real world about him, he was in a daze; he felt as he sometimes had after being dead drunk. His pillow was drenched, his clothes disheveled; his shirt-sleeves were both torn below the elbow, as if he had wrenched at them in some sort of frenzy. His body and mind felt drained. He lay now on his back in a twisted welter of bedclothes.

He turned his head slowly to the window. Twilight . . . How long had he lain here? He couldn't remember. Some dreadful disaster had befallen him. Maria's face, as he had last seen it, shrunken and bereft of life in her coffin, swam before him. No, that was long ago. A vague, hideous memory of the swarming, hotly desired bodies of the Irish laborers, rolling on him, piercing him, disfiguring his image of himself forever, tortured him briefly, and faded also. No, no—not that either. Something worse, worse . . . He threw his ragged arm over his eyes and gave a choking cry of anguish.

All the Robinsons except young Edmund left for Scarborough the next day. No one bothered with Branwell. Mary alone asked where he was, but nobody knew, and she forgot about him, too, in the bustle of departure.

By noon the house was quiet; only the servants' quarters were still occupied, and the stables. Edmund was down there playing with his ferrets. Devoted as he was to Branwell, he was not about to hunt for his tutor, whose company might involve lessons; and Edmund, who was irredeemably slow at learning, would rather be lonely than risk that. Anyway, William was about. William Allison was the Robinson's chief groom, a sour, suspicious man, but steady and responsible. Edmund always felt safe with him.

He was feeding the female ferret through the wire of her cage. William had warned him not to take chances, but she seemed so docile, and he longed to stroke her. Cautiously, after looking around, he opened the door and reached in to pick the sleek little beast up.

The next instant he was shrieking with pain and outrage, and the ferret was snaking off across the yard.

William came running, but when he saw what had happened he had little sympathy.

"I told thee! Tha's lost 'un now, and thi finger's bitten to t'bone, I reckon! Let's see it, tha daft bairn—"

But Edmund wanted to be made a fuss of.

"I want Mr. Brontë! I don't want you!"

"Then go and find 'un," said William. "He'll dress it for thee, dainty as any lass, no doubt." And he stumped back to his horses.

Edmund rushed into the house calling for Branwell. Alone in

his room at the top of the house, Branwell finally heard him and roused himself. He needed a drink. And Edmund was below, calling him. Smoothing his hair uselessly and groping for his glasses, he staggered downstairs.

Edmund, clutching his hurt finger, stopped crying as Branwell descended and gaped at him.

"Are you ill, Mr. Brontë?"

"No, I'm all right. What's the matter? Good God—what's all that blood?"

"My ferret bit me!"

The sight of the boy's blood and his crumpled wet face tore Branwell's heart. He had a sudden moment of complete empathy; he even felt the sharp rodent teeth in his own flesh. It was hard to be fond of Edmund—he was not an attractive child—but Branwell was aware of the boy's devotion to him, and now, seeing his need of comfort, he suddenly loved him.

"Poor lad—poor little lad! Come, I'll bathe it, I'll make it well."

He took the boy's hand tenderly in his and kissed it. Then, holding it still and with his other arm around Edmund's shoulders, he led him upstairs.

"What on earth is all that hullaballoo in the dining room, Tabby?"

"'Tis the curates, Miss Charlotte. They've coom busting in, *four* on 'em, if you please, fresh and 'ungry from a walk, and our new 'un, that Mr. Nicholls, 'as cheek enow to say 'appen we've some tea to give 'em. Seemingly Mr. Grant's told 'em Monday's our bakin' day."

"Oh, really, they are too bad! Why can't they wait to be invited?"

"'Appen they know 'ow you feels about 'em, miss, and that they'd never get past t'door!" And the old woman bent over to laugh.

"Well, it can't be helped. You'd better lay the things, Tabby, and I'll set out as few of our cakes for them as Papa would think decent."

Patrick never minded the neighborhood curates invading the parsonage at teatime, but it infuriated Charlotte, especially when, as now, she was hot and tired from baking. However, she would have done her duty and served them their ill-deserved tea in peace had they not begun talking "curate-talk"—in other words, indulging in self-glorification at the expense of less enlightened members of other sects.

"The heretical absurdity of this man Maurice, daring to put it about that sinners will not be eternally damned!" expostulated one, a Mr. Smith from Keighley. "How does *that* pious notion sort with the doctrine of a just deity?"

"Why, there would be no containing evil if such an idea took hold!" exclaimed Mr. Nicholls. He was the newcomer to Haworth, and in Charlotte's opinion, as narrow-minded a bigot as ever put on a surplice. "Dr. Pusey has declared war on this whole pack of so-called Christian Socialists, who are no more than Dissenters in a new guise."

"I'm surprised such a great man as the Doctor bothers himself about a few prating heathens who seem to set more stock by science than Holy Writ," said Mr. Grant from Oxenhope, already a fast friend of Mr. Nicholls' and an avid supporter of his Puseyite views and rabid anti-Dissensionism.

"Ah, well," put in the fourth curate, a little pale prim-lipped man called Bradley, "let us be thankful that our good Lord has vouchsafed *us* the light to lead our flocks in His appointed ways." And he cast his eyes up in an attitude of smug self-satisfaction that proved just too much for Charlotte's overstretched temper.

"How happy must you all be," she snapped out, "to have received God's personal attention! Did you hear His very voice whispering the eternal truths to you which lesser mortals still find they need to discuss and puzzle over? And how fortunate *we* are, here in this remote country parish, to have men at the helm more confident of their enlightenment than the greatest prelates and theologians of London!"

"*Charlotte!*" cried her father, scandalized. But Charlotte, smacking down the teapot almost hard enough to crack it, flung herself out of the room and banged the door.

The curates gaped, while their minister, flushed with angry embarrassment, stammered out apologies. Mr. Nicholls recovered first. Something like a slow, reluctant smile lengthened his lips between his heavy mutton-chop whiskers.

"Say no more, sir," he said in his deep, resonant voice. "It may be we were guilty of the sin of pride. Your daughter did right to chastise us."

No voice was raised in agreement, and the four intruders, having polished off the last pinch of cake crumbs, took their leave.

When Branwell unexpectedly arrived at the parsonage everyone was very surprised to see him. He would not answer any questions, but retreated to his room, where he sat hunched up, remaining motionless and unresponsive till nightfall, when he was heard slamming out of the house by Emily, Anne and Tabby. They looked at each other in speechless anxiety. They all knew where he was going. Mr. Nicholls was in with Patrick discussing parish matters.

"Would that be your son, sir?" he asked, on hearing the front door slam.

"It would," said Patrick heavily.

"I look forward to meeting him."

Patrick said nothing. He was utterly cast down by Branwell's ominous sudden appearance. Somehow the old man felt doom hanging over them. For a moment, looking at the bland eyes and heavy, stolid features of the dark young cleric opposite him, he felt a stabbing pain of loss for Willie. But what was the use? Arthur Nicholls was dependable and conscientious, and he, Patrick, needed all the help he could get. He couldn't expect this man to take any of the family burdens off his weary shoulders. Charlotte was away, visiting Ellen; Patrick missed her and was short-tempered as a result.

"Let us get on," he said tersely. Then he pressed his hand suddenly to his abdomen.

Mr. Nicholls leaned forward. "Have you that pain again, sir?"

"Yes. It comes when I am tense. It is trying, but after long experimentation I have learned what medications best ease it."

"I notice you keep Dr. Graham's *Modern Domestic Medicine* always by you. An excellent volume."

"Are you interested in medical matters?" asked Patrick, brightening.

"Indeed, yes! My uncle, you know, who adopted me and brought me to Ireland, was a doctor—"

Patrick waved this away. He was not interested in his curate's supposedly elevated origins, and privately doubted them. He himself had occasionally been guilty of some harmless falsification in his early days, to conceal the humbleness of his Irish background, and he was not likely to be put upon by such another as himself.

"I hope," he said invitingly, "that *you* have no troubling symptoms of internal disorder?"

"Occasional rheumatic twinges. I, too, suffer more when I am tense or agitated. Happily that is not often the case. Dr. Graham has some useful advice on the subject of rheumatism—"

"But more on that of digestive irregularities!" interrupted Patrick eagerly. For the first time in the several months of their association, he actually warmed to the young man. "Perhaps you would care to glance at my copy. I have made copious notes in the margins. I find compensation for my chronic ill health in seeking cures and experimenting on myself. My results are all noted here," he added, tapping the book complacently.

"I shall be greatly interested to see them," said Mr. Nicholls with gratifying enthusiasm. No more parish matters were discussed that night.

Branwell, dead drunk, was brought home by John Brown at midnight. Anne helped Emily get him to bed. They said little, their hearts cold with apprehension.

He was still in bed the next day when a letter arrived for him from Scarborough. Anne took it up to him. She watched him snatch it eagerly, then saw his face fall.

"This—this is not from Lydia!" he exclaimed, looking up at Anne wildly, as if she were to blame.

"I know."

He began to pant as he stared at the letter. He made a feeble attempt to open it, but his hands shook so badly he could not do it. At last he muttered, "Open it. No! Not you. Fetch Emily."

Anne did so, and tactfully stayed outside. She heard Emily's deep voice steadily reading, and she listened against her will.

" 'Your proceedings have been discovered. I can only describe them as bad beyond expression. That you are dismissed from my service needs not to be said, but I add this: If you do not wish the world at large to know the *whole truth* of your vile behavior, you will instantly and for ever break off all communication with every member of my family.' "

There was a deathly silence from the room. Emily either had no more to read, or could not bring herself to go on. From Branwell there was no sound. After a moment, Emily, white-faced, came out. She and Anne took hands and stood mutely together, as if waiting for the house to collapse about them.

Suddenly the silence of the parsonage was rent by an animal howl. Others followed. Patrick stumbled out of his room below and called up the stairs, "What? What in heaven's name is the matter?" And Tabby hobbled from the kitchen and stood beside him, clutching his arm and whimpering.

Emily recovered first.

"Go down," she ordered Anne. "Take the letter. Break it gently to Papa, but tell him all you know. I will deal with—that."

She thrust the fatal letter into Anne's hands and returned to Branwell's room, from which shortly issued loud, compelling commands for quiet. These gradually took effect. By the time Anne had begun her grueling ordeal of explanation below, the howls had subsided to sobs and groans.

8
HOPE
RENEWED

THE CATASTROPHE FELL ON THE parsonage while Charlotte was away staying with Ellen, and the first indication she had of it was when, on her return, she was met by a distraught and red-eyed Tabby.

"Oh, my poor lass—tha'd a done best to stop away than coom back to this house of grief and shame!"

Charlotte, her heart thumping with dread, put Tabby aside and ran upstairs. Anne met her on the landing.

"Don't go in to Branwell, Charlotte! He is—ill."

Charlotte shrugged grimly. She was all too familiar with this family euphemism. But Anne shook her head and drew her into her own room.

"Listen, I must tell you everything quickly. Branwell has been dismissed for—for making love to Mrs. Robinson."

Charlotte was dumbfounded.

"He made love to his employer's wife? A *married woman?*"

Anne nodded, and suddenly Charlotte burst out, "But that is dreadful! It is quite, quite dreadful!"

"Well of course it is, Charlotte, but there's no doubt that he really does love her, and also that she encouraged him. I can promise you it was mainly her fault."

"That does not excuse him!"

Emily came in, grim-faced, her hair in disorder. "Are *you* judging him, Charlotte?" she asked bluntly. "*You?*"

Charlotte, stung to the quick, turned on her. "Yes! And I, of all people, have a right to!"

"Because you had prudence to flee—finally. But what if the *married* man you loved had loved and encouraged you? What then?"

In a terrible state of agitation, Charlotte rushed from the room.

"You shouldn't have said that, Emily," said Anne quietly.

"I know. But I cannot bear this self-righteousness that condemns the weak. Branwell is a hopeless being—I knew it long ago. But he can't help it, so how can one blame him? If we must be angry, let it be with that wretched woman. Presumably she betrayed him when the affair grew inconveniently intense on his side."

"You think she told her husband herself?" Anne asked incredulously. "Never! It would endanger her position too much. No. Either Lydie or Eliza must have done it. Or even Edmund . . ."

"Edmund," echoed Emily musingly. "Branwell raves about Edmund when he is drunk. Edmund is Mr. Robinson's name too, isn't it? Which Edmund haunts him, I wonder—and why?"

The answer to Emily's question might have shocked even her, but luckily she was never to learn it. In fact, after a remarkably short time, it would have been impossible for Branwell to reveal it even when drunk, for it shamed him so unutterably that he buried it in some deep, dark part of his mind, covered it over, locked door upon door above it and in that way obliterated it from his consciousness forever.

Only sometimes, in a drugged or drunken dream, he saw the boy—always from the back, faceless, nameless—running down the steps of a great red brick house, across a green silent space and into a stable-yard. A looming presence brooded over this area, ceasing soon, in Branwell's stifled memory, to be identifiable as William Allison, the Robinson's groom; nor could he hear anymore—as he had heard in reality—the shrill cries of the boy, intolerably, crudely, brutally describing the gentle, tender things Branwell had attempted, and the sharp loud bark of the man's rejoinder:

"He *what?* Tha' shalt go to Scarborough wi' me this hour, lad, and I shall 'ave a word wi' thy father about that young nancy!"

None of this was able to penetrate the locked doors imposed on memory. Only the boy, running, running through the green stillness and Branwell, shouting at him soundlessly to come back, come back, come back . . .

But this was seldom. For the most part, the more endurable horror took command of all waking and sleeping thoughts. He could recall in the smallest detail every exchange that had ever passed between him and Lydia Robinson, excluding the last. That, too, was buried. She loved him, she yearned and hungered for him. Robinson had discovered it from one of the girls. Now here Branwell lay in torment and despair while in distant Scarborough *she*, too, must be writhing on a bed weeping and wailing. For what would such a husband not inflict as punishment on a wife, however pure and faithful in deed, whom he thought guilty? Thoughts of what she must be suffering added to Branwell's agony, for before long he totally believed in his saving fiction, and he raved as often about her imagined misery as about his own.

After a week of turmoil, by which time the village was seething with gossip and the entire story (or Branwell's version of it) was on every tongue, Patrick roused himself from his stupor of shame and summoned John Brown.

"John, I must send him away. I should have done it sooner—now they all know. It's all come upon me too late in life, John, too late in life! Take him to Liverpool for a few weeks."

From Liverpool, at John's instigation, Branwell wrote a short letter to Charlotte. He didn't care so much about the others. It was Charlotte's cold, closed face that he saw, her wordless reproaches that hummed in his ears, her forgiveness and restored love that he suddenly needed. His apology, his promises of amendment, came straight from his heart, though it was hard to form them into words she might accept.

But after he had posted the letter, he broke down and wept to John.

"All my vows are made to be broken!" he muttered. "I meant all I said to her, yet I shall not keep to it. This time I am defeated before I begin. But if Charlotte wholly loses faith in me, I am done. I must win it back somehow. It is the only thing left to me now."

Branwell's trouble had come at a bad time for Charlotte.

If M. Héger had supposed that by ignoring her letters he was helping her to get over her "infatuation," he underestimated the depth of her feelings for him. However frail her body, her heart was great, her capacity for love and suffering almost infinite. The canker of her passion for him had plenty to feed on, and lived its parasitic existence on and on, long after it should have succumbed from lack of nourishment. Charlotte could feel it like a malignant living creature and realized despairingly that it would not die until all about it was gnawed to a hollow, burned-out emptiness.

But she bore her sufferings more quietly now. She no longer cherished her love, but determinedly tried to crush it with silence. She refused to indulge it by speaking of M. Héger to Emily, or writing of him to Mary. But the desire she felt went on unabated, and she lived with it in her own private hell.

One thing she could do—the only thing—she could try to write it out of her. Slowly, laboriously, in utter secrecy, she began to write a novel. She dared not write the truth or anything close to it, yet she must somehow exorcise her demon. So, to distance herself, she tried to see her Brussels experience through alien eyes—the eyes of a young man. *He* would be the professor; and the poor, plain, insignificant, yet high-principled and loving girl, who was herself in thin disguise, would cross his path by chance when the story was well advanced, when Charlotte could hope that the effort of describing her and her love would not be painful enough to stop the flow of narrative.

She deliberately avoided making her protagonist in the least like Monsieur in any particular. Only when she came to write of the headmistress of the girls' seminary in the story did she at all let herself go, for her miseries at the hands of Madame cried out for revenge. Still Charlotte was careful not to draw a portrait of Madame, for she seemed to see every word she wrote as if Monsieur were reading over her shoulder. She disciplined herself, only spicing her fictitious creation with passing flavors of a purely subjective reality.

At first she had been afraid for her sight. Yet, oddly, when she was deeply engrossed in her writing, her eyes seemed to grow stronger. She assumed they were "better," not realizing that their previous weakness had been other than physical. Gradually the effort, the discipline, the growing pile of pages, served as a tonic. The pain eased, at least while she worked; her listlessness improved. But there were still moments of the darkest despair.

Earlier in the year, some months before Branwell's dismissal, Charlotte had been invited to visit the Taylors to say good-bye to Mary, who was at last setting off on her New Zealand adventure.

The Taylor household, never a quiet one, was in ferment. Mary had tried to animate Charlotte with some of her own excitement, but in vain; all Charlotte could think of was that in a little while Mary would leave her and she would never see her again. Her sorrow affected her physically: she was blinded by headaches and felt perpetually nauseated. Watching Mary, full of zest and vigor, darting about among her boxes and trunks, laughing at any mention of the dangers of the voyage or the uncertainties of the future, Charlotte felt like an old woman. It was as if her own life were nearly over, while Mary's was just beginning.

At last, Mary forced herself to calm down. She sat by Charlotte and held her hand.

"Charlotte, I see you've not got over it. You know, as I see it, all your energies, which should be used to bring you to a better situation, are being channeled into this hopeless love."

Charlotte stood up. There was a stabbing pain in her head and she felt sick; yet she remained on her feet and began to pace the room.

Mary went on, "You must not stay at home forever. You must go abroad again. Go to Paris—now *there* is a city, you would love it! And English families there are always seeking gov—"

A sharp movement from Charlotte pulled her up.

"All right then, some other way. But don't, I beg of you, stay at home."

"It's no use. I must stay. It's my duty. Besides . . ." Charlotte gave a sharp sigh. "A new place is not the answer. Oh, I daresay I should like any change at first, as I liked Brussels at first. But the impediment to enjoying a free life is *in me*. One part of me longs for variety, communion with human beings. Yet bodily and even mentally I haven't the energy to grasp such a way of life— it's not for me! To me it will all come at second hand, through books, through letters like yours perhaps. I feel I'm doomed always to live through others."

"I know nothing about that," said Mary bluntly. "But I do know that if you spend the next five years at home, in solitude and weak health, you'll be finished. You'll never recover. Oh, Charlotte—think what you'll be in five years hence if you do not take hold of life now!"

Such a dark shadow passed across Charlotte's face that Mary could have bitten out her tongue.

"Oh, I'm sorry, Charlotte! Don't cry."

But Charlotte was not crying. She resumed her pacing of the room and after a while she said dully, "I intend to stay at home, all the same, Mary. You must venture for me."

The loss of Mary threw Charlotte more than ever back on Ellen. Dear, faithful (and, best of all perhaps, *un*intrepid) Ellen! And Ellen was good for her in another way, for she knew nothing about Charlotte's love, so Charlotte was never tempted to break her vow of silence with her as she was with Emily. Visits to Ellen, Ellen's return visits to Haworth, soothed and cheered Charlotte, and sometimes, after one of them, it seemed for the time being possible never to write to Monsieur again.

But the balm wore off.

She wrote in May, even though she had heard nothing, even though she knew she should not, even though a hateful voice within her coldly assured her that her letter would be ignored, perhaps even spurned. And then she set herself, as a duty, a challenge, a trial of strength, to wait out six months *without hope*. And it was near the beginning of these six months, eons from the time when she might with *any* kind of justification allow herself the relief of writing another letter, that Branwell's disgrace fell on them.

She would, in fairness, have allowed Branwell his moment of uncontrolled grief. But that it went on and on, that he imposed it ruthlessly on all about him, that in the public house he babbled his woes to any curious villager who happened to be there, and that these uninhibited outpourings continued despite the fact that he allowed himself alcohol to help him dull the keen edge of misery—all these aspects of Branwell's behavior alienated Charlotte more and more. If she, a mere woman, could subdue her emotions—at least to the point where only she suffered from them—why could not he do the same?

At first he openly begged her for sympathy, pouring out the full story of his love for Lydia Robinson, hers for him, Mr. Robinson's heartless cruelty to them both, and so on. Charlotte listened in silence, though she could hardly bear this catalogue of immorality.

But when he chanced to mention "the estate" and the leisured yet productive life he had hoped to lead as the husband of this lady, Charlotte could take no more. Without a word—but not without a look of horrified contempt that shriveled his heart—she stood up and left the room. That the desire for fortune and ease should have played an admitted part in this disgraceful amour was too ignoble! In all the years of their closeness, the desire for fame, freedom and opportunity had run parallel in both of them, and burned equally in each; yet *she* had never allowed such a motive to influence her for one moment in her dealings with any man or circumstance. Love she might have understood, or tried to. But *this*! It was too mercenary, too horrible. It gave her the final excuse she needed to withdraw herself completely from her brother. The deepest truth was that the sight of him wallowing in a grief whose cause was so akin to her own, afflicted her unendurably.

Mrs. Robinson was not wallowing in grief—far from it.

Though naturally very upset by William Allison's revelations, having interrogated Edmund and subjected him to a medical examination by the family doctor, she was satisfied that no actual harm had befallen him. This being so, perhaps all was for the best. Branwell had been getting troublesome beyond a doubt, and now he had been fortuitously disposed of. It was Mrs. Robinson who had insisted upon the proviso in her husband's irate letter forbidding Branwell to contact *any* member of the family again; it had cost her a pang or two, for he had been a dear boy and very good for her morale—but the danger, once her daughters had grown rebellious, had been far too great.

For the length of the family's sojourn in Scarborough she fancied herself safely out of the wood; but on their return to Thorp Green Hall, her maid Ann Marshall, who had been privy to her foolish flirtation, lost no time in informing her that Branwell had written her a wild letter saying he was losing his mind with misery and begging for news of her mistress. At first, Mrs. Robinson flew into a rage engendered by panic: What, did he still threaten her from a distance? Ann stolidly remarked that the letter contained no threats, and no demands either, only wretchedness and concern for her. But Mrs. Robinson had a habit of judging others by herself. Branwell had an ironclad hold over her. She would do best, she felt, to forestall him before the point of blackmail was reached.

"Should I answer his letter, madam?"

"Yes," her mistress replied at last. "You had better. Tell him . . . tell him I am in as deep distress as himself. . . . Describe my grief at losing him. If he thinks I am indifferent, it may work upon him, who knows how? Men scorned can be as furious as women! If he writes again I will give you a trifle of money to send, to keep him quiet. Say it is a token of my remorse for his dismissal."

Thus it happened that Branwell, who had been improving slightly simply because he had no money with which to buy drink, suddenly found himself again in funds, and furthermore with a motive stronger than ever for spending them in the Black Bull. The maid's letter (dictated by Mrs. Robinson) described his Lydia's condition in such harrowing terms that his heart was torn, for he truly loved her and now could not doubt that she loved him. Only one thought sustained him and gave him strength to go on living: if she still cared for him, his hopes *for the future* were not at an end. But meanwhile the thought of her grief, and his own, forced him to bouts of drunkenness that kept the household in a turmoil.

Throughout this time of disquiet and upheaval, the three sisters withdrew into their own private worlds as often as they could. Never had they so desperately needed the solace each of her own room and of her own inner resources. Anne found Gondal less and less of an attraction, and only "played" at it—they still used this word for their imaginings—with Emily; when alone, she worked steadily on her governess story. This had started as a sort of journal of her experiences with the Ingham family, but gradually she broadened it, changed names, fictionalized incidents and introduced new characters. Soon she was no longer calling it *Passages in the Life of an Individual* but *Agnes Grey*, after the heroine. She grew rather excited as its length increased. Was it a real novel? She began to hope it might be, especially when, daring to read bits of it to the other two, they lavished praise and encouragement on her.

Charlotte was still at work on her story, *The Professor*. She reined herself in more strictly as it proceeded, for she wanted it above all to be a *real* account, a true thing, not a romance in the usual sense. She allowed nothing exaggerated, nothing coincidental, nothing even highly colored or dramatic to tincture the plain tale she was meticulously unfolding.

"It must be honest and true to life," she kept saying doggedly to the others when they protested it was "too ordinary."

"Any fool can write a gripping story full of wild incidents and uncontrolled passions. I want to show that normal, decent individuals can be fascinating, too."

"Well, at least listening to Crimsworth's placid narrative is a contrast to the drama upstairs," said Emily drily. "Still, he's a bit of a dull dog, you know, Charlotte—not much go in him."

Charlotte bridled.

"By 'go', do you mean the passion and violence that ruled our characters of the Nether World?"

"And which rule many here above," said Emily, nodding upwards. "They may be very trying to live with, but their doings are what people like reading about just the same."

"Have we not enough of dissipation, and egotism, and blasphemy in the house without writing about it? I reject your criticism. Crimsworth is far from dull—or if he is dull, then so are the majority of worthy, decent men whom worthy women love and marry. What you object to really, I think, is that his failings are not those of a Byron, but those of the run of mankind."

She was annoyed, and Anne, seeing it, said quickly, "And when are we going to hear some of your work, Emily?"

"When indeed?" asked Charlotte acidly.

"When I am ready, which may well be never," Emily answered.

"You are not fair!" Charlotte burst out. "We read our work to you, and you say your say without much care for our feelings. While you—whom I know to be hard at work on something or other—protect it from *our* criticism as if our eyes might mar it somehow."

"That's just what I feel. What is profoundly personal *cannot* be exposed without—" Emily stopped.

"Without what?"

"Betraying it."

"Well! But what about our work?"

"That's fiction. It's the stuff of your experience, perhaps, but not the stuff of your souls." She spoke quite matter-of-factly and without any special emphasis; yet Anne and Charlotte were silenced.

But if Anne accepted it without question, Charlotte, who had had more stings to put up with from Emily's blunt criticisms, could not. She was determined to find out what Emily was doing alone in the little nursery study for hours in the afternoons. And when she found that no amount of hints and coaxings would move Emily, Charlotte waited till she was alone in the house one day and then, quite aware of the enormity of the act and the dire consequences of discovery, she crept into Emily's room.

On the table stood the writing desk, a portable box with a sloping lid, left trustingly wide open. Inside were a jumble of papers, on the top of which lay a number of penny notebooks. Charlotte's hand went out—and drew itself back. She was conscious of a strong mixture of ignobility in her motives and was frightened of the guilt that would surely afflict her mercilessly if she proceeded. Yet she reached out again. Her fingers touched the topmost cover. On it was written: *Gondal Poems, transcribed January 1846.*

Stop again! Was she a Mlle Blanche, a spy, and on her own beloved sister? She felt the first pangs of conscience already, and yet curiosity, the need to have knowledge of Emily equal to that which Emily had of her, was stronger.

In a compulsive spasm she snatched up the notebook, opened it and read.

The first poem scarcely made sense to her, for her heart was beating so hard that her eyes could not take in its meaning. But the second struck through her like a shaft—of sunlight, of clarion music, of steel. She stood riveted, reading the same poem again and again. When she came to herself she was sitting on the bed, dazed with some emotion that had no name. It was not envy, it was more like awe. She turned a page and read another. The same feeling assailed her. She was amazed. These were no ordinary poems; this sister of hers was no ordinary poet. She had the right to be critical! Charlotte felt suddenly abashed at the thought that she had shown any of her own—by comparison with these, singularly uninspired—productions to Emily. Sitting limp and dazed, staring blindly ahead after reading half a dozen magnificent poems, Charlotte wondered numbly whether she would ever be able to look at her in the same way again. She had a strange sense of loss, for work like this set Emily apart from herself and Anne: they had their gifts, yes, but not like this!

Suddenly Charlotte was seized by a violent excitement. She swiftly lifted the notebook again, holding it close to her eyes. She read all the rest straight through; then, panting and trembling, snatched up the next notebook, and the next. Each poem was dated and neatly copied, though few had titles. This, then, had been Emily's work these last months—transcribing all the poems she thought worthwhile and no doubt destroying the rest. Charlotte abruptly clasped the books to her breast. It was Emily, their own Emily, who had written these—and might have kept them forever hidden if she, Charlotte, had not been bold and treacherous! Well, out of evil would come good.

Charlotte had not, of course, intended Emily ever to know that she had looked. But now, because of the nature of what she had seen, she must brave a wrath she could scarcely imagine in order to bring these poems to the light. A greater sin than hers in breaking into Emily's secretiveness would be to let this talent lie forever hidden. To avoid that, Charlotte felt she could face anything—even Emily.

Yet she feared her own cowardice. To forestall it, she forced herself to take the notebooks with her to her own room. That would inevitably bring the denouement swiftly upon her. She lived through an hour's nightmarish apprehension before she heard Keeper's bark and knew that Emily was back from her walk. With held breath and starting eyes she listened to Emily's sharp, decisive footsteps coming up the stairs and crossing the landing. At the door of the little study, they stopped dead. There was a moment of deathly silence, during which Charlotte thought she would swoon with terror. Then, unerringly, Emily called out:

"*Charlotte!*"

Through dry lips Charlotte croaked out, "I am here."

Emily burst in like a thunderbolt. Charlotte rose, the notebooks openly in her hands. The two sisters faced each other, Emily scarlet in the face, Charlotte white as death.

"You stole my poems!"

"I didn't steal them—they are here. I stole a look at them. And I am glad I did."

Charlotte had once, not very long before, seen Emily thrash Keeper almost insensible with her fists. It had appalled her, for even a strong man would have feared to set upon the brute without so much as a stick in his hand; Keeper was of mastiff extraction and quite capable of flying at the throat of anyone who abused him. But he had disobeyed repeatedly, and at last Emily had given him punishment he would never forget—and neither would anyone who had witnessed it.

Now Charlotte saw the same look of barbaric fury in Emily's face, the same trembling rigid arms and fists, the same stiff-clenched jaw. It seemed impossible that she should be physically afraid of Emily, yet it was with the greatest difficulty that she prevented. herself from turning to flee, or dropping to the floor in supplication. She stood up to her, for the magic power of the poetry was still on her.

"Emily, strike me if you like, but you can't make me forget what I have read. I wanted to criticize them, as you've criticized my work. But I can't. They are beyond criticism. They are brilliant."

If she had thought to soften Emily with praise, she was disappointed. Emily lowered her head and growled, as savagely as a dog herself:

"*They were mine*—that is all they were—that is all I wanted them to be! And they are not mine anymore!" Then, as Charlotte wordlessly held out the books, she shouted, "No! I don't want them now. You can burn them to ashes for all I care! What's the use of them to me now someone else has seen them? I could kill you, Charlotte. Do you hear me? I mean every word I am saying. I wish you were dead so that my work would be whole again."

She turned swiftly and walked out, leaving Charlotte's door open but slamming her own violently behind her. Charlotte, shocked and crushed, stood silent for many minutes. Then slowly her muscles unlocked. The notebooks were still in her hands. She felt she must look into them again, to make sure, to regain her conviction. But as she opened the top one it was as if this silent movement had summoned Emily. In a sudden whirlwind of movement she reappeared, almost frightening Charlotte into a faint, and grabbed the books in both hands. But Charlotte, though tottering on her feet, hung on.

"So you do still want them!" she panted. "They are not wholly spoiled for you!"

"You shall not keep them or look at them again. I shall destroy them myself!"

"That you shan't do—not while I have breath!"

"Let go! They will tear!"

"You said I might burn them!"

"I shall burn them myself."

"Emily—Emily—please—don't harm them—I dare not let them go—please!"

Charlotte knew she had not half Emily's strength; in fact, she did not know how she had held onto the books for so long with Emily pulling with all her might. Now Emily gave her a heavy push that sent her spinning onto the bed, still clutching the books against her thin chest. Emily's heavy body landed on top of hers and they struggled. Suddenly Charlotte cried:

"I shall scream for Papa!"

Breathing heavily, Emily stopped, and they lay still, one on top of the other and the books still in Charlotte's hands.

"Give them to me."

"I will! But you must promise me not to harm them."

"They are mine—"

"You have no right to destroy them yourself. You have a duty to share them."

"I don't recognize any such duty!"

"Then you'll have to tear them to pieces to get them."

Emily wrestled with her again briefly, but the fury had abated—she had no spirit to throw her full strength against Charlotte now. And Charlotte was adamant, determined—Emily could feel it. She could have got her books back piecemeal, but when she thought of the long happy hours she had spent transcribing and editing, month by month, the fight went out of her. She turned away, and for the first time in many years began to cry.

Charlotte sat up.

"Emily, you must forgive me. I know I did wrong, but now I'm sure it's for the best. Your poetry is—it's—I can't describe what I feel about it. You *must not* keep it hidden. God's given you a talent—you know what it says about talents in the Bible—"

Emily turned her tormented face away. "Be quiet, Charlotte! Let me cry in peace, I don't want to hear about God just now."

It took days to reconcile Emily to the fact that other eyes had seen "the stuff of her soul." But at last Charlotte persuaded her to show Anne; and when Anne, too, had been struck into raptures, little by little Charlotte began to put into effect a plan she had conceived, subconsciously at first, almost as soon as she had first read the poems.

They must be given to the world—and not only for the world's sake. Their hope of Branwell was dead. Well, then they had only themselves and their own talents to depend on. And here, she saw, was a talent of no common stature, a talent that could well serve to introduce the name of Brontë to literature, and on the strength of which her own and Anne's admittedly lesser but not undeserving talents might gain a hearing.

The trouble was not merely Emily's inviolable sense of privacy, but her apparently total lack of ambition. Anne was diffident and unsure of her worth, but she did have ambition in a modest way, and Charlotte had enough for the three of them. Once she saw a glimmer of light at the end of this long tunnel of obscurity and half-living, she became fanatical, with all a fanatic's single-minded energy and persuasiveness. She could not tolerate Emily's repeated refusals; she overrode them remorselessly until at last even Emily's resistance was worn down. But it was Anne's mite of persuasion that carried the day.

"If we all contributed to a volume of poetry," she said, "and if we use *noms de plume*, wouldn't that meet your main objections, Emily? In that way no one could possibly identify any of the poems with you."

It was this prospect of anonymity that finally won Emily over. Besides, she was practical enough to see the necessity of trying to make their own way now that Branwell had shown himself (in her pet phrase) "no go." All else had been tried: she, for one, was not willing to go out governessing again, and if not she, then why should the others? No, there was sense in trying to turn to effect whatever abilities they had. But she was still uneasy.

"Who will want to publish a motley collection of rhymes by three nameless nobodies? Or read it, for that matter?"

"Your poetry is unique," said Charlotte firmly. "And ours is not bad. Anyway, we must try. We *must try*."

And if any of them tried, it was Charlotte.

All that winter she kept them hard at it. Where before they had read to each other and wrestled over revision for pleasure, now they did it in deadly earnest. By December they were on their way to achieving an edited and neatly copied selection comprising the best of their joint output, and Charlotte, lambent with hope, was ready to assail the great publishing houses of London, starting her campaign with letters to the publishers of Wordsworth and Byron.

She was not rejected. She was not *answered*.

"Just as I expected," said Emily. "No go. They don't want our rhymes."

"But not even the courtesy of a reply!"

Anne was more practical. "We aimed too high. Let's write to some less exalted firm and just ask advice."

Charlotte cobbled her battered hopes into shape again and wrote to a firm in Edinburgh. This time they received a brisk and sensible reply advising them to write to a small firm that specialized in religious poetry. *Their* answer was prompt and encouraging.

"We march!" cried Charlotte ecstatically, and ran at once for brown paper and string.

9

DECLINE AND
ASCENT

*T*HE BOOK OF POEMS CAME OUT
in May. The girls had had to help pay for them to be printed
and even to defray the cost of advertising; but they had expected
that and regarded the outlay as well worthwhile, especially when
the advance copies arrived.

They carried the parcel to Emily's room—the old study above
the hall—closed the door upon their secret treasure and tore off
the wrappings in a fever of excitement. There they were, bound
in handsome dark-green cloth with the title stamped on in gold:
Poems by Currer, Ellis and Acton Bell.

They stood crowded together, each with a volume in her hands,
and even Emily was struck speechless with pleasure.

"The names look splendid, don't they? No one could guess if
we were men or women!"

"How would Mr. Nicholls feel if he knew we had appropri-
ated his middle name?" Charlotte asked, and suddenly they all
burst into suppressed laughter, choking behind their hands. It
was too funny to think of the reaction of their father's sober-

sides curate to the idea of lending his name to a book of poetry!

"Oh, *do* let us show Papa!" Anne exclaimed. But Emily was adamant.

"No. He could never keep silent. You swore we would tell no one."

They were subdued for a moment. Individually, the thoughts of each had flown to Branwell, just then lying in a darkened room groaning under the discomfort of a hangover. *He* above all must never know—it would only undermine him further—and Charlotte, who even a year before could not have imagined such an event passing unshared, felt her resentment slide a notch deeper in her soul.

"Well, it is a start at least," said Emily at last. "But no more than that. For my part, this experience has fairly set me off. I am determined to do something by myself now—and no more rhymes. We must finish our novels."

Since getting the poems off to the printers, they had all been working on their novels. *Agnes Grey* and *The Professor* were nearly finished, and Emily's—started later than the others—well advanced. She said she was basing it on a story she had heard at Law Hill, about a local man who had adopted an orphan and raised him among his own children. The boy had made himself hated by supplanting the man's own sons, and had brought disgrace and ruin upon the family. A fair basis for a plot, the others agreed, yet what Emily was building upon it was like a gothic cathedral raised on the foundations of a modest Georgian manor! After reading a passage aloud, Emily, her tight sardonic smile pulling at her lips, would glance from one openmouthed, popeyed face to the other; she would wait a few moments as if unaware that they had been too stunned by her narrative to offer the least coherent criticism, and then quietly close her notebook, stretch, and say, "Well! So much for Heathcliff and Cathy. Now let's hear how old Crimsworth and Agnes are getting along."

And tame indeed did the doings of Crimsworth and Agnes appear in contrast with the wild actions of Emily's hero! Though neither Charlotte nor Anne could approve of him, he certainly made them anxiously reexamine their own, suddenly pallid creations, for irresistibly they felt his power.

"Compared to my hero he looks like Lord Byron stood next to—to the Reverend Mr. Arthur Bell Nicholls," said Charlotte ruefully.

"No, not Byron—Northangerland, or Zamorna," said Anne. "But don't worry, Charlotte. Your character will find easier acceptance among the readers than Emily's, for he is real, whereas Heathcliff is a fearsome monster whom they will neither understand nor care for."

"He is too big for them," said Charlotte, "as Emily's strange talent is too big for us."

"I only hope she will not be too disappointed if it is not found acceptable," murmured Anne.

"Are you so confident our more modest, homely tales will fare any better?" said Charlotte quietly. "Our poems are not exactly selling like hotcakes."

They fell silent. It was a sore subject, one they seldom referred to. Their lovely little green volume, in which so much hope had reposed, had been damned with faint praise by one critic and had sold scarcely a single copy. Yet there was a peculiar magic in the mere fact of its publication. They were launched on the literary ocean; they must row hard, set their sails or do whatever was needful to stay afloat and make way.

At the beginning of June, the tavern-maid at the Bull, looking out of the back window, saw a sight to make her gape.

Branwell was by no means an unfamiliar figure to her; but to see him leaping like a dervish among the gravestones, waving a newspaper in his hand and laughing crazily was something quite out of the common.

"Look at yon!" she called to the proprietor. "What's brought on that? He were in last night, lookin' as whey-faced as ever, cryin' into his whiskey and havin' to be lugged home as usual."

The landlord glanced out. "I can make a guess," he said shortly. " 'E's read news in t' paper."

"What news?"

"Mr. Robinson—tha knows, his light o' love's better half—is dead."

Branwell was beside himself with joy. At last! At long last, his torment, and hers, was at an end. His ex-employer, whose treatment of Branwell and of his wife had grown viler in Branwell's imaginative estimation with the passing of each hellish month, was dead, and deserved not one sad thought. One effect of a year's dissipation had been to heighten Branwell's desires and depress his sensibilities. His sisters and his father could hear him talking animatedly to himself as he capered around the house making preparations to leave for Thorp Green:

"Begone, you callous rogue! Begone from mind as from sight! It is now the turn of a worthier than you to love and tend her whom you slighted and neglected!"

The listeners looked at each other wordlessly. Again their hearts, only slightly prepared by the previous uneasy situation, pounded with fear. Was he mad, in truth? What would happen? They soon found out.

The very night before Branwell was to set off to claim his lady, the taproom boy from the Bull came to the door.

"There's one coom to see Master Branwell. No, 'e won't coom oop to t' house, 'e's waitin' in t' snug for a private word."

"Who? Who is he?" cried Branwell, rushing pell mell downstairs, wild-eyed and disheveled.

"Name o' Gooch. George Gooch."

Paralyzed for an instant by sheer happiness, Branwell stared openmouthed. George Gooch was the Robinson's coachman. Lydia had sent for him! With an inarticulate sound, he dashed back upstairs to tidy himself. His thoughts raced out of control. Could he be ready to travel at once, tonight? He must leave nothing behind, nothing he would have to fetch or send for: he would not be beholden to the family who despised him, he would not return here, no, never again! If Papa desired to see him he could come to Thorp Green Hall. Panting as he struggled with his cravat, Branwell remembered how Patrick had visited him once during his service there. He let out a jubilant laugh. Next time he came, his son should welcome him as master of the house, married to the finest woman on earth. He should have royal entertainment to wipe out at a stroke all memories of the unhappy past. But not his sisters! No, none of them, ever, for they had failed him, and he cast them off. He would not even bid them good-bye! How good it would be, he thought, looking around at the room that had witnessed so much of his misery, to leave this place forever!

He clattered down the stone stairs, tore out of the house leaving the front door swinging, and bounded down the lane. He did not slow his steps when he reached the Bull, but ran straight through the public room to the snug at the rear, bursting in, his face alight. Gooch rose heavily.

"Gooch! It's good to see you! Tell me at once, how is she? When are we to leave? I need an hour to pack my things, then I am at your service—"

"Mr. Brontë—"

"Why, you are not provided with a tankard, Gooch! Let me call for a drink for you—"

"I've had one, thank ye, sir. Now if tha'lt sit down, I've things to tell thee."

"Right! I am sitting, Gooch! Proceed, for you never had a more eager listener!"

"Firstly, sir, as to the lady. She were in sad case indeed when last I saw her. Halfway to dyin' o' grief, she were."

"Dying of grief?" asked Branwell, his eager smile changing to a blank look of bewilderment. "Grief for what?"

"Why! For t' Master's death, to be sure."

Branwell stared at him. Gooch, after a quick, covert glance at him, continued, "Aye . . . in pitiful case she were, hardly able to rise from her bed except to pray by t' side of it. But she sent for me. 'Gooch,' she said—on her knees she were, her face all swollen wi' cryin'—'Gooch, go at once and tell Mr. Brontë not to come.' "

Branwell sprang to his feet, a wildness of apprehension in his face.

" '*Not* to come,' she said, 'for if he does, now or ever, I am undone. Tell him for my sake he must never try to see me again.' "

"But why? Why, Gooch, in God's name, why?"

Gooch coughed. "Well, sir, seemingly it's this way. Before Master died, he changed his will. If Misses ever has owt to do wi' thee again, she's to lose all, and her children'll be give into other hands."

"He—*did that?*"

"Aye, that's how it lies, Mr. Brontë, so tha'd best accept it, for fear of makin' things worse for one who's already near her wits' end wi' sufferin'. Seemingly, at his death, Master repented of any despiteful use of her and offered her love and kind words. She's a prey to her conscience now summat' cruel on your account, sir, feelin' she wronged him. Tha'lt not persist in coomin' at her, sir? It would but harm her more, and more harm would surely kill her."

There followed a lengthy silence. The two men stood in the small smoky room, lit by the fire and candlelight. Branwell, clutching his head in his hands, swayed on his legs. Gooch watched him keenly, for he had been ordered to bring back detailed word of "how he takes it." He was being well paid for playing this role; nonetheless he was disturbed by Branwell's rigid silence more than he would have been by ranting. The young man was a puzzle, and no mistake—all that business with young master Edmund, and yet at the same time in love with the Mistress. Very odd, the servants thought it, and it would not only be the gentry's questions he would have to answer when he got back.

At last he shifted uncomfortably and picked up his hat and whip. He coughed.

"Well . . . I mun be on me way," he muttered.

Branwell did not stir. Gooch dawdled a few moments at the

door, then went out, closing it after him. He paid his bill, called for his horse and rode off.

An hour or so later, the tavern-maid, happening to pass the door to the snug, stopped and bent her head to listen to a strange sound she had heard from inside. It was the queerest noise—not like a person—more like some poor farmyard beast in pain—like a calf bleating! Her hand pressed to her bosom in sudden fear, she threw open the door.

There on the floor lay Branwell, face up. His spine was arched and his body was jerking in spasms. His head was across the hearth, and she could see the red embers reflected in his rolling eyeballs. From his gaping mouth came the gargling, bleating sound she had heard before.

Branwell was finished. This final, callous blow was the end of him, except that it did not quite kill him. He dragged through the motions of living month after endless month, a torment to himself and everyone around him, like the victim of a bungled execution who waits in vain for the *coup de grâce*.

Patrick took him to sleep in his own bedroom, and lent his strength to him whenever he needed it, day or night. And that meant that many nights neither of them slept at all. Patrick sat by Branwell, holding his hand or even restraining him in his arms when he grew violent; he listened to his blasphemous ravings, dried his tears, soothed him as well as he could. In the intervals, he levered himself onto his knees and prayed silently beside the bed. He had always prayed with fervor, yet not since Maria lay dying had he prayed as intensely as he prayed now. And not only for Branwell, but for forgiveness for himself. No brilliant, beautiful boy comes to such a pass solely through his own fault, and Patrick, who had always secretly feared he was mishandling him, now took upon his own soul the guilt for his son's downfall— or at least part of it. The Christian tenet that urged him to pray also for the woman who had seduced Branwell proved beyond his power. His thoughts of Mrs. Robinson were filled with virulent poison. It was with difficulty that he could restrain himself from wishing her dead and damned.

She was far from dead, however, and the letters Ann Marshall wrote to Branwell at her instructions, describing her plight and hinting at thoughts of entering a nunnery, could scarcely have been more misleading. Her one desire in connection with Branwell was to keep him well out of her way, and to this end she was prepared to invest as much money as seemed necessary. She discreetly saw to it that he was furnished not only with the wherewithal but with good cause to drink: Ann Marshall's letters were soon supplemented by more from the family physician, Dr. Crosby, who was prevailed on for a consideration to confirm, from a medical viewpoint, Ann's harrowing descriptions of Mrs. Robinson's decline.

So it was hardly surprising that Branwell's condition constantly worsened, and that his family, always excepting his father, drew irrevocably away from him, further and further the more intolerably he behaved. The money from "one whom he might never see again" (as he wrote despairingly to Joseph Leyland) was irregular, and in between remittances his needs did not cease. He ran up debts that made his youthful extravagances in Bradford look trivial. Soon duns were at the door. Branwell's craven or blustering behavior on these occasions was a poignant source of shame to his family.

Charlotte could hardly bear to look at him anymore, but a sense of duty to her father, who was bearing the brunt alone, stirred her to try to talk to him. One day, she came upon him in the dining room, sitting in the window obviously in deep distress. Swallowing her repugnance, she said, "What ails you, Branwell?"

Her voice came out more coldly than she had intended. Branwell turned to her slowly and fixed her with a look of such brooding melancholy that she felt a pang of pity.

"I suppose you think I've been out drinking," he said bitterly. "Well, for once you're wrong. I've been to visit Susan Braithwaite."

Charlotte looked surprised. Susan was one of her Sunday school pupils.

"Is she ill?"

"Ill enough. She won't last out the week, they say."

"I didn't know that!"

"No," said Branwell with pathetic triumph, "*you* did not know it, yet you see *I* did, and much as it may astonish you, she was glad of my call and grateful that I sat with her. I felt like praying with her, too—" He broke off, his voice trembling, but then straightened himself and went on, "But of course that would be nonsense. I am not good enough to pray, and in any case I don't believe in God, so why should He listen to my prayers, even for an innocent child like that? So she will die, and I will go on living, though *why* is a mystery, for the longings of each of us are exactly the contrary. And I am sure you all long for me to die, too, as much as Susan's poor parents desire her to live."

Charlotte stared at him. She was thinking mainly of the child, and not of Branwell at all; the accusation he had just made, she had hardly taken in—he often said such things. But to Branwell, looking despairingly for one glimmer of love or pity for himself, her look displayed a variety of reactions, every one like a stab. He felt she doubted his word, his deed, she would not credit him with a kind action, an unselfish thought, so must conclude his story was a lie. Once—oh, once she would have believed him; would have supported and succored him; would have defended him against all the world! Now her look told him she despised him and had not one positive thought to spare for him.

"She is my little scholar, and I will go and see her," said Charlotte. She smiled at him as she left the room. But even her smile was the kiss of death, for it was forced, unnatural. And he saw it.

That day he traveled alone to Halifax and spent three days carousing with Leyland and his brother and other old friends. They were shocked at his appearance, for his dissipation was already telling on his slender physique; but they concealed their dismay and made much of him, lent him money and tried to bolster his morale. It was quite useless. Branwell was like a ghost at their feast, and when he returned home he indulged in a display of blind rage and destructiveness that resulted in Patrick and Emily eventually having to overpower him and tie him to his bed.

At the beginning of this long drawn out domestic nightmare, the girls somehow managed to finish their books, and having obtained a list of publishers of fiction from the firm that had brought out their *Poems*, sent off the three manuscripts in one package to the first name on it.

They spent upwards of a month in a state of buoyed-up excitement and hope that did much to mitigate the trials and discomforts of life under the same roof with Branwell. And there was another anxiety, too: Papa's eyes had now failed to a point where an operation was the only hope of saving his sight. It was an ordeal he had long dreaded, and he had almost thought that blindness would be preferable. But now, with the responsibility of his son heavy upon him, he needed every faculty; so at the age of nearly seventy, he agreed to the operation, provided Charlotte would stay with him all the time.

In August the two of them left Haworth and traveled to Manchester.

"If you hear anything from the publishers," Charlotte whispered to Emily before she left, "don't wait for my return—forward it at once."

In Manchester they took lodgings. The specialist, Dr. Wilson, declared the cataracts ripe for removal and said there was every hope of success. This, together with the relief of being removed from Branwell's vicinity for a brief respite, cheered Patrick somewhat, though he was a prey to awful fears about the pain he was to suffer. He prayed for strength to support it when the time came so that Charlotte might not suffer too much, for he wanted her to be in the room when it was done.

"Others endure far worse," he reminded himself. It had occasionally been his agonizing duty to listen to the ghastly shrieks of members of his parish—even children—being operated upon.

Death was a frequent, and merciful, attendant upon these occasions. Patrick, whose tenacious hold on life age had done little to weaken, despite all his troubles, wondered if any bodily pain, however severe, could make him wish himself dead. He doubted it. He loved life still; and looking across the rented sitting room at the dim figure of Charlotte, sitting bent over the table writing, he thought that the only circumstance that would remove his will to live was the loss of this dear daughter.

"I love you, Charlotte," he said suddenly.

Charlotte looked up, surprised and touched.

"Papa! Dearest Papa—" She came quickly over and hugged him. "And I you, more than ever lately."

"I am so glad and grateful you are with me."

"I wouldn't wish myself anywhere else in the world."

"What are you working at so quietly? A letter to Mistress Ellen?"

"No, Papa, not a letter. It is just something I am writing."

"A story?" he asked, with almost childish eagerness. "Will you read it to me?"

"One day, when it's finished. I have only just begun it."

"What's the name of it?"

"*Jane Eyre.*"

"That is a good plain name."

"And it will be a good plain tale."

She returned to the table and went on writing. Her heart was heavy, for that morning a packet had been delivered to the lodgings. Emily had sent it on to her unopened. The publisher had rejected the novels, and without a word of explanation! The disappointment was cruel, especially coming at this particular time. But Charlotte, who in the days of her deepest misery over M. Héger would have sunk under such a blow, now let it fall on her like the cut of a whip that made her leap forward. That very day she determined to begin a new novel, one having nothing to do with Brussels, a novel in which she could lose herself, Monsieur, Branwell, Papa, all real-life pain and sorrow. Soon she was so deeply immersed in her theme that later she was able to sit quite calmly through the operation, for her thoughts were following Jane Eyre. And Patrick did nothing to disturb them. He conducted himself as he would have hoped to do had he been a soldier on a field of battle. The surgeons were most impressed.

While the "possession" of *Jane Eyre* lasted, Charlotte noticed and cared for little else. Papa recovered and took over his duties once more from his curate, Mr. Nicholls. Branwell continued to try them all—his habit of running up debts, which his family later had to pay to keep him out of jail, infuriated Charlotte from time to time, but her anger was soon submerged in the swamping rush of creativity that was sweeping her along. The other two were working too—Anne on a new novel and Emily on Gondal poetry—and in the evenings they loved to sit in the dining room together and read to each other. The others were wild with enthusiasm for *Jane Eyre*, and this would have encouraged Charlotte had encouragement been necessary; but in fact she needed nothing but the freedom to write and write and go on writing.

Meanwhile, what of their first novels?

Some publishers were prompt in returning the manuscripts, while some were dilatory. Some enclosed a polite note; others hardly appeared to have opened the package before reconsigning it to the post.

Usually when it came back, Charlotte simply crossed the name of the previous publisher off and wrote the next address from her list on the same wrapping. She never stopped to ask herself if this might make a doubtful impression. But after nine months, the wrapping was getting so worn that she opened the parcel to rewrap it, and while it was open she reread the contents.

She could not help enjoying her own book. It seemed to her singularly real and believable, and the characters still pleased her. She read *Agnes Grey* next. No doubt about it, Anne had the art that conceals art—a lightness of touch, a kind of tripping quality that she, Charlotte, delighted in; yet at the same time, her inner puritan, ever lurking at the ready, wondered if something so easy to read could be seriously regarded. But nothing in it precluded publication, for this was just what could be popular.

Finally, with a sense of reluctance, she picked up *Wuthering Heights*. This was the name Emily had given her book. Charlotte had heard every word of it read by its author; she supposed nothing in it could shock her now, yet she began to read it with a quailing sensation like fear. Hearing it read piecemeal in Emily's deep, uninflected voice had been shattering enough; but now she felt the impact of the words upon her sensibilities directly. After nearly a year, the people, the scenery, the events, struck Charlotte with a fresh and stunning impact.

She had read her own manuscript and Anne's at intervals over a week or more; yet *Wuthering Heights* she read almost at a sitting because she could not pull herself away from it. When she was called to meals, she kept silent and let them think she was out visiting in the parish. She read on and on, tense in every fiber, half thrilled, half appalled, wholly possessed. At the end she sat still in the dusk of her bedroom, the text on her knee, feeling as if she had—in Tabby's phrase—"bin dragged through t' mangle." Such emotions had been roused in her as she could never remember receiving from a book before, for it was like no book she had ever read. It was not like a work of art. It was too raw, too savage—crude, even! She had told Emily originally that certain vivid and fearful scenes had banished sleep at night and disturbed her thoughts for days after hearing them, but Emily had let out an incredulous snort of laughter.

"Oh, stuff, Charlotte! What an affectation! Catharine is no worse than Zenobia, nor Heathcliff than what you finally did with Zamorna."

"But—those were childish fantasies! Adult writers must be more moderate. Such extreme characters are not acceptable."

"Why not? They are not extreme, anyway. People *are* like that."

"But not in books!"

Emily roared with laughter. "Charlotte, really! You're the one who insists on the unvarnished truth! You see people as essentially decent and ordinary; I see them as essentially violent and passionate. We must both be true to our ideas of what life is, mustn't we?"

And here was Emily's truth, which neither Charlotte's criticisms, nor Anne's had modified in the slightest degree. Charlotte, sitting there alone in the gathering darkness, still under the spell of that strange tragedy and those desperate, awful, yet somehow pitiable, human beings, shuddered as she thought over certain passages. The scene in which Heathcliff actually dug up the coffin of his beloved Cathy and looked at her face—ten years in the earth—and still found her beautiful enough to love, was an image so terrible, so graphic, so outrageous and yet so real that Charlotte knew it would haunt her till the end of her life.

Yet she cringed at the thought of any other person reading this manuscript. In some queer way she was ashamed of it. The power that had held her inexorably for many hours was somehow a dark power. She did not blame Emily, for she knew—who better—how creativity can flow from some outside source over which, on occasion, the writer has no more control than a tube through which water is poured. But she thought she knew now the cause of those repeated rejections. It would take a bold publisher indeed to bring such a—a monstrous talent before the public.

Nevertheless, she wrapped up the three scripts carefully and dispatched them once again on their weary rounds. But she transferred her hopes for an independent future to the growing text of *Jane Eyre*.

Her hope was not great and fluctuated strongly during that arctic winter of 1846, when quite abnormal cold immured them in the little stone box of the parsonage with a succession of ailments (a bad attack of asthma for Anne, raging toothache for Charlotte) and a miserable conviction that they would never be really warm again. Charlotte was now in her thirty-first year—always a time of reckoning in a woman's life—and sometimes in the small hours, when the creative flow stopped owing to the sheer tiredness and chill of the small body it passed through, Charlotte did the dismal female arithmetic. Youth gone . . . no real *use* made of her life, no solid achievements. At these depleted moments the sorry failure of their book of poems knifed her afresh, and all their efforts seemed futile and hopeless. But when she confided these feelings to Emily, she retorted sharply:

"Nonsense. Your blood's slowing down through cold, that's all. Wrap up well and go out for a walk—keep in the hollows though, the wind's like a sword on the heights. *Jane Eyre* is superb, and you'll know it again when spring comes."

The fifth publisher to whom the joint manuscripts were submitted was Thomas Newby of Cavendish Square. The girls had little hope left for these much-traveled tales by now and were all concentrating on new material. Therefore, when in July the postboy brought a *letter* and not a parcel from London and handed it to Charlotte, who was cutting flowers in the garden, she thought at first it must be from somebody else.

But when she saw the letterhead she flew into the house in a state of breathless excitement and called the others to come upstairs before reading a word more. It was only when they were safely shut in the study that she read the letter—and her mind seemed to freeze.

Mr. Newby was prepared to consider *Wuthering Heights* and *Agnes Grey* for publication, providing the authors would bear the costs up to fifty pounds. *The Professor*, on the other hand, he rejected as being too devoid of dramatic incident to appeal to the circulating libraries.

There was a painful silence in the study. Then, with a dredging effort of will, Charlotte pulled herself together.

"Two out of three is better than none," she said. "It is the terms you must now consider. They are not good, but are they miserly enough to preclude acceptance? Is publication on any terms your aim, or—" she hesitated "—or would it be better to try somewhere else?" Her voice was firm, her eyes dry; yet she cringed inwardly when she thought how she had assumed it was

Emily's production that was holding back the chances of the others.

A long discussion resulted in a decision to go ahead with Newby. Charlotte, who had always dealt with their joint correspondence, quietly handed over the business to Emily and retired to think over what she should now do about *The Professor*. On its own it was too short for the usual three-volume format. It had failed as part of a joint production; its chances by itself were that much smaller. Nevertheless, she decided to try one last name on her depleted list, and using the same brown paper wrapping it had been returned in, sent it off to a firm called Smith, Elder & Co.

A reply was returned within two weeks.

"Dear Mr. Bell."

Her eyes, dreadingly slow at first in following the lines, moved faster down the page and on to a second. At the end she sank back with a sigh of released breath and closed her eyes. It was indeed another rejection—but not, no, not at all, like the others! It came from a Mr. Williams and contained all that its predecessors had lacked in the way of serious discriminating criticism. The main reason given for refusing the work was its shortness. It concluded: "A work in three volumes from your pen will, you may rest assured, meet with our careful attention."

Jane Eyre was nearly finished. Roused to her fullest intensity of effort, Charlotte got down to work, determined that Smith, Elder & Co. and no other should publish it. Perhaps everyone was right—perhaps *The Professor was* too flat, too unexciting. Well! But they would not say so of her second book!

She had promised Mr. Williams it would be ready to submit in a month, but some new urgency drove her on at such a speed that by August 24 she had it finished. Emily and Anne were busy correcting their proofs for Thomas Newby. Could it be that Charlotte was—*racing* them to get into print? The question occurred to her, but she refused it an answer. The day she wrote the final paragraph, the manuscript went off in brand-new brown paper, unsullied by prior failures.

10

NOVELS
IN PRINT

*T*HE DOOR OF THE DIRECTOR'S inner office at Smith, Elder & Co. in Cornhill swung open and banged shut behind Mr. Williams, a thin, graying man who rarely showed any excitement. Mr. Smith, his young and handsome director, looked up from his desk in astonishment.

"A *faint* knock is considered customary, m' dear fellow—" he began jocularly.

"Never mind that!" interrupted Mr. Williams. "You must read this. You must give up the whole of tomorrow to doing so!"

"But tomorrow is Sunday!" exclaimed young George Smith, amused. He drew toward him the manuscript Mr. Williams had slapped down on the desk. "I'm going riding in the country."

"Cancel it. You might as well. Once you are launched upon this tale, you will find yourself unable to get away in any case."

"Really, Williams! It's not like you to get so carried away. What is it, anyhow? That queer chap in the North who sent us that rather dull production with our rivals' names all over its wrappings?"

"Queer he may be, naïve he certainly is, but I'll stake my reputation on his being also a master storyteller. I tell you, I read all night—I have not closed my eyes! My consolation is knowing that you will be equally exhausted and equally elated by this time on Monday morning."

"I beg leave to doubt it. I am too old a hand to lose sleep over any raw scribbler."

"We shall see."

Alone in her room, a very few days later, Charlotte sat quietly before the window with Mr. Smith's letter in her hands.

Happiness was not the word for what she felt; nor was she conscious of surprise. All the recurrent agony of hope deferred, resuscitated, confounded, that had been her cross for so many years, seemed, now that it was lifted from her and replaced by the blessing of certainty, simply the pilgrim's rough path leading inevitably to the Mecca of acceptance. How had she ever doubted it would come? It had to come. She had groped her way around the last bend in the dark tunnel: the light burst into her eyes and the warm sun bathed her tired spirit, feeding it with peace and elation. The dark, cold, futile, frightening years dropped away as if they had never been, and she stood clear of them, safe at last on the sacred pinnacle of ratification by kindred minds.

When she had recovered herself a little, her first need was to share this moment of ecstatic triumph with her sisters. Thank God she had been brave in *their* moment of triumph, for now she need feel no qualms! And their response was wholehearted indeed. So unhappy had they been at Charlotte's being left out of their prospects with Newby that now, seeing her even better placed, they were almost overcome with relief.

"Charlotte, how wonderful, they have not asked you for a penny!" cried Anne. "They are to pay *you*! How highly they praise your book—oh, it is thrilling! And now we will all go into print together!"

But of course someone had to be first, and it was only to be expected that it would be Emily and Anne. But Thomas Newby and George Smith were two very different men, with vastly different ways of doing business. *Wuthering Heights* and *Agnes Grey* were subject to endless delays. The corrected proof-sheets were lost; letters went unanswered; things went wrong at the printers that nobody bothered to explain to the anxious authors. Promises made by Newby were broken by him with great regularity. There were times, as the months went by, when Emily declared herself ready—almost—to break her incognito, storm down to London and strangle that slippery gentleman with her own two hands.

Meanwhile Charlotte was quite embarrassed by the contrasting efficiency and courtesy *she* received. She was kept informed at every stage, and within a few weeks her proofs were ready for correction. They arrived, inopportunely, long before she had expected them. She was staying with Ellen when Emily forwarded them to her, accompanied by a stern note reminding her of her solemn promise to preserve anonymity.

Never had Charlotte's loyalty to Emily been so severely tested! She knew how much it mattered, how deeply Emily would be hurt by "people knowing." It would take away all the joy of having her book published; she might do something wild, like stopping publication altogether. And yet . . . Had Charlotte no rights? No right to share her joy and excitement with her closest friend? Her longing to do so was all but irresistible. Apart from all else, how would Ellen feel if she found out later by chance? How would Charlotte explain why she had kept it from her?

She decided to leave it in the hands of fate. She had to correct the proofs, and since she and Ellen were always together, she must do so in her presence. If Ellen asked what she was doing, she would tell her and swear her to secrecy.

They sat together at the same table, Ellen sewing, Charlotte working. They did not speak. Every now and then Ellen glanced up, and once or twice their eyes met. Ellen was dying to ask— but she didn't. Friendship and her knowledge of Charlotte's nature kept her silent. If Charlotte wished to tell her what she was doing, she would; to ask outright would be intrusive. So Charlotte was allowed to keep her vow, and when she came home and was met by Emily's passionately questioning eyes, she was grateful to Ellen as never before.

Six weeks from the date of acceptance, and while Newby still procrastinated and the younger girls chafed impotently, George Smith sent Charlotte a neat parcel containing her complimentary copies of *Jane Eyre*.

They were beautiful and perfect. Her gratitude to these men knew no bounds; she felt they had crowned her life with the accolade of their best treatment. She could scarcely hold in her joy and satisfaction. A score of times a day she would run upstairs to look at her books, spread out upon the bed or stood on end on the table. Sometimes she couldn't resist opening one and reading a few paragraphs. She imagined how the passages would strike the great men of letters of the day. Would they ever read them?

They were doing so, even as she wondered. For George Smith was confident enough of his judgment to disseminate copies, not only to the press, but to every leading literary figure. And these men were just as delighted, just as impressed as he had anticipated. Soon the name of Currer Bell ("Such an obvious alias," said Mr Williams. "How I do *wonder* what manner of person it is!") was being discussed in all the fashionable salons of London.

Charlotte knew nothing of this at first; but, in keeping with their meticulous courtesy in all matters, Smith, Elder & Co. were prompt in posting to her all reviews as they appeared. They were quite staggering—not all favorable, but all treating the book as a serious and important event. Charlotte tried not to be upset by the more negative ones; in fact, she was almost glad of them. They made it possible for her to read all the notices aloud to her sisters without laying herself open to suspicions of conceit—for the good ones were flattering indeed.

And then came an accolade she had not dared to expect. It was a letter from George Smith, quoting one he had received from William Thackeray, one of Charlotte's idols. That such a giant should have *read* her book, let alone found it praiseworthy, was almost unthinkable; yet he even claimed that she had made him cry! Charlotte cried herself at this—she felt overwhelmed by it. She had reached out through her story and touched a great heart. She felt that nothing in her life to come could transcend this moment. Safe in her distant retreat, she hugged her secret treasures to her and rejoiced in them, the more poignantly, perhaps, because her life went on as usual: she walked about the village, and taught in the Sunday school, and visited parishoners, and went to church on Sundays, and no one knew, no one guessed!

So she supposed. But there are few total secrets in a small village, and if an alias is adopted that involves a village post office in the deception, it is not usually long before speculation reaches the public houses.

"Has Parson taken a lodger?" the publican asked Branwell one evening.

"What?"

"Just wondered who this Bell might be that gets so much post."

"Bell? That is Nicholls' middle name. Our curate."

"Nay, 'tis not him! This be a Mister Currer Bell, and there be some mix-up with other forenames too, so postmaster says."

Branwell looked at him stupidly. "Some mistake."

"If so, it be a rum 'un, for none o' t' post is ever turned back."

Befuddled as he was, Branwell determined to wait for the postman, intercept the post and find out for himself what the mystery was. But the post arrived in the mornings and Branwell never woke before noon. Soon the matter had drifted from his mind, but it left a new turbulence, a new source of bitterness. They were keeping things from him—ever shutting him out! He knew he deserved no better, and that distressed him more. He drank more, drugged himself more heavily; his relative torpor the past months erupted with the pressure of this subterranean resentment and he threw the household once more into an uproar with his brawling and cursing.

"He guesses something," said Emily. "He senses it."

"Impossible," said Charlotte flatly. She refused to contemplate the idea that the cause of her first real happiness could be damaging Branwell further.

In December the smoldering buildup of sales for *Jane Eyre* suddenly burst into flame. The first edition sold out, and when a new edition was issued, Charlotte, in a moment of impulsive gratitude, asked Mr. Smith to insert a dedication to Mr. Thackeray.

She had some doubts about it—he might regard it as an impertinence—but she never dreamed what trouble it would actually cause him. How could she know, when even George Smith did not, that Thackeray, like her hero, had an insane wife? That gossip was already suggesting that *Jane Eyre* had been written by a governess he had once employed, and that he was writing *Vanity Fair*—then appearing in installments in a magazine—as a riposte? The malicious and idle tongues of Mayfair wagged, and their butt, who was a part of their world in a way Charlotte could not have imagined, suffered.

It was some time before he could collect himself to acknowledge the dedication, which he knew to be a well-intentioned gesture by the much-discussed unknown; and when he did, it was so late that he felt obliged to explain.

Charlotte was appalled, the more because she could think of no way to cancel out one pang he had suffered because of her. Emily said:

"You see how right I was to maintain our privacy? What if *we* were subject to ugly, vicious gossip? I would die of it, I know."

But total silence could not be maintained. One day, early in the rush of sales of *Jane Eyre*, Charlotte somehow let Tabby beat her to the door when the postman came.

"Tabby, give me the letters please."

"They're for t' maister."

"There's one there from London—I can see it."

"Anyways, 'tis not for thee."

"Tabby! Hand it to me!"

"Nay, I'll not! There's been enow o' keepin' things from fowks. Post goes straight to t' parson, that's my orders."

Papa handed her her letter at lunchtime without comment. But that afternoon, following an urgent consultation with the others, Charlotte walked into his study.

"Papa, I've been writing a book."

Patrick's heart bounded. Here it came—the confidence he had waited for! But he replied mildly, "Have you, my dear?"

"Yes, and I want you to read it."

A teasing demon entered into Patrick.

"I'm afraid it will try my eyes too much."

"But it is not in manuscript. It is printed."

Patrick appeared aghast. "My dear! You've never thought of the expense it will be! It will be almost sure to be a loss, for how can you get a book sold? No one knows you or your name."

"But, Papa, I don't think it will be a loss; no more will you, if you will just let me read you a review or two and tell you more about it."

With that she sat down primly and read him the reviews, not omitting the one from the *Spectator*, which said that there was a low tone of behavior in the book. Her tongue burned, but she had to be fair. Papa said not a word till she had read them all, and then, still in the same mild, unimpressed tone, said, "And am I to read the book for myself, did you say?"

"Yes, Papa. Here is your copy. I—I shall await your verdict with —some trepidation."

She handed him the book. His eyes were kindling behind his glasses, and a grin, not unlike one of Emily's, was tugging at his mouth. She looked at him narrowly for a moment. Had he known all along? But he had a right to his own secrets. She bent and kissed him and quietly left him alone with *Jane Eyre*.

Outside, the others were waiting.

"What did he say? What did he say?"

"Nothing."

And he had meant to go on saying nothing, or at least to

maintain his casual pose. But after five chapters of the book he could not restrain his pride and excitement another moment. Bursting out of his room, he hurried across the hall and into the dining room, where the three girls were having tea.

"Girls!" he cried, his face alight. "Do you know Charlotte has been writing a book, and it is much better than likely?"

"Papa!" Charlotte jumped to her feet. "You like it?"

"My child, it is splendid! Splendid! But why have you not published it under your own name?"

They exchanged looks. "We wished to be anonymous, Papa."

"*We?*"

Another exchange of glances, and then Anne, seeing that Emily had a mulish look, timidly explained. "Yes, Papa. You see, Emily and I have written books, too."

"Also to be published?"

They nodded, their eyes fixed on him anxiously and eagerly. All four had fast-beating hearts and a strong awareness of the thrill of this moment. Patrick looked around at his three surviving daughters, and even while his face glowed with pride, his thoughts flew to his poor life-defeated son.

"We must at all costs keep this from Branwell," he said soberly. "I fear it would be the end of him."

"We wish to keep it from every living being except you, Papa," said Emily. "That is why we are publishing under *noms de plume.*"

"Ah, I see. It was for your brother's sake. That was good of you, my dear ones, very good."

It was only when they were alone again that Emily broke a thoughtful silence to say brusquely, "Of course, I did not do it for Branwell."

"Nor I," said Charlotte.

"We should have told Papa," said Anne.

Silence fell once more.

The wild success of Currer Bell's novel stimulated Thomas Newby as nothing else could have done, and the combined volumes containing *Wuthering Heights* and *Agnes Grey* appeared at long last just before Christmas. The shrewd and shady Mr. Newby was hoping to cash in; but Emily and Anne didn't know that. When they received their advance copies, they at first rejoiced that the long procrastination was over; but their pleasure was short-lived.

"Why, here is a mistake I remember correcting in the proof!" exclaimed Anne. "And here is another—*and* another! How *could* they let this happen? It's as if we had made no corrections at all!"

And it was badly printed, too, on inferior paper; nor was its binding to be compared with Charlotte's lovely trophies. Charlotte was wild with indignation, but there was nothing she could do except wait, with her heart in her mouth. Would the critics, who had on the whole been so kind to her, compensate her sisters for their long wait and their subsequent disappointment?

It was lucky for her that her book came out first, and that she had had some months of unalloyed pleasure from its gathering success, before the emergence of the others' books. For from then on, her joy was effectively undermined for some time.

The distressing element in most of the reviews was that the two later novels were not judged on their own merits, but as part of a general speculation about the identity of their authors, and within this pattern each book was compared to and measured against the first. The fact that, when so compared, they were "found wanting," hurt Charlotte the more; for although in her most secret heart she recoiled from *Wuthering Heights* and felt some lack of vitality in *Agnes Grey*, nevertheless she perversely wanted them to stand equal to her own book—not higher, but not lower. To read wounding or slighting critiques of her sisters' books gave her pain no less than if they had been directed against hers. At least she did not have to pretend to indignation; it was genuine.

But Emily rejected all sympathy.

"These reviews are not *bad*. They are just uncomprehending. You remember saying of the one in *The Spectator* about yours, Charlotte, that it was that view of the book which a certain class of mind would naturally take? In other words, the reviewer didn't

grasp what you were doing, and neither do many of these understand me. Why should they? I'm not a familiar type. As to my
characters . . . well, I'm sure the critics are all acquainted with
a Heathcliff or two—perhaps not endowed with his depth of
soul or capacity for pain and love, but certainly with all his vices
—only they are not used to seeing him thus stripped for their
edification. No, Charlotte, I forbid you to be upset on my account,
for I swear that all their sharp comments touch me not at all."

By the time a winter of numberless ailments had passed, gossip about the "brothers Bell" had reached new heights. People in
London who had relations up north were commissioning them
to look about their neighborhoods for any persons who could
be the elusive trio. Or was the trio in fact one person? This was
suggested in more than one quarter, and it was a suggestion that
was exploited to the full by Mr. Newby. It suited him excellently
to have it thought that his Bells were in fact the famous Currer
in an earlier phase, and he was not too scrupulous to use quota-
tions from reviews of *Jane Eyre* in advertising his production.

Anne spent the winter and spring working on her second novel.
It was called *The Tenant of Wildfell Hall,* and Charlotte hated
it. If *Wuthering Heights* had dismayed her, *Wildfell Hall* dismayed her more, simply because Anne and not Emily had written
it. She had long ago accepted the strong animal element in
Emily. Those primitive, even brutish characterizations flowed
from her strong natural link with the earth and the lower kingdoms. But that Anne—gentle, refined, pious little Anne—should
undertake the task of describing the downfall of a rake, sparing
no detail of his dissipation and depravity, was too staggering!

Even Emily was astonished, though not censorious. It was dis-
concerting, they both found, to hear these scenes of nightmarish
degradation read aloud, and especially by Anne. They were
obliged to recognize that these insights had evolved in this cherished younger sister through bitter personal experience. She had
seemed to bear it all so patiently and uncomplainingly: her
dreadful time at the Inghams; the long ordeal at Thorp Green
Hall; and subsequently what they had all endured, each in her

own way, the agony of watching Branwell's decline at close range, month after month. Yet inwardly Anne's soul had recorded it all in blood and fire, and here it was, written in her delicate handwriting and read out in her quiet, prim little voice.

Charlotte begged her to be more reticent in describing her villain, Arthur Huntingdon. Her treatment was too frank, too painfully honest! "Some elements of human nature should and must be veiled in the retelling," she insisted. "To expose them as you have is an artistic blunder. Readers will not tolerate it, nor should they be asked to."

"Don't listen, Anne," said Emily. "You must do it your way."

"But if she is making a mistake, spoiling her story, which is otherwise excellent—"

But Anne stood firm by her rake and her treatment of him.

"He is true," she said. "Who knows that better than we do? Am I to soften drunkenness and its direct effects? It would be quite wrong to do so."

So the manuscript went off to Newby unsoftened. And that was another thing Charlotte opposed. Why would Anne give her second novel to that scoundrel who had so mishandled the first? Why was Emily still referring to him as "our publisher"?

"Mr. Smith has said he's willing to take you on. Why don't you leave Newby and come to a decent firm?"

"We don't want to be in your shadow, Charlotte. He is only willing because you asked him."

"Nonsense! Both your first books are selling excellently. He is a gentleman, but he is also a businessman. He sees a good thing and he wants it."

"I prefer to function independently," said Anne. "I'm sure Mr. Newby will not misbehave this time. His letters are much more mannerly of late."

Her hopes, however, were misplaced.

One July morning Charlotte flew to her sisters in high excitement and indignation.

"You see, I was right about that scoundrel Newby! See what he is about! Here is a letter from Mr. Smith, saying that Newby has offered *Wildfell Hall* to an American publisher as *my* second book, and my American publisher has heard about it and written to Smith, Elder & Co. asking for an explanation! *My* next work is promised to them, and they are very angry to think it has been offered elsewhere. Newby has dared to claim we are all one person, and my Mr. Smith very naturally asks for a clarification. What are we to do, what *are* we to do?"

They looked at each other for a moment. Then Emily shrugged and turned away.

"Nothing. Let them untangle it. It is just business of the sort that such men love to indulge in. It is no concern of ours at all."

"Oh, Emily, what nonsense. Of course it is to do with us!" exclaimed Charlotte in great agitation. "Our honor, and Mr. Smith's, too, is involved here. Anne, I look to you for support."

"What do you think we should do?"

"I think we should go down to London and show ourselves."

"What?" barked Emily. "Not me. You go if you like, but you go with my complete disapproval."

"Emily, you must come!"

"I won't."

"Anne?"

After a pause, Anne said slowly, "Yes, I think it's necessary. We had better start at once."

Emily turned, and Charlotte saw that same look of untamed ferocity in her eyes as she stared at Anne that she herself had received when she stole the poems. Anne had betrayed Emily, and that withering look was her punishment. But Anne was not to be swayed from the right course, and that was not to allow Mr. Smith to suffer because Anne had insisted upon continuing with Mr. Newby.

Anne and Charlotte quickly packed a few things in a box and were arranging for it to be transported to Keighley Station by cart when they felt Emily watching them, and turned, somewhat guiltily.

"One thing," she said coldly. "No doubt when you have introduced yourselves to the gentlemanly Mr. Smith, he will at once begin to lionize you. In the world you are recklessly entering, such a chance would be irresistible to him. You will be carried through the salons of Mayfair and displayed to all the gossips of London like minor foreign royalty."

"Why minor?" asked Anne, with an uncharacteristic flash of pertness.

"I'll just say this," Emily went on stolidly. "Enjoy yourselves as seems best to you, I cannot stop you. *But leave me out of it.* And if you must give the name of Brontë to Mr. Smith and Mr. Newby, you will tell them in addition that if they reveal it to any-one else, if our secret should become common property, Ellis Bell at least shall never pen another line."

The cart could only carry their box, not themselves, so they had to walk to Keighley, or rather run, for they wanted to catch the night train to London; and besides, it looked like rain. Thunderclouds gathered as they hurried along talking excitedly about what they would do when they got to London, and when they still had a mile to go the heavens opened, drenching them to the skin.

They climbed into the train, laughing and panting. Their ring-lets had fallen into elf-locks and their clothes were steaming. The train racketed through the night; soot entered their carriage and settled on their faces and clothes as they dozed. When they ar-rived at Euston the next morning, stiff and weary but more excited than ever, they were a sorry sight indeed.

They repaired straight to the only inn Charlotte knew, the Chapter Coffee House. It hadn't changed; it was still the same dark, low-ceilinged, masculine sort of place that Charlotte remem-bered from their pre-Brussels visit, and for a moment she was seized with nostalgia, recalling her emotions as she first set off for Brussels, and all that had followed. The proprietor of the Coffee House seemed both surprised and amused to see these two prim travel-worn little countrywomen, but he politely showed them to his best rooms and offered them breakfast, which they accepted gratefully, though when it came Charlotte couldn't touch a morsel.

They washed and tidied themselves as best they could. Charlotte could do nothing with her hair but comb it smoothly down over her ears from a center parting. Anne thought it aged her dreadfully, but she said nothing. Then they sat on the beds and looked at each other.

"We should go," said Anne.

"Yes," said Charlotte.

They rose resolutely and made their way into the street. They'd previously agreed to take a cab to Cornhill, but somehow when they were out in the bustling morning city it seemed simpler just to walk. Anne had never seen London before, and Charlotte, whose head had begun to give her sharp warning stabs, recovered a little in the delight of pointing out landmarks like St. Paul's and the churches around Fleet Street.

"We're nearly there. What shall we say?"

"Oh, I don't know—I don't know!"

Sixty-five Cornhill turned out to be a large bookshop. There were a lot of people about, but they made their way through to a counter, behind which stood a supercilious-looking clerk.

"I would like to see Mr. George Smith," said Charlotte boldly.

The clerk raised his eyebrows, glanced at her shabby clothes and flicked a look at Anne, who was half hiding behind her.

"Who shall I say is calling?"

"Just say—two ladies wish to speak to him. On private business."

"Take a seat," he said pertly, and disappeared into the rear of the shop.

Anne and Charlotte sat down on a padded bench. There were tables and shelves and stands full of books all around them, all published by Smith, Elder & Co.

"Look," whispered Anne, pointing. "There is the volume Mr. Smith sent you last month as a present." She was overtaken by a sudden fit of nervous giggling, which she stifled in her mittened hands.

"I do hope Mr. Williams will be here!" said Charlotte. "I'm sure he will be kind and understanding!"

There was a sudden cough, and she became aware of a smart

pair of striped trousers at her side. Her eyes moved upward and
met with a handsome face; large dark eyes were looking down
at her inquiringly.

"Did you wish to see me, madam?"

"Is it Mr. Smith?" asked Charlotte timidly, peering up at him
through her spectacles.

"It is."

She stood up. She felt smaller than ever beside him. Out of her
reticule she took his letter, which had arrived at the parsonage
the day before, and wordlessly put it in his hand.

He stared at it in astonishment, then looked at her, then back
at the letter.

"Where did you get this?" he asked, rather sharply.

"It is addressed to me," said Charlotte primly, yet with her
whole face aching to break into laughter. His comic look of per-
plexity made the whole very serious matter suddenly seem like a
huge and glorious joke; she only wished Emily had been here to
share it.

"*You?*" cried Mr. Smith, so loudly that the clerk gave a start
and several people nearby turned to stare. "You are not—you
cannot be—you are not Currer B—"

"Shhh!" begged Charlotte, a finger to her lips.

"Come into my office! Jim! Run and fetch Mr. Williams!"

The sisters found themselves in a small, high room behind the
shop, with only enough space for a desk and three chairs. Mr.
Smith hardly seemed to know what to do with himself or them.
He drew out two chairs for them, urged them to be seated, then
rushed to and fro, letting out little inarticulate sounds of excitement and agitation. At last he stood before them.

"What is your real name? Who are you? Who is this lady?"

"I am Miss Brontë, and this is my sister, Anne. Acton Bell. My
Christian name is Charlotte. You see, we all kept our own initials.
Ellis would not come—but she does exist, as much as we do."

Mr. Smith gaped. "The writer of *Wuthering Heights* is also a
woman? A young woman, like yourselves?"

"I am thirty-two. Ellis is thirty—nearly. Acton—that is, Anne— is twenty-eight. We are not, I think, quite young."

"Incredible. Utterly incredible! Ah, Williams, come in, come in at once! See what we have here!"

Mr. Williams, who had put his head in at the door, now came in. He was just as Charlotte had imagined him from his letters, a middle-aged, pale, stooping gentleman with a mild but at present rather astonished countenance.

"Williams, I have the honor to present to you . . . Currer and Acton Bell."

Mr. Williams gratified them by appearing to be about to reel back against the door with stupefaction. The girls both burst out laughing and leaned against each other, stifling their mirth unavailingly. Even Mr. Smith couldn't restrain himself and let out a great bellow of delight.

"Yes, Williams, it is truly they! What a come-uppance for that scalawag Newby! Oh, how I shall enjoy putting him down with this! But, ladies, this is a very special occasion. I can hardly express my pride—*our* pride and delight at seeing you—meeting you—oh, really, it is too rich! Ladies, young and pretty ladies! I don't know when I have felt so excited—so amazed—you have fairly taken us by storm, Miss Brontë—yes, yes, Williams, that is their real name. Pray let me shake your hand, ma'am, and yours, ma'am. Come, Williams, don't be bashful, shake the hand that wrote *Jane Eyre!*"

Their hands were shaken to all but a jelly, and Charlotte felt Mr. Smith would fairly offer to embrace her if she did not take charge of the situation, so she sat down very firmly and said, "Gentlemen, perhaps some little *éclaircissement* is called for."

So the gentlemen sat down, and Charlotte quietly explained why they had come. Mr. Smith asked questions, one leg kicking excitedly against the side of the desk. Mr. Williams simply sat and looked at them, and smiled, and nodded; every now and then Anne put in a word; and an hour passed before their publishers even remembered to offer them refreshments.

"This is too rich—too rich!" Mr. Smith kept repeating, rubbing his hands in glee. "I must introduce you to my mother and sisters. How long do you intend to stay in London?"

"Oh—" The girls exchanged questioning looks. "Only till tomorrow—"

George Smith threw up his hands. "Impossible! So short! You must make the most of the time. Tonight you must go to the Italian opera—"

"No, really—!"

"—and tomorrow, the Exhibition. Mr. Thackeray would be pleased to see you, and if G. H. Lewes knew 'Currer Bell' was in town he would have to be shut up to be kept from meeting you. I will ask them both to dinner at my house—"

Charlotte put her hand to her heart, which was leaping about in her breast. Mr. Thackeray! And Mr. Lewes, who had written to her and given her that splendid notice in *Frazer's Magazine*! How tempting—how irresistibly tempting! But Anne, her eyes modestly on her lap, was gently treading on her toe to remind her of Emily's parting words.

Charlotte hauled herself back from the clouds.

"Gentleman, I fear none of this can be. We are most determined to preserve our incognito. We have only announced ourselves to you, whom we trust—you have been discretion itself till now—to spare you any inconvenience that has arisen from our little mystery. To all the rest of the world, we must be 'gentlemen' as before."

George Smith's boyish face fell.

The two girls rose.

"We must not take more of your time."

"Pray don't go yet! Where are you staying?"

"At the Chapter Coffee House, in Paternoster Row."

The two men exchanged amused but almost scandalized glances.

"But that is not at all a suitable place! You must come to my house and be my mother's guests. She would be enchanted—"

Both shook their heads very vehemently at this. "No, truly! We are happier where we are—thank you."

With the deepest reluctance, Mr. Smith and Mr. Williams at last allowed them to depart, but at the street door Mr. Smith stopped them to wring their hands once more and insist that he would bring his sisters to call upon them that evening. He offered to find them a cab; but inevitably the meeting ended with him and Mr. Williams standing out on the pavement watching bemusedly as the two little figures trotted away on foot along the busy street.

"Well, Williams," said George Smith when they had disappeared in the crowd, "I swear that is the most singular circumstance of my professional life—or my private life either, come to that. That—that strange little woman—I called her pretty, but I lied and she knew it—she is the reverse of pretty, and yet— the power, the genius, that lies buried in that frail, quaint, improbable little head! I guessed all along it was a woman, yet not such a one as that! What did you think of her?"

"She has very fine eyes," said Mr. Williams. "Bless her," he added unexpectedly.

Smith glanced at him, amused.

"I am taking her to the opera tonight," he said, "whether she will or no."

"She will not thank you for it," said Mr. Williams.

Charlotte was lying on her bed with a wet cloth across her forehead when the potboy came up to announce the arrival of Mr. Smith "and ladies."

Anne flew into a panic.

"Charlotte, get up, oh, do! I can't receive them alone! Have some sal volatile—"

"Stop, take it away! My head will fly off!"

Summoning up her few reserves, Charlotte dragged herself to the door leading to their small sitting room. Together she and Anne timidly crossed the threshold—and stopped dead.

Crowding the tiny room in a blaze of color stood two elegant young ladies dressed as gorgeously as if for a ball. Between them George Smith, smiling blandly, in full evening dress, stood slapping snowy gloves against his palm.

"Ladies! Are you ready for the opera?"

The mouths of the two fell open so comically that he could hardly keep his face straight.

"But we cannot! We have no suitable dresses!"

"Nothing could be of less importance. Come just as you are. Let me introduce you to my sisters. Eliza, Sarah—the Misses Brontë. Our Mama was unfortunately indisposed, and has cried off."

Happy Mama, to be allowed to cry off! While Charlotte shook hands with the silk gloves, her eyes dazzled by white, bejeweled décolletés, her memory carried her back agonizingly to her first day at Roe Head, when she had stood in her green stuff dress and been greeted by Mary and Martha and the others in all their finery.

She made one despairing effort to escape.

"Mr. Smith, I beseech you—do not insist—"

"Oh, but I do, Miss Brontë!"

He gave her his arm to help her down the dark stairs, the two young ladies going ahead to the carriage that waited in the narrow street. Charlotte whispered to him anxiously. "Do they know . . . ?"

"No. To my eternal credit, I have preserved your secret."

A pleasant surprise awaited them: Mr. Williams, also in evening dress, but more homely and less formidable, was in the carriage. The Smith girls, though unable to hide their bewilderment, chatted to them in a friendly, unaffected manner, while their brother seemed fairly bursting with a sort of inner glee.

Suddenly Charlotte thought, *What is the use of caring how ridiculous I look*? If Mary were here, she would scoff at me for letting silly conventions spoil my pleasure—or a sick headache either! I shall put headache and embarrassment in my pocket.

It was as well she did so, for otherwise the grandeur of the Opera House would have utterly daunted her. Mr. Smith tucked her hand into the crook of his arm to conduct her up the wide red-carpeted stairway, and kept it there, though she gave it one or two tugs to free it; so she stood at his side, in her spectacles and her high-necked country dress, her head scarcely reaching his shoulder. Yet he constantly bent to talk to her, while kind Mr. Williams paid similar attentions to Anne, who, judging by the dancing looks she threw at Charlotte, was as excited as Charlotte herself. In this mood they both managed to rise above the supercilious smiles cast at them by numbers of elegant strangers.

The opera was *The Barber of Seville*. It fulfilled very well Charlotte and Anne's elevated ideas of what a dazzling stage performance should be; at the same time they managed not to be carried away by it. They privately agreed later that there might be things they would enjoy better. Nevertheless, it was a spectacular treat, from which they did not return to their humble inn until just after midnight. Mr. Williams' parting words were that he would collect them for church early next morning.

"I shall never rise in time!" said Anne, as they undressed for the first time in over forty-eight hours.

"I doubt if *I* shall ever rise again," groaned Charlotte.

"Oh, but was it not thrilling? I do so wish Emily were here!"

"She would have laughed at the little fat barber and his buxom beloved."

"She would not have laughed at Mr. Smith. He's very dashing, isn't he? And how kind to us both—especially to you!"

But Charlotte was fast asleep.

PART V

The Tragic Years

1848–49

THE SLOW
APPROACH

MILY WAS VERY WITHDRAWN
after the others returned from London. In vain they tried to
regale her with funny anecdotes of their adventures there, to
draw her back to them. She sat silent, unresponding. If pressed,
she would get up abruptly and retreat to her own room. Anne
was very upset.

"I wish you would talk to her, Charlotte!"

"I'm afraid of her when she's in this mood."

"But it's so awful like this! I miss her."

Anne's look was so pitiful that Charlotte was suddenly determined. She got up sharply, went upstairs and tapped on the closed
door. Emily opened it a little way and stood before her.

"Well?"

"May I come in and talk to you?"

"I don't feel like talking just now."

"Emily, what's the matter? You've changed so much lately. You
never read to us anymore, though I know you're working on a
new novel—"

"Have you been spying again?" asked Emily fiercely.

"No, darling, of course not! Emily, it's bad enough living in this house with Branwell, remembering how things were once. Don't *you* turn in on yourself. Do tell me what's the matter. Let me help."

"I don't need any help."

"Emily! Don't shut the door! Listen to me about this. Then I'll never mention it again, I promise. Mr. Smith and Mr. Newby both gave their words of honor that our secret was safe. We *had* to do what we did. Don't punish us more for it. Our secret is still safe, or we should have heard by now."

"And haven't we heard?" burst out Emily suddenly. "Why do you suppose those worldly Robinson girls have suddenly begun to write to Anne after all this time? Could it be because their little governess has blossomed into a much-talked-of novelist?"

Charlotte was greatly startled. "How could that be?"

"Because the secret is out, as I knew it would be as soon as one link in the chain of privacy was broken."

"Nonsense! Even if you are right about their guessing, it is probably because they recognized incidents in *Agnes Grey* that she may have related to them. And then, in *Wildfell Hall* there is a drunkard who they might well realize had some basis of reality in our own family, for they have certainly heard about Branwell's condition—he is often in touch with the family doctor, begging for money to pay his debts. It is a matter of their putting two and two together."

But Emily was beyond reason. "Our citadel is crumbling," she said. "I did not need proof of it. I knew it before. I felt the cold drafts blowing on me—" She actually took hold of her own shoulders as a shiver passed over her, and her eyes took on a wild look, as of panic. "Without privacy I cannot write—I cannot *live.*"

"But, Emily, it's not my fault!"

"It is!" cried Emily. "It was you who urged me to publish, who brought it all about! Now my thoughts, my feelings, my people, are scattered everywhere, exposed to thousands of eyes.

They've damaged me—it won't mend—there's no escape anymore. I can't get out—"

She stopped herself sharply.

"Emily—!"

"No! Leave me alone."

She kicked Charlotte's foot out of the door and slammed it
shut. Charlotte, listening outside, thought she heard strange
noises, like stifled groans.

It was late at night when Patrick finally crawled to bed.

For some hours he had been kept wakeful. Branwell, after
spending the early evening in a speechless stupor, had suddenly
become alert at about ten o'clock. Leaping from his bed, he had
begun pacing the room with unsteady steps, gesticulating, pulling
at his disheveled hair, darting wild, unseeing looks about him and
uttering indecipherable sounds. All efforts to calm him were
vain.

Sometimes when he was in this state he would hammer on the
door like a prisoner in a cell, shouting out to be released—"she"
was coming, he must meet her—only to fall again into mumbling
and curses. Later, he might fling himself about the room until
Patrick, fearing he would hurt himself, found courage to set himself in his son's way. Sometimes Branwell would thrust him aside,
shouting the foulest abuse.

Tonight, he had unexpectedly thrown himself into Patrick's
arms, sobbed on his shoulder and allowed himself to be laid on
his bed, where he stayed for a while, crying like a child, clutching
his father's hand and muttering anguished syllables of remorse
and wretchedness. Usually, as tonight, this phase would end in
sleep. But the whole ordeal could last for several hours, wearing
the old man threadbare in nerve and body. His emotional response had been all but worn away by so many weary months of
misery. He had given up all attempts to judge whether his son
was mad or sane, wicked or merely unfortunate, or whether he
himself was guilty or innocent of this tragedy being endlessly

played out before him. Duty and the battered remnants of his love kept him from giving in. But sometimes the strain was too great for him and he wept bitterly himself, praying for strength, which never seemed to come. Yet somehow he struggled on.

This particular night Patrick fairly cried himself to sleep. And his sleep was so profound that he did not hear when Branwell woke again, lit a candle with shaking hand and looked for a long time at the tormented face of his sleeping father.

"Poor old man. He's a hard enough time of it," he muttered aloud.

He got up cautiously. A quite different mood was on him. He was now lucid. He pulled on a dressing gown, and taking the candle, tiptoed to the door. He easily unbolted the locks that had held him fast imprisoned in his earlier frenzy, and silently he crept downstairs, past the loudly ticking clock, the shadows of his passage flickering eerily on the whitewashed walls.

Then began the search that he often made of such rooms as he had access to—a search that was in itself a symptom of dementia, for it was carried out with exaggerated, almost theatrical furtiveness, and with strange, fussy little movements accompanied by birdlike glances about him.

Ordinarily these nocturnal prowlings yielded nothing, and he would creep back to his room, no whit soothed in his fears by failure to unearth "proofs." But tonight his search was rewarded. For there on the parlor table was Anne's writing box.

He pounced on it almost gleefully. It was not locked. Here was treasure trove! Now he would *find out*, and in the morning he would confront them all with evidence of their treachery toward him! His hands shook wildly as he pored over the contents of the little desk, and it was not long before he found Mary Robinson's letter.

At first he could not read it, for his glasses were upstairs. But he found a magnifying glass in his father's study, and with its aid he read the contents of the letter. One sentence stood out:

"Our mother is to marry again—a rich old man—"

Had any of his family seen what he was about, they would have expected some violent outcry. Yet astoundingly there was none. Branwell stood bent over the dining table for many, many minutes in motionless silence while the clock ticked away in the sleeping house. Then he lifted his face. The candlelight flashed across his cheeks, which were covered with tears.

"Oh, my dear love," he said quietly. "Why have you betrayed me?"

They found him in the morning, sitting on the floor near the table. The candle had burned out, and the papers from Anne's desk were strewn about. Branwell was not asleep; his eyes were open and his facial muscles twitched every now and then. Mary's letter had fallen to the floor near him. When Emily raised him under the arms, he was quite limp. Charlotte had to help carry him to bed. They stood together, gazing down at his unseeing eyes, listening to his shallow breathing.

"That is the end of him," said Emily.

"We must not tell Anne," said Charlotte. "I told her to hide it—"

"It didn't make much difference," said Emily.

"My boy, a friend has come to see you—Francis Grundy."

For the first time since reading Mary's letter, Branwell looked at his father directly.

"Grundy? Here?"

"He is down in the Bull. He has ordered a fine dinner for the two of you. Let me help you to dress and go down to him."

Branwell jumped up convulsively.

"It is a trick!" he muttered. "Another vile trick—but I am prepared—well prepared, you'll see! No, no help, no help—let me quite alone. Get out, old man, leave me, will you!"

Minutes later, a scarecrow figure stumbled from shadow to shadow down the lane and in at the rear entrance of the pub. Grundy, hearing a sound at the door, hurried to open it.

A head of wild red hair made a slow, almost ludicrous appearance around the doorframe, but when Grundy saw the face under the hair, he had much ado to prevent himself gasping. Here was change indeed. Ill as his friend had looked at their last meeting, he was now almost unrecognizable. His skin was yellow, his eyes sunken, his lips not so much trembling as gibbering; his expression hovered between terror and a mad resolve.

"Come in, old man, come in!" Grundy cried, hiding his dismay in an excess of bonhomie. "You look perished with cold!"

Branwell looked around dazedly as Grundy led him almost by force toward the table and the fire.

". . . left a warm bed . . . come down here . . ." he muttered.

"Very good of you, my dear Brontë! Come, here's some hot brandy for you, to warm you up! Then we'll eat, eh? And talk!"

"Eat? I've not broken bread for a week—"

"Well you'll break that glass if you're not careful! Here, let me hold it steady for you. There! That's better, isn't it? Come, sit down. Have another. Your color's returning as I look! Now have a bite of this good roast mutton and let me hear all your troubles."

With this mixture of banter and physical comforts Grundy gradually induced Branwell to relax a little, and after half an hour (and three hot punches) he was recognizable, at least, as the Brontë Grundy had known.

"There, you are better! Now I know you again!" cried the railwayman cheerfully.

"You will not know me much longer," said Branwell quietly.

"Eh? What's your meaning in that?"

"I am going to die, Francis."

Suppressing a shudder, for he had spoken so strangely, Grundy said heartily, "Rubbish!"

Branwell shook his head. "No. Nor is it morbid. I don't dread it at all. I long for it of all things. And it will come soon, regardless of what you and the old man may do, or even the doctor. I've no will to live, but much to stop living. And there's naught any father, friend or surgeon can do against that complaint."

"But my dear fellow, is it so hopeless?" asked Grundy, no longer straining after cheerfulness, but dropping his voice to the same solemn level.

"It has been entirely so from the beginning. Only now I have realized it."

Grundy was silent. After a long pause, Branwell went on:

"I had much given me, and if I have to face my Maker and answer to Him, as in the parable of the talents, truthfully I must just hang my head and hold out empty hands and ask His forgiveness. It has all been wasted, Francis—all squandered and thrown away . . ." Branwell passed his translucent hand over his face, let it drop and threw back his head. "Oh, God, how I wish I knew what to believe! Is it worth trying to pray at this stage, after denying belief for so long? My father prays for me . . . perhaps that's enough . . . my prayers must seem worthless, as worthless as myself. Yet I long to try, sometimes. Perhaps I'm reverting to childishness . . . The end is very close now, I see it just ahead. I long for it, and yet I'm afraid . . ."

Slow tears of weakness slipped down his cheeks. Grundy, very much moved, took his hand in both of his and held it.

"You hold my hand like Willie used to," Branwell said faintly.

"Who, dear old fellow?"

"A friend I had once . . . Come! I'm spoiling your evening. Let's eat and drink, and talk of other things than me."

With what amounted to a really heroic effort, Branwell now pulled himself together, and for an hour sat facing Grundy, trying to smile and talk normally. He even managed to eat something. Grundy, relieved by this turn, let himself hope that the previous mood had been a passing one and was not to be taken too seriously. Yet at heart he knew what this semblance of normality was costing his old friend, and he felt a great, heavy sorrow pressing down on him.

At last he got up to go. "Shall I see you home, old lad?"

Branwell didn't answer. He seemed to be thinking. With a deep frown, he suddenly reached up his sleeve and drew out—of all things—a carving knife. He laid it, very gently, on the table.

Grundy tried to laugh.

"Do you want to do for me, Brontë?"

"No, Francis, not you. It was for another."

"Who?"

"When I heard you were here, I thought—I get confused sometimes—I didn't believe it could be you. I thought—I thought it was Satan, come to fetch me."

Grundy was horrified. "You're not serious!"

"Oh, yes . . . And although he did not come this time, come he yet may, unless I look about warily . . . You'd say it would be no more than I deserve, if you but knew all."

"You're no worse than the rest of us!"

"Oh, yes, I am. The more that is given, the more that is expected. Never you mind, Francis. Go on now. It was good of you to come—very good. I will make my own way—home."

Grundy left Branwell standing in the road, one hand raised to wave good-bye, but his head lowered, not looking at Grundy, who feared he was weeping again. *I must come again soon*, he thought. But he knew he could not face another such meeting.

Two days later, William Brown was walking home late from the Masons' Lodge. The streets of Haworth were empty, and the faint hissing of the few gas lamps was the only sound other than that of his own ponderous clogs across the cobbles. Suddenly he stopped. Up ahead of him, making its way along the main street, was a figure he knew. It would take a few stumbling steps, then stop, leaning motionless against a wall for a space; then, pushing itself outward with one hand, would lurch on a few more yards before halting again. The halts were worse to watch than the slight progress, for the figure appeared half dropping with stress or fatigue; the head lolled forward, the shoulders stooped and at the same time heaved with sobbing breaths.

William ran forward.

"Branwell! What art about, lad? Tha should be in thy bed!"

The poor haggard face turned toward him. William was not and never had been a very sensitive man, but he could not remain unmoved at the sight of this shattered countenance lit eerily by the lamp nearest them. He stifled a gasp, for he saw death there quite clearly.

"Come! I'll help you home."

"Thanks, William," whispered Branwell, and then, as the older man put an arm under his shoulders, he added, "Can you get me in without waking my father? The poor old man—it will be a relief to him as me when all this is over—"

As they toiled up the steep lane, Branwell stopped, as William thought, to rest. But he raised a shaking arm and pointed at the parsonage, standing foursquare on its rise, dark but for a point of light in one downstairs window.

"Do you see that, William? That lamp?"

"Aye."

"That's Emily's work. She leaves one shutter open and a lamp well trimmed and clear-burning in that window for me every time I go out on my miserable wanderings. What do you think of that?"

Puzzled, William answered, "A kind thought—natural in a sister."

"Natural! You think that! But my sisters are not natural sisters to me, William. Charlotte, who was once closer to my heart than my own lung, now withholds herself from me as if she feared to become a drunkard and a wastrel herself just by looking at me. Anne, for all her religion, cannot bear to be near me. And as for Emily, she is my nurse, uncomplaining, duty-bound; but I swear, without a quarter ounce of real feeling about me, for she seldom speaks; and when I dare to question her about the mysteries and secrets that crawl and whisper through our house like termites, she cruelly refuses to set my mind at rest. What are they up to, William? Tell me if you know! Not to know is poison to me."

William scratched his head. "There's no telling for sure. But there's been talk . . . Some say there's been books written by one or more in t' parsonage, though no one hereabouts has read them. Why, what ails thee now? Stand up, man, don't faint on me! Lord, I must carry thee then."

2

RELEASE

N THE MORNING OF SEPTEMBER
24 Emily woke earlier than usual. The cloud of oppression that
hung perpetually over her mind, waking or sleeping, pressed down
on her the moment she opened her eyes, making a mockery of the
first delicate rays of sunlight entering through the curtainless
windows.

Immediately below, she heard Martha Brown opening the front
door to let the dogs out, and the next moment they were racing
around the small garden, barking ecstatically at the first whiff of
impending autumn that floated tantalizingly down from the
moors. It was the merest prickle in the early morning air, but
Emily caught it too.

With an indefinable feeling of reluctance, she knelt on her narrow bed and looked out. A lemon-colored sun had just lifted
itself clear of the farthest hills. Mist was everywhere, completely
submerging all but the tallest gravestones below her, so that the
few preeminent crosses and marble angels loomed up like the
tips of wrecks from the calm milk-and-water sea.

Quivering with sorrow, Emily took a deep breath. She tasted

autumn. Its sharp invigoration in her throat reminded her cruelly of late September days in the past when she had been able to make a spiritual leap through the window and race with the dogs, all but barking like them in an excess of joy. Yet now it was all gone. That wondrous faculty stood somewhere outside her possession, taunting her with its residual power, calling her mockingly, knowing her to be outcast, deprived, betrayed. Or was she the betrayer?

She would have liked to shutter the windows, bolt the door, shut out the scent and sight and knowledge of it, to obliterate all memory of what had once been available to her—to mourn in utter darkness and solitude. But that was forbidden. She *must* look at it, feel and remember and long for it. Her soul seemed to cry out within her, "Let me come again! Pity me! I cannot endure it!" Yet she would not even bury her face on her arms, but stared out stonily, showing nothing.

A harsh knocking broke into her revery.

"Emily!" It was Charlotte. "Come quickly! Papa needs you!"

Still in her nightgown, Emily snatched a shawl and ran across the landing to the room Papa and Branwell shared. Papa knelt beside the bed holding Branwell, who was lying with his back arched and his head thrust deep into the pillow. A ghastly grating, rattling sound came from him. Without hesitating, Emily hurried to the top of the bed and tried to force a corner of her shawl between the clenched teeth, but it was too late for that, so she wiped the flecks of froth from the grimacing lips and supported the rigid neck with her arm. Anne and Charlotte stood together at the foot of the bed looking on in helpless horror.

After a while the spasm passed and Branwell lay prostrated, his face corpselike but for the film of sweat covering it. The watchers drew breath again in a succession of trembling sighs.

"Fetch a doctor," said Patrick.

The doctor came.

"He has taken a severe turn for the worse," he said. "I'm sorry. I had not expected this or I would have warned you. I think, sir," he continued, rising to face Patrick, "that you would do best to keep to the house today and let your assistant serve your turn in church."

Patrick swayed on his feet and bowed his head. Charlotte, without bidding, hurried out to Mr. Nicholls' lodging at John Brown's house. Her mind was a blank. She knew what the doctor's words meant, and she made a weak attempt to force herself to contemplate the thought *Today Branwell will die*. But her brain rejected it.

When Mr. Nicholls stood before her, she told him briefly, almost coldly, that he must take the morning service. She felt vaguely astonished when he replied firmly and calmly that that would be perfectly all right; she was to tell Mr. Brontë not to concern himself further about it. She looked up for a numb moment into his bland face, and suddenly saw something in it— remote but benign, a sort of placid strength—that made her want to lean against him, as against some tall, passionless tree, and shut out the remorseless daylight against his broad chest.

"Thank you," she said faintly, and turned to go.

"Miss Brontë—"

"Yes?"

"I shall call after the service. You need not come down unless there is something you need. But I shall call. And again this evening."

"This evening . . ." *By this evening, Branwell will be no more.* Charlotte put her hand to her eyes and pressed the thought back. "Thank you," she said again. A few moments later she was hurrying back up the lane.

She overtook John Brown on his way to the cemetery, carrying his stonemason's tools. She grasped his sleeve.

"John, Branwell is worse. Will you come?"

He hurried on with her. The church clock was chiming eight as Tabby met them on the steps. She was holding a handkerchief to her rheumy eyes and heaving with sobs.

" 'E's woke," she said. " 'E's 'imself. 'Tis t' change before death! Ye'd best to 'urry."

"Martha told me he was better these last two days," John murmured as they hurried upstairs.

"Yes—gentler and quieter—yesterday he spoke about things we used to do. Games . . ."

For a flashing second, the thing came real for Charlotte, the true meaning of it. When Branwell had talked of their plays she had not allowed herself to feel. It would have been insupportable, and threatened to become so now. She stopped suddenly, clutching the banister.

"Go in," she said abruptly. "I am going to church. I must get my bonnet."

John looked at her curiously, then went into Branwell's room.

His daughter Martha was there, standing by the bed with Emily and Anne. The parson knelt on the floor, praying aloud, his head thrown back, his hands hard-clasped and trembling with the force of their grip.

"Oh, God!" he was saying, with the force of a shout. "He has sinned, but Thy mercy is infinite and shall encompass all who cry to You in the name of Your blessed son! We who have loved this boy know only a fraction of his true self, that beautiful creation modeled upon Your own image and sullied only by the Evil One! Beneath the burden of his sins, surely You see him still as white and clean of soul as when I first held him in my arms . . ."

Tears coursed down Patrick's cheeks and wet the high white stock around his neck; for a few moments he could not continue, but then he drove himself on.

"Have pity upon him. Forgive and cleanse him in the sacred blood of our Savior. Take him unto Yourself. If You but will it, it can still come right."

He spoke the last words in quite a different voice, undeclamatory, utterly sincere, as if, owing to their long relationship, Patrick in his extremity might approach the holy throne stripped of the vocal trappings of his office and claim intimacy with God. And something in this personal tone seemed to reach Branwell, who was lying quietly watching his father, for suddenly he said,

"Amen."

Anne burst into tears.

Patrick seemed dazed. His face had an expression half startled, half beatific, as if an impossible prayer had been abruptly answered. Bending over Branwell, he took one wasted hand in both his old ones and whispered, "My boy, you *are* penitent—you *are* aware of God—that is all that is needed—"

Branwell grew restless, his eyes roving. "Where is Charlotte?"

At that moment she entered, putting on her bonnet for church. Instantly Branwell's eyes fastened on her.

Brother and sister looked at each other. Charlotte's face between the wings of her plain bonnet was ashen, her huge eyes burned with feelings she had desperately tamped down; her body shook with the pressure of them. Branwell gazed at her with a wild hunger and tried to sit up and speak.

Suddenly his eyes glazed and he drew in his breath with a sharp sound of pain.

"John!" he called out urgently. "I'm dying!"

Brown didn't stay till the end; he couldn't bear the stress in the room. As he slipped out, he beckoned his daughter after him.

"It's all but over. I'll go to church and prepare to ring the bell for him. Run to the garden gate when his time comes and signal me—I shall stand by the church door."

Martha, dour and tearless, nodded.

He walked down the lane. Flossy and Keeper were shut up in the kitchen now, and there was a Sunday silence upon the village, broken only by the occasional footsteps of early comers to church. The Reverend Nicholls approached from the opposite direction, and the two men met and stopped.

"Well?" said Nicholls.

Brown shook his head. "A few minutes and he'll be out of this world. For his sake I hope it's no longer."

"Is Miss Brontë in the room?"

"Of course."

Nicholls looked up at the gray square front of the parsonage. His eyes rested on the upper right-hand window. Then he said:

"Your daughter is coming."

John swung around, then turned back.

"It's over," he said shortly. He stood still for a moment, his eyes on the cobbles. "Only thirty-one he was—I knew him from a lad, you know. From a fiery, funny little lad. Well," he said, straightening up but avoiding the other man's eyes, "I must go and ring the bell."

Branwell's death prostrated his father and had a scarcely less overwhelming effect on Charlotte, who immediately succumbed to an attack of jaundice.

Arrangements for the funeral were put in hand by Emily. Martha and Hannah Brown laid out Branwell's body; John and William placed it in its coffin and carried it to church. The service was attended, for the parsonage household, only by Emily, Tabby and Martha, for Anne stayed at home to look after Charlotte and her father.

Meanwhile, Arthur Nicholls had kept his word to Charlotte. He had been calling at the parsonage twice a day. Charlotte seldom saw him—she could face no one—but she heard his regular step on the path, his unassuming knock. Tabby would shuffle to the door, and then would follow always the same inquiry:

"How is Miss Brontë? How is Mr. Brontë? Is there anything I can do?" A negative murmur from Tabby, followed by, "I'll call again this afternoon" or "tomorrow." These visits meant little to Charlotte, consciously; yet she came to expect them and would have felt a shade more wretched if they had stopped.

Her guilt and grief reached their climax on the day of the funeral. The thought that Branwell, whose body was just now being lowered into the family vault under the church aisle, might in his spiritual form be undergoing torment, was unendurable to Charlotte's grieving mind. A pang of sympathetic agony, much like a burn running up the skin of her arms, assailed her; she hugged herself and began to rock and moan.

Anne held her tightly.

"Don't, Charlotte, don't! We can't know!"

"I was so cruel, so unforgiving—I betrayed him—but for me, he might have had more will to live—"

"You must never, never think that," said Anne strongly. "It is untrue and useless. It can only undermine your strength, just when we all need it—especially Papa."

Charlotte struggled for control.

"How beautiful he looked," she whispered between her sobs. "His face when he was dead tore my heart. I remember everything so clearly! When we were young, before all went wrong—I did love him, Anne! I did!"

"Of course you did."

"But I stopped loving him," she said drearily. "Why did I stop?"

Anne held her and said nothing, looking out at the scene now lit by a sullen, sulfurous light. There was a blinding flash. Thunder sounded almost right overhead, and then the clouds burst and rain deluged down. In a few minutes the cobbled lane was a tumbling stream.

Charlotte stared. "How fitting!" she said strangely. "He would have liked this. The Genii might have arranged it specially for him."

But Anne only said, "Emily didn't wear her pattens. Her feet will get dreadfully wet."

3

PRISONER
IN THE FLESH

 MILY GOT MORE THAN WET AS
she walked home from the funeral arm in arm with Tabby. She
caught a cold, an unusual thing for her. She had been hardy all
her life.

And the cold clung. In a fortnight it had dropped to her chest.
She wheezed when she breathed, and her hollow cough began to
frighten everyone.

"Darling, you must see a doctor," said Patrick one evening in
the middle of October. Emily had been seized by an attack of
coughing that had forced her to go out of the room. When she returned, her eyes were bloodshot, her hair damp at the temples.

"I need no poisoning doctors," she said shortly, and sat down
again in the windowseat with her book.

"But my own dear girl—"

"No, Papa."

"Just because you have never needed one before—"

Emily's head came up and she fixed him with a hard, glittering
stare.

"You may leave nagging me, if you please, Papa. I will not see
a doctor, and there's an end."

Patrick looked helplessly at Anne, who was sitting by the fire with Flossy across her feet. Keeper, also on the hearthrug, was watching Emily with his bulging mastiff's eyes. Now he got up and went over to her. Sitting down on the cold flags near her skirt, he put his head on her lap. Her hand moved stiffly till it lay across his nose.

Anne, watching her averted figure, shook her head at her father. When Emily rose after a few minutes without a word of good-night and left the room, Anne said quietly:

"It's no use, Papa. We have all tried. She is absolutely set against it. To Charlotte she denied there was anything wrong, and me she has entirely forbidden to mention the word 'doctor' again."

The old man's voice rose.

"What's to be done then? I—we cannot sit by and—" He brought both hands up to cover his face for a moment. He could not say the words.

Anne quickly said, "Don't worry, Papa! It is only a cold, you know, such as all of us get two or three times a winter."

"Do you really think so, my pet?" asked the old man piteously, taking a little comfort from the assurance in Anne's tone.

Charlotte, whose conscience ached perpetually from her self-belaboring about Branwell, could scarcely endure to contemplate the possibility of anything happening to Emily. It was not only the loss of a beloved sister that she could not face, but the fear that she herself might leave something undone, neglect some avenue of effort or persuasion that could save her.

So she laid siege to Emily's "citadel" of silent noncooperation. She followed her about in a fever of anxiety, trying to do her jobs for her, offering to carry things, to relieve her of every slightest exertion. Whenever she dared, she urged her to keep to her bed, to lie on the sofa at least, or to allow the servants to wait on her a little.

"You are ill, Emily! Why do you persist in denying it?"

Emily shrugged coldly. "If you go on wishing it on me, no doubt I shall soon be as ill as you now imagine."

A word more, and she would jump up with unconcealed anger

and stride from the room. For hours or even days after a really persistent attempt on Charlotte's part to remonstrate with her, Emily would seem to punish her with silence, icy looks or withdrawal from rooms when Charlotte entered them, as if in trying to help her Charlotte had mortally offended her.

But Emily was not angry all the time, only when a member of the household was trying to "get at" her about her illness. For the rest, she seemed calm enough, only too silent. When several days had passed since anyone had offered her medicine disguised as tea, or suggested feeding the dogs for her, or (dreadful day!) dared to bring her her breakfast in bed, which Martha once did, she would seem easier, and would sit in the parlor with the family in the lengthening evenings, reading her book on the hearthrug with Keeper close at her side.

The only concession she paid to her illness was that she never left the house. Her beloved moors, bleak now and hardening their sinews for the coming winter, were shut out; but Charlotte felt that it was not from prudence that Emily no longer walked upon their fierce heights, but because to do so would give her some unendurable spiritual pain.

In desperation Charlotte at last called in the doctor who had attended Branwell, telling him to make the call appear a social and not a professional one. But when Emily, making her slow, painful way from the kitchen to the parlor, encountered him in the hall, she threw Charlotte one look of blind rage and ran—or rather, struggled—up the stairs. The little group below heard her bedroom door slam as she jammed the bolt home.

Charlotte turned to the doctor with her hands outspread.

"Did you see? How she reeled back against the wall when the wind from the open door struck her? Did you hear her breathing? You can hear it all over the house!"

The doctor shook his head.

"Without her cooperation there is little I can do. Keep her warm. Do not let her exert herself. She ought to stay in bed—"

"In bed! She rises punctually at seven each morning, and will not retire till ten at night. All the duties she has assigned herself around the house she still performs, and *will* perform, no matter what we say or do. To see her kneading bread or down on her knees brushing the carpet every day more slowly, more effortfully, and yet more doggedly—is a nightmare to all of us."

"Kneading bread? Brushing carpets?" exclaimed the doctor, appalled. "She will kill herself!"

Charlotte stared at him.

"From the brief look I had, I fear her case is far advanced," said the doctor soberly. "I am sorry."

"Then there is in any case nothing you could do?"

The doctor shrugged. "Perhaps transfer to a warmer climate— one never knows—"

"Perhaps that is what she fears," whispered Charlotte. "That we would send her away . . ."

The doctor left some medicine. Anne, who was less afraid of Emily's anger, quietly offered it to her that evening.

"It might do you good," she said gently.

"Rubbish," said Emily harshly—and at once burst into a long, racking spasm of coughing. Listening to it in anguish, Charlotte could hear Maria's cough in the church at Tunstall all over again, and knew suddenly that she should renounce hope.

But it was impossible—*impossible* to contemplate life without Emily. Hope was like a thin rope stretched across the tilting, wave-washed deck of a ship in a storm; it was essential to get from one point, one day, to another, essential for each forward step. Without that thin line, Charlotte felt she would collapse and be swept into a bottomless ocean of regret.

In early December the weather turned really cold. Snow fell and the keen winds, lent a knife-edge by frost, cut through every crack and crevice around doors and windows of the parsonage, giving the air within a perpetual, undefeatable chill. Even opening the door briefly to let the dogs in or out sent a blast of biting cold through the house.

To see what this cold did to Emily was heartrending. It afflicted her like the lashes of a whip. Yet she would wear no extra clothing beyond her usual winter shawl. Her hair was lank, her hands chilblained and raw, and each breath she drew was a noisy agony to herself and all within earshot. Her body was racked by spasms of trembling which so infuriated her that she would grip with both hands any table edge, doorframe or chair-back near to her, set her teeth, bow her head, and strain all her aching muscles in a furious effort to control the ague. When a wave of hard physical pain struck her, however, she would not deign to take hold of anything. Perforce she would stand motionless, eyes not closed but strained wide open, nostrils flared, mouth clenched, her elbow—not her hand—pressed against her side, breath hard-held until the attack passed. Then slowly she would move on about her business. She hardly ever spoke.

None of them dared any longer to so much as reach out to steady her when she swayed, or even affect to notice her sufferings. But theirs were scarcely less in watching so helplessly and uncomprehendingly.

"If she would but expend half the willpower on fighting the illness that she does upon subduing its symptoms," said Anne despairingly, "she would be cured in a week. One might almost think she *wanted* to die!"

Charlotte turned on her. "No! Don't say that. I won't believe it!"

She turned sharply and went and shut herself up in her room. She sat on her bed in an agony of mind too deep for movement or tears.

One night they were all sitting by the fire. Emily was clearly desperately ill; yet she still refused to go to bed a moment before ten. Usually she sat in a chair, her eyes half closed, fighting silently for breath, while Charlotte read aloud to pass the terrible hours until they could all go upstairs. The climb was sheer torture, for not so much as a comforting arm might be offered. Emily dragged herself up step by step unaided, and the inevitable prospect of this ordeal weighed on Anne and Charlotte throughout the evening.

Tonight Emily would not sit in her chair. She had lowered herself to her old place on the hearthrug, and there she sat with Keeper near her, slowly going through some piles of papers in her portable desk, which stood next to her on the floor.

Charlotte was reading from Emerson's essays, sent by kind Mr. Williams. Anne was sewing. Suddenly they both noticed an odd brightening of the fire and looked up. Emily was slowly feeding pages into the flames.

"What are you burning?" Charlotte asked.

Emily did not seem to hear.

Charlotte leaned forward. "What are those papers, Emily? It's not your new book, is it?"

Emily jerked her body, turning her shoulders deliberately so that Charlotte could not see. She hunched over her box, and now her weak hands tried to move more quickly, crumpling the pages and thrusting them into the grate several at a time.

"Emily—"

Emily hunched still more, her back fully turned to Charlotte, but to Anne on the other side of the fireplace she cast a speaking look of appeal. Anne signaled with her eyes to Charlotte, and then put her sewing aside and went down on her knees beside Emily.

"Shall I help you, love?" she said tenderly. And for once, Emily did not protest. Charlotte watched helplessly until the box was nearly empty and the grate filled with black ashes.

The next day was cold and clear. It was less than a week to Christmas. Charlotte, Anne and Patrick watched Emily drag herself from one chair-back to the next until she was seated at her usual place at the breakfast table. This was a mere formality: she would not or could not eat, and could scarcely carry a cup of tea to her lips, even using both hands. Her face was all shades of gray, light to whiteness on the skeletal cheekbones, dark to blackness around her eyes and jaw. Sweat stood on her upper lip, and she rasped as she took each breath. Yet she was dressed, the last button fastened by herself, though it had taken over an hour to achieve it, and after her "meal" she would walk to the kitchen, leaning at every step against the wall to get strength for the next, to mix the dogs' food in their bowls. Tabby and Martha were at this moment hurrying to get every other possible job out of the way before Emily's inevitable appearance.

She returned to the parlor, Keeper as always with his nose an inch from the back of her skirt. With great difficulty she lowered herself into an armchair. Last night she had not been able to rise from the hearthrug without the assistance she despised. The piece of sewing that Anne had been doing lay on the arm of the chair, and rather than seem idle, Emily picked it up. The infinitely painful slowness of all her movements struck Charlotte like blows to the face. She was sitting writing a letter to Ellen, struggling to hide her tears:

"I should have written to you before, if I had had one word of hope to say; but I had not. She grows daily weaker . . . Moments as dark as these I have never known. . . ."

She looked at Emily again. The sewing lay in her lap with Keeper's chin on it. She was staring out of the window. A pale reflection of sun on snow gave a faint lightening to Emily's face, a little glow. And abruptly Charlotte got up.

"Would you like some heather, darling?"

For the first time for many days, Emily looked at her. She did not say anything, but her eyes had a beseeching look.

"I know it's late in the year, but there might be a sprig left somewhere. It will be a bit of the moors, won't it? I'll bring it for you—wait here!"

Wait here . . . Why had she said that?

In a flurry of desperate, impetuous haste, Charlotte threw on a cloak and bonnet and left the house through the kitchen door. In five minutes she was climbing the snowy breast of the first familiar slope. It was an almost fruitless mission. She knew it quite well. Heather in December? Yet Emily had responded, if only a little. She must find some—she must. In the first hollow she dropped to her knees and burrowed in the snow with her ungloved hands, scraping it away from the scrub and dead bracken-stalks, searching, combing the rotted growth with her fingers. Nothing. She clambered to her feet and ran on.

Her search took her two hours. But at last, panting with exertion and a growing conviction of urgency, almost weeping from repeated disappointments, she uncovered a heather plant. On the underside she found one last dismal sprig on which the colorless crumpled bells of blossom could still be seen. Cupping it in both hands, she turned and ran for home, not stopping to brush the snow off her skirt.

"It will make her remember spring," she kept thinking. "It will make her want to live!"

She stumbled into the kitcnen, dropped her wet cloak on the floor and rushed into the parlor.

Anne was there, and Patrick. And Emily. But Emily was not sitting up in the chair. She was lying on the black horsehair sofa.

Charlotte stopped dead. It was the first time Emily had ever consented to lie down in the daytime. Her face was turned toward the window, where the noon sun now shone in. When Charlotte came up and gently laid the heather in her hand, she suddenly realized that Emily's eyes could not see the heather, or her, or anything. Yet the terrible hollow rattling breaths went on, coming and going from the ravaged lungs.

"If you'll send for the doctor," Emily suddenly whispered, "I'll see him now."

They did not look at each other. None of them wanted to go. Anne at length went and found Martha, grim-faced, outside the door, and bid her fetch Dr. Wheelhouse.

"Did *she* say so?" asked the girl. Anne nodded. "Then it's too late," she muttered. And even as she spoke, they heard the old man's tragic cry from behind the parlor door.

4

RESIGNATION

*M*R. WILLIAMS DID NOT USUALLY share Charlotte's letters with George Smith. But he carried the one he received after Emily's death to his partner.

"This sad event may have repercussions for us," said Smith. "Currer's new novel has naturally been in abeyance since October. For her sake as well as ours she ought to bring out another before too long. Work is the best healer. You have her confidence. Perhaps you might point that out—tactfully, of course—"

Mr. Williams looked at his feet in their neat patent-leather boots.

"I don't think I'll mention it, Smith, if you'll forgive me," he said. "Not just now. She has another sister ailing. All her strength and energy will be needed. We have no right to make claims on her at such a time."

George Smith fixed his fine bright eyes on the older man and suddenly smiled.

"You're a good fellow," he said heartily. "You make me ashamed of my wretched ambition."

No persuasion could have caused Charlotte to resurrect her

aborted novel. The sunny uplands of Yorkshire at the time of the Luddite riots, carefully chosen as its background, seemed as remote from the Satanic landscape that hemmed her in now as the Antipodean bay where Mary lived.

Her main need was the comfort of a visit from Ellen, whom she had dissuaded from visiting the parsonage since before the death of Branwell. Now Charlotte sent for her, and she arrived only a few days after Emily's funeral.

"My poor dear—how have you borne it?"

"I haven't—I don't. It is not to be borne, Ellen! Can you conceive of it—never to see her anymore? The house is desolate! And if you'd seen her at the end! No quiet, easy death for her— she was fairly torn out of life—"

"Oh, don't! I can't bear to think of it."

"And I cannot stop."

"Where is Anne?"

Charlotte's face clouded with a new dread.

"In bed."

"What? Is she poorly?"

"Yes. Listen—do you hear?"

Ellen listened. After a moment, a cough she had not noticed before grated through the house. She looked wide-eyed at Charlotte, who had gone white.

"That might be Emily's, but it is Anne's."

"*Charlotte!*"

"We shall know soon. A specialist is coming from Leeds. One thing at least—Anne is tractable. She acknowledges her illness and is willing to help herself. At all events we shan't have to bear the absolute horror we had with Emily, the total and forced neglect—"

"Charlotte, don't, you'll upset yourself more!"

Charlotte wiped her streaming eyes again and again.

"You're right. I must be more composed now you are here. But my heart is all bruised, every thought makes me wince. And Ellen . . . her dog has upset me so terribly since she died . . ."

"Keeper? How?"

"Papa let him come to the funeral like any human mourner. He walked behind her coffin and lay in our pew, and afterward he went straight up to her room and has lain outside her door almost ever since. Poor brute, he can't fathom the source of his misery, and so he howls, and sometimes I feel I could howl with him. He won't let anyone enter her room—not that I could bear to go in."

"Shh, darling, stop now! Let's go up and see Anne. When is the doctor due?"

"On the fifth. Papa is in a worse way than I am. I think he would rather not know the truth—so would I. It's Anne who insists, so that we may take proper steps, so she says."

"The courage of her!"

"Courage!" Charlotte dragged a sigh from her depths. "Oh, yes, courage is notable in my sisters. Emily met death like a warrior, defiant to the end."

And you were a casualty in her battle, thought Ellen, as they went upstairs arm in arm.

The three girls managed to be tolerably comfortable together for the next week or so, though they were all oppressed, as much by the impending visit of the Leeds lung specialist as by the awful absence of Emily. The truth was that at this stage Emily's death was in some tragic way a relief to those who had had to witness and been forbidden to relieve her sufferings. Whenever they felt the cutting winter wind blowing through the house, or looked out in the mornings upon the start of another dark, icy day, they could comfort themselves by thinking that at least Emily was beyond reach of the hostile elements. But these affected Anne severely: her fever worsened and her cough began to bedevil the household as Emily's had until so recently.

One evening, after Anne had gone to sleep, Charlotte and Ellen sat by the fire. Conversation had petered out, and Charlotte, rising restlessly, suggested they walk as they had used to do. Ellen took her arm, and they circled the table for some time in silence.

"Charlotte, I want to ask you something," said Ellen timidly at last.

"I think there is nothing, now, that I wouldn't tell you," said Charlotte wearily.

"Some time ago I wrote you a letter, passing on certain rumors I'd heard concerning your—literary activities. You were very angry with me and wrote back that whoever said so was no friend of yours and must have dreamed what she heard, and much to the same effect—in short, you as good as gave these rumors the lie direct, and authorized me to say, to any who asked me, that you had never published a book in your life."

Charlotte said nothing. They circled the table once more. Then Ellen drew them both to a stop, and turning Charlotte to face her, forced her friend to look her in the eyes.

"Charlotte, I did as you told me. I have gone on doing it in the face of a veritable storm of rumors—rumors now amounting to a certainty. The book they say you have written is none other than *Jane Eyre*. I have read it myself and I cannot doubt you wrote it. Yet as lately as last week I denied flatly to three gossiping friends—schoolfellows of yours, Charlotte—that you had any hand in it. Tell me now, frankly. Have you made a fool and a liar of me? And if so, I am entitled to know why."

Tears of chagrin came into Charlotte's eyes as she looked into the trusting, puzzled face of her friend. She put her face down on Ellen's shoulder, but for once Ellen's arms did not come up to comfort her.

"Tell me the truth, Charlotte, *please*."

Abruptly, Charlotte pulled away and ran from the room. Ellen waited. After a few moments Charlotte came back with six volumes in her hands. She spread them out on the table.

"You are right about *Jane Eyre*," she said. "And these are Emily's and Anne's novels. You may put them in your box—they are for you. As for what you accuse me of, I confess to it, and I am humbly sorry. But Ellen, there was a reason—perhaps not good enough to justify my deceiving you, but you may judge me when you know it." And she told Ellen everything, with special emphasis on Emily's fanatic insistence on secrecy.

"It was for her sake chiefly," Charlotte concluded. "For my part, I would never have hidden it from you. I nearly did tell you once, when I was staying with you—you remember?"

"Oh, yes, I do."

"You guessed then, and refrained from asking?"

Ellen nodded. Charlotte sighed deeply.

"You are the best friend in the world," she said. "Can you forgive me?"

"Yes."

But there was still something troubling her, Charlotte could see. As she stooped above the table, looking at the books that Charlotte was inscribing to her, she suddenly asked, "Did you tell Mary?"

Charlotte blushed, began to speak, but shut her mouth and simply met Ellen's eyes dumbly.

"You always confided in her more than in me," said Ellen quietly.

Dr. Teale came while Ellen was still there. He found his patient dressed and sitting up on a black horsehair sofa, looking, he thought, very pretty with her soft fair hair and expectant eyes. But her flushed cheeks, which added color and life to the picture, caused him misgivings. It was a symptom he was all too familiar with.

He sent everyone out of the room, asked Anne to open her bodice and carefully applied his stethoscope to her chest and back. He straightened up and said cheerfully,

"Thank you, my dear! That will be all. Not so bad, was it? Now I will send your sisters in to you again while I have a little word with your Papa."

Anne had her eyes fixed on him in a way he was not accustomed to. As she calmly buttoned up her dress, she said,

"It would really be better if you told *me*, Dr. Teale. My father is too old and too unhappy readily to stand any shock."

"I said nothing of giving him a shock," he replied heartily. "Now you are to rest yourself and not worry about anything at all. Let others work and worry for you. How lucky you are to have two sisters to care for you, eh?"

"One sister," corrected Anne quietly. "My other died recently. Of consumption," she added, still gazing at him with those insistent blue eyes.

"How recently?" asked the doctor uneasily.

"Seventeen days ago," she said.

The doctor could not repress a visible start. He said no more, but left the room at once, crossed the hall and knocked on the parson's door. He felt gravely shaken by what he had just heard, and now looked at the elderly parson, with his eccentric collar and ravaged face, with more compassionate eyes. Were there only a son in the household to whom he might more safely confide his diagnosis! Of course, telling the elder daughter was not to be thought of. Death was a matter for men.

Patrick sat alone in his study after the specialist had taken his leave. Charlotte had been called to show him out, and Patrick had heard him talking to her politely and cheerfully at the front door. The burden of ill news, then, was upon him alone, and he bore it with a terrible fortitude, half dependent upon the merciful initial numbness that follows a fatal wound.

The old man prayed for strength, but his faith was faltering. Now the tenor of his prayers kept wandering into querulous question form: why that sweet creature still in her youth, and not me in my dotage? What have I done to deserve these terrible losses, one after the other, with scarcely time to recover in between? The fervor with which he had prayed for Maria and Branwell—prayed essentially that they might be spared—was enfeebled now, for he had received no encouragement to hope that God might be good to him. So he whispered his unanswerable questions to an unanswering deity; and then, wearily and without resolution, only because he knew they were all waiting across the hall and that there was no avoiding it, he painfully struggled to his feet and went to them.

The three were on the sofa. A pretty sight they made together, despite their black dresses and crepe ribbons, a picture of youth and life. They had been chatting as he entered, rather forcedly perhaps, but with a greater degree of courage than he had been showing, alone in his room a few moments before. As he entered, the two older girls rose and stood like sentinels on either side of Anne, and they all looked at him, calm and apparently resigned— waiting.

Patrick walked unsteadily to the sofa and sat down at Anne's side. She had already read his message, and he was appalled to see the sudden raw blaze of fear that for a second overlaid the patient acceptance she had set upon her face. His heart was wrenched, as painfully as any other muscle upon which too much strain is put; he felt sick and faint as he looked for that moment into the depths of his youngest child's terror of death.

"My *dear* little Anne!" he muttered brokenly, and took her in his frail arms.

The situation was too much for Ellen—she was not accustomed to such trials as Charlotte was. She went home as soon as she decently could, promising to come again later. When she kissed Anne good-bye, she could not help crying.

"No valedictory tears, Miss Ellen," said Anne briskly. "I shall last out a good while yet, I dare say. We'll meet again in this world, for I intend to do all I can to prolong my life, even though, what with these blisters and doses of cod-liver oil, I begin to feel the treatment is worse than the disease!"

Dr. Teale had left a list of detailed instructions that Charlotte had set herself to carrying out to the letter. She did so almost fanatically, as if, now she had a willing patient, she could make up in loving zeal all that had been frustrated in Emily's case. She shut her eyes to all signs that the prescribed medicines and treatments were not only doing no good, but actually causing harm; for the blister was painful and the oil made Anne feel wretchedly sick.

"It tastes like train-oil, and smells like it, too!" she gasped. "My spirit is willing, but my stomach rebels. Ugh! Oh, is there not some more palatable alternative?"

"Dr. Teale said it was invaluable," said Charlotte implacably.

The weakness, fever and coughing persisted, however, until early in February, when Charlotte was able to write to Mr. Williams that the symptoms were a little easier. And at that point Anne began to pester Charlotte in her turn.

"Charlotte, is it not time you returned to *Shirley*? You must not make me the excuse for idleness on other fronts, for I won't be thus used, and so I tell you frankly."

Reluctantly Charlotte took out the aborted manuscript and reread it. She became immediately anxious about the similarities to a newly published first novel, *Mary Barton*, by a Mrs. Gaskell, which had gained great popularity. She wrote to Mr. Williams and asked if he would agree to read her own book and see what he thought of it so far. It was the first time she had ever felt the need of such reassurance from an outsider, or dreamed of showing any portion of unfinished work. But without Emily's acerbic criticisms she felt lost, insecure. She began for the first time to *miss* Emily, to comprehend fully what it was going to mean to live without her, and at that point her spirits took such a sudden downward plunge that it was like black walls of water closing over her head—she literally felt she might drown in grief. Yet she fought her way to the surface. As she had written to Ellen, "I avoid looking forward or backward . . . This is not the time to regret, dread or weep." One look at Anne, one look at her father, proved this to her over and over again. She dared not flag, she dared not even be ill, though she was often a prey to aches and pains. She treated them as meticulously and conscientiously as she treated Anne's graver symptoms.

The verdict from London on her novel was favorable. The three men who had read it—the third was a trusted reader called James Taylor—had some cautious criticisms, but all heartily urged her to continue and not to worry about Mrs. Gaskell's work. Dear Mr. Williams's letter was particularly generous and encouraging.

"There!" said Anne. "Now be obedient. I desire my due portion of reading-to *every* evening, and promise to pine without it."

Anne was wonderful in every way. She was a joy to nurse, especially after Emily. And there was the additional relief of not needing to conceal anything from her. She knew the ultimate hopelessness of her case, yet was determined to oppose this verdict as long as she could; and Charlotte got great comfort from being able to talk to her about her condition. They drew Papa into these conversations, and sometimes the old man, ever fascinated by medical matters, could almost forget whom they were talking about in his enthusiasm for the minutiae of symptoms and treatments.

And Anne's urgings drove Charlotte back to her book, which grew by fits and starts during the long, dark, testing weeks of winter and early spring.

In April the first trickles of clemency in the weather brought a mixed cup of new hope and new anxiety to the household, for Anne began talking animatedly about a change of air.

"I've been thinking a great deal about it," she said. "Dr. Forbes, you know, when *he* saw me, told me that a warmer climate, and sea air, might do much, provided we do not leave it too late— in the illness, I mean of course, not in the year! And to say the truth, during these dismal weeks I've found myself often dreaming of Scarborough as I used to see it when Mr. Robinson took us there. It was ever my idea of heaven on earth—and, Charlotte, to think! You have never seen it! I should like above all things if you and I could go there together, and I could show you all the prospects I love. Perhaps we could go by way of York, and I could get another glimpse of the Minster before I die. That would be glorious! And *perhaps*, if we went, I need not die at all, or not yet . . . Oh, don't you think it might be beneficial, Charlotte?"

Charlotte did not know what to think. When she looked at Anne, every week thinner, more hollow-eyed, sometimes too weak to get up, and even on her "good" days barely able to creep around the house, she dared not let herself hope, and was deathly afraid of the effects of the long journey to this distant Mecca Anne dreamed of. Yet, to deny her, and to deny the *chance* of an improvement, seemed worse. She spoke to Papa.

"Take her to Scarborough."

"Are you sure, Papa?"

"If you can bear it, I can. It is what she wants. There is nothing to lose, and it is her heart's last longing."

Charlotte wrote to Ellen—Would she come with them? Charlotte prayed she would agree, for the thought of making the trip without help frightened her beyond measure. Meanwhile, Anne, despite increasing weakness and illness, chatted happily whenever she had enough strength about the coming "holiday," as if the prospect contained nothing but pleasure; and when Ellen wrote accepting the invitation, Anne was overjoyed.

"With Miss Ellen to share the burden of looking after this wretched invalid, all will be perfect. Oh, I cannot wait! Charlotte, are you not excited? Pray do be, just a little!"

Charlotte tried to seem so, but it was hard work. She was too worried about the journey. If only it were well over! Looking at Anne, with her sticklike arms and hollow-eyed, sickly countenance, lying in her chair scarcely able to lift a finger, Charlotte wondered how on earth they would ever get there at all.

The date of the journey was set for May 23. They were to meet Ellen at Leeds Station and proceed together. Ellen arrived at the arranged time and waited for three hours, but the others did not come. Night fell; she put up at a hotel, scarcely sleeping at all for anxiety. Had the worst happened? What else could have prevented their coming? The next morning she hurried to Haworth in a hired carriage, arriving in mid-morning at the parsonage, in time to see the strapping curate, Mr. Nicholls, carrying Anne down the path from the front door.

Charlotte had written warning Ellen not to react to the shocking change in Anne's appearance, and since they did not at once see her, she had a chance to collect herself. Anne was as thin as a child, a mere bundle of shawls and rugs, with a peaked and shadowed face, hedged in by a bonnet, resting against the young man's shoulder. The driver of the chaise, which stood in the lane, was standing in his vehicle ready to receive her; Charlotte followed. Martha and Tabby stood by, both with streaming eyes, and Mr. Brontë stood on the front doorstep with Keeper.

Flossy leaped up into the chaise after his mistress. The driver tried to shoo him down, but Anne, now settled in her seat, said faintly, "Let me say good-bye to him." The spaniel jumped onto her knee, and she put her face down to whisper to him, and stroked his silky ears for a few moments. Then she signaled to Charlotte, who lifted him gently down and put him into Mr. Nicholls' arms.

At that point they saw Ellen standing in the shadow of the wall, and everyone became very animated while explanations were exchanged. Anne had been too ill yesterday, it seemed, to start the journey, and they had had no way of letting Ellen know. How good that she had come! Now they could make the whole journey together. Good-byes were said. Anne leaned over the side of the chaise to kiss her father, who clasped her hands in both of his and gazed up at her.

"Come back to me," he said at last, and stepping back from the chaise, waved the driver on.

It was a trying journey, but not as bad as Charlotte had feared. They were shown tremendous kindness at every stage of it. The chaise driver carried Anne into the train; porters ran hither and yon fetching and carrying; gentlemen gave up their seats to enable the three to sit together by the window. Anne slept most of the way to York, and when they reached that halfway house she rallied amazingly.

"This is my favorite city!" she exclaimed as they helped her into a cab. "You may keep London, for my part, so I may have York. No," she interrupted firmly, as Charlotte was directing the cabbie to a hotel, "I don't want to go there till we have seen the Minster. I have had a rest and I feel much, much better—Come, to the Minster, with all speed, while the sun is still on it, for I'd have you see it at its finest."

So they were driven to the Minster, and the cab drew up outside its front entrance. The three sat silent, staring at the magnificence before them. Anne, flushed and with clasped hands, looked at it as she might have looked at the gates of paradise.

"Is it not splendid!" she breathed, and suddenly the others noticed she was panting and trembling with exhilaration. "Oh, if finite power can do this, what is the—?" She stopped short and caught her breath in a brief, hacking cough. Ellen put her arm around her. Charlotte hastily signaled to the cabbie.

The next day they drove on to Scarborough. On this leg of the journey, Anne did not sleep. Excitement was unavoidable now, for her dream-town was approaching, and familiar landmarks were everywhere. She was as thrilled as a child, crying out every minute, "Look! Look there! Isn't it beautiful! That is where we stopped to picnic once . . . Oh! Now I smell the sea!" The others had no option but to echo her enthusiasm and promise themselves to put her to bed the moment they arrived.

The host of the lodging house hurried out as they drew up at his door and offered to carry Anne to her room, but she said firmly, "No, thank you. Just lift me down and I will walk in. Isn't it wonderful, Charlotte? I can *feel* the sea air doing me good!"

They had to help her upstairs, but she walked unaided into her bedroom and straight to the French windows, which commanded a glorious view of the bay. She stood there, subtly supported by the other two, gazing over the misty blue sea with the gulls wheeling over it and the boats with their bright sails gliding across its smooth surface. Her companions felt the thinness of her elbows, and her faint, ecstatic trembling, and trembled in their turn. But Anne said quietly:

"I'm so glad we came. To see this again! I'm happy—really happy. And I do thank God gratefully for it, and for strength to enjoy it."

The next morning they breakfasted together with the other lodgers, and Anne, who had dressed with only a little help, seemed full of life and talked brightly to everyone. After the meal, the landlady drew Charlotte aside.

"Your sister does not seem to be in as much danger as you wrote to me," she said. "She is very thin of course, poor thing, but she has a good color and she ate more than I had expected. May we hope matters are not so bad as you feared?"

"We must take great care of her," was all Charlotte would say.

They walked very slowly to the beach after breakfast the next day. Anne did not talk much now, but neither did she seem especially tired; she looked about her contentedly and sometimes drew the others' attention to various especially pleasing sights. They strolled on the smooth golden sands, just below the shingle, and once Anne stopped and said, "I once gathered shells just here with the children. Edmund had no patience, but Mary ran to me every minute with a new variety." Charlotte stooped, picked up three or four shells, and put them in Anne's hand. Anne smiled, playing with them. "How complex, how delicate," she said. "God is such a craftsman!"

Suddenly she stopped again. "Oh, look," she said, pointing. "Donkey carts!" There was a row of them, with their drivers. It was still early and there was no custom. Ellen and Charlotte looked at each other—*Why not?*

"Would you like—?"

"Oh, *yes!* If no one would laugh."

They helped her up. The driver was a lad of about fourteen. "Not too fast," Charlotte said, but he had not stirred all morning and was in the mood for a spin. A little way along the sands he smacked the donkey's flank with his whip. "Gerrup!" he called. The little thing broke into a gallop and the cart careered down the beach.

"Stop," said Anne sharply.

Startled, the boy pulled on the reins.

"Now get down. I will drive."

"Doosta know 'ow?"

"Don't be silly."

The boy reluctantly climbed down. Anne clucked and shook the reins and the donkey moved forward. The boy walked alongside.

After a while, Anne spoke to him. "You should not strike them, you know. They are God's creatures like you. *You* wouldn't like it if someone struck you with a whip."

"Someone does," said the boy bitterly.

"Well then. Don't do unto others."

Ellen came panting up, having chased the cart all along the beach.

"Are you all right, Anne?"

"Perfectly. And so is my little friend. Come. We'll go back now; I've had enough for today."

The next day was Sunday, and after lunch they went for a little walk.

"Oh, here's a comfortable seat for me," said Anne. "Let me sit here, and you two walk on. Walk toward the castle. It's well worth seeing close to, but I don't feel up to it today—perhaps tomorrow. Anyway, I'd like you to see it."

They walked on, not too far. Ellen said, "She is amazing. Is it really as she makes it seem? Can she be as calm and cheerful as she would have us believe?"

"She has convinced me of it. But then, I want to be convinced. How different it all is from Emily! It is the worst thing in the world, Ellen, to see someone you love suffering and be unable to help them. The memory of it grows more agonizing, not easier. I could not bear to think Anne is suffering inwardly from fear that I couldn't alleviate. But she has always been very much upheld by faith—her own brand. It's possible she is truly unafraid."

That evening they drew Anne's chair up to the French windows and together watched the most glorious sunset that could be imagined. The castle stood on its cliff in gilded glory; every wave of the ebbing tide and every little craft bobbing at anchor reflected the last splendid brilliance of the dying light. Anne's rapturous face, too, was fingered with warm color, and Charlotte, silently watching her, remarked the difference between the lupus glow on Emily's face from the chill winter sun, and this bonny radiance which gave Anne a look of total health. Then the sun sank, and the pallor and sickly shadows returned. Charlotte's heart sickened, too, and she was assailed by such horrible forebodings of loneliness that she felt herself weaken.

"Come on, let's go back to the fire," said Anne. "But did you ever see anything so heavenly? Perhaps heaven is like that— perpetual awareness of God in all His majesty and glory . . ." When they had settled her comfortably, with a rug across her knees, she went on, "Do you know, I was thinking while I was alone this afternoon. Am I not being very selfish? What if I were to die here? No, now don't protest, you both know it's possible I may. How would you manage? It would be simpler all around if it happened at home. And yet when I think of poor Papa, having to bury yet a third child in such a short space, I wonder if perhaps it would be kinder to him if it were all got over somewhere else, and he were spared the worst. What do you think, Charlotte?"

"I think you should stay here, if here is where you're happiest."

"I haven't much strength to face another journey," said Anne. Relieved, she leaned back and closed her eyes. Then she opened them and sighed. "If only I could get my breath easily, I would be very comfortable. Really, dying is not so bad, if one just tries not to struggle."

At eleven o'clock next morning, while they were sitting in the sun on the terrace, Anne suddenly turned to Charlotte and said, "I feel different. Something has happened."

Both the others jumped to their feet in alarm, but Anne said, "Now don't be frightened. We've all expected it. But perhaps you'd better ask our hostess to call a doctor."

The doctor had been warned and arrived speedily. He'd expected to find his patient in bed, but she was sitting up in a chair by the window and she greeted him with a smile and a feeble handshake, and at once said:

"Doctor, I think the end is coming soon. I'm worried about my sister. Do you think, if we set off at once, we could reach my home in Haworth before I die? I don't want her to have the trouble of making arrangements in a strange town."

The doctor was astonished at her calmness. He examined her and then looked down at her, folding his stethoscope.

"I understand you want me to be quite straight with you?"

Anne nodded.

"I'm afraid you would not survive the journey."

"How long have I got to live?"

The doctor pursed his lips. "A very little while. Long enough to make your peace with God, no more."

Anne closed her eyes and her lips moved. The doctor noticed that although her face was calm, it was deathly white, and the knuckles of her clasped hands were livid, too. He knew fear when he saw it, no matter how disguised, and leaning over, he covered her cold hands with his big warm one and said, "There will be no pain, you know."

At once the blue eyes opened wide. "I'm not afraid of death," she said. "But it is terrible to leave life with so little achieved. I had a lot to do here, and almost none of it's done."

When the doctor had gone, promising to return shortly, Ellen and Charlotte came and sat down near Anne. None of them had anything to say, and oddly, there was no grief yet. After a short rest—her breathing was an increasing trial—Anne said, "I think I'd like to say a prayer." She folded her hands, without strain this time, and said:

"Dear God, be good to Charlotte. Look after her, and do not let her be too lonely. May she find comfort in her writing, and strength enough to get some pleasure from life, and to look after our father. And bless dear Miss Ellen, who has been such a true friend." Then she turned to Ellen and said, "Will you be a sister to Charlotte in my stead? Give her as much of your company as you can. And thank you both for looking after me so kindly. And now I'd like to lie down. Just over there, on the sofa."

They carried her there between them, and now, seeing her lying still and hearing the terrible labored breaths so akin to Emily's and Branwell's, Charlotte began to feel the towering wall of grief moving in upon her again.

"Are you feeling easier, dearest?" she managed to ask, though her voice nearly failed her.

"Not very much, but soon I shall be easy indeed. I do believe it, and now it seems truer than ever—God will look after me. And I'll be with Emily. I'll give her your love."

Charlotte clenched her teeth, but her face was crumpling. Anne's hand crept over the rug and tried to touch her.

"Oh, poor Charlotte! Take courage!" she whispered.

She said no more. She lay still, her eyes on Charlotte's face. Ellen sat on the floor nearby, and they both held Anne's hands. Once more the doctor called, but he did not disturb them, seeing there was nothing he could do. And at two o'clock—the exact hour Emily had died—something almost tangible went out of Anne's face. The blue eyes went blank, the slow pulse stopped in the childlike wrists. Charlotte leaned over and drew down the lids, feeling their warmth and delicacy and softness, like an epitome of Anne. She let her fingers move gently down the quiet face, all the way down to the chin.

There was a tap on the door, and the landlady put her head in.

"Dinner is ready," she said in her brisk Yorkshire accent.

"Thank you," said Charlotte.

The landlady, still not realizing the situation, withdrew, and suddenly Charlotte's grief swept over her like a moorland storm. As she sobbed in Ellen's arms she gasped out over and over again:

"I wish it were me! I wish it were me!"

5

THE LONG
SOLITUDE BEGINS

*I*T WAS A MONTH BEFORE CHAR-
lotte returned to Haworth.

They decided to bury Anne in Scarborough cemetery, high on
the cliffs overlooking the sea that she'd loved. And when it was
done, they stayed on in the lodging house. Mr. Brontë himself
suggested it. He longed for Charlotte unspeakably, but when he
thought of the emptiness she must return to, his better part took
command and he wrote urging her to stay at the coast as long as
possible.

When their booking at Scarborough ended, Charlotte and
Ellen moved on to Filey, and later still to Easton, there to spend
a week with the Hudsons as they had ten years before. The
weather was warm. They took gentle walks, arm in arm, and
spent many hours sitting by the sea talking. There was a lot to
say. Charlotte told Ellen all about the novels, how they came
to be written, the story of the visit to London and all that followed. Sometimes, speaking of Anne, they both cried; but their
tears were somehow healing, not the sort Charlotte still shed for
Emily and Branwell. The very nature of Anne's death comforted

her, for if ever anyone "made a Christian end," it was she, and Charlotte was assured that she had gone to a happier place and was reunited with the others. What, she wondered, if one didn't believe in an eternal life? How could such events then be endured?

In this placid interlude, surrounded by peaceful beauty and in company with her dear Ellen, Charlotte felt quite tranquil. The sorrow was there, but it was not sharp. It was like moving through a gentle mist of pain which gave before her advance and closed in again behind her.

At Easton she got a good deal of writing done in the privacy of the Hudsons' summerhouse. *Shirley* must be finished now— there was nothing to prevent and everything to urge it. For what else had she left but her work? It was to Ellen that she now read her day's output. It was not the same—how could it be? But it pleased Ellen, and Charlotte felt it was something she owed her for her former deceit. They grew closer than ever.

The one thing they never discussed was the thing Charlotte could not even look at in her mind—the prospect that lay before her when the interlude should be over.

At the end of June, her conscience would be quiet no longer. It suddenly seemed to her quite wickedly selfish to have left Papa alone for so long. In any case, Ellen had to go home to her family. They packed up and traveled back to Leeds, where they parted rather abruptly: some of Ellen's family were there to meet her and they whisked her away almost before she could say good-bye to Charlotte, who was left outside the station feeling suddenly bereft, as if the sun had gone in and would never reappear to warm her.

When she got home the dogs rushed out to greet her, and then seemed to sniff about expectantly, especially Flossy, who ran up and down the lane whining. Papa, Tabby and Martha hugged and kissed her. There were no tears—evidently they had bound themselves not to make her solitary homecoming harder. The parsonage, she found, had been prepared to welcome her as cheerfully as possible—everything sparkling clean, flowers in her room, some little touches of newness to brighten the place, which, alas, only seemed to emphasize all that was familiar and shabby and darkened with sad associations.

Tabby served tea to refresh her after her long journey, and she and Papa shared it in his study. Papa asked about Anne's grave, and sought reassurance that he had not done wrong in failing to come for the funeral.

"Papa, pray don't trouble yourself! You could not have got there in time anyway."

"And how are *you*, my dearest?" he then asked for the fourth or fifth time, gazing at her with love and anxiety. "Your eyes are not so sunken, but I don't like that little cough. And does your back still pain you? I noticed you wince just now when you lifted the teapot—"

"Nonsense, Papa, I am quite all right."

"You know there is nothing more important to me in the world now than your health, my love," he said. "You *must take care* of yourself, Charlotte. You *must*."

"Of course I shall, Papa. Don't—" She had been about to say "fuss," but changed it to "worry." In fact she had caught a cold in Easton. But she realized that she would have to endure, apart from all other trials, a constant stream of anxious inquiries, and to protect them both, would be obliged to hide any signs of ill health.

The old man ate his meager evening meal alone as always, while Charlotte presided over a dining-room table once crowded but now a polished blank. After Martha had cleared away her uneaten meal and made up the fire, Charlotte took her place beside it—and waited.

At precisely nine o'clock she heard the study door open and close, heard footsteps, very slow now, mounting the stairs, heard the clock being wound. The steps continued. Papa's bedroom door closed with a barely audible click, and there were a few muffled sounds as he prepared for bed. Then the house settled into a profound stillness, broken only by the old clock ticking away on the landing.

Charlotte sat motionless in her chair. She knew the worst was now upon her—the dreaded, fearful hour; the blackest hour of any ordeal because it is the first, when all lies ahead. This horror had to be faced and passed into—not passed *through*, for she could envisage no end to it except her own death, and she must not wish for that because of Papa.

Her mind darted about, seeking some relief; but it was trapped, and her imagination merely tortured her further by leading her through the empty rooms of the house—past the shuttered windows and pillowless beds, the little portable desks gathering dust together with abandoned work-baskets, trinket boxes, drawers of folded clothes still interleaved with Aunt's lavender sachets.

And now her mind jumped to the vault under the flagstones in the church, where Emily's and Branwell's bodies lay in their coffins. She twisted her head about, trying to avoid the vivid pictures that came, for she saw them both as they must look now, and even so she longed for them, and understood Heathcliff for the first time. If Emily could rise from the grave, if Anne's gentle spirit could come into the room, would she flee them, fear them? *No—no*—she would welcome them—any trace of them—any proof that they were still near her. A whisper, a cold touch, a supernatural breath on her cheek, the rustle of a ghostly skirt on the flags! Oh, if they would only come!

But she must not allow this. To crave proof was a kind of doubt of God's mercy and of her faith in a future life. She stood up resolutely and began to walk around the table, around and around. She must not let her mind wander into these paths. She clasped her hands and twisted her fingers together. The tears she had shed for Anne were infinitely more wholesome than these morbid thoughts; she grew angry with herself. But as her anger took hold of her, it turned outward—upward.

Why was she alone, why had she been robbed of her dearest companions and comforts? Why had she been left to struggle on through this horror of solitude that lay—not just ahead anymore, but all around her? She had done all she could. She had had boundless faith. "Pray for strength and it shall be given you." Well, she had prayed continuously, and how had God fulfilled His pledge? Was *this*, this quivering, shrinking pulp that was all the core she could feel within her, was *this* the best God could offer? If so, she was defeated before she began. And who was at fault?

She flung herself down in her chair again and buried her face in her hands. The Devil was tempting her in her loneliness, tempting her to doubt the only Being who ever sustained and comforted her. God had not failed her till now. She must believe he would give her the necessary courage! This was a trial. She must set herself to pass it.

But could she—was it possible to survive this truly appalling pain?

Her head came up suddenly. Someone was knocking very quietly on the front door.

There was something like a flash of fire in her head, a blind, insane moment of hope. But she quenched it instantly. Rising, she took a candle and went to open the door. On the step stood the tall, heavy figure of her father's curate.

"Miss Brontë?"

Charlotte, holding tightly to the door frame, clenched her teeth and breathed deeply to try to keep control of herself. This man was an outsider and he had intruded upon her at the nadir of her life. She could easily have poured out upon him all the bitterness and resentment that was in her. But in the candlelight his eyes had a strange glow of sympathy, so strong that they stilled in her any desire to inflict her pain upon him.

"Yes, Mr. Nicholls?" she said flatly.

"I have come to tell you," he said slowly, "I have come to tell you—" He stumbled over the words, stopped for a moment, and then, as she waited blankly, went on more strongly: "To tell you that if there is anything—anything at all that I can do for you— to help you through this—ordeal you are facing now—the lightest hint will suffice. Anything. At any time."

She stared up at him. The candle began to shake in her hand.

She put both hands to it and made it be still. There was a silence. Then she said, as steadily as she was able:

"I appreciate your kindness."

She could manage no more. The tears were coming, the storm she had fought to suppress because, once it was upon her, she did not see how she would ever stop it. A few formal words of sympathy from this semistranger had been her undoing. She caught her breath and her head snapped back.

"You must go now!" she gasped.

He gave a small, stiff bow, and backed down one step. Then, as she was about to close the door, he did a most curious thing. He reached out toward her with both hands, and his own breath came in a short gasp, almost as if her pain had lashed out and struck him like a lance.

A moment later he was gone, into the darkness.

Charlotte did not think about him again from the moment the door shut on him. He was the unwelcome agent of her lost control—that was all. Her grief for the past, her blinding terror of the future, swept her away from all reason—discipline—religion. Rarely in her life had she been so lost to all command over herself. Now this terrible violent helplessness took charge of her, tossing her like a cockleshell upon a great ocean of anguish.

Still in the midst of it, care for her father restrained her from making any noise. While she paced to and fro across the room she stifled her cries, bottling in the pain as best she could.

At last the storm died down—for the time. Beaten and exhausted, she was able to crawl back into her chair by the burned-out fire. And little by little her strength of will mysteriously crept back to her. An hour she sat there—two hours—her mind and spirit so ravaged they seemed empty. And then a desperate courage began to fill her.

"I shall not give way like that again," she thought. "Not many women can have lost as much as I have. But then not many have my Godsent remedy."

She sat quite still for a long time, allowing her mind to rest. Then her spirit roused itself again.

"I shall go to bed now. When I wake up tomorrow morning I shall not lie for even one minute thinking of what is past or what is to come. I shall get up at once and go down and help with the housework. Before lunch I shall take the dogs for a walk, and that will help to keep me healthy. In the afternoon, if Papa does not need me, I shall write in the parlor. Yes, I shall write! A thousand words a day—more, if my eyes will let me. For the evenings, and the nights, there is no remedy. I must bear them as best I can. But though I am mortally wretched and bound to remain so, I am *not* crushed, nor robbed of elasticity, nor of hope, nor—best of all—endeavor."

With that resolve, she got up. The candle was nearly finished. Taking a fresh one from the box, she lit it from the stub, and fitting it into the brass holder, pressed it firmly down into the pool of wet wax. At the door she paused, and looked around the silent room. Then she went out into the hall and walked quietly up the stone stairs, past the ticking clock.

POSTSCRIPT

*W*HEN THREE MEMBERS OF A quartet are dead, it is a quartet no longer. But in some ways the zenith of Charlotte's life was still to come. Not only spiritual triumph lay before her—the courage to transcend the terrible losses she had sustained and continue to live and write. Two great books, *Shirley* and *Villette*, were still to appear. And her life, what remained of it, was to be lived on two strikingly contrasting planes. The fame she had longed for, the freedom, acceptance on terms of equality by the great figures of her age in the glittering, "Verdopolitan" world of London—these became hers for the taking. Yet at the same time the lonely hell of her isolated moorland home, inhabited by her ever more difficult and demanding old father and haunted by the ghosts of her dead, remorselessly called her back.

Between these two worlds, while she did not change outwardly, she continued to develop and grow as a woman and as a writer. The newest and most daring ideas of her time—emancipation of women, atheism, urbane cynicism and the breaking down of social barriers—impinged upon her through those with whom her fame brought her into contact. Nor was her heart dead. She fell in love with one of her publishers, while being ardently pursued by another. She married, at the age of 39, the same Mr. Nicholls who was her father's curate and who cared so much for her. She entered into this union in a spirit of resigned pessimism, but it brought her extraordinary happiness. It also, by a terrible irony, brought her death.

Charlotte's last years, then, comprise a story that is too important, too moving and too full to be compressed into a few chapters attached, with an air of aftermath, to a history of the four Brontës together. It deserves a book of its own.